Political Philosophers of the Twentieth Century

CW00952177

To *David Raphael*, my first teacher in politics

Political Philosophers of the Twentieth Century

Michael H. Lessnoff
Department of Politics
University of Glasgow, UK

BLACKWELL
Publishers

First published 1999

2 4 6 8 10 9 7 5 3 1

Blackwell Publishers Ltd
108 Cowley Road
Oxford OX4 1JF
UK

Blackwell Publishers Inc.
350 Main Street
Malden, Massachusetts 02148
USA

British Library Cataloguing in Publication Data

A CIP cataloguing record for this book is available from the British Library

Library of Congress Cataloging-in-Publication Data

Lessnoff, Michael H. (Michael Harry)
     Political philosophers of the twentieth century / Michael H.
Lessnoff.
          p.   cm.
     Includes bibliographical references and index.
     ISBN 0–631–20260–9 (alk. paper). — ISBN 0–631–20261–7 (alk.
paper)
          1. Political science—Philosophy—History—20th century.
     2. Political science—History—20th century.   I. Title.
JA83.L39   1999
320.5′09′04—DC21   98–22987
                                                          CIP

Typeset in 10½ on 13 pt Bembo by Ace Filmsetting Ltd, Frome, Somerset
Printed in Great Britain by T. J. International, Padstow, Cornwall

This book is printed on acid-free paper.

Contents

Acknowledgements

My thanks are due to a number of people who helped me in various ways with the writing of this book. Various chapters were read and commented on by Glasgow colleagues, including John Fowler on Weber and Robert Grant on Oakeshott. Paul Graham was very helpful in relation to the 'Frankfurt' authors, Marcuse and Habermas. The entire typescript was read, once again, by Mary Haight. Of course, responsibility for the text remains my own. But it could not have been completed without a huge amount of help from the Glasgow Politics Department secretaries, Elspeth Shaw, Avril Johnstone and Jeanette Berrie. I have relied greatly on their expertise with computers and other such paraphernalia involved in the production of books in the high technology age. In the course of our joint labours they also achieved a notable improvement in the legibility of my manuscript material.

1
Introduction

I must begin by making plain the scope of this book, and justifying its inclusions and exclusions. Its subject, as indicated by the title, is the major political philosophers of the twentieth century. The book is, however, also intended to have a thematic unity, which cannot be expected to correspond exactly to chronological divisions. I therefore confine my attention (with one exception, to be explained below) to what the historian Eric Hobsbawm has called the 'short twentieth century' – the era bounded at one end by the First World War and the Russian Revolution, and at the other by the dramatic collapse of the USSR and Bolshevism as a result of the advent to power of Mikhail Gorbachev and the subsequent 'revolutions' in East and Central Europe.[1] Roughly speaking, the period of interest coincides with the lifetime of the Soviet Union, 1917–91. The period has not only a political but also a cultural unity, at least in Europe and America ('The West') – using the word 'cultural' in a broad sense, to refer not just to intellectual issues, but to the general shape of society and the conditions of life of individuals in it, which rested, largely and increasingly, on an industrial economy and technology. The recent striking and far-reaching technological developments known as the 'information revolution' seem to portend the rise of a radically different kind of society and, quite possibly, a different set of social and political problems.

What I am suggesting, therefore, is that Western society during the 'short twentieth century' was a society of a specific kind, faced with specific kinds of problems. These problems, naturally, preoccupied the political philosophers of the period, so that the perennial problems of political philosophy took on, for them, a particular form, or slant. In part, then, the political philosophy of our period is shaped by the particularities of its social structure. But only in part – equally important, needless to say, has been the need to grapple with the implications of the great shaping events – and, one must say, catastrophes – of the century: two world wars, revolutions, and the threat to human values posed by totalitarianism in its various forms.

These latter issues are familiar. But it is also necessary, as indicated, to pay attention to issues of fundamental social structure. That is why I begin this study with Max Weber. Weber, although he lived almost entirely before our period (he died in 1920), is nevertheless the greatest sociologist of 'modernity', that is, of twentieth century society. It is his work, above all others, that identifies the crucial social and cultural trends of our time, and the problems to which they give rise – trends and problems summed up, in particular, by the twin terms 'rationalization' and 'disenchantment'. Although these phenomena are in part cognate (since disenchantment is, in fact, the consequence of rationalization in the intellectual sphere), together they produce an ironic predicament. In brief, there is, on the one hand, an ever greater capacity to achieve ends, based on ever greater intellectual understanding of the physical world; on the other a loss of confidence in the objective value of ends. Our stock of means (in the form of wealth, knowledge, etc.) is enormously superior to that available to previous generations, but the worth of the ends they are used to pursue is uncertain and disputed. The collapse of religious belief is of course crucial here.

In a fairly obvious way, liberalism is a response to disenchantment in Weber's sense – whether it takes the form of Isaiah Berlin's value-pluralism, or John Rawls's doctrine of the priority of the right over the good – this being the appropriate response to 'reasonable disagreement' about the good, which individuals should be free to define for themselves and to pursue subject to the restraints imposed by rules of right. Michael Oakeshott and Friedrich Hayek also, in their different ways, seek to limit the scope of public authority to the enforcement of rules, and correspondingly to reserve the pursuit of ends to the free choices of private individuals and associations or oganizations. Rawls, however, goes further than the others by proposing a method for determining the constraining rules of right ('principles of justice') – notably, a contractarian method based on hypothetical agreement rather than objective right or natural law, since the latter is not available.

In so far as rationalization and disenchantment are two sides of the same coin, the currency in question involves the monopolization of reason and knowledge by science and technology – knowledge of facts and of means. This 'technical' view of rationality, and its societal implications, have been a major focus of attention – often hostile – on the part of twentieth-century political philosophers. This is preeminently so in the case of 'critical theorists' of the Frankfurt School, represented in this volume by Herbert Marcuse and Jürgen Habermas. Marcuse's rejection of the 'technocratic' (or 'positivist') vision is the most sweeping, and is in the interest of revolutionary liberation. Yet it is striking how theorists of the most opposed ideological tendencies can concur in a similar if less sweeping rejection of the same vision, that is, of its social implementation in the form, for example, of 'dehumanizing' bureaucratization that turns men into 'objects of administration'. The conservative Oakeshott, for example, warns against the over-estimation of 'technical knowledge', in the interest of tradition and established practice; the right-wing economic liberal Hayek repudiates attempts at thoroughgoing organization of society as destructive equally of freedom, efficiency and progress; the view of bureaucratic administration taken by the radical social democrat Habermas coincides to a remarkable degree with that of Hayek. Among the political philosophers discussed in this book, only Karl Popper gives a (strictly limited) endorsement of technical reason in the form of 'piecemeal social engineering'. In so far as 'technocracy', 'bureaucracy' and the 'administered society' are found objectionable on the grounds that they involve treating human beings purely as means, the critique thereof is at one with the Kantian categorical imperative, which forbids precisely that, and which is taken as fundamental by the libertarian Robert Nozick.

While left-wing and right-wing theorists can make common cause in hostility to bureaucratization and the administered society, they part company when it comes to another major aspect of Western rationalization, the market, especially in its capitalist form. While Hayek lauds the market as the epitome of freedom, to Marcuse consumerist capitalism is the locus *par excellence* of dehumanizing manipulation in our time. Hostility to modern consumerist culture is also a leitmotif of other theorists, notably the republican Hannah Arendt and the liberal Marxist C. B. Macpherson. Although Arendt and Macpherson agree with Marcuse in seeing consumerism as a form of enslavement, or self-enslavement, and a denial of human creativity, unlike him they do not see it as a manifestation of technocratic reason. Indeed, Macpherson, in a Marxist spirit, is inclined to see technology as liberating rather than enslaving.

Of course, the ideas of the theorists named above, all of whom are discussed in subsequent chapters, cannot be wholly reduced to the themes mentioned. I therefore make no attempt to confine my discussion to these themes. The aim, rather, has been to give a fully adequate account of the ideas of the most significant and illuminating political philosophers of the twentieth century. There are, I should add, two things I have not attempted to do. I have not tried to cover the most prominent themes or schools of thought manifest in the political philosophy of the century – though I hope that many of these arise in my discussions of particular political philosophers. Such important movements as feminism and environmentalism are, however, absent for this reason. Nor have I sought to include those theorists who have been most influential, prominent or celebrated. That status is, unfortunately, as often the result of fashion as it is of intrinsic intellectual quality. My aim, in brief, has been to put before the reader accounts of the best twentieth-century political philosophers I know.

This accounts for certain omissions which perhaps should be mentioned. Inevitably my knowledge is not unlimited, and there are doubtless some omissions due to ignorance – Carl Schmitt may be a case in point. Other well-known and admired figures have been omitted deliberately, because, in my opinion, their contributions are not such as to merit inclusion. Legions of neo-Marxists, existentialists, phenomenologists, post-structuralists, post-modernists and deconstructionists are absent for this reason. Thus the reader will find in the pages that follow no discussion of, for example, Sartre, Merleau-Ponty, Althusser, Foucault, Rorty or Derrida, simply because none of them seems to me to have said anything about politics that is both original and significant – in so far as their writings are comprehensible at all. Another notable omission that may surprise some readers is Alasdair MacIntyre, considered by many to be a leading contemporary exponent of communitarian political philosophy. MacIntyre is in fact a special case, a theorist whose career exhibits so many extraordinary changes of position – from Catholic to Marxist to Aristotelian to Thomist (for all I know there may be other phases that I have missed) – that it is quite hard to take him seriously, and equally hard to give a coherent account of his thought. It is true that one consistent thread does run through all these tergiversations – a hatred of liberal individualism. The arguments offered for that view, however, at least in MacIntyre's later post-Marxist or right-wing communitarian phase, are in my opinion, for the most part crude and unoriginal.[2]

Whatever the validity or otherwise of these value judgements, they have guided the process of selection which is inevitable in a work of this kind. And even if readers disagree with my selection and the judgements that have guided it, they will perhaps agree that there is a good deal to be said for writing about what one believes to be genuinely worthwhile. That at least has been my strategy in this book.

As well as this strategy, the structure of the book requires some explanation. As mentioned above, the substantive discussion begins with Max Weber (chapter 2). Thereafter the book is divided into three parts: within each section authors are discussed in chronological order, and the order of sections is also chronological, but the overall order in which individual authors are discussed is only approximately so. Part I groups three 'Critics of Consumerist Capitalism' (Marcuse, Arendt and Macpherson); part II, entitled 'Embattled Liberalism', brings together four (more or less) liberal writers who defended that position against the background of the Cold War (Oakeshott, Hayek, Popper and Berlin); finally, the third part, entitled 'Contemporaries', discusses the three most important living political philosophers (Rawls, Nozick and Habermas).

Notes

1 E. J. Hobsbawm, *Age of Extremes: The Short Twentieth Century, 1914–1991* (Michael Joseph, London, 1994).
2 See, for example, *After Virtue: A Study in Moral Theory* (Duckworth, London, 1981); *Whose Justice? Which Rationality?* (Duckworth, London, 1988); and *Three Rival Versions of Moral Enquiry: Encyclopaedia, Genealogy and Tradition* (Duckworth, London, 1990).

2
Max Weber and the Politics of the Twentieth Century

Although humanity has been grappling with the problems of politics for literally thousands of years, we cannot understand the political philosophy of the twentieth century without an understanding of the twentieth century itself — of the very specific evolution, in our century, of human life and society. Needless to say, that is too vast a topic to treat fully here. What we need, however, is not an encyclopaedic description, but rather a diagnosis of essential trends. What have these been? Where should we look for such a diagnosis? I propose to turn to one particular source, which seems to me particularly fruitful for the purpose, namely the work of the German sociologist Max Weber. Not only did Weber, who died in 1920, devote his exceptionally acute mind to analysing modern society within the context of world history, he was also keenly interested in the political dimension of life. This chapter, therefore, will be devoted to an exposition of his insights, and his own political responses.

Science and the Human Condition

Before looking at Weber's view of modernity, we need to consider some more general issues on which, as a social scientist, he had occasion to ponder. The social sciences, of course, are a part of science in general, that is, of the search for systematic knowledge of the world. Their subject, however, is the human world — hence social science is, or seeks, knowledge of the human condition. Deep philosophical issues arise, therefore, in relation to the presuppositions, definitions and basic concepts of social science, issues which, notoriously, remain in large measure controversial and unsettled up to the present day. Let us therefore look at Weber's commitments on these fundamental matters.

According to Weber's well-known definition, sociology is the science that seeks to understand a particular kind of human action, namely, social action. For present purposes, the genus is more relevant than the species. According to Weber, 'action' is human behaviour to which 'the active individual attaches a subjective meaning'.[1] Already, in this simple definition, Weber has introduced a concept fundamental to his world-view and to his diagnosis of his times – that of 'meaning'. What exactly does it imply, here? The answer is, something both simple and profound. Human action does not exist except in so far as human beings see some point in acting – something that makes the action worthwhile, or *meaningful*. What can do so? Simply and briefly, it must seem to serve some purpose, or embody some value.

Perhaps that answer is too simple and too brief. If we turn to Weber's celebrated fourfold typology of (social) action, we find that actions oriented to purposes and values respectively are two out of the four types.[2] Significantly, they are said to be two types of *rational* action (introducing another key Weberian concept) and contrasted with traditional action, oriented (consciously or unconsciously) to the continuation of customary practices, and affectual or emotional action 'determined by the specific affects and states of feeling of the actor'. Nevertheless, the two forms of rational action are the kinds Weber considered most significant – the other two, he says, are on the borderline of what can be called meaningful action, and often indeed are 'on the other side'.[3] This is because they tend to be automatic and unthinking. When this is *not* so, Weber says, they tend towards one or other of the two forms of rational action. In other words, in so far as traditionally oriented action becomes self-consciously so, it tends to be the expression of a specific value (traditionalism); in so far as affectual/emotional action becomes controlled rather than automatic, it tends towards the purposive or value-oriented type. So it is, after all, not wrong to say that for Weber, the 'meaning' that constitutes human action is its orientation to either purpose or value – an orientation that may be more or less 'rational'. More will be said later about these concepts.

The centrality of meanings, for Weber, is not limited to their role in motivating (and hence, for the social scientist, understanding) individual human actions – on the contrary, it extends much further, to the whole of human life, and even to the entire universe. Human beings, according to Weber, have a need, an 'inner compulsion', to conceive the world as a 'meaningful totality', or 'meaningful cosmos'.[4] Not only religions, but secular metaphysical philosophy also are born of the endeavour to find a coherent meaning in 'the world as a whole and [human] life in particular'.[5] Just what might suffice to render the world meaningful or imbue it with meaning in this sense is a difficult question, to put it mildly. However, one must not lose sight of the semantic continuity linking meaning in this context and in that of individual human actions – here, as there, the 'meaning of the world' has to do with the purposes and/or values that it subserves, and give it point or worthwhileness. As we shall later see, the relation between the meaningfulness of the world and the meaningfulness of actions is of central importance to Weber's analysis.

Since social science aims to describe human life and human action, meaning, it might be said, constitutes its subject matter. On the other hand, Weber famously insisted that social science is value free (*wertfrei*). Not, be it noted, that it should be value free, but that it *is* value free: anything not value-free cannot be social science, as a matter of logic and epistemology. Given the close conceptual connection between value and meaning, this may seem paradoxical, but it is not. Social science, by its nature, is incapable of making, or in any ultimate sense validating value judgements (defined by Weber as judgements of the 'desirability or undesirability' of phenomena, including in particular 'social facts').[6] The methods of social science, as of all sciences, are rationally adapted to establishing what the facts are or were, and what causal and other relations exist between them, but not in the least to evaluating them 'from ethical, cultural or other points of view'.[7] Science, including social science, can be action-guiding only in a secondary sense; it can show what *means* if any are necessary or possible for the realization of *given* ends or purposes, and also what further consequences are likely to follow from the employment of these means. But that is all: it cannot even *prescribe* the use of such means, much less the pursuit of any ends, because such prescriptions necessarily rest on extra-scientific value judgements.

If science, including social science, by its nature does not yield practical prescriptions nor any rational assessment of values and purposes, does that mean that *no* rational assessment or validation thereof is possible? That was indeed Weber's view. 'To *judge* the *validity* of [ultimate] values' he wrote 'is a matter of *faith*'.[8] This does not mean, of course, that such judgements of value are not significant – on the contrary, they 'determine our conduct and give meaning and significance to our lives'.[9] But it does entail that all meaning is subjective rather than objective, not only from the point of view of social science, but also in an ultimate metaphysical sense. Objectively speaking, the world is meaningless. To put it in another way, which belongs to the vocabulary of Weber's analysis of the history of Western civilization, the world is disenchanted. To that historical analysis we must now turn.

Rationalization

Weber's sociology is at once historical and comparative – it is an analysis of the major world civilizations, and of their differing evolution through time. More precisely, Weber's interest focused on the unique evolution of Western civilization, which he sought to define and explain. Central to this analysis are the concepts of rationalization and disenchantment, which are closely related and, up to a point, two sides of the same coin. But it is rationalization that is the more inclusive and complex of the two, and which we must examine first.

By common consent, Weber's concept of rationalization is very complex indeed. In brief summary, he saw the history of Western civilization as a particular kind of rationalization of life and society. What does this mean? Let us return to Weber's definitions of rational action already mentioned. As we know, Weber distinguished two kinds of rational action, purpose oriented (*zweckrational*), and value oriented (*wertrational*). He also offered a second dichotomy – between formal and substantive rationality. This latter dichotomy, however, is less general than the other (it is applied by Weber to particular areas of social life such as economics and law). The contrasting fortunes of purpose-oriented and value-oriented rationality are centrally implicated in the historical trajectory of Western civilization, as Weber saw it. To understand Weber's sociology, therefore, we must examine these contrasted terms.

Unfortunately, Weber's definitions of his concepts are not wholly consistent (or else he uses some key terms in non-standard ways). At first, *zweckrational* action is said to be action oriented to the agent's consciously held 'system of individual ends', with external objects and other individuals being looked on as potential means or obstacles to these ends.[10] This implies a conscious weighing of different ends, and calculation of appropriate means in the light of all the likely consequences, welcome and unwelcome, of alternative courses of action. When *zweckrational* action takes place, the action is chosen as a means to an end, rather than as being valuable in itself. By contrast, *wertrational* action is action dictated by belief in the 'absolute value' of the behaviour in question, whether for ethical, aesthetic, or religious reasons, or out of a sense of duty, honour, personal loyalty, or whatever, and without regard to conse-

9

quences.[11] This contrast seems clear enough. Later, however, Weber distinguishes between two ways of weighing up differing ends or purposes that an agent may have in mind: he may treat them as 'subjective desires' and weigh them in terms of their 'relative urgency', aiming to 'maximize his utility'; or he may assess them in terms of 'absolute value' and choose accordingly.[12] The latter, Weber says, gives rise to a mixed case involving a form of rationality which is both value oriented *and* purpose oriented – it is, Weber confusingly says, *zweckrational* (purpose oriented) only in so far as it involves choice of means. Weber thus seems to have two quite different criteria for distinguishing his two kinds of rational action: whether it is driven by subjective desires and their urgency, or by value judgements and their subjective importance; and whether it has regard to consequences, or not. An action driven by value judgements, but also by attention to consequences, is a mixed case of rational action (the other mixed case, action determined by the urgency of desires and without regard to consequences, is presumably not rational action at all – perhaps it is affective/emotional action).

Several problems remain with this picture. Thus, the pure case of so-called purpose-oriented rational action appears to be completely amoral – neither belief in values, nor concern for other individuals, plays any part in it, by definition. It is surely a pathological kind of rationality, the 'rationality' of the psychopath. The pure case of value-oriented rational action seems to be pathological in a different way, namely its total neglect of the consequences of actions, born of an obsessive concentration on one single value to the exclusion of all others – the 'rationality' of the fanatic. Perhaps Weber would agree that the two pure cases are pathological – we shall see evidence for this later in his political theory. Also, he remarks in the course of his discussion of the two forms of rational action that it is very unusual to find concrete cases of action oriented in only one of these ways,[13] perhaps meaning, taking one of the pure forms. If so, the norm of rational action is the mixed case, and the point of the two pure cases is, presumably, to serve as analytical tools. For the *balance* between the two elements, *Zweckrationalität* and *Wertrationalität* – that is, between the calculation of means and consequences on the one hand, and the motivating role of values on the other – is of great significance, not least to the history of Western civilization as seen by Weber. It is worth mentioning, however, although parenthetically for the moment, that Weber's analysis of action, including rational action, omits to mention one very important motivating factor, namely, the influence of internalized *constraints*. The role of constraints (most significantly, moral constraints) is to *rule out* possible actions, thereby often inducing the agent to choose some alternative action (or, in some cases, inaction). As we shall see in later chapters, it is of the utmost importance, politically speaking, not to assimilate constraints (like, for example the precept 'Thou shalt not kill') to purposes or values, even though they may derive from value judgements of a negative kind, just as purposes may derive from positive value judgements.

Our concern just now, however, is to explicate Weber's key concept of *rationalization*, which is notorious for its complexity and many-sidedness. Rationalization, or increasing rationality, is obviously related to what Weber calls rational action, but is even more complex or inclusive. For one thing, it involves the notion of *degrees* of rationality. What is entailed in the idea that one form of action is 'more rational' than another? The answer to this should become apparent as the discussion proceeds. But in addition, Weber's concept of rationalization embraces not only forms of action but also systems of thought, theoretical rationality as well as practical rationality. Weber never tired of stressing that rationalization can take many different forms with dramatically different historical consequences. Indeed, it has done so, in the divergent development of the different world civilizations. The focus of Weber's attention was the contrast between the civilizations of the East and of the West, of Asia on the one hand and of Europe and America on the other. For Weber the contrast is fundamentally one of mentality or world-view, and is therefore rooted in the differing religious traditions dominant in these civilizations.

Religion and the World

We saw above that Weber conceived of the great world religions (as well as secular metaphysical systems) as attempts to grapple with the problem of universal meaning. This problem can, however, be tackled at two levels: the meaningfulness of the entire universe or cosmos, and the meaningfulness of human life. Of course the two cannot really be separated but the emphasis can vary. By and large, Weber suggested, the problem of the meaningfulness of the universe as a whole has been the particular concern of 'intellectual strata', whereas concern as to the meaningfulness of human life has by no means been so limited.[14] In the latter context, the all too obvious problems requiring solution are, as Weber says, the prevalence of suffering, especially of (apparently) unmerited suffering, and what he called 'ephemerality' – in other words death.[15] Often religions solve, or claim to solve, both of these problems at once, as in the Christian concepts of heaven and hell, or the Hindu and Buddhist concepts of karma, transmigration and nirvana. Religions of this kind, Weber says, are religions of salvation[16] – they offer the believer salvation from (unmerited) suffering and the ephemerality of death. In this way they make the believer's life meaningful to him and, at least up to a point, render the universe meaningful in his eyes.

It seems obvious that these various conceptions of salvation must carry implications for the way a human life is lived. What are they? In Weber's view, there are marked differences between the major Western and Eastern religions – between Christianity on the one hand, and on the other Hinduism, Buddhism and Taoism, the major salvation religions of the Indian and Chinese civilizations (Confucianism is something of a special case). According to Weber the South and East Asian salvation religions were in origin religions of intellectual strata oriented to problems of meaning of the universe as a whole, though they did not remain so, but spread widely through large populations, changing their characteristics as they did so. Nevertheless they remained marked by their origins, and by 'techniques of salvation' markedly different from those of European religion. The contrast, of course, is not total, in that the kind of techniques prevalent in one were not totally absent in the other: nevertheless the difference, in Weber's eyes, was great and of great significance.

Weber conceptualized the difference between Eastern and Western religion in terms of their differing 'rejections of the world'. It must be stressed that, in this phrase, 'the world' means not the universe as a whole, the totality of being, but the ordinary secular or workaday world or society in which most people, of necessity, spend most of their lives. The Asian (especially Indian) religious intellectuals, unable to find meaning in this world, devalued it and sought salvation elsewhere, in a characteristic fashion: through other-worldly contemplative mysticism. The clearest example is Buddhism, which adopted what Weber called the 'ultimate ethic of world-rejection', one which seeks the annihilation of all desire and of the very self.[17] In Western religion world-rejection is also to be found, but it characteristically took a different form – what Weber called 'asceticism'. The contrast between asceticism and mysticism is so important to Weber's thinking that his definition of it should be quoted:

> Asceticism . . . is God-willed *action* of the devout who are God's tools . . . . Mysticism intends a state of 'possession' [of the holy], not action, and the individual is not a tool but a 'vessel' of the divine.[18]

Obviously this contrast is related to differing concepts of divinity – the transcendent personal deity of the Judaeo-Christian tradition as opposed to the more diffuse divinity envisaged by the Eastern religions. The crucial point, however, is the Western concept of a holy life as a divine tool or instrument, devoted to carrying out the will of God. Weber saw this conception as having important potential (absent in the Eastern religions) for the rationalization of action (in fact, Weber's term *Zweckrationalität* has often been translated as 'instrumental rationality'). Western religious asceticism sometimes rejected the everyday secular world in a quite radical way, as in early Christian and medieval monasticism; but it also had a potential (lacking in the contemplative mysticism of the East) for transforming that world. Other-worldly contemplative mysticism has indeed rather little relevance to a life lived in the ordinary world: hence, when a religion like Buddhism became a popular religion with a mass following, it came to depend on what Weber calls the staples of popular salvation religion – magic, and personal saviours. Neither of these is in any sense rational. According to Weber's famous comment, for popular Asian religiosity, 'the world remained a great enchanted garden',[19] in which the way to find security was 'to revere or coerce the spirits and seek salvation through ritualistic, idolatrous or sacramental procedures'. Not that personal saviours or magical attitudes or practices were by any means absent from Western popular religion – however, unlike the contemplative mysticism of the East, Western asceticism was capable of taking an 'inner-worldly' form in which individual salvation was conceived as requiring action (as God's instrument) *in the world*, world-rejection taking the form not of flight *from* the world but rather mastery *of* the world, the taming of the 'creatural and wicked'[20] ('in the world but not of the world'). In this activity in the world the individual finds his 'calling' or 'vocation', and thus the meaning of his life.

Economic Rationalization

As every student of Weber will recognize, the last sentence above encapsulates Weber's famous thesis about the role of the 'Protestant ethic' in generating modern Western capitalism. What Weber called the 'spirit' of this capitalism looked on ceaseless effort to acquire more and more profit from economic activity without ever lapsing into idleness or self-indulgence as a vocation (the 'calling of making money', as Weber put it).[21] At first it was for many a religious vocation – obedience to the will of God – but as the Western world became increasing secularized, as a consequence not least of the spread of modern capitalism itself, its vocational status also became secularized and attenuated. Though it never disappeared, it became secondary and indeed unnecessary as a motivating factor for the businessman – profit maximization is now for him simply a systemic imperative of the modern economy. To describe this change in different but still Weberian terms, capitalistic economic activity has become much less *wertrational* and much more *zweckrational* – much less the embodiment of values, much more nearly a pure calculation of means to 'maximize utility'. However, it cannot be purely *zweckrational* so long as the pursuit of money is constrained by legal and moral norms (forbidding violence, theft, deceit, etc.) – constraints strongly emphasized by Weber in his account of modern Western capitalism, and without which the system probably cannot function, but, as we saw, omitted from his typology of action.

Weber himself frequently described modern Western capitalism as a peculiarly rational type of economic activity. The meaning of this assertion is, however, once again complex. Not only does Weber refer in so many words to 'economic' rationality (contrasted, sometimes, with 'ethical' rationality'),[22] he also introduced, in this context, a distinction between 'formal' and 'substantive' rationality.[23] The concept of formal economic rationality is closely tied to the money economy: Weber defined 'formal rationality of economic action' as the extent to which 'calculation or accounting' is applied to economic ends. Money is the most efficient means of this accounting. So far as economic producers are concerned, it involves monetary calculations of the prospective costs and benefits of every activity as well as retrospective assessment of these costs and benefits, comparison of alternative courses of action, periodic calculation of the money value of the assets of the economic unit, and 'systematic distribution of utilities as between present and future' (i.e. calculation of the optimum sum to devote to current expenditure, as against saving and investment), all in the interests of maximizing long-term money gain.[24] Formal rationality, according to Weber, is dependent on the market, because rational economic calculation in money terms is not possible without money prices set in the market. The market is an arena of 'rational exchange', from which both parties expect to benefit.

Weber is clear that modern capitalism is formally a highly rational system. When (in *Economy and Society*) he lists the conditions of formal economic rationality, many of the items on the list are structural features of a modern capitalist economy – not only a money economy and freedom of contract and exchange but also separation of the economic enterprise from the household, private ownership of the 'non-human' means of production, non-ownership of jobs by workers and non-ownership of workers by employers ('formally free labour' which can be hired and fired, or in other words a free labour market). Weber has an interesting analysis of the relative 'rationality' of free and slave labour, from the standpoint of the employer.[25] Use of free labour is more rational, he argues, because (*inter alia*) purchase of slaves requires a much larger and riskier capital investment than does employment of free labour (which can always be fired, and payment of wages thereby terminated); the employed worker is more likely to be good at his job because 'part of the selection according to aptitude is turned over to the workers themselves' (or, in other words employees, but not slaves, have some choice over the job they do and are likely to try to choose jobs that they are good at); and slaves, unlike employed workers, cannot safely be given tasks involving a high level of responsibility (free employed workers presumably wish to keep their jobs, while slaves have so little wish to do so that they frequently try to escape). Free labour, therefore, is more 'formally' rational, in the sense not that it gives greater scope for numerical calculation of economic costs and benefits, but rather that a rational employer aiming at maximum profit and making the relevant calculations would prefer to employ free labour. The preference for free labour *follows from* formal economic rationality.

Does that mean that employment of formally free labour in capitalism represents greater *substantive* economic rationality? The answer depends on what is meant by substantive rationality, a concept which Weber admits is 'full of difficulties'.[26] Certainly formal rationality is no guarantee of substantive rationality, or even of economic rationality *tout court*. It has to be asked: rationality from what point of view, and from whose point of view? The concept of substantive rationality, unlike formal rationality, raises issues of overall judgement of the workings of an economic system, not of the modalities of individual action within such a system. To put the point in another way, maximum opportunity to calculate costs and benefits in monetary terms is something quite different from maximum capacity to achieve ends – more especially since, as Weber often stressed, the economy is *inter alia* an arena in which conflicting interests struggle.[27] Judgements of substantive economic rationality therefore depend on the values of the judge. Thus formal and substantive rationality may be held to be actually contradictory by, for example, those who think that to calculate everything in money terms is an evil in itself.[28] (Weber noted the extreme 'impersonality' of the market, its hostility to 'spontaneous human relations' and all similar distractions from the economic goal.)[29] If, on the other hand, 'the standard used is the provision of a certain minimum of subsistence for the maximum size of population', then experience suggests, Weber says, that formal rationality and (this) substantive rationality coincide to quite a high degree. However, as Weber was well aware, market economies respond not to needs or even wants as such, but to 'effective demand'. Hence, from an egalitarian standpoint (based on a principle of equal want-satisfaction), capitalism is substantively irrational, though formally highly rational. Conversely, a planned economy dedicated to want-satisfaction is from this point of view substantively more rational, at least in its aims, but at the price of much reduced formal rationality because of its abolition of free markets and consequently of market prices. It thus sacrifices an important tool of economic efficiency.

In sum, whereas formal rationality is an objective matter, or a matter of fact, substantive rationality is purely subjective because it depends on value judgements, which Weber viewed as purely subjective. It should also be noted that, whereas formal rationality is closely connected with what Weber called purpose-oriented rationality (*Zweckrationalität*), substantive rationality is quite different from value-oriented rationality or *Wertrationalität*. Action is *wertrational* to the extent that it is motivated by value judgements: whether and to what extent this is so in any given case is a matter of fact. Nothing, however, is substantively rational as a matter of fact, because this description depends on a judgement based on subjective value standards. *Wertrationalität* is a descriptive category for the empirical analysis of actions: substantive rationality is nothing of the kind. Very probably, it was introduced by Weber in order to signal that, in characterizing capitalism as economically rational, he did not mean to convey his moral (or other) approval of it.

What, in fact, was Weber's overall judgement of this powerful and pervasive element of modern Western rationalization? A summary answer is given in a much-quoted passage near the end of his famous essay on *The Protestant Ethic and the Spirit of Capitalism*: capitalism, Weber wrote, has become an 'iron cage', in which 'material goods have gained . . . an inexorable power over the lives of men'.[30] Two elements are combined in this denunciation: first, the loss of individual freedom (most people have now no choice but to live according to the 'inexorable' dictates of the capitalist system, to function as parts of a profit-maximizing machine); secondly, the near total triumph of materialistic (or economic) values. Weber himself never ceased to pillory 'hedonism' or utilitarianism (maximization of pleasure, happiness or want-satisfaction) – what nowadays might be called 'consumerism' – as a philosophy of life. Such a life, one might say, was for Weber meaningless. Like the Puritan forebears of modern capitalism, Weber was, in his own way, an ascetic and a believer in the ethic of vocation. It is, of course, one of the ironies of Western history that – if Weber is right – a development driven by vocation and ascetisism has culminated in the triumph of materialistic hedonism.

Rational Administration

When Weber referred to modern Western civilization as an 'iron cage', in all probability he did not have in mind only the imperatives of the market. Equally important is another of its major structural elements – bureaucracy. Bureaucracy was defined by Weber as the most rational – that is, most efficient – form of administration. Clearly we have to do here with rationality in the sense of *Zweckrationalität*. Weber frequently described bureaucracy as a living tool, or instrument, a means for those who control it to achieve their aims. The political relevance of the phenomenon is obvious enough, but it is of course not limited to the political sphere in the narrow sense of the term. Rather, it extends potentially to every organization dedicated to the pursuit of ends, and not least the capitalist economic enterprise. Weber pointed to a dual affinity between capitalism and bureaucracy. In the first place, since capitalism means a particularly 'rational' pursuit of profit, capitalist enterprises can be expected to adopt the most efficient organizational means to that end – in the case of large enterprises, bureaucracy. Secondly – in ways to be explained later – there is a symbiotic relation (at least up to a point) between capitalism and the bureaucratic administration of the state.

As is clear from the above, bureaucracy, as a means or instrument, can be turned to any of a wide variety of ends. Why is it a particularly efficient means? (Perhaps it would be better to ask, why is it capable of being an efficient means? Like any tool, it will actually *be* efficient only if those using it know how to use it intelligently.) To answer this question, we need to attend to Weber's definition of bureaucracy, but also to realize that his analysis is historical and comparative, so that bureaucratic administration is always implicitly or explicitly conceptualized in contrast with alternatives. A bureaucracy, then, is a hierarchical structure of offices.[31] Each office is a clearly defined sphere of competence and responsibility. Incumbents (officials) are appointed by means of a free contract, on the basis of technical expertise or ability more generally. (Offices are not inherited, therefore.) They are paid a money salary, graded according to position in the hierarchy (they do not appropriate – own – their positions, as in some 'traditional' systems). They use but do not own the means of administration. They devote themselves to their official duties as a full-time job, and can make these a career through successive promotions depending on the decisions of their superiors. Last but not least, they are subject to official discipline – they must abide by the rules (usually written rules) that specify their function, and which are enforced by superiors. A bureaucracy is a rule-bound organization.

Bureaucratic state administration, according to Weber, is an aspect or arm of one particular type of political authority, which he called legal authority. Here careful definition of terms is necessary. A functioning political system or state means, normally (and, in Weber's view, universally) that the many are ruled by the few. Although coercion plays a greater or lesser part in this process (Weber defined the state as a body claiming the right not just to exercise but to monopolize coercive power in its territory), nevertheless in most cases most of the ruled accept the situation as legitimate – that is, they accept the political authority of the rulers. Why? Weber, famously, distinguished three types of reasons: belief in the sanctity of tradition (traditional authority); devotion to a saintly, heroic or otherwise exceptional individual and to that person's 'message' (charismatic authority); or belief in 'legality' and the powers of those duly authorized according to legal norms (legal authority). It might perhaps be wondered why anyone should accept authority on grounds of its legality: however, according to Weber there are specifically *rational* grounds for doing so, in that legal norms can be and presumably are established 'on grounds of expediency or rational values or both'.[32] Hence he sometimes referred to this kind of authority by the dual description of 'rational-legal'. It is clear that it is defined as rational in both the *zweckrational* and the *wertrational* (or value-oriented) senses. Although traditional authority has of course been very important and widespread in the history of the world, and bulks large in Weber's political sociology, nevertheless he saw little future for it in contemporary Western civilization. As we shall see, his normative theorizing about politics concentrates almost wholly on the 'rational-legal' and the 'charismatic' forms and, more particularly, on the polarity between charisma and bureaucracy.

As already mentioned Weber saw a close affinity between the capitalist economy and the legal-cum-bureaucratic state: the reason is that the latter offers a (potentially) optimum combination of flexibility and predictability in the economy's political environment. Rational long-term planning in the interests of profit maximization (or anything else) requires a stable, predictable environment, and this the rules of law and bureaucracy provide. Tradition-based politics are perhaps more stable, but they are often less predictable, because of the large degree of discretion exercised by traditional rulers; and they are of course much less flexible, less adaptable, therefore to the needs of capitalism (charismatic rule is generally unpredictable and unresponsive to economic needs). Thus, although the legal–cum–bureaucratic Western state has its origins, in large part, in the heritage of Roman law, it has been greatly strengthened in modern times by the needs and pressures of the capitalist economy, whose development it in turn facilitates.

In brief: capitalism, bureaucracy and the law-based state mesh together well because all manifest to a high degree a certain kind of rationality, purpose-oriented rationality (*Zweckrationalität*). It is interesting that Weber reintroduced, in his sociology of law, the distinction between formal and substantive rationality that bulks large in his analysis of the capitalist economy.[33] It is also noteworthy, however, that the way these terms are defined is not completely analogous in the two cases. The reason, I think, is partly that the relation between the system and individual action is quite different in the two areas: judges are expected to carry out the will of legislators (if there are any), but economic agents are not necessarily expected to carry out the will of economic policy makers (if there are any). Thus, Weber says that law is formally rational to the extent that it makes use of (1) general legal rules, integrated into a consistent system; and (2) rational procedures for finding evidence of guilt (as opposed to recourse to oracles, ordeals, or the outcome of battles); and it is substantively rational to the extent that it is influenced by ethical norms, or political or utilitarian considerations. (Rather strangely, he describes *khadi* justice, in which each case is decided 'on its merits', i.e. directly by ethical or political criteria without recourse to formal legal rules, as 'substantively irrational'.[34] He should have said that in this kind of legal system formal rationality is sacrificed to substantive considerations.) In a fully rational legal system, formal and substantive rationality would be combined, i.e. the legal rules and procedures would reflect ethical, political, etc., criteria. Thus, in the case of law, unlike economics, 'substantive rationality' is a purely sociological category, referring to the degree to which legal rules are designed to serve a purpose or reflect extra-legal norms - are, in other words, either *zweckrational* or *wertrational*.

Bureaucratic administration and rational law are not unique to modern Western civilization. For example, several ancient empires – notably ancient Egypt, imperial Rome and classical China – developed administrative systems having bureaucratic features to a greater or lesser extent. The Chinese case is particularly interesting in that it developed, not just a quasi-bureaucratic administrative state, but a civilization dominated culturally by the official stratum (the mandarinate) and by its religion or ethos – so-called

Confucianism. Compared to other religions of the great world civilizations, Confucianism is, Weber believed, uniquely worldly – uniquely focused on this (secular) world, and accommodated to it.[35] It is, therefore, not a salvation religion – it did not posit any need for salvation. Its social effect was stabilizing and conservative, serving to maintain the political and cultural continuity of China over thousands of years. To use Weber's categories, Chinese civilization was in some respects highly rational, but lacked a strong drive to increasing *rationalization*. The same is true (or apparently true) of pre-modern Occidental civilization and religion, largely because of the heritage of Roman law. Weber pointed out that the pre-Reformation Christian Church, being in large measure the inheritor of imperial Roman law and Roman state structures, exhibited a rationality unique among salvation religions in its development of a bureaucratic organization and of a system of sacred rational law (canon law – this Weber contrasted with, for example, the unsystematic Islamic sacred law, with its reliance on *ad hoc fetwas* issued by religiously qualified individuals and 'the disputatious casuistry of the [four] competing orthodox schools').[36] The great difference, however, between Christian Europe and China is that the former, but not the latter, also contained a powerful ascetic ethic capable of entering, and influencing, the everyday secular world – its economics, that is, rather than its politics – in the direction of an unprecedented rationalization.

In Weber's view, then, bureaucratic structures and values lack the dynamism needed to help establish a modern capitalist economy in the first place, though they can be very useful and even necessary to it once that system has come into existence for other reasons. Indeed, capitalism is probably responsible for creating, in the modern Western world, a society that is bureaucratized to an unprecedented degree. Weber's attitude to this development was complex. On the one hand, he accepted bureaucracy as the most efficient form of administration and for that reason, and to that extent, indispensable and unavoidable in the modern world. On the other hand, he saw it as a threat to some of the most important human values. It is a rule-bound, impersonal force that imposes itself on human beings and threatens to destroy creativity and individual freedom. It makes the individual into a cog in a living machine dedicated to carrying out someone else's will, a machine that works better the more it 'de-humanizes' the individual and eliminates all non-calculable, 'irrational' human emotion. It leads to what Weber called 'the parcelling out of the soul',[37] fragmenting the integrity of the individual personality. Or at least it tends to do all of these things, if not somehow checked. As we shall later see, much of Weber's political thinking is dominated by this problem – how to check the 'excesses' of bureaucracy. For now, it can be noted that fear of bureaucracy was the main ground of his unrelenting opposition to Marxian socialism, whose effect, he foresaw (quite apart from the problems of economic efficiency involved, mentioned above) would be to merge the bureaucracies of the state and of the large economic enterprises into a single over-arching super-bureaucracy that could crush all individual freedom and creativity out of society.

Disenchantment

The rationalization of Western social institutions, clearly, has been a mixed blessing, the huge gains in wealth and efficiency being offset by important costs. But so far only half the story – perhaps the less important half – has been told. We have to turn our attention now to the other half – intellectual rationalization. By 'intellectualism' Weber meant, roughly speaking, the drive to understand the universe. 'The intellectual' said Weber 'conceives the "world" as a problem of meaning'.[38] We have already noted the importance of this motive in the generation of the great world religions. Religion, however, is not its only manifestation – metaphysical philosophy is another, and a more intellectually rational one. In the West, the whole intellectual culture, including the dominant religion, Christianity, has been powerfully influenced by the tradition of rational philosophical thought inherited from the Greeks. The early Christian Church, Weber noted, developed in a Greek-educated milieu and felt constrained to develop, in opposition to it but also influenced by it, a uniquely 'comprehensive' and 'systematically rationalised' dogmatics of a theoretical type concerning cosmological matters'.[39] Perhaps more important was the later development in Europe of a philosophically influenced theology. Eventually this tradition of thought gave birth to natural science, in which, it might be said, the ancient Greek spirit of free enquiry re-emerged, liberated from the dogmatic strain in Christianity with which it had coexisted for centuries.

That, however, is an over-simplified account of natural science, which has a dual character: it is on the one hand philosophy, on the other technology. *Qua* technology, it is a supremely important aspect of social and economic rationalization in the instrumental or *zweckrational* sense. As a tool of bureaucracy and especially of capitalism, it has greatly enhanced the calculability (predictability) of actions and the capacity of agents to achieve desired ends. Historically speaking, however, large-scale technological application of Western natural science developed rather late (only in the later nineteenth century): early modern capitalism owed almost nothing to it, and natural science made its debut as a theoretical intellectual movement, a 'new philosophy' – natural philosophy. Our concern here is with natural science as a philosophy, a fruit of the intellectual drive to understand the world through reason.

As such it is profoundly ironic. According to Weber, the motivational wellspring of philosophy is the desire to comprehend the meaning of the universe – to grasp the world as a meaningful whole: and the culmination of this most urgent human enterprise, in its most rational manifestation (Western philosophy, issuing in Western 'natural' philosophy/science) has been what Weber famously called 'the disenchantment of the world' – the conclusion that no such meaning is or can be rationally discernible, or even that it is non-existent.

Why exactly is this so? Accounts of world 'disenchantment' (not least by Weber himself) often stress the elimination of magic from the modern, scientific world-view. This, however, is I believe a secondary matter. The issue of magic arises in two different contexts. Let us define magic as the attempt to manipulate other-worldly (possibly divine) forces for human ends. Then, these ends may themselves be worldly or other-worldly. Where the ends are worldly, magic is a kind of non-rational, relatively ineffective proto-technology. Its supersession by rational, science-based technology appears to give rise to no *problem* of 'disenchantment'. But magic also has had another role, as a means to the 'other-worldly' end of salvation – what Weber called a salvation technique. Weber viewed ascetic Protestantism as a religion peculiarly hostile to magical salvation techniques, such as abound in many other religions including pre-Reformation Christianity: it is, rather, a notable example (perhaps the most notable) of what he called 'ethical religion', or even 'rational ethical religion' (ethical behaviour is not, however, a technique of salvation but a manifestation of one's state of grace in those versions based on the doctrine of predestination). This is another aspect of the elimination of magic from the modern world-view – but once again it carries no threat of disenchantment *so long as belief in the religious ethic holds firm.*

It is just this belief that intellectual rationalization, culminating in modern science, has destroyed. In essence, Hume's view of reason and rational knowledge has triumphed (but with consequences far beyond those Hume envisaged): rational (human) knowledge is in principle limited to matters of observable fact and logical reasoning. In a universe thus conceived there is no place for an invisible God or gods, despite the efforts of innumerable theists to evade this conclusion. As Weber often remarked, belief in God and theistic religion is today impossible without a 'sacrifice of the intellect' (dramatized by the notorious formula *credo quia absurdum*, a deliberate decision to believe the unbelievable).[40] Nor can ethical beliefs be unaffected by this 'death of God'. They become, as Weber said, a matter of personal faith, not reason, and thereby inevitably dubious – and doubly so, because, contrary to Hume's view, there is no general human consensus of moral sentiment. There are no objective values, only subjective and conflicting value judgements.

Some of Weber's most eloquent passages refer to this predicament. The theologian Swammerdam's belief that he saw 'proof of God's providence in the anatomy of a louse' was typical of a pietistic view that 'in the exact sciences . . . where one could physically grasp His works, one [could] come upon the traces of what He planned for the world'. And today?

> Who – aside from certain big children who are indeed found in the natural sciences – still believes that the findings of astronomy, biology, physics or chemistry could teach us anything about the *meaning* of the world? . . . If the natural sciences lead to anything in this way, they are apt to make the belief that there is such a thing as the 'meaning' of the universe die out at its roots.[41]

If the universe has no meaning, does it follow the human life has no meaning? Weber quotes Tolstoi: 'Science is meaningless because it gives no answer to our question, the only question important for us: What shall we do and how shall we live?'[42] In Weber's view Tolstoi is right that science cannot answer this question (it is value free). But it does not follow that science is meaningless, nor – in Weber's view – that for modern man life has no meaning because (as Tolstoi put it) death has no meaning. We can *give* 'meaning and significance to our life' by espousing, and living by, the highest values in which as individuals we can believe.[43] It is difficult to say whether this prescription is intellectually or psychologically coherent: we are enjoined to hold fast to our values, while recognizing that there is no ultimate rational ground for them – to pursue a meaningful life in a meaningless universe.

Weber's personal solution to the dilemma went further than the choice of values, to the choice of a vocation – the vocation of science. Science is value free, but the decision to devote oneself to the life of a (social) scientist is of course far from being value free. The vocation of the scientist is to seek the truth by scientific methods because the truth about something matters profoundly to him. Weber's use of language freighted with religious overtones is of course not accidental, and it is striking how his description of the scientific calling parallels the old Puritan concept. The scientist (and the great artist also, for that matter) must 'serve his work and only his work', and must do so 'with passionate devotion'.[44] 'Nothing is worthy of man as man unless he can pursue it with passionate devotion'. But enthusiasm alone is not enough. Science is a *discipline*, in more than one sense of the word. It requires of the scientist a combination of enthusiasm and 'very hard work'. He who lacks 'a firm and reliable work procedure', no matter how brilliant his ideas, remains only a 'dilettante', a dabbler.[45] Clearly Weber's conception of his own vocation is thoroughly secularized, the task itself being its own justification without reference to the will of God. But another difference from the Puritan concept may be slightly less obvious. Weber, we might think, was lucky in that he was able to find his vocation. Whereas the Puritans postulated an earthly calling for everyone, a calling to fulfil a divinely legitimated social role, the secularized Weberian vocation hardly seems possible for most people in the bureaucratic and market-dominated 'iron cage' of modernity. The Weberian vocation has to be meaningful in itself, whereas the Puritan's calling could be meaningful no matter how 'soul destroying' it might appear. Yet there is also a parallel here, as well as a difference. According to Calvinistic Protestantism the saved are a small elite (though many are called, few are chosen); likewise, it would seem that only a relative few can find meaning through a secular vocation in the rationalized, disenchanted world.

Politics in the Modern World

Weber did serve his 'work', his scientific calling, 'with passionate devotion', but he did not serve 'only his work'. The unique calling, to which one must dedicate oneself if one's life is to have meaning, was not after all enough. Perhaps it is too akin to the narrowly specialized life role imposed by bureaucratic and market rationality, which leads to the 'parcelling out of the soul'. Although Weber was not a political philosopher in the usual sense of the term, he was a profoundly political animal, with strong and frequently expressed political views. Just as much as Machiavelli or Tocqueville he deserves the name of political theorist. Although the 'vocation' of the politician was not his vocation, it was one to which he attached enormous importance. For Weber, politics as much as science gave meaning to life. Here, Weber's views on politics will be considered under four headings – liberalism, nationalism, democracy and (most fundamental of all) the nature of politics itself.

Weber's liberalism is completely of a piece with his view of the human condition in a disenchanted universe and a 'rationalized' society. In a disenchanted universe no values can be discovered, they can only be chosen; and the individual must choose them, because without values he cannot act, still less lead a meaningful life. And he must choose them *for himself* (not accept values dictated by others) since in the choice of values to live by, Weber believed, lies the dignity of the human personality. This belief is, of course, an article of (humanistic) faith, in itself a choice – Weber rejected as scornfully as Bentham the idea that the individual has 'natural rights' (no rights can be found in, or deduced from, nature). Nor has Weber's belief in individual liberty anything in common with support for the so-called 'free market' of capitalism. On the contrary, 'rational' capitalism governed by market forces and bureaucratic organization, which Weber recognized as the inescapable economic system of modern society, threatens to destroy genuine freedom and individuality for all but a small number of entrepreneurs. This theme was sounded with striking consistency throughout Weber's work. Already in his famous youthful inaugural lecture at Freiburg, 'The nation state and economic policy', delivered in 1895, Weber celebrated the German agricultural labourers who, at significant material cost, rejected dependent wage-earning status on the developing capitalist estates of the East German *Junker* landowners, for the sake of 'freedom'. Ten years later, in an article on the abortive Russian Revolution of 1905, he ridiculed the suggestion of an affinity between developed capitalism and '"freedom" (in any sense of the word)'.[46] Freedom and individuality must be fought for 'against the tide' of economic trends, as well as (Weber added, returning to the theme in an article written during the First World War) ever-growing bureaucracy in the state as well as the economy. To Weber the fundamental question was: in view of these irreversible institutional developments, 'How is it at all possible to salvage any remnants of individual freedom?' – not for an elite only, but for the masses. Only, Weber argued, by means of a liberal and democratic political system.[47]

In the Freiburg inaugural lecture, however, Weber was not yet concerned with political democracy, but rather, as its title suggests, to give expression to the nationalism that was then his strongest political sentiment, and always remained a powerful one (we shall see later that it was in fact nationalism that made him a democrat). But what is nationalism? What is a nation? How are the two connected? Weber was, of course, social scientist as well as political being, and his analysis of these matters shows the extraordinary combination of passion and dispassion that was such a singular feature of his

25

personality. 'Nation' is a political concept: a nation is a 'community of sentiment' which not only exhibits 'solidarity' *vis-à-vis* other groups but also
seeks to establish or maintain 'a state of its own'.[48] This political solidarity
can have many different bases – a common language is usually (not always)
necessary but is often not sufficient, while other important predisposing factors are a shared religion, or 'memories of a common political destiny' (this
is why the Alsatians are Frenchmen not Germans).[49] Racial homogeneity is
of some importance, though much less so than the belief in it. Nationality is,
clearly, a cultural phenomenon. Particularly stressed by Weber, however,
was the role of intellectuals and intellectual culture. The idea of the 'nation'
is a construct of intellectual strata who identify with the 'national' culture,
and so corresponds to what Weber called their 'prestige interests'.[50] In thus
diagnosing the role of nationalist intellectuals, Weber was diagnosing himself. Such intellectuals play an important role in initiating and propagating
nationalist sentiments, whose spread among the masses has to await the spread
of literacy. This is one connection between nations and nationalism. As Weber
remarked, nationalism – the idea of the nation as a value – commonly rests
on a belief 'in the superiority, or at least the irreplaceability' of the nation's
peculiar culture.[51] In Weber's own case, as we shall see, it was its irreplaceability, not superiority. Weber was a nationalist in general as well as a German nationalist. In both the general and the particular cases, the justification
of nationalism, for him, was that, amid the dangers of world power politics,
the national culture needs the protection that only the state can afford it. To
put the point slightly differently: the state's world power political role is
defensible as a guarantor of national culture.

Weber's maturity, roughly the thirty years from 1890 to 1920, coincided
with a period when German nationalist sentiments among his contemporaries were intense and often extreme. Weber's own German nationalism was,
by the standards of the time, not extreme, but it was intense – just how
intense is shown by his famous remark, in the immediate aftermath of the
First World War, when Germany lay prostrate and humiliated, that he had
'never felt it so much a gift of destiny to be born a German'.[52] Nevertheless
Weber's German nationalism was not extreme, because it was checked by
his recognition of the value of *other* national cultures. As he remarked, it was
quite impossible to prove the superiority of German culture over French, or
vice versa. It would, indeed, have been strange if Weber, the *verstehende*
sociologist *par excellence* of the many and diverse civilizations of the world,
had not acknowledged the multiple manifestations of cultural achievement.
Though an enthusiastic supporter of the German cause during the Great

War, he was outspoken in his opposition to the territorial annexations advocated by, for example, the Pan German League. The justification of the war, in his eyes, was to enable Germany to achieve equality with the other Great Powers, and to prevent a world hegemony of Russia, the English-speaking states and France – as he put it, to prevent world culture from being dominated by 'the regulations of Russian officials on the one hand and the conventions of English-speaking "society" on the other, with perhaps a dash of Latin *raison* thrown in'.[53] This was Germany's duty, not merely her interest. But Weber did not even wish to unite all German speakers in a single state – 'we have every reason to be grateful', he wrote, that there are Germans (and others) in small states like Switzerland, able to develop cultural values unrealizable by a Great Power.[54] Germany and Switzerland had different world-historical tasks.

Weber's concern for the world-historical role of the German state and nation was the mainspring of his reflections on political systems. In Weber's view the German system failed dismally to match up to this role. In the 1895 inaugural lecture, he famously lamented the legacy of Bismarck, whose very greatness, together with his determination to monopolize political power, had left the nation bereft of a political class capable of genuine national leadership. Instead, power was shared (very unequally) between the state bureaucracy and a dilettante monarch both equally unsuited to exercise it. The result was a succession of disastrous political blunders, especially in foreign policy, in the period after Bismarck's fall. Bureaucrats, in Weber's view, make poor political leaders. By their nature bureaucracies are uncreative, rule-bound, intrinsically *unpolitical* organizations, supremely efficient executants of policy (and as such indispensable), but quite unfitted to set the nation's political agenda. They nevertheless always tend to usurp power because of their expertise – a tendency which must be fought. Bureaucracy (like capitalism, which is also indispensable) must serve the political goals of the nation, not determine them.

Throughout his mature life Weber was preoccupied with the problem of establishing a framework for national political leadership, and it was this that made him a champion of parliamentary democracy. However, the world 'democracy' should not be understood too literally – despite his support for universal suffrage, Weber was scornful of the idea that the people could genuinely 'rule'. Rather the point was to give recognition to their interests and their dignity as members of the 'nation', to increase the influence of 'public opinion', and to unify and mobilize the nation behind national political leaders. Parliamentary democracy, in Weber's eyes, could bring about both the national unity and the political leadership he desired. In a genuine parliamentary democracy party leaders struggle with one another for power and the responsibility that goes with power – this *struggle* being precisely the training needed to make an effective politician, on the world stage as well as the domestic one.[55] International politics is by its nature a scene of struggle, for which the party struggle is excellent preparation: what party politicians do, Weber said, is 'fight with words'.[56] Furthermore, the victor in this fight is the politician who can best claim to represent the nation because he has won the support of the people.[57] The function of the 'political class' in this system is to provide, not a ruling group or party, but rather a recruiting ground and a following for a 'plebiscitary' leader arising out of the party struggle and ratified by the popular vote. According to this conception, the democratic political leader wields what Weber called charismatic authority – he gains support through his 'charismatic qualities'.[58] Thus, parliamentary democracy can be said to combine the advantages of two types of political authority, legal and charismatic. Charismatic leadership by itself, while it injects a dynamic element into history, more necessary than ever in the modern bureaucratic age, is unstable and impermanent because it lacks a firm institutional structure. Parliamentary democracy, however, can serve as a mechanism for continual charismatic renewal.

Weber made clear that his constitutional ideas, like those of Montesquieu before him, drew largely upon what he saw as the successes of the British system of government.[59] Beyond any question Weber was deeply impressed by the fact that a liberal parliamentary at-least-semi-democracy (based on a mass electorate, though not yet universal suffrage) was the most powerful state of the late nineteenth and early twentieth century, and ruled an empire 'on which the sun never set'. The link in his view was causal, not coincidental: the British system produced great 'demagogic' leaders such as Gladstone and Lloyd George, both explicitly named by Weber as models.[60] But when German parliamentary democracy was at last born in 1918 Weber could not celebrate the triumph of his hopes, for the birth occurred in almost the worst possible circumstances, as the consequence of military defeat and the forced abdication of the Kaiser. The new democracy was beset by powerful domestic enemies. Furthermore, to Weber's dismay, it rejected the British voting system and instead adopted proportional representation. Thus, almost at the end of his life, Weber found himself forced to seek Germany's national political leader elsewhere than in the parliamentary system he had so long championed. He now advocated direct election of a president, who should be no mere figurehead but should have significant and even vital powers. In the event, the fact that the Weimar Constitution did incorporate a directly elected president with not insignificant powers has frequently been credited to Weber's influence.

Weber has been much criticized for championing what he called 'leadership democracy' (or 'Caesarist democracy') and especially for his late advocacy of a strong president.[61] Some critics, writing with hindsight, have thought him partly to blame, for this reason, for the catastrophic failure of Weimar democracy through the rise of the charismatic demagogic leader, Adolf Hitler. It would, however, be absurd to suppose that the highly cultivated Weber – who was, besides, famous in his lifetime as a scourge of anti-Semitism – would have harboured any admiration whatsoever for Hitler or National Socialism, or have sympathized in any way with Hitler's seizure of power. The presidential power he advocated in 1919 was to be firmly limited by the rule of law. 'Let us ensure', he wrote, 'that the president of the Reich sees the prospect of the gallows as the reward awaiting any attempt to interfere with the laws or govern autocratically . . . But let us put the presidency of the Reich on a firm democratic footing of its own.'[62] In any case, when Hitler seized power and suppressed democracy he was not president but chancellor of the Reich.

It is, of course, true that Weber failed to foresee the rise of Hitler. Did anyone foresee this, in 1919? If Weber is to be criticized in this regard, it can only be for adopting an over-optimistic attitude to charismatic authority. In one way this is surprising, since in Weber's political sociology it is clear that he uses the term in a value-neutral way, to refer to phenomena that may or may not be admirable from an 'ethical, aesthetic or other such point of view'.[63] Why then did he so unreservedly support charismatic leadership in a democratic context? Was he over-optimistic about democratic institutions, in the sense of assuming that democracies could be relied on to choose a desirable kind of 'charismatic' leadership? Or was charismatic leadership so important to Weber that he was willing to risk the bad kind for the sake of a real chance of the good?

Another answer is possible, namely that in Weber's view evil cannot be avoided in politics; at best it can only be minimized. That is the implication of the very nature of politics, and its place in a disenchanted world. In his famous lecture-essay 'Politics as a vocation', Weber referred to the world's 'ethical irrationality', a phenomenon encountered in its sharpest form in the political sphere.[64] As we know, Weber believed that in a disenchanted universe, bereft of objective values, each individual must choose the values by which to act and live – so and only so can he confer meaning on his life and dignity on his personality. But, as Weber never tired of pointing out, to choose certain values is to reject others which, from an objective point of view, are equally valid. Thus, the soul of every individual is torn, so to speak, by an inner war. One who lives in this world 'can only feel himself subject to the struggle between multiple sets of values, each of which, viewed separately, seems to impose an obligation on him'. Often Weber referred to these competing values as rival 'gods', one or some of which the individual must serve and, by that very token, *fight* against the others. More graphically, 'the individual has to decide which is God for him and which is the devil'. For example, he has to choose between the Christian ethic of the Sermon on the Mount – resist not evil, turn the other cheek – and an ethic of worldly manliness – 'resist evil – lest you be co-responsible for an overpowering evil'. Weber made it clear that he himself chose the latter.[65]

But what exactly did Weber mean when he asserted that by choosing the one set of values he must fight against the other as if it were the devil? To be sure the two values are logically contradictory, so that no individual can espouse both – but what should be the attitude to one another of those who make different choices? Must they fight one another like intolerant sects?

Weber's views on this matter are complex, and to understand them it is necessary to appreciate the peculiar cast given to his thinking on the subject by his sociological interests, which focused so largely on religion, and in particular the concept of 'vocation'. To choose one's values is (in a semi-religious or post-religious sense) to choose one's vocation, to commit oneself to a particular sphere or way of life. Thus the choice or conflict of values in Weber's thought is often presented as a choice or conflict between value *spheres*: that is, between different spheres of life having their own inherent, but differing values and norms among which the individual has to choose. Weber's most extended discussion of these 'value spheres' is to be found in the so-called *Zwischenbetrachtung* (or 'parenthetical comment') published posthumously as part of his *Collected Sociology of Religion* (*Gesammelte Aufsaetze zur Religionssoziologie*).[66] There, the economic, political, aesthetic, erotic and intellectual spheres are discussed, significantly, in terms of their relation to, and tension with, religion (or, the religious sphere). Such tensions and conflicts are inescapable, though sometimes at least a temporary reconciliation is possible (for example, the religious and economic spheres were for a time reconciled by the affinity between the 'Protestant ethic' and the 'spirit of capitalism'). No ultimate reconciliation is possible however, between religion and the 'intellectual sphere', especially science (Weber's own vocation), which has disenchanted the world. Weber notes, interestingly, that the erotic, aesthetic and political spheres can become *rivals* of religion, offering 'meaning' and even 'salvation' in their own terms. Politics, in particular, can perform the quintessentially religious function of *making death meaningful* – through death in battle, in which the individual 'can believe that . . . he is dying "for" something'.[67] Presumably this 'something' might well be the nation. It seems that, for Weber, political nationalism was a substitute for religion in the disenchanted universe.

Weber once described himself, in a much-quoted phrase, as 'religiously unmusical'. This is somewhat misleading. To be sure, Weber rejected religion, for two main reasons. One was intellectual honesty – for Weber one of the highest of all values. Religious belief is now intellectually untenable. But Weber also rejected the religious, or at least the Christian ethic, which he considered to be anti-political and, in a specific sense, irresponsible, particularly in the political sphere. On the other hand, there is no doubt that he felt powerfully the pull of what he rejected – not only the 'consolations' of the religious world-view, but its ethic also.

This is apparent from his discussion of 'Politics as a vocation'. Probably the most famous part of his lecture-essay is Weber's distinction between two ethics, or two kinds of ethic – the ethic of responsibility and the absolute ethic (also called by Weber – confusingly and not very appropriately – the ethic of ultimate ends). Weber rejects the 'absolute ethic' in politics, because it is an ethic that ignores the *consequences* of action: it is 'irresponsible'. And he cites several examples. One is provided by a faction of revolutionary socialists, committed to promoting revolution through prolonging the First World War, even though objectively there was no realistic chance that such a revolution could bring about socialism. Another example is the Christian ethic, exemplified by the principle 'resist not him that is evil by force'. This principle is absolute, and has no regard for consequences: 'The Christian does rightly and leaves the result with the Lord.' By contrast, the politician's ethic of responsibility has to reckon with the 'foreseeable results of one's action'.[68] Of course the politician's ethic of responsibility is not purely a matter of instrumental nationality or *Zweckrationalität*: the politician must serve a cause (his nation, for example) and thus follow the principle of value-rationality also. But he must serve his cause (his ultimate ends) responsibly, as well as passionately.

Although Weber rejects the religious ethic, he undoubtedly feels its grandeur. To reject it, as one must, is to be conscious of loss – to be conscious of the necessity to reckon with evil. This is the 'ethical irrationality of the world' – the necessity to use evil means in order to achieve good. As he wrote: 'the proponent of an ethic of absolute ends [sic] cannot stand up under the ethical irrationality of the world', which is a kind of cowardice.[69] This ethical irrationality, the necessity to use evil means, is nowhere more apparent than in politics, for the specific and ultimate political means is violence. The very existence of politics is a recognition of the ineliminability of evil from human life. Weber's well-known definition of the state is an organization that (more or less) successfully claims a *monopoly of the legitimate use of physical force* within a given territory (Weber's emphasis). Trotsky was therefore right to say that 'Every state is founded on force.'[70] It is because the ultimate political means is violence that the ethic of responsibility is quintessentially a political ethic, part of the politician's vocation. He must confront violence, and hence must use violence – responsibly. But still the politician cannot avoid evil, as Weber proclaims in many stark and sombre phrases: 'he who lets himself in for politics . . . contracts with diabolical powers'; 'political action operating with violent means and following an ethic of responsibility endangers the "salvation of the soul" '; 'he who seeks the salvation of the soul . . . should not seek it along the avenue of politics'.[71] Of course, Weber did not believe in the soul, in the literal sense; but he felt the force of the religious ethic powerfully enough to express his sense of 'necessary evil' in religious terminology.

To clarify fully Weber's views on the political it is necessary to distinguish between domestic and international politics. In domestic politics, the state's (near-) monopoly of physical force is two-edged. On the one hand, it (largely) pacifies the territory of the state, and makes it possible for the adherents of different values to coexist peacefully. Thus it makes liberalism possible. In particular, the conflict between value–spheres need be no threat to civil peace, no matter how great the emotional turmoil it may create within the individual psyche. One man may devote his life to economic values, another to religious values, a third to intellectual values. They will disagree, but they need not fight. In politics the values that should guide policy are contested but in, for example, a democratic (or any functioning) political system these conflicts can be resolved peacefully – at least up to a point. However, monopoly of force is not absence of force. The state – even the liberal democratic state – always holds violence in reserve, to be used if necessary. Sometimes it is necessary – not only to punish lawbreakers, but to put down insurrections and revolutions. Even in domestic politics, the politician has to be prepared to use violence.

In international politics the overt use of violence is much greater. According to Weber it has to be, at least for a nation (state) that aspires to Great Power status, as the recently unified Germany must, in Weber's view. Often, he referred to this necessity as Germany's 'fate', and even an 'accursed duty' and 'tragic historical obligation'.[72] To withdraw from the Great Power struggle would be dishonourable, in Weber's opinion. Yet it is strange that he should speak of fate in this context, since, as he so often emphasized, value judgements in a disenchanted universe are and must be a matter of *choice*. No one needs to choose tragedy or to embrace a historical curse. This is the aspect of Weber's political thinking that seems most outdated and least acceptable at the end of the twentieth century, in the era of weapons of mass destruction. What is more, it is arguable that Weber should have foreseen the development of these weapons. After all, as we have seen, a leading theme of his sociology is the rationalization of Western culture – including its technological rationalization. Ever greater rationalization, applied to the technology of war, was more or less bound to lead to the present perilous situation, in which national cultures are more likely to be destroyed than preserved by military means.

Notes

1   Max Weber, *The Theory of Social and Economic Organization,* tr. T. Parsons (Free Press of Glencoe, 1964), p. 88.
2   Ibid., pp. 115ff.
3   Ibid., p. 116.
4   Max Weber, *Economy and Society,* tr and ed. by G. Roth and C. Wittich (Bedminster Press, New York, 1968), vol. 2, pp. 450–1, 479.
5   Ibid., p. 451.
6   Max Weber, *The Methodology of the Social Sciences,* tr. and ed. by E. A. Shils and H. A. Finch (Free Press, New York, 1949), p. 10.
7   Ibid.
8   Ibid., p. 55.
9   Ibid.
10 Weber, *The Theory of Social and Economic Organization*, p. 117.
11 Ibid., p. 116.
12 Ibid., p. 117.
13 Ibid.
14 Weber, *Economy and Society,* vol. 2, p. 506; Max Weber, *From Max Weber: Essays in Sociology*, tr. and ed. by H. H. Gerth and C. W. Mills (Routledge and Kegan Paul, London, 1948), pp. 280–1.

15 Weber, *Economy and Society*, vol. 2, p. 627.
16 Weber, *From Max Weber*, p. 353.
17 Weber, *Economy and Society*, vol. 2, pp. 544, 627.
18 Weber, *From Max Weber*, p. 325. Arguably 'of the holy' in this translation should be 'by the holy'.
19 Weber, *Economy and Society*, vol. 2, p. 630.
20 Weber, *From Max Weber*, p. 325.
21 Max Weber, *The Protestant Ethic and the Spirit of Capitalism*, tr. T. Parsons, (George Allen and Unwin, London, 1930), p. 72.
22 For example, in Weber, *Economy and Society*, vol. 2, p. 584.
23 Weber, *The Theory of Social and Economic Organization*, pp. 184ff., 211ff.
24 Ibid., p. 168.
25 Ibid., pp. 276ff.
26 Ibid., p. 185.
27 Weber, *Economy and Society*, vol. 2, p. 211.
28 Ibid., p. 212.
29 Ibid., p. 636.
30 Weber, *The Protestant Ethic and the Spirit of Capitalism*, p. 181.
31 Weber, *The Theory of Social and Economic Organization*, p. 333.
32 Ibid., p. 329.
33 Weber, *Economy and Society*, vol. 2, pp. 656ff., 809ff.
34 Ibid., p. 820.
35 Ibid., p. 630.
36 Ibid., p. 820.
37 Quoted in D. Beetham, *Max Weber and the Theory of Modern Politics* (George Allen and Unwin, London, 1974), p. 81.
38 Weber, *Economy and Society*, vol. 2, p. 506.
39 Ibid., p. 462.
40 Ibid., p. 567.
41 Weber, *From Max Weber*, p. 142.
42 Ibid., p. 143.
43 Ibid., pp. 151–2; Weber, *The Methodology of the Social Sciences*, p. 55.
44 Weber, *From Max Weber*, pp. 136–7.
45 Ibid., pp. 135–6.
46 Max Weber, *Political Writings,* tr. and ed. by P. Lassman and R. Speirs (Cambridge University Press, 1994).
47 Ibid., p. 71.
48 Weber, *From Max Weber*, p. 176.
49 Ibid., p. 173.
50 Ibid., p. 176.
51 Ibid.
52 Beetham, *Max Weber and the Theory of Modern Politics,* p. 143.

53 Weber, *Political Writings*, p. 76.
54 Ibid., p. 75.
55 Ibid., pp. 166, 219.
56 Beetham, *Max Weber and the Theory of Modern Politics*, p. 77.
57 Weber, *Political Works*, p. 220.
58 Cf. W. J. Mommsen, *The Age of Bureaucracy: Perspectives on the Political Sociology of Max Weber* (Basil Blackwell, Oxford, 1974), p. 90.
59 Weber, *Political Works*, pp. 181–2.
60 Ibid., p. 342; Beetham, *Max Weber and the Theory of Modern Politics*. p. 107.
61 Weber, *Political Writings*, pp. 331, 351.
62 Ibid., p. 305.
63 Weber, *The Theory of Social and Economic Organization*, p. 359.
64 Weber, *From Max Weber*, p. 122.
65 Ibid., pp. 148–9, 151–3.
66 Ibid., pp. 323–59.
67 Ibid., p. 335.
68 Ibid., pp. 119–20.
69 Ibid., p. 122.
70 Ibid., p. 78.
71 Ibid., pp. 123, 126.
72 Weber, *Political Works*, pp. 76–7.

Further reading

By Weber

M. Weber, *The Protestant Ethic and the Spirit of Capitalism*, tr. T. Parsons, George Allen and Unwin, London, 1930.

M. Weber, *The Theory of Social and Economic Organization* (Part I of *Economy and Society*), tr. T. Parsons, Oxford University Press, New York, 1947.

M. Weber, *From Max Weber: Essays in Sociology*, tr. and ed. by H. H. Gerth and C. W. Mills, Routledge and Kegan Paul, London, 1948.

M. Weber, *The Methodology of the Social Sciences*, tr. and ed. by E. A. Shils and H. A. Finch, Free Press, New York, 1949.

M. Weber, *General Economic History*, tr. F. H. Knight, Collier Books, New York, 1961.

M. Weber, *The Sociology of Religion*, tr. E. Fischoff, Methuen, London, 1965.

M. Weber, *Economy and Society*, 3 vols., tr. and ed. by G. Roth and C. Wittich, Bedminster Press, New York, 1968.

M. Weber, *Political Writings*, tr. and ed. by P. Lassman and R. Speirs, Cambridge University Press, 1994.

On Weber

P. Anderson, 'Science, politics, enchantment', in J. A. Hall and I. C. Jarvie (eds), Transition to Modernity, Cambridge University Press, 1992.

C. Antoni, 'Max Weber', in *From History to Sociology*, Merlin Press, London, 1959.

D. Beetham, *Max Weber and the Theory of Modern Politics*, George Allen and Unwin, London, 1974.

R. Bendix, *Max Weber: An Intellectual Portrait*, Methuen, London, 1966.

A. Giddens, *Politics and Sociology in the Thought of Max Weber*, Macmillan, London, 1972.

W. J. Mommsen, *The Age of Bureaucracy: Perspectives on the Political Sociology of Max Weber*, Basil Blackwell, Oxford, 1974.

Part 1
Critics of Consumerist Capitalism

3
Herbert Marcuse and the Frankfurt School: The Tyranny of Instrumental Reason

Max Weber died in 1920, two years after the surrender of Germany put an end to both the Great War and the German monarchy. In its place arose the democratic Weimar Republic, which was to prove ill starred, unstable and short lived. Battered by colossal economic problems, undermined by the harsh peace terms of the Treaty of Versailles, and harried by powerful internal enemies to left and right, the Republic succumbed after only fifteen years to Hitler's brutal Nazi dictatorship. The Nazi regime led Germany into a second world war in 1939 culminating in a second humiliating defeat in 1945. In a word, the history of Germany in the generation after Weber's death was catastrophic, and political catastrophe was the background that helped shape the ideas of German social thinkers of the period. A case in point is the group of thinkers associated with the Frankfurt Institute of Social Research, the so-called 'Frankfurt School'.

In 1931, Max Horkheimer, one of the 'founding fathers' of the Frankfurt School, became director of the Institute. Just over two years later, Hitler's advent to power forced the Institute to flee, first to Geneva, then to other European centres, eventually to the United States of America. A second member of the founding Frankfurt generation, Herbert Marcuse, joined the Institute in 1933: the third, Theodor Adorno, Horkheimer's life-long friend, colleague and co-author, did not formally adhere until 1938. Of the trinity of Horkheimer, Adorno and Marcuse it was the last named who produced the major work of Frankfurt political theory; accordingly, he is the focus of this chapter. Unlike his two colleagues, who returned to Frankfurt after the Second World War, Marcuse remained in the United States, writing now in English, and also remained truest of the three to the political radicalism of the Institute's early years. Thus it came about that a body of ideas originally forged against the backdrop of Nazism and global war achieved celebrity and influence with a new and very different generation of radicals, those of the 1960s.

The 'critical theory' of the Frankfurt School is often referred to as 'neo-Marxist'. Certainly, in its origin, it owed much to Marxism, but it was never wholly orthodox; and as time went on it became less so, and even became distinctly un-Marxist in some major respects. Put briefly, what it shared with Marxism is a hostility to bourgeois civilization; but the bases of this hostility were, or became, different from those of Marx – so much so, that in the Frankfurt case the hostility broadened out to encompass the very foundations of modernity. In their diagnosis of modernity the Frankfurt theorists were greatly indebted to Weber, though they had little sympathy with his political or philosophical views. Although it is the work of Marcuse which is mainly our subject here (because he is the most political of the Frankfurt theorists), nevertheless the reader should bear in mind that many, perhaps most, of his arguments are not his alone, but are rather the common property of the Frankfurt School.

Marcuse's most celebrated and most important contribution to political theory is *One-Dimensional Man*, published in 1964; this was followed by the essay on 'Repressive tolerance' in 1965, and by *An Essay on Liberation* in 1969. Also significant are two earlier books, *Eros and Civilization* (1955), and *Soviet Marxism* (1958). Some relevant articles, mostly written in German in the 1930s, were reprinted in a collection entitled *Negations* in 1968. These are the main sources for Marcuse's political thought, though of course others of his works may also be relevant.

To understand and assess the thinking of Marcuse, and indeed of the Frankfurt School as a whole, it is necessary to keep in mind the political history of the Western world from the School's foundation up to the present, as well as the original 'neo-Marxist' theoretical orientation of the School. Marxist theory predicted the collapse of the capitalist system under the strains and stresses of its 'internal contradictions' – and, sure enough, Germany's bourgeois democratic republic did collapse soon after the foundation of the Frankfurt School. But it was overthrown and replaced, not, as Marx predicted, by socialism or communism, but instead by Hitler's Nazism (just as the Fascism of Mussolini had earlier destroyed and replaced 'bourgeois democracy' in Italy). Not only was Nazism an extreme right-wing movement, as vehemently anti-communist as it was anti-democratic, it proved to be one of the most barbaric and murderous regimes in world history. To the Frankfurt theorists this was not only a profound shock and a source of personal danger, it was also a theoretical puzzle and challenge. In due course the Fascist and Nazi dictatorships were defeated in an exceedingly destructive war and eliminated from world history: what emerged from this, in Western Europe and North America, however, was not any fulfilment of the Marxist prophecy but a strongly entrenched, reinvigorated and apparently highly successful capitalism. Meanwhile, of course, the Bolshevik revolution of 1917 had seized power in Russia in the name of Marxism, but here, too, the hopes of many Marxists were disappointed (to put it mildly) by the onset in the 1930s of the Stalinist regime based on institutionalized terror (though this was not widely acknowledged until much later), and by the continual postponement therefore of the communist millennium (despite a softening of the most violent elements of Stalin's system after his death). These developments, too, were not only a disappointment but a theoretical challenge requiring explanation.

The Frankfurt theorists, and Marcuse, did indeed develop an explanatory theory designed to make sense of these developments, a theory fashioned by infusing into neo-Marxism large elements of Weber, and of the founder of psychoanalysis, Freud. What is perhaps most striking about the Frankfurt synthesis is that the *same* explanatory framework is used to understand all three of the (from a Marxist standpoint) historical anomalies of the twentieth century – Fascism, resurgent post-war capitalism and Sovietism. To a certain extent, all three, in Marcuse's view, are similar – for example, he describes (and condemns) all three as 'totalitarian'. Of course, this does not mean that he was blind to the large and obvious differences between them. Let us begin with Marcuse's analysis of post-Second-World-War capitalism, or 'bourgeois democracy', which he observed at first hand as a resident of the USA. This analysis, which brought Marcuse a wide measure of popular fame, is the main subject of *One-Dimensional Man*.

From an orthodox Marxist point of view, the theoretical problem posed by the 'mature' capitalism of America and Western Europe in the 1950s and 1960s is the following. Marx viewed capitalism as an irrational, anarchic and ultimately inefficient system which, as its productive technology developed, would encounter such severe economic problems that its main victims, the proletariat (the employed working class), finding their position increasingly intolerable, and enlightened by Marxist theory, would rise and overthrow the system. Nothing of the kind was happening. Instead, the workers, like the rest of society, were growing steadily more affluent and, if not totally contented with the system, were in the main, completely unrevolutionary. There was no need to suppress them by violent means. Despite an apparently liberal and democratic political 'superstructure', the capitalist system seemed perfectly stable.

None of this reconciled Marcuse to the system, which in his eyes remained unjust, oppressive and – most importantly – a deformation of human nature and the human spirit. Not that he failed to recognize the economic successes of mature capitalism – on the contrary, he refers to it as 'the affluent society' (a phrase coined by the economist J. K. Galbraith).[1] This general affluence, as Marcuse recognizes, was based on three factors – the economic productivity of capitalism, Keynesian countercyclical economic policy which had apparently (if only temporarily) cured the capitalist economy of the recurrent depressions that previously afflicted it, and the welfare state.[2] However, instead of viewing these developments as welcome achievements, Marcuse sees them rather as means by which the population, and especially the working class, are manipulated into acceptance of a repressive system. To him, they are instruments of domination. It is perhaps particularly striking to find the welfare state, so long and so bitterly fought for by the working class and their political representatives, thus denounced from the political 'left' (as well as, of course, by other theorists, from the 'right').

In order to grasp Marcuse's viewpoint it is necessary to understand what he finds objectionable about 'affluent capitalism', and also his explanation of how it has won such widespread acceptance – two issues which to him are virtually one. But it must be said that some serious difficulties arise from Marcuse's manner of exposition. As he explicitly admits, *One-Dimensional Man* 'vacillate[s] between two contradictory hypotheses: (1) that advanced industrial society is capable of containing qualitative change for the foreseeable future; (2) that forces and tendencies exist which may break this containment and explode the society'.[3] This, perhaps, is in itself no more than an honest avowal of uncertainty; however, the avowed contradiction is by no means the only one to be found within *One-Dimensional Man*, or in other works of Marcuse's, or between them – nor do they relate only to peripheral issues. What is more, admission of uncertainty is not necessarily a virtue, particularly if, as with Marcuse, it tends to produce argument by speculation rather than affirmation. A notable, and troublesome, feature of Marcuse's work is the large number of (sometimes important) statements that carry the qualification 'perhaps', or its equivalent. The reader is left uncertain as to what exactly Marcuse has committed himself to. These problems may or may not be related to Marcuse's explicit rejection of 'formal logic' in favour of 'dialectical logic'.

Notwithstanding these difficulties, Marcuse's 'Frankfurt interpretation' of the modern predicament is a challenging and interesting one, in which capitalism and its evils appear as only one example of a broader trend. Nor is this trend simply, or even mainly, a political or social one – it is also intellectual and philosophical. Unlike Marx, Marcuse does not seem greatly concerned about the direction of causality between the social and the intellectual; however, being himself a philosopher he tends to give pride of place to philosophical and theoretical issues. The social malaise he diagnoses is also a philosophical malaise, which can be summed up in one word – 'positivism'. Marcuse's critique is, *inter alia*, a critique of 'positivist' understandings of knowledge, truth and reason.

The critique of positivism was a staple of the early Frankfurt School, and can be found, for example, in Marcuse's 1936 article 'The concept of essence'. According to Marcuse, positivism has always rejected this concept as 'metaphysical'. Positivism adheres to an empiricist epistemology, according to which all human knowledge of reality derives from our *experience*, or from *observation*, and is therefore necessarily knowledge of empirical facts only. However, according to Marcuse, positivism goes beyond mere empiricism by asserting the 'cognitive equi-valence [sic]' of all facts and all reality.[4] The positivist world of facts (Marcuse says, anticipating the title of his famous book of thirty years later) is 'one-dimensional'. Positivism is, therefore (and is proud of being) non-critical and non-evaluative. According to positivism, reality and knowledge are 'value free' and 'ethically neutral'; to take up a critical or evaluative position therefore, involves, as Marcuse puts it, 'delinquency in rigour' (or, less satirically, at least a departure from rigour).[5] It is obvious that, from this point of view, Weber's conception of value-free science (including social science) is a form of positivism. (Indeed, positivism could be summarized, only a little crudely, as the view that scientific knowledge is the only true knowledge.) Marcuse (in 1936) calls positivism 'bourgeois', but it would be a more accurate expression of his opinion (and more in accord with his later arguments) to call it 'conservative': such a theory, Marcuse claims, 'can only be one of resignation';[6] it helps to protect 'powers concerned with the preservation of [the existing] form of reality', against 'the already real possibility of another form of reality', presumably a better one.

Positivists may well protest at Marcuse's political interpretation of their epistemology; they may say, quite accurately, that the implication of their doctrine is neither to criticize nor to support the social status quo, but rather that to do *either* goes beyond knowledge, properly speaking. And indeed, Marcuse himself admits that, in past centuries, positivism was a radical force, politically: 'Its appeal to the facts then amounted to a direct attack on the religious and metaphysical conceptions that were the ideological support of the *ancien régime*.'[7] Religion and metaphysics, or *that* metaphysics, *are* genuinely false, then, as positivism claims. To Marcuse, however, its *reason* for so claiming cannot be the right one, for, even if an individual positivist today happens to be politically progressive, his theory 'succumbs to helpless relativism [in relation to value judgements], thus promoting the very powers whose reactionary thought [he] wants to combat'.[8] If, that is, he does want to combat them. Marcuse often gives the impression that he sees, in particular, social scientists who adhere to the positivist programme as more or less willing servants of the powers that be.

There are many illustrations of this charge in *One-Dimensional Man*, where positivistic social science is frequently attacked under the labels 'empiricism', 'behaviourism' and 'operationalism'. An example is a typical piece of research into the functioning of democracy in America, in which 'democracy' was defined, quite deliberately and self-consciously, in terms of *what could be observed in America*, namely 'competition between opposing candidates', rather than 'a method for insuring that representatives comply with directives from constituents' (the latter conception was rejected '"because it assumed a level of articulated opinion and ideology not likely to be found in the United States"' or any other modern country).[9] Thus the sociologists in question, by opting for 'operationalizable' concepts only, excluded any critical judgements about the quality of existing so-called democracies, and therefore any searching analysis of the systemic causes of their shortcomings. For these systemic factors are not in any simple sense observable. They are a

> context [which] is larger and other than the plants and shops investigated [or] the areas and groups whose public opinion is polled . . . And it is also more real in the sense that it creates and determines the facts investigated, polled and calculated. This real context in which the particular objects obtain their real significance is definable only within a *theory* of society . . . an analysis which is capable of identifying the structure that holds together the parts and processes of society and that determines their interrelation.[10]

In sum: positivist social science is superficial as well as uncritical, and superficial *because* it is uncritical. It serves, therefore, as an ideological support for a repressive society.

We have not yet explained, in any detail, Marcuse's objections to mature capitalist society. Such an explanation can, however, be approached by examining another aspect of 'positivism', namely its conception of *rationality* – and doing this will also bring us into contact with Max Weber's theory of *rationalization* and disenchantment. According to positivism (and Weber), value judgements cannot be rational because there are no objective or 'true' values. Accordingly, the only genuine rationality is what Weber called *Zweckrationalität*, or, as it is sometimes translated, instrumental rationality – a term often used (pejoratively) by Marcuse. According to this positivist, instrumental conception of reason, the only genuine rationality is the efficient adaptation of means to ends – the ends being outwith the sphere of rational judgment and hence incapable of being judged rational or irrational. Marcuse often calls this instrumental concept of rationality 'technical' or 'technological' or 'technocratic' reason, since techniques and technology are means to achieve given ends. Technology and technological reason are, he holds, utterly characteristic of modern society, and in particular of mature capitalism. This is one major reason why he objects so strongly to it.

It is important to be clear that Marcuse has *two* reasons for objecting to the technological conception of rationality, one positive and one negative. The negative one is the denial of rational status to ends and values – that has been discussed above. More complex is Marcuse's distaste for alleged technological rationality as such. Technology is applied science, but in Marcuse's view the technological applicability of science has a meaning and a significance not generally acknowledged, especially by positivism. Natural science rests on a particular view of nature. In Marcuse's words: 'The quantification of nature . . . separated reality from all inherent ends and, consequently, separated the true from the good, science from ethics' – as one might say, facts from values.[11] Aristotelian 'final causes' have been banished from nature. To put it in Weberian terms, the universe has become 'disenchanted'. What is the implication? Inert nature is viewed as mere resource for technology, for instrumentality: 'The science of nature develops under the *technological a priori* which projects nature as potential instrumentality, stuff of control and organization. And the apprehension of nature as (hypothetical) instrumentality *precedes* the development of all particular technical organization.'[12] In brief, natural science is intrinsically an instrument for the control of nature.

Marcuse's evaluation of natural science thus conceived is a question to which I will return. Meanwhile, let us note a corollary: social science modelled on this natural science (i.e. positivistic social science) must also be an instrument of control – control, not of nature, but of human beings.[13] It is thus inherently adapted to serve as a means by which the powerful can effectively exercise their power over the rest of society. In mature capitalist society the powerful are the bourgeoisie and their adjuncts in the state apparatus. Again, Marcuse gives a number of examples of technical, and hence manipulative, social sciences in *One-Dimensional Man* – industrial psychology and sociology, scientific management, motivation research, public relations theory, public opinion studies, the psychology of advertising.[14] But these are only the most blatant examples. Avoidance of economic depressions by Keynesian demand management is (or was) a means of stabilizing the capitalist system and thus also has served as a tool of the 'ruling class'. Not only that – the same is true of the welfare state, and of economic affluence itself. These economic and social developments, Marcuse seems to imply, are really applications of a manipulative form of psychological knowledge – a political psychology – which indicates how the people can be bribed to accept the system. The manipulativeness of affluence is the central message of *One-Dimensional Man*.

We can now begin to understand why Marcuse is such a vehement critic of mature, affluent capitalism. It is a society whose members are so effectively controlled through economic affluence and the application of manipulative social science as to justify the description 'totalitarian'. But it is the economic affluence that is more fundamental, because it is the main reason why the manipulation is successful – why people *allow* themselves to be manipulated. They are, in effect, like voluntary slaves. It would probably not be correct to say that Marcuse is opposed to affluence as such, but he is most definitely opposed to capitalist affluence. Why? In the first place, because capitalist affluence is not only a bribe to induce the people to surrender their freedom, it is a *false* bribe. Capitalist affluence does not satisfy genuine needs, but rather caters to false needs, which it itself creates, but whose falsity it conceals. Its success – its stability in the context of 'liberal democracy' – depends on what in the Marxist tradition is called false consciousness. The generation of false consciousness is therefore an essential part of the system, and is achieved through the advertising industry, the mass media and the use of manipulative social and psychological sciences. The leisure and entertainment industries also play their part – an important one – in stabilizing the system (rather in the manner portrayed by George Orwell in the novel *1984*) by filling workers' free time and providing them with a certain satisfaction of a cheap and second-rate kind. Marcuse refers to these various processes that reconcile people to the system as 'moronization'. They are corrupted, blinded and enslaved by 'consumerism'.

In Marcuse's eyes, all of this reinforces his view that Max Weber's concept, and ideal, of value-free social science is, in reality, a monstrous sham. Weberian social science is perfectly structured to serve the interests, and thus endorse the values, of rulers and oppressors. What is more, Marcuse charges, that was exactly Weber's intention: 'His theory of the intrinsic value-freedom, or ethical neutrality of science, reveals itself [in his analysis of industrial capitalism] as an attempt to make science 'free' to accept obligatory valuations that are imposed on it from the outside.'[15] The values thus accepted are, of course, those of the wielders of social power.

At this point, however, a critic of Marcuse may suggest that his analysis puts the cart before the horse, and pins the blame in the wrong place. Technical science, including technical social science, may surely in principle serve *any* interest, and *any* values. If in practice it serves the powerful (judged by Marcuse to be oppressors), does not the fault lie in the political structure rather than in technical social science? Must not radicals and revolutionaries also have recourse to technical means–end rationality, such as is embodied in technical science, in order to achieve their goals? To answer this criticism two arguments are available to Marcuse. One draws attention to the basic empiricist epistemology of positivism: all genuine knowledge derives from experience (or empirical observation). If so, this must apply also to technical knowledge of means–end relations, and equally to the scientific laws of cause and effect of which the former is an application. For this reason, positivistic technically oriented social science will consist essentially of 'empirical correlations' between facts observable in existing societies or discoverable in earlier ones. Such empirically based 'laws' cannot, by definition, embrace the radically new and different sort of society envisaged by Marcuse. They can show only how to bring about minor changes, or how to stabilize the status quo. Empirical social science, therefore, is of no use whatever to radicals and revolutionaries. It is of interest to notice that this disjunction between revolution and orthodox scientific method, which makes Marcuse such a fierce critic of orthodox social science, is in the view of Karl Popper precisely an argument against revolutionary politics.

Marcuse has a second possible reply to his imagined critic. In so far as technical social science can be used to bring about desired ends, even desirable ends, its use still involves manipulation of human beings, just as technical natural science is used to bring about desired ends by manipulation of nature. It thus denies to human beings their essential freedom and dignity.[16] But there may be a different way of bringing about the radical social transformation desired by Marcuse – namely, by the enlightenment of those involved through rational persuasion, by making clear to them the oppressive and degrading nature of mature capitalist society, and by showing them a better alternative. One might, indeed, wonder if this is likely to be an effective revolutionary strategy – we have seen that Marcuse himself, in *One-Dimensional Man*, was dubious about the likelihood of radical transformation. In later writings, however, he became more optimistic.

Unfortunately, however, these writings show that the line of self-defence suggested above is after all not open to Marcuse. In the essay 'Repressive tolerance', Marcuse calls for '*intolerance* towards prevailing policies, attitudes [and] opinions' (emphasis added):[17] freedom of speech and assembly should be denied to proponents of various policies considered unacceptable by Marcuse, including 'armament' and opposition to the extension of public services. Rigid restrictions on educational institutions 'may' also be necessary.[18] 'Revolutionary violence', however inhuman, is justified, according to Marcuse, in order to usher in a better society ('since when is history made in accordance with ethical standards?', he asks rhetorically).[19] These means, however regrettable in themselves, are in this case justified by the end.[20] Perhaps so, perhaps not: the relevant point, however, is that Marcuse, in endorsing the use of coercive means, undercuts his objection to technical social science as inherently manipulative.

What is more, the revolution to which Marcuse, in his optimistic moments, looks forward, must be (like most revolutions) the work of an élite, not the people as a whole. 'Repressive tolerance' and *An Essay on Liberation* were written during the period of student unrest in the United States and Western Europe[21] – a radical movement which adopted Marcuse as a mentor and, at the same time, gave him hope that the system might not be impregnable, but which, of course, involved only a small minority of the population. Marcuse is explicit that, since most people in mature capitalist societies are in the grip of false consciousness, they must be liberated, even against their will, by those who know better, using 'apparently undemocratic means' against the 'tyranny of the majority'. Those who know must necessarily be a minority in a society based on systematic moronization, manipulation and indoctrination. A truly free and democratic society, therefore, has to be achieved by coercive and 'apparently undemocratic' means.[22]

Even if one grants one of Marcuse's premises here, that of widespread false consciousness (and it certainly has to be admitted that the general population in mature capitalist societies is subjected to a considerable effort of indoctrination) he must still, it seems, justify a further premise – that he is in possession of the truth. That is not easy, and Marcuse's efforts to do it are not very impressive. Here is how he states the problem, in the introduction of *One-Dimensional Man*. In the first place, value judgements are needed, in terms of which existing and alternative forms of society can be judged as rational or irrational (presumably these value judgements, therefore, must have objective truth status); the second requirement is 'the judgment that, in a given society, specific possibilities exist for the amelioration of human life and specific means of realizing these possibilities. [It is necessary] to demonstrate the objective validity of these judgments . . . on empirical [sic] grounds'. These are the elements of a 'critical theory of society', which, Marcuse claims, 'is opposed to all metaphysics by virtue of [its] rigorously historical character'.[23] Unfortunately there is not much genuine rigour, because Marcuse goes on to confuse facts and values in a way which turns critical theory into a circular argument. The goals of critical theory, he says, must be 'expressive of an actual tendency – that is, their transformation must be the real need of the underlying [sic] population'. Of course, the 'real need' of a manipulated population suffering from false consciousness will not manifest itself as an 'actual tendency' except, perhaps, in the protests of an enlightened minority. Nothing validates the value judgements of this minority except their confidence that they are right.

However, it is not Marcuse's value judgements that are the real problem; indeed, his characterizations of the good society are largely unexceptionable – they include peace (often called by Marcuse 'the pacification of existence'), justice (unfortunately not further defined), the free development of human needs and faculties (but which faculties?), freedom from ugliness and from unnecessary toil.[24] Few will disagree with this list of goods – the problems to which it gives rise are, in some cases, interpretation of Marcuse's rather vague terms, and, more importantly, what kind of social system will maximize these goods. On this crucial matter Marcuse, who is no social scientist, has nothing to offer, and has to fall back on familiar Marxist nostrums with which history has not dealt kindly. Marcuse, therefore, has no right to be a revolutionary, as distinct from a social critic – and in fact, the latter role is one he has frequently seemed to prefer, speaking not of revolution but of 'The Great Refusal' and praising 'negation'.[25] In these moods, perhaps, he sees himself as a voice crying in the wilderness, a prophet of doom, driven to bear witness, to echo Luther's 'Here I stand, I can no other', regardless of consequences.

Let us therefore return to Marcuse the critic – of modern capitalist (but not only capitalist) society and culture. Two features of the latter are important to Marcuse: the culture of modern society is a scientific culture, and also a culture of productivity. Both features are objects of his criticism. We saw above that, in Marcuse's view, modern science and technology form a seamless whole whose true meaning inheres in technology rather than science: 'The science of nature develops under the technological *a priori* which projects nature as potential instrumentality.' Science, in other words, is an instrument for the mastery of nature. It is also, of course, an instrument for the mastery of men, in Marcuse's eyes, a 'mastery' which is objectionable to him *as such*, and also because of the masters who make use of it. Science and technology provide ways in which powerful groups protect and exercise their power. The argument here is similar to Marcuse's case against instrumental *social* science, and is open to similar objections.

But Marcuse's objection to modern science goes deeper, and also extends further – for example, it extends to formal logic. In Marcuse's view, the fault of formal logic is that it refuses to tolerate contradictions ('contradictions are the fault of incorrect thinking'), (whereas dialectical logic recognizes contradictions in reality, for example between essence and appearance). Thus, says Marcuse, well-defined concepts 'become instruments of prediction and control', and formal logic is therefore the first step towards scientific thought (which is also an instrument of prediction and control).[26]

But only the first step. Full-fledged science uses formal logic *inter alia* in its project of mastering nature or, as Marcuse often puts it, for the domination of nature. To Marcuse this attitude *to nature* is objectionable for several reasons. In the first place, the 'dominative' attitude naturally spreads from nature to man, also seen as part of nature, both 'objects' being treated in accordance with what he calls the logic and rationality of domination. Furthermore, domination takes place, as Marcuse puts it, 'not only through technology but *as* technology', particularly in economic life, where men are actually dominated *by* the technology of the productive apparatus; a domination legitimized by the fact that this apparatus 'enlarges the comforts of life and increases the productivity of labor'. Once again we are corrupted by affluence and at the same time enslaved by technology, and thus, ultimately, by science.[27]

But the full scope and character of Marcuse's objection to science has not yet been made clear. Marcuse objects to mastery or domination of nature *as such*; he objects on behalf of nature itself. The 'scientific universe' projects nature as 'quantifiable matter', 'the mere stuff of control', 'raw material', lacking in inherent ends or value (one might say, in Weberian terms, 'disenchanted'). The rationality of domination, he says, 'tends to be fatal to this universe as a whole'.[28] Marcuse indeed complains not just of domination but even of 'the ferocity of man against Nature'.[29] At this point, Marcuse's thought links up with (and perhaps to a degree inspired) that of the environmental movement – by the ferocity of man against nature he means destruction of the soil, wholesale deforestation, ruthless exploitation of natural resources and so on. But still more is involved. Marcuse aims at what he calls the pacification of nature itself, the reduction of its blind ferocity. 'In Nature as well as in History', he writes, 'the struggle for existence is the token of scarcity, suffering and want.'[30] Here he is presumably referring to animal forms of life and to the process of Darwinian selection in which they are trapped. Human mastery of nature actually makes things worse, not better – our ill-treatment of animals, Marcuse says, creates a Hell, a Hell which he blames on our conception of nature as sub-rational matter to be comprehended, organized and transformed by human reason – that is, the technical-scientific conception of nature.

Marcuse's anger at ill-treatment of animals is admirable; beyond this, it is not clear in what way nature literally suffers as a result of human 'ferocity'. Destruction of the environment, surely, is foolish rather than cruel. But Marcuse carries his concern for nature to what seems to be incredible lengths. He describes as a 'terrible notion' the view that 'the sub-rational life of nature' must forever remain 'a helpless and heartless universe' of suffering, violence and destruction.[31] But for this universe to be pacified (or, as Marcuse often puts it, liberated) it is of course not sufficient that humanity abstain from cruelty to animals – somehow or other the whole Darwinian struggle for existence would have to be eliminated. This, alas, is only a utopian dream (and as such, unfortunately, not untypical of Marcuse's way of thinking).

There is yet more to be said about Marcuse's concern regarding the ill-treatment of nature; indeed one of his most important and characteristic themes in that area remains to be explored. But before embarking on this, it is important to note the conclusions that Marcuse draws from what has been already discussed. As we know, he blames the technical-scientific conception of knowledge, rationality and nature, for most of the ills he discerns in modern industrial society. It is therefore natural that he should advocate changes to the dominant conceptions. And so he does. 'Established science and scientific method' he suggests, is inherently limited to 'rationaliz[ing] and insur[ing] the established *Lebenswelt*' because it fails to envisage '*a qualitatively new mode of "seeing"*' and qualitatively new relations between men and between man and nature' (emphasis in original).[32] The necessary 'change in the direction of progress', therefore, must change 'the very structure of science'; in a pacified world, science would be based on 'essentially different concepts of nature', and would establish 'essentially different facts'.[33] Unfortunately Marcuse gives no inkling what this 'new science' would be like, except to disclaim any desire to revive teleological philosophies, or to establish any kind of 'qualitative physics'. On the basis, however, of his proposed 'new science' would be established a similarly 'new technology', adapted to pacification and liberation rather than domination and manipulation, requiring, he says, a 'catastrophic transformation' of orthodox ideas.[34]

Is such a development conceivable, let alone desirable? It is a noteworthy fact that the idea has been repudiated by Marcuse's successor in the Frankfurt School, Jürgen Habermas, who interprets Marcuse as attributing 'subjectivity' to nature (animals, plants and minerals) and seeking a relation of 'fraternal intersubjectivity' between nature and humankind. Habermas concludes that 'The idea of a New Science will not stand up to logical scrutiny, any more than that of a New Technology.'[35] There is no 'more humane' substitute for a science 'oriented to possible technical control'. Habermas's criticism of Marcuse marks a decisive break between the old and the new Frankfurt School, and may be said to have launched Habermas's career as a major independent political and social theorist, of whom much more must be said below.

It may also be suggested that Marcuse's polemic against orthodox science and technology and their allegedly repressive political implications conflates two elements which should be distinguished – they may be called the *technical conception of reason* and the *technological conception of nature*. The technical conception of reason is relatively modern – it dates from David Hume in the eighteenth century, and the triumph of his view that reason has to do *only* with 'matters of fact' and 'relations of ideas'; thus, in relation to action, reason can only be a 'slave', not a master: in other words, can judge means only, not ends. The technological conception of nature – by which I mean the idea that (non-human) nature is essentially a resource for human use – is much older. It is, for example, a part of orthodox Christianity (as John Locke put it in the seventeenth century, the earth was given by God to mankind as his property and for his benefit), and can even be traced back to the Old Testament. It is the *combination* of these two ideas that has been so potent in modern times.

Let us return to Marcuse on the mis-treatment of nature – to what he calls the *repression* of nature. This is not primarily a matter of orthodox science and technology, though it has much to do with the repressiveness of modern industrial society, as Marcuse sees it. The source of this repression is, roughly speaking, the cultural attitudes explored in Weber's famous thesis linking the 'Protestant ethic' and the 'Spirit of Capitalism', interpreted by Marcuse in the light of Freud's theory of civilization – a theory which runs in terms of the subordination of the 'pleasure principle' to the 'reality principle'. The nature repressed in 'productivist' civilization is *human* nature, or human instinctual nature.

Although reference to this aspect of Marcuse's views can be found in *One-Dimensional Man*, its main exposition is in the earlier *Eros and Civilization*, which is sub-titled (a little misleadingly) 'A Philosophical Inquiry into Freud'. Freud's view, as explained by Marcuse, is that civilization and instinctual behaviour stand in opposition to one another. In order for civilization to develop and continue, it was and is necessary that the life of instinctive, natural pleasure-seeking, enjoyment and play give way to (self-) restraint, work and productiveness; in sum, immediate satisfaction to delayed, but more secure satisfaction. *Reason* is a function of the 'reality principle', and is thus of an instrumental type – but one whose logic leads to a loss of *freedom*, as part of the price of civilization and its benefits. In large part this loss of freedom manifests itself in social institutions and their rules, which are to a degree externally enforced ('repression from without'); but they operate also though a kind of self-censorship put in place by education and socialization ('repression from within'), in Freudian terms the function of the superego.[36] For the necessity of this repressiveness in civilization, Freud gave an explanation at root economic, in terms of scarcity. Human energies, for this reason, must be directed to *work*, and away from instinctive behaviour – including, notably, sexuality.[37] Civilization, in this sense, rests on repression of instinctual nature. Marcuse traces the repression back at least to classical Greece, whose philosophers (for example Plato) defined virtue as subjugation by reason of the individual's 'lower' faculties – his 'sensuous' and 'appetitive' ones. Conquest of 'internal nature' paved the way for conquest of 'external' nature through work, science and technology.[38]

According to Marcuse, Freud's theory of civilization requires revision in the light of the teachings of Marx and Weber on capitalism (though neither is mentioned in *Eros and Civilization*, their presence is palpable). What Marx showed, for Marcuse, is that not all civilization need be equally repressive: capitalist civilization is highly repressive, as *it* needs to be, though civilization as such does not. This excess of repressiveness over what is necessary for civilization Marcuse terms 'surplus repression' (also defined as 'the restrictions necessitated by social domination').[39] Among the institutions that give rise to surplus repression are 'a hierarchical division of labour' and 'the monogamic-patriarchical family' – the one an organization of *work*, the other an organization of *sexuality*. Marcuse quotes Freud's view that civilization directed men's energies 'away from sexual activities on to their work'.[40] One historical 'ideology' in particular has focused on both sexuality and work (the repression of sexuality and the repressive celebration of work) – Puritanism, or as Weber put it, ascetic Protestantism, the ancestor in his view of the 'spirit of capitalism'. Marcuse does not use this phrase, but refers (pejoratively) to 'the philosophy of productiveness'[41] and (in effect) to the 'work ethic' – the idea that hard work is a virtue rather than a curse. These values are sources, in our capitalist culture, of surplus repression ('from within').

Sexuality, its repression and expression are favourite themes of Marcuse (a fact presumably not unconnected with his popularity in the 1960s); for, as he puts it, 'The sex instincts bear the brunt of the reality principle'.[42] What Marcuse mainly refers to here is the subjection of sexuality to what he calls (following Freud) 'the primacy of genitality' – in other words, the limitation of legitimate sexuality to the function of procreation (yet another triumph of instrumentalism). As much as possible, sexuality should be separated from pleasure and play, and the body freed for 'productive' labour.[43] To this end, non-procreative manifestations of sexuality were branded as 'perversions'. According to Marcuse, 'the reduction of Eros to procreative-monogamic sexuality' completed the subjection of the pleasure principle to the reality principle; and this coincided with the individual's becoming 'a subject-object of labour in the apparatus of his society'.[44]

But this puritanical 'work and sex ethic' has not, in modern times been limited to capitalist society: Marcuse, in his 1958 book *Soviet Marxism*, found a quite similar ethos to be prevalent in the USSR, once again as part and parcel of a repressive, productivist and instrumental society and culture. Marcuse may indeed be described as, in his own way, a member of the 'convergence' school of social theorists: 'Both systems [Western and Soviet]' he writes 'show the common features of late industrial civilization – centralization and regimentation . . . there is joint rule of economic and political bureaucracies; the people are coordinated through the "mass media" of communications, entertainment industry, education.'[45] There is mechanization, rationalization of labour and general conformity. And there is an ironic symbiosis between the two systems, in that each uses the threat posed by the other to justify its own repressiveness. Soviet Marxism has even abandoned dialectical for formal logic![46] But over and above this the USSR has developed its own 'work ethic', its own philosophy of productiveness ('Stakhanovism'), its own ideology of self-restraint, and its own celebration of the monogamous family and the corresponding procreative definition of sexuality.[47] Up to a point, all this is the functional equivalent of the Calvinist or 'Protestant-capitalist' ethic, but with a difference: the justification offered for present puritanism and repression is the achievement of a free and good society in the future, rather than the demonstration of predestination to eternal salvation.[48] Marcuse, therefore, judged that 'Soviet man' could more readily throw off the ideology of restraint than his Western counterpart; both because its explicit justification was temporary only, and because it was much less strongly internalized, much more a matter of external coercion, than in the West.[49] Subsequent history suggests that Marcuse may have been right about this, but that the consequences have been unhappy rather than happy. Soviet Marxism has been replaced, not by genuine communism, but by a very immature, undisciplined and predatory form of capitalism that seems to suffer precisely from lack of internalized constraints.

Let us return to mature industrial capitalism. Marcuse uses Freud's phrase 'the return of the repressed'[50] to refer to what he (Marcuse) calls 'the tabooed and subterranean history of civilization', exemplified in periodic but normally unsuccessful revolts of the younger generation against the authority of their elders, and, in symbolic form, by the arts:[51] witness the fact, Marcuse suggests, that the great literature of our culture in so largely a celebration of 'unhappy love'. Such art posits a different, free existence – but only in imagination: it poses no real challenge to repressive reality. The repressed does not truly return.

Marcuse, however, wants it to. That is to say, he calls (in the first place) for the liberation of the 'all but unlimited erotogenic zones of the body', for 'a non-repressive reality principle' which, he is confident, is perfectly compatible with civilization and social order.[52] He is eager to stress that what he intends is 'not simply a release but a *transformation* of the libido: from sexuality constrained under genital supremacy to erotization of the entire personality . . . a spread rather than explosion of libido'.[53] The abolition of surplus repression would thus in fact '*minimize* the manifestations of *mere* sexuality by integrating them into a far larger order, including the order of work'. I must confess that I cannot conceive what Marcuse means by the integration of sexuality and work; however, it would, he says, give work the character of *play* and of *freedom* – 'the free play of human faculties'.[54] Also his 'far larger order' of sexuality would, he tells us, have a place for the so-called 'perversions',[55] including homosexuality and even sado-masochism.

Marcuse published *Eros and Civilization* in 1955, before the growth of the 'permissive society', which put an end to the old sexual puritanism, freed sexuality from 'genital primacy' and granted greatly increased toleration to the 'perversions'. None of this, however, has destroyed or seems likely to destroy the capitalist-industrial-administrative social structure seen as so oppressive by Marcuse. It is therefore not surprising that he does not see so-called 'permissiveness' as in any way constituting the liberation he sought – on the contrary, it is just one more tool for manipulating the people into acceptance of the system (again Orwell's novel, *1984*, with its concept of 'prolefeed', seems to the point). Marcuse calls it 'scientific management of libido'.[56] He also detects a falsity, a narrowness, in the erotic experience of urban, industrial man. Truly fulfilling eroticism seems to demand a setting of unspoiled nature, in Marcuse's view. Technological transformation ('violation') of nature (the natural environment) fatally cramps the expression of human nature (the natural instincts).[57]

That is a matter of opinion; but a more general comment on Marcuse's polemic against the repression of nature (or natural instincts) is in order. Throughout this polemic he takes it for granted that the natural instincts are good, that their expression is desirable (other things equal), and that they should be repressed as little as possible (as little as is compatible with 'civilization'). Is there not a large element here of the romantic utopianism that is so typical of Marcuse? And is not such romantic utopianism liable to be dangerous, and therefore irresponsible? Here it is to the point to consider Fascism and Nazism, and what Marcuse and other Frankfurt theorists have to say about these historical phenomena. Marcuse himself says rather little, and that little is hardly adequate. In an early essay of 1934, he treated it simply as the continuation of capitalism by other means;[58] later, in *Eros and Civilization*, *Soviet Marxism* and *One-Dimensional Man*, he sees it simply as one more embodiment of the technocratic repressive society – the most complete and indeed the most efficient of all.[59] But a more adequate diagnosis is found in the work of other Frankfurt School theorists, such as Horkheimer. Horkheimer does not contradict Marcuse, but he also asks the question, what factors enabled Fascism and Nazism to be so effective? His answer is given in the title of an article written shortly after the end of the Second World War – 'The Revolt of nature' (roughly speaking, what Marcuse calls 'the return of the repressed'). Modern man has submitted to the authority of civilization and the suppression of instinctual human nature it involves, but he has not really accepted it: adjustment to it 'involves an element of resentment and suppressed fury'. He cannot bear 'the painful repression of natural urges', which therefore 'always lie in wait, ready to break out as a destructive force'.[60] When this happens, men 'abandon themselves to tabooed urges with hatred and contempt'. Nazism took advantage of, and organized for its own purposes, this 'revolt of nature', which provided it with much of its motive power and popular support. 'In modern fascism, rationality [instead of] simply repressing nature . . . now exploits nature by incorporating into its own system the rebellious potentialities of nature', says Horkheimer.[61] But even more significant is his comment that 'the rebellion of nature . . . always involves a regressive element, [hence] it is from the outset suitable for use as an instrument of reactionary ends'.[62] This analysis by his old friend and colleague should have given Marcuse pause, for it indicates clearly enough the dangers of seeking to 'liberate' repressed human nature by casting off the shackles of society. A good deal of human nature is better repressed. Of course, Marcuse can reply that it is only the harmless, life-enhancing human instincts that he seeks to liberate; but that would require a more skilful and precise form of psychological engineering than we have at our command. Once again, Marcuse, whatever his merits as a critic of our society, appears as an unreliable guide to action and to policy.

Notes

1   J. K. Galbraith, *The Affluent Society* (Hamish Hamilton, London, 1958).
2   H. Marcuse, *One-Dimensional Man* (Beacon Press, Boston, 1966), p. 21.
3   Ibid., p. xv.
4   H. Marcuse, *Negations: Essays in Critical Theory* (Penguin, Harmondsworth, 1972), pp. 64ff. See also H. Marcuse, *Reason and Revolution*, 2nd edn (Routledge and Kegan Paul, London, 1955), p. 327.
5   Marcuse, *Negations*, pp. 77, 65.
6   Ibid., p. 66.
7   Marcuse, *Reason and Revolution*, p. 341.
8   Marcuse, *Negations*, p. 45.
9   Marcuse, *One-Dimensional Man*, pp. 114–15.
10   Ibid., p. 190.
11   Ibid., p. 146.
12   Ibid., p. 153.
13   Cf. H. Marcuse, 'From ontology to technology: fundamental tendencies of industrial society', in *Critical Theory and Society: A Reader*, ed. S. E. Bronner and D. M. Kellner (Routledge, London, 1989), p. 126.
14   Marcuse, *One-Dimensional Man*, pp. 10, 75, 107.
15   Marcuse, *Negations*, pp. 202–3.
16   Cf. Marcuse, 'From ontology to technology', p. 126.
17   Marcuse, 'Repressive tolerance', in R. P. Wolff, Barrington Moore Jr. and H. Marcuse, *A Critique of Pure Tolerance* (Jonathan Cape, London, 1969), pp. 95–6.
18   Ibid., p. 114.
19   Ibid., p. 117.
20   H. Marcuse, *An Essay on Liberation* (Penguin, Harmondsworth, 1972), pp. 75–6.
21   Ibid., p. 30.
22   Ibid., pp. 26, 96–7, 104; Marcuse, 'Repressive tolerance', p. 114.
23   Marcuse, *One-Dimensional Man*, pp. 10–11.
24   Cf. H. Marcuse, 'Liberation from the affluent society', in *Critical Theory and Society: A Reader*, ed. Bronner and Kellner, p. 283; Marcuse, *One-Dimensional Man*, p. 220.
25   Marcuse, *One-Dimensional Man*, pp. 63, 70.

26 Ibid., pp. 137ff.

27 Ibid., pp. 155, 158.

28 Ibid., pp. 146, 153, 156, 160, 166.

29 Ibid., p. 240.

30 Ibid., pp. 236–7.

31 Ibid., p. 237.

32 Ibid., p. 165.

33 Ibid., pp. 166–7.

34 Ibid., p. 227. Cf. also Marcuse, 'Liberation from the affluent society', p. 283.

35 J. Habermas, *Toward a Rational Society*, tr. J. J. Shapiro (Heinemann, London, 1971), p. 88.

36 H. Marcuse, *Eros and Civilization* (Routledge and Kegan Paul, London, 1987), p. 16.

37 Ibid., p. 17.

38 Ibid., p. 111.

39 Ibid., p. 35.

40 Ibid., p. 17.

41 Ibid., p. 221.

42 Ibid., p. 40.

43 Ibid., p. 49.

44 Ibid., p. 90.

45 H. Marcuse, *Soviet Marxism: A Critical Analysis* (Routledge and Kegan Paul, London, 1958), p. 81.

46 Ibid., p. 227.

47 Ibid., pp. 229, 232–4, 243, 255.

48 Ibid., pp. 239, 242.

49 Ibid., pp. 262–7.

50 Marcuse, *Eros and Civilization*, pp. 16, 69.

51 Ibid., pp. 144–5.

52 Ibid., pp. 23, 131.

53 Ibid., p. 201.

54 Ibid., pp. 212, 214–16.

55 Ibid., p. 203.

56 Marcuse, *One-Dimensional Man*, p. 75.

57 Ibid., p. 73.

58 Marcuse, *Negations*, p. 10.

59 Marcuse, *Eros and Civilization*, p. 10; *One-Dimensional Man*, p. 189; *Soviet Marxism*, p. 265.

60 M. Horkheimer, *The Eclipse of Reason* (Oxford University Press, New York, 1947), pp. 100, 113, 116.

61 Ibid., p. 121.

62 Ibid.

Further reading

By Marcuse

H. Marcuse, *Reason and Revolution: Hegel and the Rise of Social Theory*, Oxford University Press, London, 1941 (repr. with supplementary chapter, 1955).

H. Marcuse, *Eros and Civilization: A Philosophical Inquiry into Freud*, London, Routledge and Kegan Paul, 1956.

H. Marcuse, *Soviet Marxism: A Critical Analysis*, Routledge and Kegan Paul, London, 1958.

H. Marcuse, *One-Dimensional Man*, Beacon Press, Boston, 1966.

H. Marcuse, 'Ethics and revolution', in R. T. de George (ed.), *Ethics and Society*, Doubleday, New York, 1966.

H. Marcuse, *Negations*, Allen Lane the Penguin Press, Harmondsworth, 1968.

H. Marcuse, *An Essay on Liberation*, Penguin, Harmondsworth, 1968.

H. Marcuse, 'Repressive tolerance', in R.P. Wolff, B. Moore Jr. and H. Marcuse, *A Critique of Pure Tolerance*, Jonathan Cape, London, 1969.

H. Marcuse, *Studies in Critical Philosophy*, New Left Books, London, 1972.

H. Marcuse, 'From ontology to technology: fundamental tendencies of industrial society', 'Liberation from the affluent society' and 'Philosophy and critical theory' in S. E. Bronner and D. M. Kellner (eds), *Critical Theory and Society: A Reader*, Routledge, London, 1989.

On Marcuse

V. Geoghegan, *Reason and Eros: The Social Theory of Herbert Marcuse*, Pluto Press, London, 1981.

J. Habermas, 'Technology and science as ideology', in *Toward a Rational Society*, tr. J. J. Shapiro, Heinemann, London, 1971.

B. M. Katz, *Herbert Marcuse and the Art of Liberation: An Intellectual Biography*, New Left Books, London, 1982.

D. M. Kellner, *Herbert Marcuse and the Crisis of Marxism*, Macmillan, London, 1984.

A. C. MacIntyre, *Marcuse*, Fontana/Collins, London, 1970.

G. A. Steuernagel, *Political Philosophy as Therapy: Marcuse Reconsidered*, Greenwood Press, Westport, Conn., 1979.

4
Hannah Arendt: Classical Republicanism and the Modern World

Hannah Arendt is one of the most distinguished and distinctive intellects to be found among the political thinkers of the twentieth century. The distinctiveness of her thought is, naturally, in part a consequence of intellectual power; but it is equally or more the result of her life experiences, and the originality of her response to them. Of no political thinker of our century is it more obviously true that the thinker's biography is crucial to an understanding of the thought; and the life of no political thinker has been more emblematic of the political history of the century. In this respect – the relation of history, life and thought – it is illuminating to compare Arendt with Marcuse. Both were German Jews who came to adulthood under the Weimar Republic, who witnessed its overthrow and replacement by Nazism, who fled first to Western Europe and then to the United States of America. Both were born Germans and died Americans. Arendt's experience of Nazism, however, was more direct, personal and menacing. Before fleeing Germany in 1933 she was detained by the police for political reasons and interrogated for eight days; later in France she was held in an internment camp before escaping to the USA in 1941. When Arendt came to write, in the perspective of political theory, on the plight of refugees and stateless persons, she knew at first hand that of which she spoke.

Arendt's theoretical response to the experience first of Nazism, then of post-war America, is in some way comparable to Marcuse's. The political thought of both is, in part, directed against two evils – totalitarianism and capitalist consumerism. Arendt, however, did not, unlike Marcuse, view the latter as a form of the former. Arendt, also, was a much more intellectually isolated and, perhaps for that reason, a more original thinker. She never belonged to any intellectual group comparable to the Frankfurt School, nor was she ever a popular icon of any political movement. Her independence of mind made that impossible – rather, her frequent interventions in public affairs embroiled her in a number of notoriously acrimonious disputes. Nor, despite Arendt's keen interest in Marx and acknowledgement of his importance within the Western intellectual tradition, is her political theory in any sense Marxist. Her main quarrel with Marx, indeed, was that his thought was anti-political. Arendt's reflections on her own experiences and that of so many of her contemporaries as refugees and 'displaced persons' convinced her that no-one was safe who did not enjoy full membership and protection of a *political* community. As she herself puts it, 'The Rights of Man . . . were supposed to be independent of all governments; but it turned out that the moment human beings lacked their own government and had to fall back on their [human] rights, no authority was left to protect them and no institution was willing to guarantee them'.[1] Here undoubtedly is one of the roots of Arendt's mature political theory, *republicanism*.

It is not, however, the only one. Another is more purely intellectual and philosophical. Indeed, before the Nazi threat to Jews and others became manifest, Arendt was first and foremost a philosopher with no interest in politics. Crucial to her intellectual formation is the fact that she studied under two founders and leaders of philosophical existentialism, Martin Heidegger and Karl Jaspers. Although the relation with Jaspers was the more lasting, becoming indeed a lifetime friendship, that with Heidegger – considered by some the greatest philosopher of the twentieth century – was probably more important theoretically and even personally. It became, for a year or so, a relation not just between student and teacher, but between lovers also. She could not, of course, know then that Heidegger would later betray her, and philosophy as well, by supporting Hitler's Nazi regime. Her political republicanism is, again in part, a response to the concerns of Heideggerian existentialism, and to the political failure not only manifested by Heidegger personally but also, in Arendt's view, inherent in his philosophy. This will be discussed in much more detail below.

Although Arendt had by the early 1930s been jolted into political activism and concern, her major book of political theory, *The Human Condition*, did not appear until a generation later, in 1958 – after, that is, seventeen years' residence in the United States. This book, in which her idiosyncratic conceptual system is set out and applied to Western social and intellectual history, both ancient and modern, is generally and rightly considered to be, not only her single most important contribution to political thought, but also the key to her political thought as a whole. It was not, however, her first significant book-length contribution; that title belongs to *The Origins of Totalitari-anism*, which first appeared in 1951. But, as Arendt herself admitted, that long book is oddly structured. Of its three parts, the first two (on 'Antisemitism' and 'Imperialism') are of relatively marginal significance: only the third part is in fact on 'Totalitarianism'. This third part, which analyses the Nazi and Stalinist regimes, is indeed of central importance, and, quite appropriately, has also been published separately. The relation between it and *The Human Condition* is also important. While it cannot of course be claimed that *Totalitarianism* is literally an application of the theory set out in *The Human Condition* to the totalitarian regimes, the relation is close. That Arendt's system of ideas grew out of her analysis of totalitarianism is clearly shown by the fact that the second and later editions of *The Origins* add to its third part a new chapter ('Ideology and terror: a novel form of government') which first appeared as a separate article in 1953, and in which the conceptual system of *The Human Condition* unmistakably appears in embryonic form. *Totalitarianism* thus, to a degree, provides an illustration of Arendt's theoretical system *avant la lettre*. Likewise, Arendt's third major political book, *On Revolution*, applies it to the American, French and (more briefly) Russian revolutions, as well as to the contemporary situation. The three books together, therefore, provide a systematic and original normative political theory, combined with an extended analysis, informed by that theory, both of relevant Western thought and of several major landmarks of Western political history. Mention should also be made of three collections of shorter pieces, occasional and other: *Between Past and Future, Crises of the Republic,* and *The Jew as Pariah,* all of which appeared in the 1970s (though some of the collected items had been published as early as 1943); and of Arendt's many contributions to leading American journals of opinion such as *Dissent* and *Partisan Review,* often though not always on issues of the moment. (It is probably obligatory, also, to mention Arendt's most notorious and controversial publication, *Eichmann in Jerusalem*,[2] which reports and reflects on the capture, trial, conviction and execution of the high-ranking Nazi official, Adolf Eichmann, by the state of Israel. It will not, however, be necessary to refer to it again in this book.)

As indicated above, Arendt's political thought cannot be understood unless seen as, in part, a reaction to the existentialism she learned from her teachers, especially Heidegger. How then did she view that philosophy? Two pieces by Arendt are important here, the early article 'What is existential philosophy?' (1946), and the later lecture 'Concern with politics in recent European thought' (1969). In these pieces Arendt expounds the elements of Heideggerian existentialism as follows. The existence (being, *Sein*) of the human individual is always and essentially existence at a particular time and place (a being-there, *Dasein*), that is, it is existence in an already existing environing world (*Umwelt*) – a 'being-in-the-world'. Furthermore, 'By reason of this with-like Being-in-the-World, the world is always the one I share with Others. The world of *Dasein* is a with-world (*Mitsein*).' Heidegger thus recognized, correctly, the worldly and social (or plural) condition of human life, but immediately went on to devalue it. For Heidegger, interpretation of existence in terms of *Umwelt* or *Mitwelt* is *inauthentic*. The shared *Umwelt* appears objective, universal, durable; while the reality of human existence is subjective, singular and – above all – finite. Death – human mortality or finitude – is for Heidegger the ultimate reality. All authentic being therefore is an utterly lonely being-unto-death. That is the reality obscured by focusing on the 'chatter' of the anonymous and superficial public world – as Heidegger famously puts it, 'Publicness obscures everything [Die Öffentlichkeit verdunkelt alles]', a remark quoted by Arendt in the preface to her collection, *Men in Dark Times*. Quoted, and repudiated. Arendt's quarrel with Heidegger is that, for all the profundity of his thought, and despite his rejection of the universalism of the Western philosophical tradition stemming from Plato, he none the less shared with that tradition a misplaced scorn for, or at least neglect of, the political dimension of human existence.

For the political cannot and should not be either neglected or scorned. In a Heideggerian perspective, authentic existence accepts the anguish of inevitable finitude, and also the 'burden of freedom' integral to human life – the necessity, while one lives, to accept that one is free to live as one chooses, without guidance from any universal or objective standards, to accept responsibility for one's choices, and to live with the guilt inevitable because the obverse of choice is necessarily neglect. Apart from the notably gloomy nature of this conception of human life as necessarily laden with anguish and guilt, it is notable also for its extreme individualism, almost to the point of solipsism – an individualism much more extreme than the individualism of universal human rights, which Arendt had found by her own experience to be so ineffectual without political support. It appears, in fact, as an extreme development of the Romantic individualism of the nineteenth century. Arendt, however, read it as an expression of the loneliness of atomized individuals in a mass society – a state of affairs also implicated, in her judgement, in the rise of totalitarianism.

Hence the political dimension of existence cannot be avoided. It is illuminating to compare Arendt's response to existentialist individualism with that of another student of Heidegger, Jean-Paul Sartre. Starting from a position of extreme Heideggerian individualism (encapsulated in his famous line, 'Hell is other people'), Sartre found it necessary, after all, to embrace politics and this, via his concept of *engagement* (commitment), led him into a total surrender to Marxism and, worse, defence of Stalinism. Sartre's evolution, although not shameful, may nevertheless seem, to a degree, like an eerie replay, in mirror image, of that of Heidegger himself in the 1930s. According to Arendt, Heidegger, too, had found it impossible to cling consistently to his extreme individualism: 'Later and after the fact', she writes, 'Heidegger drew on mythologizing and muddled concepts like "folk" and "earth" in an effort to supply his isolated Selves with a shared, common ground to stand on'[3] – concepts which undeniably smoothed the way for his own surrender to Nazism. Thus, existentialism's failure to do justice to politics, and to understand its true importance, led two of its leading exponents into regrettable or even disastrous political choices when these were forced upon them – choices which seem like desperate stratagems to cope with existential loneliness and to ease the burden of freedom.

Arendt's own response to the weaknesses and lacunae of existentialism is much more honourable and more intelligent than those of Heidegger or Sartre. Nevertheless, she takes seriously Heidegger's problems and makes use of some of his concepts while also transforming them – notably, the concepts of world and publicness, and the existential problem of mortality. Even the title of *The Human Condition* is a kind of tribute to existentialism, since it signals Arendt's belief that there is no such thing as a fixed human nature or essence, that human beings are essentially free agents, though not unconditioned.[4] One of the conditions is indeed mortality. So also is *natality* – the fact that every human being is *born* into a pre-existing world and is thus, as Arendt puts it, a new beginning, free to make a difference.[5] Birth and death, in the case of human beings, are, Arendt writes, 'not simple natural occurrences', because human beings, unlike purely natural phenomena, and unlike other animals, are 'individuals, unique, unexchangeable and unrepeatable'.[6] But they depend on, are born into and die from, a relatively permanent world, 'which existed before any one individual appeared into it and will survive his eventual departure', a world which itself knows neither natality nor mortality.

Mortality, however, is not merely a feature of the human condition, it is also an existential problem for every human individual – one which human beings have, in various ways, tried to cope with and even, in a sense, to overcome. Arendt, focusing on the Western tradition, notes two such attempts – contrasting attempts to achieve a kind of human immortality – that of Christianity and that of classical pagan antiquity (Græco-Roman civilization). Her concern, however, is not which of the two is 'truer' or more plausible. Rather, the contrast which concerns her is that the Christian concept of the immortal soul is radically individualistic and not of this world, whereas that of classical antiquity was worldly and *political*. The gods of the Greeks and Romans were *immortal* (not *eternal*, like the Judaeo-Christian God); and human beings too, the Greeks and Romans held, could achieve a kind of immortality (and thus even a kind of divinity) by performing great deeds – immortal deeds – deserving to be remembered for ever, deserving of 'immortal fame'. Clearly this is a kind of immortality that depends on human plurality, on preservation in the minds of one's fellows and of their descendants. 'The *polis* was for the Greeks, as the *res publica* was for the Romans, first of all their guarantee against the futility of individual life, the space . . . reserved for the relative permanence, if not immortality, of mortals'.[7] For Arendt, the famous funeral oration of Pericles defined the Athenian *polis* as a space for 'organized remembrance' which thus conferred *reality* on the otherwise 'passing existence and fleeting greatness' of mortal men.[8]

The word 'reality' in the last sentence is important, because, according to Arendt, the Greek philosophers – especially Plato – did not share the view that Thucydides attributed to Pericles, indeed he repudiated it. To Plato, the fountainhead of the Western philosophical tradition, reality was to be found, not in worldly or human immortality but in the eternal, something extra-worldly and super-human, the object of philosophical contemplation. The contemplative life of the philosopher, therefore, was elevated above the active life of the citizen – *bios theoretikos* was elevated above *bios politikos*. In Arendt's view, Plato's insistence that philosophers must rule the *polis* as kings was fundamentally for the sake of philosophy rather than of citizens.[9] Christianity (influenced by Augustine, who was influenced by Plato) restated the viewpoint of the Greek philosophers in its own idiom, translating the Greek terms into Latin as *vita contemplativa* and *vita activa*. As with the Greeks, the former was still seen as superior, but (as Arendt notes), the latter had lost its specifically political connotation. In *The Human Condition*, Arendt sets out to re-evaluate, and to restore to dignity, the *vita activa* and (more especially) the *bios politikos* – as she puts it, to correct the anti-political bias of the philosophers.

We may now expound and explain the system of concepts used by Arendt to express her political theory. Her focus is on what medieval Europe called the *vita activa*, the active life, within which three sub-categories, she holds, must be distinguished, which she calls *labour, work* and *action*. (It is perhaps a minor difficulty that so-called 'action' is in this vocabulary only one category of the active life.) In addition to this fundamental trichotomy, Arendt also uses two dichotomic contrasts, namely, that of public versus private, and (reflecting the importance to her thinking of Greek concepts), that between *polis* and household. The relation between these categorial schemes, and the relation of politics to each, are not entirely straightforward. They should become clearer in the course of this chapter; for the time being, it suffices to note that politics is (naturally) more or less coextensive (at least in the Greek case) with the *polis*, but, while it belongs to the public realm, and to the sphere of action, it is not identical to either. Aspects of what Arendt calls 'work' also belong to the public sphere, while 'action' to some extent intrudes into the private. Nor is the private realm identical to the household. On the other hand, politics is for Arendt unquestionably the most important form of action and the most important aspect of the public sphere. While not identical, action, politics and the public sphere coincide to a significant degree.

Arendt's fundamental conceptual scheme (and her most original and characteristic one) is the triad of labour, work and action. The first distinction between them is that labour and work are both modes of activity in which human beings operate on the natural environment, whereas action is actually *inter*action between human beings. But labour and work, Arendt insists, are not the same, although earlier theorists (notably Marx) failed to note the difference. Labour is in reality a biological function, rather than a distinctively human one – like all animals, men must use the natural environment in order to sustain life. Parts of the environment have to be consumed for this purpose, and to be made consumable. The activity that serves this function is performed by what Arendt calls the *animal laborans*, indicating by this phrase her opinion that labour, however necessary, is a sub-human activity, made necessary by our animality. It is the mode of activity in which men are least free, precisely because it is a matter of (biological) necessity, and it is (or throughout most of human history was) experienced by human beings as painful. Arendt points out that the English word 'labour' and its synonyms in other languages, such as 'travail', also signify 'pain and effort' (she might have added that the word 'travail', which means 'labour' in French, means 'pain' in English).[10] It is relevant, too, that the English word 'labour' and its synonyms also signify giving birth, in which context it again carries connotations of pain, and refers to a biological function whose point is the maintenance of the life of the species. The purpose of labour, then, is the preservation of species life, and life (or preservation of life) is the highest value of the *animal laborans*. But it is not his only value, for the *animal laborans* seeks relief from his pain, from the toilsomeness of his labour – he seeks ease, comfort, pleasure instead of pain. All these are therefore characteristic values of the *animal laborans*, and all human activity that serves *only* these functions is also labour. Roughly speaking, it follows for Arendt, the scope of labour coincides with that of economic activity, embracing all production whose point is consumption (in the economic as well as the biological sense of that term). In economic activity, therefore, human beings are not genuinely free, but largely follow the dictates of necessity. In Arendt's eyes it is no accident that economics was the first 'social science' to seek, and with some success, to emulate the natural sciences, whose laws express natural necessity and where freedom does not arise.

Work (in Arendt's sense of the word), though like labour it involves interaction with the natural environment, is a creative, fully human activity. It is the province not of the *animal laborans*, the labouring animal, but of *homo faber*, man the maker – the maker of things among which he lives. To Arendt the most significant generic feature of work is that through it mankind creates a *world* – 'an "artificial" world of things', among which men can feel at home. These artefacts may be of the most varied and heterogeneous kind, and thus 'work' embraces a great variety of activities, including for example both technology and the fine arts – everything in fact. which anthropologists refer to as 'material culture'. The work-created world includes, also, such 'humble' but significant items as tables and chairs. In a brilliant and well-known passage, Arendt enlarges on the human significance of tables. Tables, of course, are used for serving meals, and thus serve the consumption needs of the *animal laborans*. At the same time, however, a table shapes the social and spatial relations of human beings, of those who sit round it, at once relating them and holding them somewhat apart, and thus placing them in relation to each other as, at the same time, separate individuals. Arendt asks us to imagine the reaction of a group of individuals sitting round a table, if the table were suddenly and magically to disappear – her suggestion is that the result would be disorientation and confusion. It is of prime importance to the human significance of the work-created artificial world that its components do *not* suddenly disappear – that they are *durable*, more lasting than mortal men, providing for the latter a 'home' to be born into and to die from. In contrast to Heidegger, Arendt sees this as a source, not of inauthenticity, but rather of solace, stability and meaning.

The analytic distinction between labour and work does not, of course, preclude overlap between them in the actual course of human life. One example of such overlap was given above – the table, which serves for consumption of food as well as forming part of the familiar world which we inhabit. Many if not most of the goods produced in the economy serve a similar dual function: in their use by 'consumers' (as economists say) they tend to get, not only used, but *used up*, or worn out, eventually disappearing from our 'world' back into the inhuman processes of nature. Though durable, they are not immortal. Their durability, indeed, varies, not only intrinsically, but – very importantly to Arendt – as a function of human attitudes. They endure the more, if we wish them to endure, and thus make them in such a way as to endure. The more this is the case, the more do they embody the spirit of *homo faber*, man the maker, the world-builder; the less it is so, the more concerned we are only to use these objects rather than to keep them, the more rapidly they are destroyed in use, then the more they serve, and express the attitudes of, the *animal laborans*, who produces only to consume. In this sense, the 'purest' form of work, or world-creation, are works of art, objects which are made, not at all to be used or used up, but only to endure for as long as possible, as part of humanity's artificial world (a*rs longa, vita brevis*). They are 'the most intensely worldly of all tangible things'. In Arendt's view these artefacts of high culture are the most valuable parts of our world, and their creation the highest form of work. Though not quite immortal, they provide 'a premonition of immortality'.[11] The preeminence of works of art in the work-made world means, to Arendt, that beauty is the preeminent value of that world, and a standard even for ordinary use objects, which are not (or may not be) intended to be beautiful. The other defining value of our world (along with beauty), is to be sure, utility. But every *thing*, as Arendt says, has an appearance, and thus cannot help but be beautiful or ugly, whatever utilitarian function it may also have.[12]

There is another interface between labour and work that is significant to Arendt. As she puts it, *homo faber* has come to the help of the *animal laborans*, has acted to 'ease his labour and remove his pain', by the making of tools.[13] Tools (which as everyone knows have become more and more complex and sophisticated in the course of human history) are made by *homo faber*, but also used by the labouring animal (as well as *homo faber* himself). But Arendt sees a categorical difference between *tools* and *machines*. Tools *can* be used by *homo faber*, because tools are under the control of human beings; whereas the user (if that is the word) of a machine is rather *its* servant, has to adjust himself to its rhythms and requirements, and so on. Machine-users (or machine-minders) are therefore labourers by definition, that is, are not free agents. Nor does a machine-labourer *make* anything, because his activity is governed by the principle of *division of labour*, and thus has no independent end of its own. Arendt insists on the difference between division of labour, and specialization of work; the latter 'is essentially guided by the finished product, whose nature it is to require different skills which then are pooled',[14] whereas division of labour 'presupposes the quantitative equivalence of all single activities for which no special skill is required'. The skilled worker creates machines, which are used by unskilled labourers. Machines, then, are indeed part of the human world – they have become, thanks to the Industrial Revolution, the world of the labourer. Or rather, Arendt says, they constitute a pseudo-world, for this 'world' fails to give mortal men 'a dwelling place more permanent and more stable than themselves'.[15]

As might be deduced from the previous paragraph, Arendt believes that the category of *instrumentality*, of means-end reasoning, belongs essentially to the activity and experience of *homo faber*.[16] The *animal laborans*, by contrast, whether he consumes, or acts for the sake of consumption, or contributes some fraction of an activity under a scheme of division of labour, does not produce or envisage an end-product. I believe that in this argument Arendt makes the same mistake as Marcuse, that of identifying means-end reasoning with men's mastery of external nature. *Homo faber* is, indeed, man as the master and shaper of nature, nature used as a resource for human ends. But means-end reasoning (called 'utilitarianism' by Arendt, as well as instrumentality) is by no means confined to this aspect of human life, but pervades every aspect of it. In all probability, terms such as 'instrumentality', 'instrumentalism' and 'instrumental reason' are both cause and reflection of this confusion. On the one hand, they are taken, as a matter of course, to translate what Weber called *Zweckrationalität*, goal-directed rationality; on the other, they imply the use of some instrument, some physical thing, as a means used to transform some other physical thing, a resource. Of course means and ends are not truly limited to such physical embodiments.

In another respect, however, Arendt's thinking contrasts starkly with that of Marcuse. Unlike him, she does not complain about the 'domination' or 'oppression' of nature; rather (in a more Hegelian spirit) she celebrates human shaping of nature into an artificial world, a home. Like Weber, she sees 'nature' as a system of meaningless processes and forces, the realm of necessity rather than freedom, eternally swinging in its endless cycles. Freedom and meaning, for Arendt as for Weber, enter reality only with human beings (the *animal laborans* has not truly emerged from natural necessity). Nevertheless, she does see the 'instrumentalism' (or utilitarianism) of *homo faber* as a threat to meaningful existence. For *homo faber* tends to see *everything* as a means, to ask, in relation to everything, 'What use is it?' i.e. what is it a means to? What is more, an end as such cannot provide meaningfulness for human life, for once achieved 'it loses its capacity to guide' our activity.[17] 'Meaning, on the contrary, must be permanent'. One is reminded of Hobbes's dictum that every end, once achieved, is but the start of the pursuit of a new end, so that men's appetites are never satisfied. Every end achieved becomes a new means to a new end, *ad infinitum*. This, says Arendt, is the 'tragedy' of *homo faber*, who 'is just as incapable of understanding meaning as the *animal laborans* is of understanding instrumentality'.[18] This, perhaps, is Arendt's way of characterizing what Weber called disenchantment.

But this tragedy, or disenchantment, is certainly not seen by Arendt as inherent in the activity of work, of *homo faber*, nor of the world he creates – it is rather a perversion of them. A more positive aspect, which belongs to work as such, is that it bridges the gap between the private and public realms. Work, in itself, is a private activity, it may even be the activity of a single person working alone. But what it creates is not just a private but, even more importantly, a public, that is a common world for men to inhabit.[19] Furthermore, Arendt holds, *homo faber* (unlike the *animal laborans*) is capable of creating a public (though not a political) realm of his own – the market. By this term, Arendt emphatically does not refer to the abstract web of economic transactions so typical of modern capitalism – she means a physical place, the market place, or exchange market, where producers display their wares and not only exchange them but also 'receive the esteem due' to them – what Arendt calls 'conspicuous production'.[20] Presumably bazaars and shops also belong to this public realm of *homo faber*. It is interesting, however, that in this connection Arendt makes no mention of art galleries or museums, which also display, and particularly for admiration, the greatest works of *homo faber*. Perhaps she sees these institutions as belonging to a completely common public world, rather than that of *homo faber* as such. It is noteworthy, also, that the 'tragedy' of *homo faber*'s instrumentalism or utilitarianism should not apply to the artist – who may thus be better able to escape from disenchantment and meaninglessness.

Be that as it may, it is clear that for Arendt work is a realm of some importance and dignity (it would scarcely be capable of tragedy, otherwise) – certainly more so than labour. It is, also, in her eyes, a realm of greater freedom; but not of the greatest freedom possible for men. *Homo faber* indeed acts freely, but the 'partner' of his activity is nature, a nature governed by necessary laws. In this sense work is not totally free of necessity. Mankind's highest freedom occurs in interactions where both (or all) parties are free, i.e. are human. This is what Arendt calls *action*. And, Arendt says, 'action is the political activity par excellence'.[21] It follows that politics is the supreme locus of human freedom: as Arendt puts it, 'The *raison d'être* of politics is freedom.'[22]

It is clear that this is the so-called classical republican concept of freedom, and of politics. Or rather (as we shall see), it is the existentialist concern with freedom politicized, and thus republicanized, through a republican concept of politics stemming from Arendt's admiration for the ancient Greeks and Romans. However, politics is not coextensive with Arendt's concept of action, which is our immediate concern. Action (that is, interaction between human beings) reflects the most essentially human aspect of the human condition – plurality, or as Arendt puts it in a phrase she repeated several times, and which is clearly fundamental to her thought, 'not man but men inhabit the earth'. Human plurality, Arendt explains, entails both *equality* and *distinction*, a combination which at the same time requires and enables men to converse with one another. 'If men were not equal, they could [not] understand each other. . . If men were not distinct, each human being distinguished from any other who is, was, or will ever be, they would need neither speech nor action to make themselves understood.'[23] Arendt's concept of human plurality is perhaps the most felicitous expression to be found in political theory of, at once, the individuality and the interdependence of human beings, and has been widely and rightly admired. It is to be noted that speech – the use of language – is an essential (not merely useful) aspect or accompaniment of action, and of action alone. Action is the supremely and inescapably human form of human activity.

What is its nature? From the standpoint of the individual (of each unique, irreplaceable individual) it is a process of self-disclosure (another Arendtian term that neatly blends individuality and interdependence): 'In acting and speaking, men show who they are, reveal actively their unique personal identities and thus make their appearance in the human world.'[24] Without thus *appearing* to their fellows, men could scarcely be human – indeed, Arendt tells us, in the Greek view (with which she clearly sympathizes) the very reality of the actor's existence is assured by appearing before an audience of fellow men.[25] And yet, Arendt also tells us, action by its nature risks futility. Unlike work, it produces no tangible end-product. Because action is always interaction of one free agent with others, it is inherently uncertain and rarely if ever totally predictable. 'He who acts never quite knows what he is doing.'[26] Without intending it, he may even bring about calamitous consequences – or rather, set in motion a sequence having such consequences. Thus, there is reason 'to turn away with despair' from the realm of human action and from the consequences of human freedom. Existential guilt and anguish seem, perhaps, inescapable.

Yet politics can redeem action and even the human condition itself – can, if it remains faithful to the fundamental norm of plurality. A man's words and deeds may not only appear to his co-agents and audience, they may enter into the latter's memory and become part of the story of his community. With the help of *homo faber*, they may be embodied (or 'reified') in books, poetry, painting or sculpture – the work, Arendt says, of *homo faber*, in his highest capacity, the artist, the poet, or the historiographer.[27] In this way, men's greatest deeds acquire *glory*, called by Arendt a 'shining brightness' which action needs for its full appearance, and which can occur only in the public sphere of politics.[28] 'Action, in so far as it engages in founding and preserving political bodies, creates the condition for . . . history.' The politics–dependent ability of action to 'produce stories and become historical', Arendt says, is one great source 'from which meaningfulness springs into and illuminates human experience'.[29]

Arendt's view of history may seem like a great-man theory, but her view of politics emphatically is not – she is a republican. The glory of great deeds must be won in the eyes and minds of one's peers, one's fellow–citizens (and every citizen is a potential hero). Political power rightly understood, Arendt insists, arises not from violence, but from individuals acting in concert.[30] Politics is a sphere of persuasion, not force (from force and violence no true political glory springs, though naturally the public realm of political action may need to be protected by armed force against external attack). Arendt's consensual view of politics, based on human plurality, creates a certain kinship with social contract theory (though her theory does not belong to that category).[31] The power to act in concert, she says, depends on mutual promises or contracts.[32] By this, however, she does not mean any kind of founding act bringing the political realm into existence, but a continuing relationship, or form of relationship, by means of which fellow citizens coordinate their actions and mitigate the unpredictability that is the price of freedom.

Arendt's view of politics as the supreme embodiment of human action, and of human plurality, enables her to combat a number of erroneous political conceptions. One such is nationalism, which she describes as a 'perversion of the state into an instrument of the nation [through] identification of the citizen with the member of the nation'.[33] Arendt was a bitter critic of the inter-war Versailles settlement, based on the national principle, which offends against the principle of plurality in its implicit assumption of the mystical unity of the nation, from which non-nationals are excluded. Hence came the harsh fate of the 'national minorities' within the inter-war European states, at best reduced to a status of second-class citizenship, at worst subjected to mass expulsions from their homes and countries. It was her hostility to nationalism that led to Arendt's disillusion with orthodox Zionism, of which she had for a time been an active supporter. For similar reasons – its denial of human plurality – she could have no truck with the Rousseauan 'general will', which was indeed the begetter of European nationalism as it emerged in the French Revolution – 'la nation une et indivisible'.[34]

Arendt also calls nationalism the most dangerous form ever assumed by political absolutism – the French Revolutionary exponents of nationalism, indeed, simply put the nation in the place of the absolute monarchy.[35] According to Arendt, all political absolutism, all despotism, all sovereignty, is a perversion of politics, which is a relation between equals – between citizens. This perversion in part arises, according to Arendt's reading of Western intellectual history, from a confusion of action (politics) with making, the activity of *homo faber*. The most distinguished example of this mistake was Hobbes, theorist of sovereignty *par excellence*, who saw the establishment of the Commonwealth as like the making of an 'automaton that moves [itself] by springs and wheels as doth a watch'.[36] More generally, the despotic or monarchical view of politics, which sees the political realm as one in which the ruler commands and subjects obey, seems to Arendt to reflect the attitude of man the maker, the master of nature.[37] (There is here some similarity to the views of Marcuse, but Arendt traces the attitude in question back to Plato, whose intellectual influence became pervasive in the Western tradition. And, again unlike Marcuse, Arendt sees the same attitude at work in the Marxist revolutionary tradition, with its desire to 'make history'.)[38] Her objection to despotism and tyranny is not merely that despots and tyrants may act cruelly and oppressively (Platonic philosopher-kings would not), but above all that even if they do not they destroy human freedom (their own, as well as their subjects') which can arise only in action, and hence destroy truly meaningful existence.

Arendt's republican politics is in an obvious way egalitarian, but the relation of her thought generally to egalitarianism is much more complicated than this may suggest. In the first place, the egalitarianism she espouses is political only – to wider, 'social' egalitarianism she was firmly opposed (this will be discussed in greater detail later). In addition, even her political egalitarianism is not unproblematic: here, the issue is whether her classical republicanism can be given adequate application in the modern world (a modern world in which Arendt finds much to deplore). This again is an issue which will occupy us, at some length, in what follows. It is an ironic fact that the theory of classical republicanism had to wait until the twentieth century to find in Arendt its greatest exponent – by which time it may have been too late.

As is apparent from what was said above about political and social egalitarianism, Arendt drew very sharp – some would say too sharp – distinctions between the political and the non-political, the public and private realms, *polis* and household (in Greek terms), action, work and labour. As she notes (without expressing either approval or disapproval) Greek thought (typified by Aristotle) excluded from the political realm all those engaged in labour, money-making or economic production (craftsmanship), making no categorical distinction between work and labour, since all these activities were held to be incompatible with freedom, fit indeed for slaves rather than free men. Thus it is clear that even the philosophers, who downgraded what would later be called the active life by comparison with the contemplative, nevertheless at the same time saw political activity (*bios politikos*) as the highest level within the former. Much of *The Human Condition* is devoted to a fascinating account of the changes and reversals that have occurred over the centuries in the relative ranking, not only of the *vita activa* and the *vita contemplativa*, but also of the various forms of the active life (labour, work and action), and of the implications thereof for politics – implications which to Arendt are largely unwelcome, to put it mildly. Whether one agrees with her or not, this approach provides a highly original and thought-provoking angle of vision on politics.

The first major change, the Christianization of the West, had the effect of depreciating the political even more than in the thought of the classical philosophers – not only was the superiority of the contemplative life reaffirmed in a new idiom, but (thanks to Christian unworldliness or rather anti-worldliness) the sense of distinctions within the active life was lost.[39] 'Glory' accordingly was redefined as 'vainglory'. Modernity has, of course, changed much by comparison with the Christian world-view, yet its relation to its Christian ancestor is complex – while much has been repudiated, important influences persist. Most significantly, in Arendt's view, Christianity's 'alienation from the world' has left its mark on a civilization that ostensibly has rejected it.[40] Following Weber, she sees the rise of modern capitalism, in significant part at least, as the outgrowth of Puritan asceticism – an asceticism working 'in the world, but not of the world'. Before the consequences of this worked themselves out, however, the most momentous of the changes involved in modernity had occurred – the reversal of the ancient and medieval rankings of the contemplative and the active life.[41] This was the work of modern science, which arose (contrary to Marcuse and the Frankfurt School) not out of practical concerns but out of the thirst for knowledge (the motive of the philosopher). The reversal due to the scientific revolution amounted to the conviction that true knowledge is to be derived, not from contemplation, but from the work of men's hands – paradigmatically, Galileo's telescope. Contemplation was not merely demoted but totally undermined, and, in the experimental method, 'thinking' became the handmaiden of 'doing'.[42]

More specifically, the rise of modern experimental science is seen by Arendt as the triumph of *homo faber* – the maker of scientific instruments. But his triumph was short-lived. Soon, and much more lastingly, the rule of *homo faber* was to be swept aside by that of the *animal laborans* – a new hegemony which would engulf the political realm also, and which has persisted until our own day.

Already in the seventeenth century the triumph of the labouring animal was being prepared – notably in the work of a theorist with affinities both to puritanism and to early capitalism, John Locke (despite – or perhaps because of – the fact that he made no material distinction between 'the labour of our body and the work of our hands').[43] Arendt refers here to Locke's 'discovery' that labour is the source and justification of property, property whose God-given function is to turn the earth into consumable goods.[44] Direct descendants of Locke's view are Adam Smith's celebration of labour (and the division of labour) as the source of all wealth, and the labour theory of value of the classical economists and of Marx. According to Arendt, it is in Marx that the apotheosis of labour reaches a climax – for him, labour was not only 'the source of all productivity', but 'the expression of the very humanity of men'[45] – a view diametrically opposed to that of the Greek philosophers. Yet Marx nevertheless agreed with the latter in his denigration of politics, which would 'wither away' in his ideal society. All these views, as Arendt notes, were responses to, and in part explanations of, the unprecedented economic growth experienced in the West from the seventeenth to the nineteenth centuries.

The triumph of the *animal laborans* is traceable in other ways: two philosophical expressions of it, in Arendt's view, are Benthamite utilitarianism, and the principle of the sacredness of life. The maintenance of life – a purely biological function – is, it will be recalled, precisely the function of labour. The sacralization of biological life, in Arendt's view, resulted from a secularization of Christian belief. For Christianity, too, the individual human life was sacred, but this was understood as a person's immortal life, or soul. Loss of belief in the immortal soul converted the Christian view into a powerful support, even apotheosis, of the highest value of the labouring animal. Hedonistic utilitarianism, too, in which good and evil are identified with pleasure and pain respectively, are again clear expressions of the value system of the *animal laborans*.

The triumph of the *animal laborans* has culminated in what Arendt calls 'the rise of society'[46]. 'Society' and 'social', it has to be stressed, are for Arendt always pregnant terms, and always pejorative ones (this is true whether she speaks of 'mass society' or of 'good society' or simply of 'society'). Latin Christendom made a profound mistake, she claims, when it translated Aristotle's '*zoon politikon*' as '*animal socialis*' — it is not man's social but his political character that distinguishes him from other animals. The rise of society is, so to speak, this mistake writ large. It means, to Arendt, the usurping or takeover of politics by the non-political, and more particularly by the *animal laborans* and his concerns. It means production subordinated entirely to consumption, rather than the building of a world (it is notorious how, in late capitalism, things are not made to last, but to be quickly thrown away and quickly superseded); and it means a corrupt politics entirely dominated by economic concerns, devoted to the facilitation of economic consumption, matters which, in Arendt's terms, are properly a concern of the private, not the public realm. It means abolition of the distinction between these two realms, of the distinction, so much insisted on by the Greeks, between *polis* and household, to the great detriment of both, and their replacement by an all-embracing, undiscriminating 'society'. The 'society' that Arendt so deplores is more or less synonymous with modern consumerism — it is a society devoted to economic consumption. Arendt calls it a society of job-holders, devoted to 'earning a living'.[47]

Why exactly does she find it so deplorable? The answer, perhaps, is obvious. The swallowing-up of work and action, of the political, by private, economic concerns means the destruction of men's freedom, the swallowing-up of freedom by necessity. It means also that in the blizzard of consumption mankind is losing his stable world, suffering increasingly from 'world-alienation'. Economic man is a manifestation of the *animal laborans* (he should perhaps be called not *homo* but *animal economicus*). If, Arendt writes, modern man was to be 'liberated' from labour by automation, his plight would be parlous indeed. The 'labouring society' we have created would be turned into 'a society of labourers without labour . . . Surely, nothing could be worse'. Arendt pens a notable Jeremiad:

This society no longer knows of those other higher and more meaningful activities for the sake of which this [liberation from labour] would deserve to be won. Within this society, which is egalitarian because this is labour's way of making men live together, there is no class left, no aristocracy of either a political or a spiritual nature from which a restoration of the other capacities of man could start anew.[48]

It is scarcely too much to say that, for Arendt, this is a society in which men have almost ceased to be human and become again a part of nature. Such, indeed, is the image of man accepted by those who proclaim the legitimacy of 'social sciences' modelled on natural science. 'Marx's contention that economic laws are like natural laws . . . is correct only in a labouring society.'[49] Again, 'The trouble with modern theories of behaviourism is not that they are wrong but that they could become true, that they actually are the best possible conceptualizations of . . . trends in modern society.'[50] Despite all their differences we can see here an agreement between Arendt and Marcuse: so called 'natural sciences of society' correspond to an un-free society enslaved by consumerism: a society of anonymous, interchangeable individuals lacking in all individuality.

The consumer society is not, however the only or the greatest evil ascribable to this state of affairs. Again in (partial) agreement with Marcuse, Arendt sees it as implicated in the great evil of totalitarianism which has so disfigured the twentieth century. (The agreement is only partial because Arendt uses the term 'totalitarianism' in its conventional sense, and hence in a more limited sense than Marcuse.) Arendt's analysis of totalitarianism was written before *The Human Condition* and therefore does not follow exactly that book's conceptual scheme, but resemblances and continuities between the two are not hard to find.

In view of its importance in twentieth-century history and her own painfully close involvement in it, it is hardly surprising that Arendt should wish to understand the phenomenon of totalitarianism. Despite that painful personal involvement, her analysis is strikingly objective, cool and incisive. As an essay in historically and philosophically informed political science, Arendt's *Totalitarianism* bears comparison with the work of one of her heroes, Alexis de Tocqueville.

Arendt had in fact a significant personal relation with both of the prime examples of twentieth-century totalitarianism. Not only was she herself a victim of Nazism, so too was her husband, Heinrich Blücher; Blücher (whom Arendt married in 1940) was an idealistic Marxist and Communist Party member who, like so many others, became disillusioned by Stalin's

Communist-inspired version of totalitarianism. The two regimes, Nazism and Stalinism, are treated by Arendt as examples of a single, completely new, political type. Her analysis, it must be said, is not a complete explanation of the phenomenon. She pays little attention to the specific historical disasters that paved the way for the development of totalitarianism in Germany and Russia – defeat in war and massive economic dislocation; her focus instead is on the organization and methods typical of the new totalitarian political form, and the state of society which proved so tragically receptive to these methods.

Arendt's analysis of totalitarian organization and methods is more insightful and more convincing than that of Marcuse. Rather than seeing totalitarianism as an extreme embodiment of Weberian rationalization in the *zweckrational* sense, of technocracy and bureaucracy, Arendt pointed out, correctly, how different was Nazi and Stalinist administration from the bureaucratic or rational–legal model, which is rule governed, hierarchical, and based on expertise; a multi-level structure of authority and of defined competencies.[51] By contrast, totalitarian organization is (or was) based on totally different principles: the leader principle, ideology and terror. By bureaucratic or rational-legal standards Nazi and Stalinist organization was notably chaotic, but this apparent chaos was in fact perfectly suited to the operation of the leader principle: it enabled the Leader to intervene at any time and at any point and thus to make the party or state apparatus a perfect instrument of his personal will. The rule of law was, of course, non-existent, but so, too, was all respect for the bureaucratic chain of command: multiplication of offices and establishment of competing jurisdictions were deliberate devices to facilitate the Leader's power. As Arendt writes, the leader principle means that 'authority is not filtered down from the top through all intervening layers to the bottom of the body politic . . . There are no intervening levels, each of which would receive its due share of authority and obedience. The will of the Führer can be embodied everywhere and at all times.'[52]

Not only is totalitarian administration remote from bureaucratic or rational–legal models, Arendt argues (again contrary to many other analysts) that totalitarian leadership is not an example of Weber's charismatic authority.[53] Rather, she believes, the power of the totalitarian leaders was based on their mastery of the totalitarian form of organization. This perhaps is more accurate in the case of the *apparatchik* Stalin (whose pseudo-charisma, the so-called 'cult of personality', was created only after he had achieved supreme power) than of Hitler. Hitler, no doubt, was also a master of totalitarian power structures, but in his case personal magnetism and oratorical skill, combined with ideological appeal, seem significant factors in his rise to power. Even Stalin may have been able to exploit a genuine charismatic appeal – not his own, but that of Lenin, whose leadership position he inherited.

Be that as it may, Arendt is far from playing down the importance of ideology in the totalitarian phenomenon – on the contrary, she insists on it. It is noteworthy that both totalitarian regimes proclaimed an ideology – socialism or racism – masquerading as a science of history. 'Nowhere does the ideological origin, of socialism in one instance and racism in the other, show more clearly than when their spokesmen pretend that they have discovered the hidden forces that will bring them good fortune in the chain of fatality', knowledge which supposedly permits what Arendt calls (in language reminiscent of Popper) 'scientific prophecy' (or rather, pseudo–scientific prophecy). 'Laws of history' or 'laws of nature' spell the doom of the enemies of the totalitarian movement.[54] As we know, Arendt did not, any more than Popper, believe in the validity of 'natural' laws of history, though for rather different reasons from Popper (she believed *all* law-like social science to be incompatible with human freedom). Since these ideologies are false, totalitarian movements and governments must, in order to hide their falsity, resort to lying on a colossal scale, as a principle of policy – hence the importance of propaganda in totalitarian regimes. But this, strangely, does not mean that belief in the ideology on the part of totalitarian leaders is insincere – this is shown by, for example, the profoundly 'un–utilitarian' behaviour of the Nazis who, even at the most desperate crises of the Second World War, 'wasted' significant resources on exterminating the Jews and others.[55] Arendt sees the imposition of totalitarian economic 'planning' by Stalin in 1929 as a comparable triumph of ideology over economic rationality – perhaps rightly, though more debatably (the Marxist economic planners, after all, could claim to be following Marxian economic theory). Arendt sees the determination of totalitarian leaders to cling to their ideologies and to implement their ideological goals in the face of all difficulties and all reality as the manifestation of a quite new belief: that 'everything is possible', given only sufficient strength of will.[56] Such delusions of omnipotence must lead, in the face of recalcitrant reality, to rule by violence and terror (concentration camps, *gulags*, the secret police), even if violence is not (as it was in the Nazi case) an explicit part of the ideology itself. Only terror can come close to giving the leaders sufficient control to realize their aims (or can appear to them to do so).

Soberly viewed, the fantastic nature of totalitarian ideology and organization must seem like a recipe for insanity and disaster. Why, then, were two totalitarian regimes able to establish themselves in Europe in the 1930s? Certainly not by terror alone, in Arendt's view, for both enjoyed a significant measure of popular support. Why? Why was the totalitarian version of reality so widely acceptable? Arendt's somewhat controversial answer is a version of the theory of mass society. Russia before 1917 was 'a country where a despotic and centralized bureaucracy governed a structureless mass population which neither the remnants of the rural feudal orders nor the weak, nascent urban capitalist class had organized.'[57] Collapse of the despotism made it relatively easy to win power over the mass. But to create a totalitarian state Stalin had to suppress and destroy all the nascent autonomous post-revolutionary bodies such as soviets and trades unions, and thus again 'fabricate an atomized and structureless mass' in the USSR.[58] In Germany, the creation of an atomized mass society, Arendt believes, was due to 'the breakdown of the class system' after the First World War.[59] According to Arendt, 'the chief characteristic of mass man is . . . his isolation and lack of normal social relationships'.[60] It is this loneliness and social atomization that opens men's hearts and minds to the totalitarian appeal: 'Totalitarian movements are mass organizations of atomized, isolated individuals', whose fanaticism and devotion to the Leader are the result precisely of the loneliness from which they seek to escape.[61]

It is arguable that Arendt tends to exaggerate the similarities between the Nazi and Bolshevik cases, and some critics cast doubt on the accuracy of her description of pre-Nazi German society (the Nazis, they argue, actually incorporated and subjugated a large number of pre-existing social bodies). More important than these historical details, however, is another point emphasized by Arendt, namely that the personnel, followers and supporters of the totalitarian movements were largely drawn from previously *non-political* individuals – people apparently too indifferent to public affairs to join a political party or even to vote.[62] The blame for this widespread political indifference, in Arendt's opinion, lies to a significant degree with the 'acquisitive society of the bourgeoisie', and their anti-political ethos – 'a way and philosophy of life so insistently and exclusively centred on the individual's success or failure in ruthless competition that a citizen's duties could only be felt to be a needless drain on his limited time and energy'. Totalitarianism was facilitated by the absence of 'a citizenry that felt individually and personally responsible for the rule of the country'.[63] It is easy to see how this analysis connects with Arendt's republicanism.

The shortcomings of bourgeois society had another unfortunate consequence, according to Arendt, namely that they led to the alienation of large parts of the intelligentsia, and thus help to explain, and apparently to justify, the shocking readiness of members of that social stratum, not excluding some of their most distinguished members, to support totalitarian movements. Of course this 'treason of the clerks' cannot be justified, but Arendt finds understandable their hatred of 'the ideological outlook and moral standards of the bourgeoisie', its acquisitiveness, philistinism, smugness and hypocrisy, to say nothing of its callous treatment of the proletariat.[64] In perverse reaction, some intellectuals 'elevated cruelty to a major virtue because it contradicted society's humanitarian and liberal hypocrisy'.[65] While deploring all this, Arendt does not wish to exaggerate its importance, sardonically remarking, 'in all fairness to those among the élite who . . . have let themselves be seduced by totalitarianism, and who sometimes . . . are even accused of having inspired totalitarianism', that in fact they had no historical influence whatever.[66]

It is clear that Arendt's study of totalitarianism convinced her of the danger posed by ignoring or devaluing politics, and, even more, by those who do so; and that this in turn led to the republicanism enunciated in *The Human Condition*. Her third major contribution to political thought, *On Revolution*, applies that theory to an earlier phase of Western history, the two great revolutions of the late eighteenth century – the American and the French.

Arendt's definition of revolution is characteristically idiosyncratic: a revolution, by definition, aims at freedom (by which she of course means, republican freedom).[67] Being a violent act, it is not strictly speaking part of politics, rather it aims at establishing a political realm, the realm of republican freedom. Arendt insists that this political freedom must not be confused with the *liberation* that is also an aspect of revolution, that is, the overthrow of a previous tyrannical regime. Such liberation does not, in itself, *establish freedom*.

That the American and French Revolutions were genuine revolutions, at least in intention, i.e. were genuine attempts to establish freedom, means, to Arendt, paradoxically, that they began as (attempted) *restorations*, events inspired by deeply traditional ideas.[68] By this Arendt means that they were largely inspired by the political ideals and practices of classical antiquity, especially Roman antiquity, and sought to recover the freedom of this classical republicanism. Lest this should seem perverse or arbitrary, it should be noted that Arendt is able to support her interpretation with copious quotations from the mouths and pens of the revolutionaries. But despite the similarities between the two eighteenth–century revolutions, it is the differences between them that Arendt finds most instructive. Simply expressed, the difference is that the American Revolution succeeded while the French Revolution failed. The American revolutionaries succeeded, not just in overthrowing

British power, but in establishing and stabilizing a constitutional republic, an achievement described by Arendt as 'perhaps the greatest enterprise of European mankind';[69] the French revolutionaries, on the other hand, though they were able to overturn the absolute monarchy, failed to establish their republic on a stable footing. And yet paradoxically, as Arendt points out, it was not the American but the French Revolution that seized the consciousness of Western man, coming to be defined as the epochal turning point of modern Western history, and accepted (regrettably) as the paradigm of revolution as such. Arendt sees an indubitable continuity between the French and Russian Revolutions: for (in the first place) Hegel's 'revolutionary' idea that the 'absolute of the philosophers' is revealed in history was, she suggests, due to the impact of the French Revolution on his thought.[70] One need only consider that this idea was inherited by Marx and in turn by Lenin to see the force of Arendt's genealogy. If one further reflects that Lenin's successor was Stalin (begetter of one of the two European totalitarian regimes of the twentieth century) it becomes rather natural to ponder the sequence Rousseau – Robespierre – Hegel – Marx – Lenin – Stalin. What Arendt sees as particularly significant is 'the most terrible and least bearable paradox in the whole history of modern thought', introduced by Hegel and restated by Marx, 'the paradox that freedom is the fruit of necessity'. Revolutionary freedom came to be seen, paradoxically, as the child of 'historical necessity'. 'Instead of freedom necessity became the chief category of political and revolutionary thought.'[71] Instead of action revolutionary politicians saw only history.

It thus becomes urgent for Arendt to analyse and to account for the differing outcomes of the two revolutions, French and American. Arendt's analysis is original, provocative and intensely controversial. It hinges on what she calls (following Robespierre) 'the social question', that is, 'the terrifying predicament of mass poverty'.[72] In brief, the point for Arendt is simply this: the American Revolution did not have to cope with that 'terrifying predicament', whereas the French and all later revolutions did, and were destroyed by it. America was the 'land of opportunity', a new land of apparent abundance where the 'economic problem', the ancient curse of human poverty, might for the first time be solved, where, as John Adams put it, 'emancipation of the slavish part of mankind' could occur, and serve as an example for the whole world.[73] As Arendt is (rather uncomfortably) aware, Adams's view sits oddly with the phenomenon of Black slavery in America: one has to conclude that, if Arendt is right in her diagnosis, the American Revolution could escape the 'social question' as much because of the powerlessness of the poor as through their relative absence. Nevertheless, the fact remains that the American Revolution, from first to last, was about the issue of creating an independent, republican form of government rather than relief of economic misery: in the French Revolution, by contrast, the issue of 'public freedom' was rather quickly overwhelmed by the social question.

The point is this: the abjectly poor are not free, 'because they are driven by daily needs', by 'the needs of their bodies'.[74] A socialist, no doubt, would agree with this; but not with Arendt's inference from it, namely, that the admission of the poor to the political realm destroys *its* freedom. Politics must be the realm of free men, if it is to remain a genuine field of human action. 'When [the poor] appeared on the scene of politics, necessity appeared with them, and the result was that . . . the new republic was stillborn: freedom had to be surrendered to necessity', as Robespierre himself asserted.[75] The entry of the poverty-stricken masses on to the historical stage in the French Revolution was more like a natural force than genuinely human action. 'Necessity, the urgent needs of the people . . . unleashed the terror and sent the Revolution to its doom'. In the language of *The Human Condition*, the *animal laborans* had invaded politics and destroyed republican freedom: and not only in France in 1790 or 1793. The French Revolution's change of aim from freedom to happiness, despite the fact that it culminated in manifest disaster, infected and corrupted the entire revolutionary tradition. Arendt sees a similar confusion at work in the theory of Marx (the greatest and most influential theorist of revolution) who, despite his ostensible (and genuine) concern with freedom, 'finally strengthened more than anybody else the politically most pernicious doctrine of the modern age, namely that life is the highest good'.[76] Economic progress, in other words, became the ultimate *raison d'être* of revolution.

Of course this economistic view is not, in the modern world, peculiar to revolutionaries. Arendt is, in her own way, a convergence theorist. Despite her obvious admiration for American republicanism, we already know her gloomy view of modern society in general – and which society is more modern than the American? The vices of consumerism are hardly absent from the modern USA – they are perhaps more pervasive, indeed, than anywhere else. Evidently, something has gone wrong; the viewpoint of the *animal laborans* has entered the political scene and threatens to become dominant. How and why? Arendt believes that the answer is urbanization, industrialization and, above all, mass immigration.[77] For mass immigration brought into the American republic millions of Europe's poor, or if not poor, persons whose aim in emigrating was economic betterment, property, wealth, abundance – the characteristic 'ideals of the poor',[78] Arendt says, or of the *animal laborans*. Mass society, in America, has led not to totalitarianism but to consumerism. It has not yet destroyed America's republican freedom (Arendt judged, writing in 1963) but it could do so. How she would judge the situation at the end of the millennium one can only guess, but the trends she deplored seem stronger than ever.

It is now time, however, to consider critically Arendt's political theory and her view of modern society. The following questions must be asked: first, what exactly is the nature of the political activity or 'action' that she prizes so highly? Secondly, is her view of politics an incurably elitist one, indifferent to the needs and desires of the majority of mankind? Thirdly, what institutions, if any, could adequately embody Arendt's political republicanism in the modern world?

As a matter of fact, the first two questions can hardly be separated, and this is partly because it is so hard to give a positive answer to the first question. It is much easier to say what Arendt wishes to exclude from politics than what she wishes it to include. Thus, as we know, she would exclude all economic matters, whether the pursuit of abundance, the cure of poverty, or distributive justice. Is Arendt lacking in compassion for the unfortunate? Or does she rather have an untenable and unrealistic ideal of politics? She writes, indeed, that 'the effort to conquer the seemingly sempiternal misery of mankind is certainly one of the greatest achievements of Western history and of the history of mankind',[79] but also that the attempt to achieve this conquest *by political means* has always led to disaster. 'Every attempt to solve the social question with political means leads into terror'.[80] For this reason, *compassion* should have no place in politics, which is or ought to be a relation between equals. 'Pity, taken as the spring of virtue, has proved to possess a greater capacity for cruelty than cruelty itself'.[81] Arendt is equally sceptical of the French Revolutionary slogan of 'fraternity' – an attitude which she considers appropriate only 'among the insulted and injured', and unable to survive their emancipation. It is therefore politically irrelevant.[82]

Arendt's category of the politically irrelevant is a wide one. For example, and notoriously, she opposed federal legislation to outlaw segregated education of Black and White in the school systems of the southern states of the USA (a fundamental demand of the Civil Rights movement of the mid-century), on the grounds that the political system should not be used to enforce social equality – even basic equality of opportunity. It seems that, like Tocqueville before her, Arendt sees social equality as a threat to individuality, that individual distinctiveness that is one side of the human plurality she so prizes. There may be something to be said for this view. However, her view about the mutual exclusiveness of politics and economics is unacceptable. How exactly does she suppose that the conquest of poverty can be achieved without any political intervention at all? To be sure, events seem to have justified Arendt's opposition to the attempt to do so by means of a politically controlled economy of the Soviet type (though she has – unlike Hayek – no adequate analysis of the *economic* weaknesses of that model). But on the other hand, as everyone knows who understands elementary economic theory, the private enterprise free market system, while it may be a most efficient wealth generator, cannot by itself cure poverty, because it is compatible with any distribution of wealth whatever. The market rewards only those endowed with marketable assets – those who lack them receive nothing. Yet Arendt denounces the welfare state ('government [in which] popular welfare and private happiness are its chief goals') as a system that has destroyed 'public freedom'.[83] It is indeed remarkable from how many points of view the welfare state has been denounced by political philosophers in the twentieth century (neo-Marxist in the case of Marcuse, conservative in the case of Oakeshott, libertarian in the case of Oakeshott and Nozick, republican in the case of Arendt).[84] Arendt perhaps has least reason of all to do so, given her analysis of the disastrous effects of poverty on republican freedom. Arguably, the latter can survive (if at all) *only* if the former is relieved by state action.

One is driven to ask, at this point, what exactly is the nature of the political action that, in Arendt's opinion, is so valuable, and why it is so valuable. What supreme form of human good does it involve? The answers are elusive. Not many participants in political action, after all, are likely to win undying glory. Unlike other thinkers in the republican tradition, such as John Stuart Mill, Arendt does not much emphasize civic virtue or 'public spirit', or the selflessness of devotion to the common weal. At one point,[85] taking seriously a light-hearted remark of Thomas Jefferson, she suggests that the *joy* of transacting public business, to the political actor, can be like a foretaste of eternal bliss to come (and if there is no eternal bliss to come, perhaps the nearest mortal man can approach to that state). More often, she refers to *courage* as the supreme political virtue, but it is not quite clear what this courage amounts to. Since politics, for Arendt, is by definition a realm free from violence, this is not the courage to risk one's life, but rather, as she says, the 'courage' to emerge from the obscurity of private life into the public glare of the political drama. And the word 'drama' is here more than a dead metaphor, for Arendt suggests that political action and its peculiar merits should be compared to the 'virtuosity' displayed in the performing arts, whose exponents need an audience to display that virtuosity, and need one another to enable them to display it, and 'where the accomplishment lies in the performance itself and not in an end product which outlasts the activity'[86]. Not only does the courage required for such performances seem unexceptional, play-acting, in which actors act a part and repeat again and again lines written by others, seems a singularly inappropriate image for a realm which, according to Arendt, is the locus *par excellence* of human freedom, individuality, and self-disclosure. Actors, furthermore, naturally aim (like other stage performers) for the applause of the audience, while Arendt, we find, castigates the revolutionary politicians of the French National Assembly precisely as 'play-actors' who rather than engaging in serious discussion and debate like their American counterparts, sought instead the 'intoxicating applause of the crowd', 'the hissing or applauding galleries which attended the deliberations of the Assembly'.[87] One has to conclude that the performing arts can tell us little about the point and value of politics.

There is, however, one aspect of Arendt's comparison which requires further consideration, for it is no mere passing analogy, but goes to the root of Arendt's conception of politics. In politics, as in the performing arts, she writes, 'the accomplishment lies in the performance itself and not in an end product'. This expresses her often-repeated view that politics is, or should be, non-instrumental. Thus, she quotes, with unmistakable approval, the ancient Greek view that political 'greatness', 'the innermost meaning of the acted deed', is quite independent of 'any eventual outcome, [of] consequences for better or worse'. Politics 'lies altogether outside the category of means and ends'.[88] In other words, politics is a self-justifying activity, not justified by the production of any results. To aim at results, to judge by results, is for Arendt the utilitarian or instrumental attitude proper to 'work', to *homo faber*, not to politics. To turn politics into a means to some 'higher' end – whether economic prosperity, the salvation of souls, or (as with Plato), the safety of the philosopher – is, Arendt says, to degrade it.[89] Politics, it seems, should serve only politics.

Why? Is it because, in Arendt's view, political agents unlike *homo faber* rarely if ever achieve the results they seek (political action is not making)? Arendt appears to believe that if politics becomes goal oriented, political agents will act on the maxim that the end justifies the means, however violent – an attitude appropriate to *homo faber*, who makes use (indeed violent use) of nature, but not the political agent, who deals with other men. *Homo faber* legitimately breaks eggs in order to make an omelette; or better, legitimately kills a tree in order to make a table. To speak of 'ends that do not justify all means', says Arendt, 'is to speak in paradoxes; the definition of an end being precisely the justification of the means'.[90] This surely is quite false. All human life involves the pursuit of ends, but certainly not by any means whatever. All pursuit of ends must be constrained by moral rules. It is absolutely crucial to grasp this point, in relation to politics as to all spheres of human activity. Arendt has here again been misled by her identification of the pursuit of ends with the use of physical instruments. In Arendt's defence, it might be suggested that her anti-instrumental view of politics aims at a limitation of the political somewhat similar to Oakeshott's theory of civil association. But Oakeshott's view (to be discussed below) is much clearer, and also consorts better with the relatively humble role he ascribes to politics in the scheme of human life. Oakeshott wants to limit politics because it is *not* (for him) the supreme locus of human freedom and self-disclosure, not because it is.

We must now confront a further questions, or rather (once again) two inseparable questions about Arendt's political republicanism. What political institutions (if any) could appropriately embody her ideal in the modern world? Inseparable from that question is another one, already broached: is Arendt's republicanism an elitist theory of politics that excludes the majority of mankind? These questions caused Arendt considerable difficulty, as is shown by some unresolved contradictions in her work. Thus, the reader of *On Revolution* notices a surprising shift of direction in that work. After developing at length her contrast between the American and French Revolutions – the former succeeded, while the latter failed, in erecting a republican polity, because the latter was, while the former was not, overwhelmed by poverty-stricken masses – Arendt's argument changes tack. Having noted that a representative system such as that of the American Republic confines political action to a small minority, she turns to lament the neglect by the American revolutionaries of native institutions of direct democracy such as the town meeting,[91] and even the suppression by the French revolutionary politicians of such spontaneous organs of popular democracy as the Paris Commune and its 'sections', and the *sociétés populaires*, although these were precisely the channels through which the destructive force of the impoverished French masses was brought to bear. In *The Human Condition*, she goes so far, at one point, against the whole trend of her argument, as to praise in the highest terms the political role of the labour movements in European revolutions of the nineteenth and twentieth centuries. However, the embodiment of this high political achievement, according to Arendt, was not the political parties of the working class or the trades unions, but the 'people's councils', organs of direct popular political participation, which, she says, have sprung up time and again, in every revolution from the American to the Hungarian in 1956, as exemplified most famously by the soviets of the 1917 Revolution in Russia.[92] As Arendt is aware, these 'systems of people's councils' never endured for long; but she seems uncertain whether this was due to their suppression by orthodox political forces, or to their unfitness to transact normal political business.

However that may be, it is on a federated system of people's councils that Arendt finally pins her faith: 'a principle of organization which begins from below, continues upward, and finally leads to a parliament'.[93] She admits that such a system would result in a kind of élitism, because most people cannot or do not wish to make the commitment of time and effort required for grassroots political participation: government would be in the hands of a self-selected élite of political activists. 'The joys of public happiness and the responsibilities for public business would become the share of those few from all walks of life who have a taste for public freedom and cannot be "happy" without it'.[94] To Arendt this is a justified aristocracy of those who care for more than their private happiness, and far preferable to rule by the career politicians who control representative democracies. No one could complain about being excluded from power, because the excluded would have excluded themselves. On this proposal, a few questions are in order. Why does Arendt suppose that her élite of political activists will conceive of and practise their political activity in the non-instrumental, non-economic way she approves? And if they do, why should we be governed according to the opinions of those whose happiness lies in politics rather than in other spheres of the active life? Would we rather be ruled by career politicians whom we can vote out of office, or by political enthusiasts whose power we can control only by devoting much or most of our lives to politics? Arendt's view that the latter is better possibly rests on an over-estimation of the value of the political by comparison with other ways of life.

Finally, let us pose the question, what is the relation of Hannah Arendt's political philosophy to liberalism? In two respects at least it is highly congruent with it – first, in her passionate individualism, her insistence on the uniqueness and irreplaceability of every individual human being. Also congruent with liberalism is a central tenet of her thought, the absolute necessity to draw a boundary between the public and private spheres of human activity. The two bêtes noires of her political theory, totalitarianism and capitalist consumerism, different though they may seem, both commit the sin of obliterating that boundary – in the former the public swallows up the private, vice-versa in the latter. The liberal, however, by definition wishes to defend the private sphere against the public: and while this is of concern to Arendt she is more preoccupied with the opposite, the defence of the public realm against the private. She has comparatively little sympathy for the liberal conception of freedom, which she terms 'freedom from politics'. Her freedom is not liberal but republican freedom, because of the exceptionally high value she places on political action.

Notes

1 H. Arendt, *The Origins of Totalitarianism*, 3rd edn (Allen and Unwin, London, 1967), pp. 291–2.
2 Notoriously, Arendt's description of Eichmann's career as a manifestation of 'the banality of evil' caused offence to many, who apparently failed to grasp her meaning.
3 Quoted in S. Benhabib, *The Reluctant Modernism of Hannah Arendt* (Sage, Thousand Oaks, Cal., 1996), p. 54.
4 H. Arendt, *The Human Condition* (University of Chicago Press, Chicago, 1958), pp. 10–11.
5 Ibid., p. 247; H. Arendt, *On Revolution* (Penguin, Harmondsworth, 1973), p. 211.
6 Arendt, *The Human Condition*, pp. 96–7.
7 Ibid., p. 56.
8 Ibid., pp. 197–8.
9 H. Arendt, *Between Past and Future* (Faber and Faber, London, 1961), p. 107.
10 H. Arendt, *The Human Condition*, p. 48 n. 39.
11 Ibid., pp. 167–8.
12 Ibid., pp. 152, 172–3.
13 Ibid., p. 173.
14 Ibid., pp. 123–5, 161 n.29.
15 Ibid., p. 152.
16 Ibid., pp. 153ff.
17 Ibid., p. 154.
18 Ibid., p. 155. Arendt blames the evils of 'instrumentalization' (as distinct from 'fabrication') ultimately on 'the life process' (p. 157) – that is, presumably, the *animal laborans*.
19 Ibid., p. 52.
20 Ibid., p. 160.
21 Ibid., p. 9.

22 Arendt, *Between Past and Future*, p. 146.

23 Arendt, *The Human Condition*, pp. 234, 175.

24 Ibid., p. 179.

25 Ibid., p. 198.

26 Ibid., p. 233.

27 Ibid., p. 173.

28 Ibid., p. 180.

29 Ibid., pp. 8–9, 324.

30 Ibid., pp. 26, 244.

31 Arendt, *On Revolution*, p. 15.

32 Arendt, *The Human Condition*, pp. 244–5.

33 Arendt, *The Origins of Totalitarianism*, p. 231.

34 Arendt, *On Revolution*, p. 77.

35 Ibid., p. 195.

36 Arendt, *The Human Condition*, p. 299.

37 Ibid., p. 161.

38 M. Canovan, *Hannah Arendt: A Reinterpretation of Her Thought* (Cambridge University Press, New York, 1992), p. 164.

39 Arendt, *The Human Condition*, pp. 53–4.

40 Ibid., pp. 251, 254.

41 Ibid., p. 289.

42 Ibid., p. 292.

43 Ibid., p. 79.

44 Ibid., p. 101.

45 Ibid.

46 Ibid., p. 321.

47 Ibid., p. 5.

48 Ibid.

49 Ibid., p. 209.

50 Ibid., p. 322.

51 H. Arendt, *Totalitarianism: Part Three of the Origins of Totalitarianism* (Harcourt Brace Jovanovich, San Diego, 1968), pp. 62–3, 91–110.

52 Ibid., pp. 102–3.

53 Ibid., pp. 59–60 n. 57.

54 Ibid., pp. 43, 48.

55 Ibid., pp. 108–9.

56 Ibid., p. 85. For the epigraph of *Totalitarianism* Arendt chose a quotation from David Rousset: 'Normal men do not know that everything is possible.'

57 Ibid., p. 16.

58 Ibid., p. 17.

59 Ibid., p. 11.

60 Ibid., p. 15.

61   Ibid., p. 21.
62   Ibid., p. 9, 11.
63   Ibid., pp. 11–12.
64   Ibid., p. 26.
65   Ibid., p. 29.
66   Ibid., p. 65.
67   Arendt, *On Revolution*, p. 11.
68   Ibid., p. 37. Arendt quotes Robespierre: 'the plan of the French Revolution was written large in the books . . . of Machiavelli'. See also Arendt, *Between Past and Future,* p. 141.
69   Ibid., p. 55.
70   Ibid., pp. 51–2.
71   Ibid., pp. 53, 54, 58.
72   Ibid., p. 24.
73   Ibid., pp. 23, 70.
74   Ibid., pp. 48, 59.
75   Ibid., p. 60.
76   Ibid., p. 64.
77   Ibid., p. 55.
78   Ibid., p. 139.
79   Ibid., p. 138.
80   Ibid., p. 112.
81   Ibid., p. 89.
82   H. Arendt, *Men in Dark Times* (Cape, London, 1970), pp. 17–18.
83   Arendt, *On Revolution*, p. 269.
84   See earlier and later chapters in this book, including that on Habermas who can be added to the list.
85   Arendt, *On Revolution*, p. 131.
86   Arendt, *Between Past and Future*, pp. 153–4.
87   Arendt, *On Revolution*, pp. 120, 125.
88   Arendt, *The Human Condition*, pp. 205, 207.
89   Ibid., p. 229.
90   Ibid.
91   Arendt, *On Revolution*, pp. 235–6.
92   Arendt, *The Human Condition*, p. 216; Arendt, *On Revolution*, p. 249; H. Arendt, *Crises of the Republic* (Penguin, Harmondsworth, 1973), p. 189.
93   Arendt, *Crises of the Republic*, p. 189.
94   Arendt, *On Revolution*, p. 279.

Further Reading

By Arendt

H. Arendt, *The Origins of Totalitarianism*, Harcourt Brace Jovanovich, San Diego, 1951 (part III published as *Totalitarianism*, 1968).

H. Arendt, *The Human Condition*, University of Chicago Press, Chicago, 1958.

H. Arendt, 'Reflections on Little Rock' and 'Reply to critics', *Dissent* 6, 1959.

H. Arendt, *Between Past and Future: Six Exercises in Political Thought*, Meridian, New York, 1961.

H. Arendt, *On Revolution*, Viking, New York, 1963.

H. Arendt, *Men in Dark Times*, Harcourt, Brace, New York, 1968.

H. Arendt, *On Violence*, Harcourt, Brace, New York, 1969.

H. Arendt, *Crises of the Republic*, Harcourt Brace Jovanovich, 1969.

H. Arendt, *The Jew as Pariah: Identity and Politics in the Modern Age*, ed. R. H. Feldman, Grove, New York, 1978.

H. Arendt, 'Heidegger at Eighty', in M. Murray (ed.), *Heidegger and Modern Philosophy*, Yale University Press, New Haven, 1978.

H. Arendt, *Arendt: Essays in Understanding: 1930–1954*, ed. J. Kohn, Harcourt Brace Jovanovich, New York, 1994.

On Arendt

S. Benhabib, *The Reluctant Modernism of Hannah Arendt*, Sage, Thousand Oaks, Cal., 1996.

M. Canovan, *The Political Thought of Hannah Arendt*, Dent, London, 1974.

M. Canovan, *Hannah Arendt: A Reinterpretation of Her Political Thought*, Cambridge University Press, 1992.

S. Dossa, *The Public Realm and the Public Self: The Political Theory of Hannah Arendt*, Wilfrid Laurier University Press, Waterloo, Ont., 1989.

M. P. d'Entrèves, *The Political Philosophy of Hannah Arendt*, Routledge, London, 1994.

G. Kateb, *Hannah Arendt: Politics, Conscience, Evil*, Rowman and Allanheld, Totowa, N.J., 1984.

5
C. B. Macpherson: Possessive Individualism and Liberal Democracy

Crawford Brough Macpherson (known always by his initials, C. B.) was born in 1911 in Toronto, Canada, and lived there almost all his life. He was both a student and (for forty-five years) a teacher at the University of Toronto (with a brief spell as a graduate student at the London School of Economics in between). Such a settled and stable life and career form a sharp contrast with the turbulent experience of the German-Americans, Marcuse and Arendt. Nevertheless his thought has something in common with theirs, and especially Marcuse's – both can be described as neo-Marxist. In some ways Macpherson is the more orthodox Marxist of the two, in some ways less so. Macpherson is less Marxist in that he never even flirted with the idea of violent revolution (his is a 'humanist' Marxism). On the other hand, both the explanatory framework used by Macpherson to analyse Western history (especially the history of Western thought), and the ethical perspective brought to bear on it, are essentially those of Marx. This does not mean that Macpherson is unoriginal – on the contrary, he is one of the few thinkers of this century to develop Marxist theory creatively. He is an untypical Marxist, also, in the clarity and elegance of his prose. To sum up (over-simply) his achievement, it is a lengthy and detailed elaboration of the Marxist theory of ideology, in application to the major political thinkers of the capitalist era. But it is not of merely historical interest; Macpherson generalizes from his historical analysis to construct his own moral critique of capitalist society, and his own vision of a better one.

Macpherson's best-known book, published in 1962, is *The Political Theory of Possessive Individualism*; and 'possessive individualism' is indeed the organizing concept (one might say, the trademark concept) of his work. In the preface to another book published over twenty years later, Macpherson expressed wry agreement with a critic 'who remarked that I never write about anything except possessive individualism'. His 1962 book charts the emergence and development of possessive individualism in the political philosophy of the seventeenth century. Perhaps the most systematic account of this concept, however, is to be found in *Democratic Theory*, published in 1973, but collecting papers mostly written in the 1960s – in particular in the important paper entitled 'The maximization of democracy'. In 1977 Macpherson returned to tracing the historical career of possessive individualism with the *Life and Times of Liberal Democracy*, which adds analyses of thinkers from Bentham to the present to those offered in the 1962 book. These three books contain Macpherson's most significant contribution; but mention should also be made of his *The Real World of Democracy* (1965) and *The Rise and Fall of Economic Justice and Other Essays* (1985), as well as his own contributions to his edited collection on *Property* (1978).

Macpherson's thesis, in a nutshell, is that the liberal democracy of which the modern West is so proud is in reality deeply flawed, because of its historical and social roots in possessive individualism. In his view, in Western society and thought liberalism preceded democracy, and possessive individualism preceded (and shaped) liberalism. But possessive individualism and democracy are incompatible; hence the modern synthesis is unstable, and its democratic component seriously disabled by its powerful but incompatible partner.

Macpherson traces the origins of 'the political theory of possessive individualism' back to the seventeenth century, and specifically to the first and greatest of modern political philosophers, Thomas Hobbes. Hobbes, famous (or notorious) for his defence of the near-absolute sovereignty of political rulers, was no liberal, but he was certainly an individualist in the methodological sense, reasoning entirely from premises about individuals and their interests. According to Macpherson, he was not just an individualist, but a *possessive* individualist. Possessive individualism is a conception of man (of the 'human essence' as Macpherson sometimes says) and of human society. The former is defined by Macpherson as follows:

> The individual [is conceived] as essentially the proprietor of his own person or capacities, owing nothing to society for them. The individual [is] seen neither as a moral whole, nor as part of a larger social whole, but as owner of himself . . . The individual is free inasmuch as he is proprietor of his person and capacities.[1]

To this possessive individual corresponds a certain kind of society – called by Macpherson a 'possessive market society'.[2] Such a society consists of free, equal individuals related to each other as proprietors of their own capacities and of what they have acquired by their exercise. Society consists of relations of exchange between proprietors. Political society [is] a . . . device for the protection of this property and for the maintenance of an orderly relation of exchange.[3]

This picture of man and society involves certain corollaries.[4] The political authority enforces contracts, but does not (unlike in earlier societies) authoritatively allocate work or rewards. Land and resources are owned by individuals and are freely alienable (through the market, for example). So too is 'each individual's capacity to labour' (this distinguishes 'possessive market society' from what Macpherson calls 'simple market society', a one-class society of small proprietors selling their products on the market, such as was advocated by Rousseau and Jefferson, but cannot in Macpherson's view exist in the modern world). 'All possessions, including man's energies, are commodities; . . . all individuals . . . must continually offer commodities (in the broadest sense) in the market, in competition with others.' So possessive market society (because of differences of 'energy, skill or possessions' as between different individuals) is a class-divided society – it is in fact capitalism, characterized by the two classes, the minority of owners of land and productive resources, who buy the 'capacity to labour' of others, and the majority who, owning no land or productive resources, must sell that capacity to members of the owning class.[5] To this society there corresponds a mentality: 'All individuals seek rationally to maximise their utilities', and thus normally want more than they have. Since this picture of society, and man in society, is derived from a view of the 'human essence', or human nature, it is seen as natural and justified, or even inevitable. Such is the standpoint of possessive individualism.

And such, according to Macpherson, is the standpoint of Hobbes. To Macpherson, it is his possessive individualism, not his celebrated theory of near-absolute sovereignty, that is the truly significant aspect of Hobbes's political philosophy – or rather, it is the former that is the foundation of the latter.

It is a commonplace that Hobbes's famous depiction of the horrors of the 'state of nature', in which 'the life of man [is] nasty, brutish and short', and which functions in his theory to justify the sovereign powers of rulers, is premised in large part on his conception of *human* nature. According to Macpherson, the Hobbesian account of human nature represents in reality, not human nature as such, but rather the nature of men in a possessive market society – men who are possessive individualists. Although mistaken in so far as it purports to show universal human traits, it is quite accurate as an account of Hobbes's own contemporaries in seventeenth-century England,[6] even though possessive market society was then only in its early stages. Macpherson is careful to stress that possessive market society need not imply a regime of economic *laissez-faire* (such as developed later, together with the view of the market as a self-regulating order).[7] Hobbes's theory (and also that of Locke) 'corresponds', Macpherson says, to the early mercantilist phase of market capitalism: this does not make Hobbesian men any less of an embodiment of possessive individualism. 'Hobbes's analysis of human nature, from which his whole political theory is derived, is really an analysis of bourgeois man.'[8]

What shows this? In the first place, Hobbesian men are by nature self-seeking, a-social beings who enter into social relations purely for selfish ends: 'We do not', Hobbes says, 'by nature seek society for its own sake, but that we may receive some honour or profit from it . . . All society therefore is either for gain or for glory'.[9] (In this quotation, the references to 'gain' and 'profit' more obviously fit with Macpherson's thesis than do those to 'glory' and 'honour', but Macpherson thinks otherwise. We shall return to this.) To put it another way, men value social relationships as a way to enhance their 'power', which Hobbes famously defined as a man's 'present means, to obtain some future apparent good'.[10] Equally famous is Hobbes's assertion that men naturally seek ever more power: 'I put for a general inclination of all mankind, a perpetual and restless desire of power after power, that ceaseth only in death.'

But why should this be so? According to Macpherson, the reason is that Hobbes sees the powers of different individuals as necessarily *opposed* to one another. A person's power, therefore, is not an absolute but a comparative quality, the 'eminence' of his power over that of others, as Hobbes puts it. But Hobbes goes further. Social life, being a struggle for preeminent power, becomes also a struggle to enhance one's own power by exercising power over others. 'Though the benefits of this life may be much furthered by mutual help, yet these may be better obtained by dominion.'[11] Domination of other men not only neutralizes their potentially hostile power, but adds it to one's own power.[12] According to Macpherson, this picture of society as a competitive struggle for power, including especially power over others, for one's own benefit, is also a description of competitive market society.

But is it? There may be two reasons to doubt Macpherson's interpretation. One might disagree with his account of competitive market society (bourgeois capitalism); or, agreeing with that (more or less), one might point out that Hobbes's picture of the state of nature could equally well apply to non-bourgeois, non-capitalist societies and men (even if not, as Hobbes has it, to 'the natural condition of mankind'). The second objection is more important, and Macpherson must confront it. He attaches great importance, therefore, to the following passage in Hobbes:

> The value, or worth of a man, is as of all other things, his price; that is to say, so much as would be given for the use of his power: and therefore is not absolute; but a thing dependent on the need and judgement of another . . . As in other things, so in men, not the seller but the buyer determines the price.[13]

As Macpherson interprets it, this passage says that the true value of a man is his market value, just as in a labour market in which some men sell their 'power' to others. Furthermore, the passage quoted above continues thus:

> For let a man (as most men do) rate themselves at the highest value they can; yet their true value is no more than is esteemed by others.

and further:

> The manifestation of the value we set on one another, is that which is commonly called honouring, and dishonouring. To value a man at a high rate, is to honour him; at a low rate, is to dishonour him.

In other words, Hobbesian men understand personal esteem and honour as similar to, almost the same thing as, a person's market value. 'Riches are honourable.'[14] Wealth is honour, just as wealth is power. Hobbes goes further, startlingly so: 'Covetousness of great riches [is] honourable', because the power to attain them is so. Thus, the struggle for 'glory' can, in Macpherson's view, hardly be separated from the pursuit of wealth. Hobbes could see the pursuit of glory as a human universal only because 'the development of capitalist relations' had led to 'the freeing of more classes of men from the old social bonds'.[15]

Thus, Hobbesian men are by nature acquisitive, a-social and a-moral individuals, who consider themselves free to compete for gain, power and glory, mainly by means of the wealth they can acquire by exploiting their market value (that is, the market value of their capacities) and that of any other individuals whom they can dominate. They are a-moral, in the sense that they have, and recognize, no obligations to other individuals, other than those they themselves choose to create, by means of contracts. Hobbes denies (against a longstanding tradition) that there is any such thing as objective natural justice, either commutative or distributive. 'To speak properly, commutative justice is the justice of a contractor; that is, a performance of covenant, in buying and selling . . . lending and borrowing . . . and other acts of contract.'[16] The value 'of all things contracted for', Hobbes says, 'is measured by the appetite of the contractors; and therefore the just value, is that which they be contented to give'. The old scholastic idea, that 'it were injustice to sell dearer than we buy', is dismissed by Hobbes as absurd.

There is some plausibility, at least, in Macpherson's view that the attitudes of Hobbesian men, which in Hobbes's view make necessary rule by a sovereign power, 'to keep them all in awe', are in fact the 'possessive individualist' attitudes that motivate participants in a bourgeois market society – though it might be objected that that interpretation elides some other highly significant 'causes of quarrel' which may have been equally or more present to Hobbes's mind, such as the religious intolerance, and warlike ambitions of great magnates, that disturbed the peace of England and Europe in the seventeenth and earlier centuries. But Macpherson's argument goes too far, and entirely loses plausibility, when he claims, or seems to claim, that the Hobbesian state of nature, the war of every man against every man, 'really is' the possessive market society, but without law or political authority. In Macpherson's view, the outstanding feature of the state of nature from which Hobbes deduces political obligation, the equal insecurity of all men, is actually derived from 'market assumptions'.[17] The notion of a market society without law is, however, a sociological monstrosity – almost a contradiction. Certainly the Hobbesian war of all against all, in which the life of men is nasty, brutish and short, cannot be equated with the undeniable insecurities of a market society. The grain of truth in Macpherson's argument, however, is that there is indeed a certain, and perhaps a significant, *similarity* between the Hobbesian state of nature, and the unregulated or *laissez-faire* free market. This will prove to be of some importance when we come to consider the disagreement between the later theorists, Rawls and Nozick.

Macpherson credits Hobbes with an outstanding insight into the realities of his own society; yet he notes that Hobbes's theory was not found acceptable by his contemporaries, or by any subsequent generation of possessive market society. Why not? Because, Macpherson thinks, of one major flaw in Hobbes's theory.[18] Hobbes deduced his theory of sovereignty from the postulate of equal insecurity of all men in a totally fragmented market society. What he failed to see is that such a society does have, also, a significant basis of solidarity – namely, class. The solidarity of the capitalist class can create a substitute for the Hobbesian sovereign, namely, a ruling class, and one which is obviously *preferred* by the bourgeoisie. This mistake on Hobbes's part, Macpherson thinks, was 'corrected' by Locke, and that is why Locke's political theory was found so much more acceptable than Hobbes's.

Locke's political theory stands at the origins of liberalism in the English-speaking world. As is well known, Locke, unlike Hobbes, asserted a natural individual right of liberty and defended a more limited and conditional form of government than Hobbes. Nevertheless, in Macpherson's view, the continuities with Hobbesian theory are considerable, not least in the matter of possessive individualism (even though Locke was, in Macpherson's judgement, a less radical and consistent thinker in this respect). Locke's arguments for government, and for political obligation, are, despite some confusions, essentially the same as those of Hobbes. It is well known, also, that Locke devotes much care to establishing an individual, 'natural', right to private property. But Macpherson stresses that he does much more: he succeeds in turning a *limited* right of appropriation into an *unlimited* one. 'Locke's astonishing achievement was to base the property right on natural right and natural law, and then to remove all the natural law limits from the right.'[19]

Locke's lesser theoretical radicalism, compared to Hobbes, is shown by the fact that the basic premise of his argument is not the nature and desires of men, but the will of God - which, according to Locke, is the same thing as the law of nature. God has created men to serve his purposes, and therefore they have a right to life. He has created the rest of the world for mankind to use in order to sustain and enhance life; but individuals cannot so use it without making what they need for these purposes their exclusive property – hence the natural property right. But the right is not unconditional: God gave the earth to the 'industrious and rational', not the covetous and quarrelsome, who wish to profit from others' labour. A man's labour is his own property. Labour then is the title to property in goods: to appropriate justly, one must 'mix one's labour' with what one appropriates. Furthermore the right to appropriate is not unlimited: since its justification is to enhance human life, no one may appropriate more of the earth or its fruits than he can use, 'to any advantage of life before it spoils'.[20] Anyone who takes more than he uses, who allows God's creation to spoil in his possession, 'takes more than his share', takes what belongs to others. If this rule is obeyed, a further requirement will be satisfied: that one may appropriate only as much as leaves 'enough and as good' for others.

A little reflection makes clear that this Lockean account of a conditional and limited right of appropriation is intended to apply to the earliest stages of human history – to the original appropriation by men of the earth and its fruits. It applies only to a primitive stage of human society – in fact, as Locke makes clear, to a pre-monetary and therefore pre-market stage. The invention and general acceptance of money does not nullify the original conditions and limitations placed on appropriation by natural law, but it changes hugely their significance. For, in the first place, gold and silver do not spoil, and so a man may accumulate them without limit – God's plan is not crossed thereby, nothing useful for human life is wasted. By this simple move, Locke justifies unlimited acquisition (so long as it takes a certain form), and also, quite explicitly, unlimited inequality in ownership of property.

However, as Macpherson points out, Locke's argument gives rise to two obvious questions, neither explicitly discussed by Locke. *How* could an individual legitimately acquire such large properties as Locke envisages (since appropriation is supposedly justified by 'mixing one's labour'); and *why* should a person wish to accumulate unlimited amounts of property, given that the point of appropriation was supposedly just the support of human life?

Let us consider the second question first. As Macpherson shows, Locke certainly did not consider the mere hoarding up of gold and silver to be rational. When he wrote that 'a man may fairly possess more land than he himself can use the product of, by receiving for the overplus, gold and silver',[21] Locke clearly envisaged a market economy. The proper function of money thus acquired, in Locke's view, was not to be hoarded up, but to 'drive trade', that is, to be used as capital.[22] Capital should be invested profitably, to beget more capital, and so on. Land likewise may and should be accumulated without limit, as capital.[23] In other words, Locke has in mind not just a market economy but a capitalist market economy – or, as Macpherson might put it, a possessive market society.

But *how* can a person legitimately acquire so much property? How is the 'labour-mixing' condition to be 'transcended'? Very simply, in Macpherson's view. If a person is the 'owner' of his labour, he can sell it – to the owner of land, for example. And if some landowners have legitimately acquired very large properties, many men will have to do so. Locke does not say this: but he assumes it. In a now notorious passage, when Locke is expounding the implications of the 'labour-mixing' condition, he remarks that both 'the ore I have digged' and 'the turfs my servant has cut', equally become *my* property.[24] The servant has sold his labour; I have bought it, and its fruits are mine. A capitalist labour market is in operation. Locke adds, in further justification, that English labourers, though landless, are better off materially – better fed, clothed and housed – than are the 'kings' of the primitive societies where land has not been individually appropriated (for example, the chiefs of American Indian tribes).[25] The greater productivity of a capitalist market economy ensures that God's creation better serves its divinely ordained purpose of serving human life. Humanity as a whole does not suffer, but benefits, from unlimited capitalist appropriation. What is more, Macpherson convincingly argues that this monetary, market, class-divided, capitalist economy and society are treated by Locke as part of the state of nature, prescribed by the law of nature, and precisely that which government was instituted to protect.[26] Macpherson argues further, that in order to do this government must be a government of the property-owning class, and that this, too, was intended by Locke.[27] This last is probably as justified an interpretation as any of Locke's notoriously unclear account of the matter.

In any event, Macpherson can fairly claim that Locke's theory accomplished a moral revolution. He 'erased the moral disability with which unlimited capitalist appropriation had hitherto been handicapped'.[28] He identified the 'essence of rational behaviour' as 'industrious appropriation'.[29] Unlike Hobbes he condemned 'covetousness', as was traditional, but redefined it, not as excessive acquisitiveness, but as the wish to take away the just property of others.[30] All this he did by his interpretations of the law of nature and of the state of nature which, Macpherson argues, reflect capitalist institutions and morality – or in other words, possessive individualism.

It was in the eighteenth century that the philosophy that Macpherson calls possessive individualism was consolidated, most notably in the work of the two great liberal thinkers of the Scottish Enlightenment, David Hume and Adam Smith. Macpherson, however, did not pay much attention to this stage in the concept's career, though he did duly note the striking view of Hume that mankind are by nature actuated by 'an avidity . . . of acquiring goods and possessions [that] is insatiable, perpetual [and] universal', a passion so powerful that, combined with the natural scarcity of goods, it would be 'directly destructive of society' were it not curbed by the *convention of property*, and the *artificial virtue of justice* (respect for the property of others).[31] As Hume points out, exclusive rules of property, though they directly curb the avidity for goods, indirectly serve it, by stabilizing society and providing an incentive to industry, though they must be supplemented by provision for its 'transfer by consent'.[32] As this argument shows, the case for possessive individualism, which Locke based on the law of nature, has become in Hume (as also in Smith) a utilitarian one. It was to remain so into the nineteenth century.

Macpherson's interest in the career of possessive individualism focuses on the seventeenth century which gave birth to it, and the nineteenth century, when the liberalism which subsumed it began to transmute into liberal democracy. But Macpherson's detailed discussion of this development, in *The Life and Times of Liberal Democracy*, is informed by an elaboration and modification of his conceptual framework, to be found in certain key essays of his *Democratic Theory*. To this we now turn.

The essays in *Democratic Theory* are, in fact, an analysis of the theory of liberal democracy in historical perspective. Macpherson discerns in the history of thought two alternative views of the 'human essence': that man is 'essentially a consumer of utilities', and that man is essentially 'a doer, a creator', an enjoyer of the exercise of his human faculties.[33] In Macpherson's view, the justificatory theory of liberal democracy claims to do justice to both these conceptions, or as Macpherson puts it, liberal democracy claims to maximize both the utilities and the powers of individuals. Macpherson begs to differ. He finds this combination an 'uneasy compromise' to say the least.

According to Macpherson, the view of man as an exerter of his powers is much the older of the two. It is dominant, in different forms, in both Greek and Christian thought. Indeed, this view dominated the Western tradition (admittedly in a highly inegalitarian form) up to the seventeenth century, the epoch that gave birth to possessive individualism. Then, a different view began increasingly to dominate: that man is essentially a consumer, indeed an infinite consumer, because an infinite desirer.[34] This does not quite mean that the conception of man as a doer, or exerter of his powers, was jettisoned; rather, it was subordinated to the other conception, and given a form appropriate to this subordination. Man came to be seen as essentially a consumer *and appropriator*; accumulation of property – unlimited accumulation – became the most valued, the most rational form of the exercise of human powers.

Why did this way of thinking, which Macpherson finds in Hobbes, Locke and later liberal thinkers, emerge? Macpherson answers the question at two levels. In the first place, it corresponds to capitalist or possessive market society, which *needs* men to behave in accordance with it. At another level, it corresponds to a view of human life as 'an endless battle against scarcity' or (the same thing) endlessly devoted to increasing productivity.[35] Macpherson allows that this view had, for a period, functional economic consequences. Nevertheless he finds it distinctly unattractive. Unending scarcity is the other side of the coin of infinite desire, which earlier ages castigated as the sin of avarice. It is clear that Macpherson fundamentally sympathizes with this judgement.

To return to liberal democracy. It is now clear that for Macpherson its claim to maximize individual powers is false – rather, it distorts and corrupts them. Macpherson implicitly distinguishes between two kinds of powers, or exertion of human capacities; those which are involved in 'materially productive labour', and others such as 'aesthetic creation or contemplation . . . religious experience . . . making music . . . playing games of skill'.[36] From this it is apparent that Macpherson's distinction between consumption of utilities and exercise of powers does not coincide with the standard economists' distinction between consumption and production. Nevertheless, Macpherson's argument is undoubtedly, like those of Marcuse and Arendt, a critique of the 'consumerist' ethos of mature contemporary capitalism, which all three theorists, in their way, despise. Macpherson adds to his critique the charge that modern capitalism in any case fails to maximize individual utilities[37] – a charge that seems largely due to Marxist blinkers. He is on stronger ground in denying the equity of the distribution of utilities in a capitalist market economy. But he is more concerned with the effect of the capitalist market on the distribution of powers. The capitalist market is an exchange of powers, but it is not a fair exchange, because ownership of the 'means of labour' is monopolized by a minority class. To be able to use one's powers to get a living, and thereby be enabled to develop and enjoy them, one must have access to the means of labour (capital). 'Those without . . . their own means of labour, must pay for access to others.' Thus the capitalist market society 'by its very nature compels a continual net transfer of part of the power of some men to others'.[38] A redistributive welfare state cannot offset this enforced transfer because to do so would destroy the incentives on which capitalism depends. Here is the Marxian theory of exploitation and alienation in a new guise. Macpherson goes so far as to claim that the normal modern understanding of the term 'power', as meaning power against or over others, is a distortion of the proper meaning, brought about by the possessive market society or (if one prefers) possessive individualism. He calls the modern concept 'extractive power', and his preferred concept 'developmental power'.

And the trouble with modern liberal democracy is that it rests on a possessive market society and therefore has never managed to escape from the possessive individualist ethos. The first anglophone democratic theorists – the utilitarians Jeremy Bentham and James Mill – did not even try to escape from it. What they sought to do was to democratize liberalism just as it was – in Macpherson's view an impossible project that was bound to end in self-contradiction. 'With Bentham and James Mill liberal democracy got off to a poor start.'[39]

There is not much doubt that Bentham and his follower the elder Mill saw man as essentially a consumer of utilities, a maximizer of his own pleasure without limit – that in the fundamental psychological postulate of Benthamite utilitarianism. It is also clear that both saw wealth as one of the major means to pleasure (or to happiness, which Benthamism equated with pleasure – though Macpherson goes too far when he claims that the utilitarians *equated* wealth and happiness).[40] Again Bentham and James Mill explicitly adopted, and indeed urged, the arguments elaborated by the classical political economists for free markets, the protection of private property, and the need for inequality as an economic incentive (all of which follows from their view of human nature).[41] Both Bentham and James Mill also argued that it was natural for men to seek power over others, for their own advantage. Thus Bentham:

> Human beings are the most powerful instruments of production, and therefore everyone becomes anxious to employ the services of his fellows in multiplying his own comforts. Hence the intense and universal thirst for power; the equally prevalent hatred of subjection.[42]

James Mill agreed: 'The desire ... of that power which is necessary to render the persons and properties of human beings subservient to our pleasures is a grand governing law of human nature.' And he added that this desire is 'the foundation of government'.[43] It is also the foundation of the Benthamite case for democracy – essentially, as a protective device against human nature.

Despite all this, Benthamite utilitarianism also has an important egalitarian element (above all Bentham's famous ethical postulate that every individual counts for one, none for more than one), without which the Benthamites could scarcely have been democrats in any sense, or even utilitarians. But according to Macpherson their advocacy of democracy was continually compromised and confused by the inegalitarian premises of the possessive individualism in which they also believed. In Macpherson's opinion, this explains their inconsistencies and compromises on the issue of universal suffrage, and even universal manhood suffrage.[44] James Mill could advocate a franchise with a working-class majority, only because he believed that they would accept the political leadership of the middle class. And Bentham, Macpherson thinks, was reconciled to democracy only by the experience of the United States, which showed that the poor majority understood the advantages of the institution of property, and did not wish to attack it.[45]

There is, of course, another explanation for these matters, namely the actual political situation which was the background to the writings of Bentham and James Mill, and the movement for radical constitutional reform, in which both were active, and which was a movement of the politically excluded, both bourgeois and working class. It was not an unambiguously democratic movement – Macpherson is quite right to say that the impulse for democracy came from the working class. Whether or not the Benthamites genuinely aimed at democracy, they did not achieve it in the Reform Act of 1832, which enfranchised the industrial bourgeoisie only. But throughout the nineteenth century the pressure for democracy from the working class became ever stronger, until, in Macpherson's opinion, it became evident that it could no longer be resisted.[46] One of the first theorists to understand this was James Mill's son, John Stuart Mill.

Macpherson's attitude to John Stuart Mill is much more friendly than it is to James Mill or to Bentham. The younger Mill's version of liberal democracy cannot really be called more egalitarian than that of his predecessors (notoriously, he favoured plural votes for the best qualified electors), but it does show a much greater respect for the aspirations of the working class, their autonomy and their rights.[47] It differs also from that of his predecessors in another way. Unlike them, J. S. Mill sought to incorporate into his theory the view of man (and woman) as essentially a creator and an exerter of his (or her) powers. The explanation for this is simply that he subscribed to the growing revulsion against the materialist capitalist ethos that was also forcefully expressed by such social critics as Carlyle, Ruskin, Marx and many others. Mill famously distinguished between higher and lower pleasures (a distinction similar in function, though not necessarily in meaning, to Macpherson's own distinction between consumption of utilities and exercise of powers), and advocated democracy primarily as a means to the development of man's active, intellectual and moral capacities – 'the improvement of mankind'. Human development was far more important to him than economic development, and he looked forward to the achievement in the future of a 'stationary state' of economic satiation, in which men and women could devote themselves to developing their capacity to enjoy the 'higher pleasures' (or, as Macpherson might put it, the exertion of their human powers). Clearly Mill did not see man as an infinite desirer or appropriator. Yet despite all this, in Macpherson's view the younger Mill (himself a leading economist) was unable to rid himself of the assumptions of possessive individualism.[48] Macpherson in fact exaggerates the degree to which Mill was committed, *pro tem*, to the capitalist market economy. As Macpherson recognizes, he saw the injustice of Victorian class inequalities and deplored their effect on the life of the working classes. He therefore advocated a fundamental (though gradual and non-violent) transformation of the economic system, in which capitalist firms would be replaced by worker cooperatives, thus ending the division of society into two hostile economic classes. Macpherson acknowledges this; but the fact that Mill proposed to retain the institution of private property, as well as a market system of coordination to provide economic incentives, in his opinion shows that Mill was still in the grip of the possessive individualist mentality.[49]

In any event, the capitalist system has not been transformed into a system of worker cooperatives. Bentham and James Mill have proved to be at least partly right about the respect of the majority for bourgeois values and institutions. Our present situation is indeed a combination of liberal democracy and market capitalism, in which Macpherson finds democratic equality and capitalist inequality to be incompatible, and in which – more than ever, one might say – the image of man as infinite desirer and infinite appropriator holds sway. As for the theory of liberal democracy, as Macpherson sees it, after a lengthy period in which it took its cue from John Stuart Mill's developmentalism, it finally, around the middle of the twentieth century (in the persons of Joseph Schumpeter, Robert Dahl and various elitist and 'pluralist' thinkers), accepted 'reality' by conceptualizing democracy as a quasi-market, in which the bulk of the population plays a largely passive role, while politicians compete for their votes just as firms compete for their money. The justification offered for both systems is the same – the maximization of utility.[50]

Needless to say, Macpherson is totally unreconciled to this state of affairs. What, then, is the way forward? It is clear, from his critique of John Stuart Mill, that Macpherson requires abandonment of the capitalist conception of property (private property), and of reliance on the market, with its dependence on an appeal to man the infinite consumer of utilities. He has, indeed, considered the issue of property on several occasions: in this regard, he calls for the supplanting of *private* property by *common* property (though quasi-Marxist historicism often makes him express this demand as a prediction). All property, Macpherson notes, is 'an enforceable claim of a person to some use or benefit of something'.[51] Private property is a right to *exclusive* use or benefit, an owner's right not only to use or benefit but to exclude others from use or benefit. Common property, Macpherson insists, is just as much a right of individuals as is private property (and must be sharply distinguished from state property): it is the right of individuals '*not to be excluded* from the use or benefit of something which society or the state has proclaimed to be for common use' (presumably by all members of the society or state in question).[52] In this sense, common property is a perfectly familiar institution – it includes 'common lands, public parks, city streets, highways'. In Macpherson's view it should include much more. The apotheosis of private property derives from possessive individualism, from the consumerist-appropriator view of man, and it inevitably deprives the bulk of society of the right of access to the means of labour, thus subjecting them to a compulsory transfer of their powers to others. The means of labour (or, as Macpherson also puts it, the accumulated productive resources of society) must therefore become common property. This is emphatically *not* the radical Marxist proposal it may seem. A common right not to be excluded from the use or benefit of society's productive resources may mean, Macpherson explains, either of two things: (1) a right to work on them, and draw an income from so working; or (2) a right to an income from the whole produce of the society, to the extent needed for a 'fully human life', independently of work. The latter, as Macpherson recognizes, is nothing other than a welfare state.[53] Such a welfare state *is* common ownership of the means of production.

This apparent endorsement of the welfare state is somewhat puzzling, given Macpherson's stated opinion that it cannot offset the 'transfer of powers' from workers to capitalists that keeps the market functioning (see above). And the welfare state undeniably is a part of the 'actually existing' liberal democracy with which Macpherson expresses such dissatisfaction (even if it is currently undergoing some quite serious difficulties and changes). Does Macpherson envisage the wealth distributed (or redistributed) by the welfare state as being produced without resort to markets and their incentives? The answer is presumably yes. In 'The maximization of democracy' Macpherson invokes 'the socialist model', as one in which no 'net transfer of powers' is necessary.[54] But what is the 'socialist model'? Perhaps surprisingly, Macpherson seems to find it exemplified by the old Soviet-style systems, to which he refers as 'practising socialist societies', regrettably disfigured however by the absence of civil and political liberties (and thus by their own form of suppression of individual 'powers'). Macpherson looks forward to a kind of convergence of the Soviet and Western models, in which the former adopts the institutions of liberal democracy and the latter the Soviet-style economic system. The sudden and total collapse of the latter was not foreseen by Macpherson, any more than by the political science profession as a whole. To the contrary: Macpherson believed (writing in 1967), that 'Western democracy from now on will have to face increasingly strong competition from the Communist nations'.[55]

How could a market-less, free, democratic communism work? How would the right mix of goods be produced in sufficient quantities to provide for people's needs and wants? Like Marx, Macpherson looks to the abolition of

107

scarcity. He envisages an attack from, so to speak, both ends of the problem, subjective and objective. Scarcity is partly in the mind, a product of man the infinite desirer and consumer, of possessive individualism. This mind-set, functional perhaps in poorer epochs, Macpherson considers now to be unnecessary as well as inhuman. We should rid ourselves of it.[56] Also, we can benefit from the help of our advanced productive technology, which, in Macpherson's judgement, enables us to satisfy reasonable, limited economic needs with the expenditure of relatively little time and effort.[57] Thus armed, reformed and liberated we can devote ourselves to the life-enhancing exercise of our human powers, much as John Stuart Mill envisaged. It is notable how different is Macpherson's attitude to technology from that of Marcuse (Macpherson is here the better Marxist). For Marcuse, our technology is itself part of the mind-set which has enslaved us; for Macpherson, it is a possible means to liberation and salvation.

Alas, things are not so simple. Comparing Macpherson's theory with that of Hayek suggests that the former has no real understanding of the economic function of markets, which is to link supply and demand. Technology, plus a devotion to the exercise of our human powers, will not alone indicate what should be produced. Nor (contrary to what Macpherson seems to think) does a devotion to the exercise of human powers (whatever exactly these are) necessarily imply a limited demand for economic production – for that exercise might also be without limit, and require material means for its pursuit (one cannot fly to the moon, or explore the mysteries of particle physics, without vastly expensive equipment). One has to conclude that, acute as Macpherson's moral critique of consumerist capitalism may be, his solutions are utopian and unhelpful. In this way, both his strengths and his weaknesses are typically Marxian.

Notes

1   C. B. Macpherson, *The Political Theory of Possessive Individualism: Hobbes to Locke* (Oxford University Press, London, 1962), p. 3.
2   Ibid., p. 54.
3   Ibid., p. 3.
4   Ibid., p. 54.
5   Ibid., p. 55.
6   Ibid., p. 61.
7   Ibid., p. 58; C. B. Macpherson, *Democratic Theory: Essays in Retrieval* (Oxford University Press, London, 1973), pp. 247–8.

8   Macpherson, *Democratic Theory*, p. 239.
9   Ibid., p. 240.
10 Macpherson, *Possessive Individualism*, p. 35.
11 Macpherson, *Democratic Theory*, p. 240.
12 Macpherson, *Possessive Individualism*, p. 59.
13 Ibid., p. 37.
14 Macpherson, *Democratic Theory*, p. 244.
15 Ibid., p. 241.
16 Macpherson, *Possessive Individualism*, p. 63.
17 Ibid., p. 79.
18 Ibid., pp. 93–4.
19 Ibid., p. 199.
20 Ibid., p. 201.
21 Ibid., p. 204.
22 Ibid., pp. 205–6.
23 Ibid., p. 207.
24 Ibid., p. 215.
25 Ibid., pp. 211–12.
26 Ibid., pp. 208–9.
27 Ibid., p. 249.
28 Ibid., p. 221.
29 Ibid., p. 233.
30 Ibid., pp. 236–7.
31 C. B. Macpherson, *The Rise and Fall of Economic Justice* (Oxford University Press, Oxford, 1985), p. 112.
32 Ibid., p. 110.
33 Macpherson, *Democratic Theory*, p. 5.
34 Ibid.
35 Ibid., p. 17.
36 Ibid., p. 54. Is pushpin (a game of skill) as good as poetry (aesthetic creation)?
37 Ibid., p. 7.
38 Ibid., pp. 10–11.
39 C. B. Macpherson, *The Life and Times of Liberal Democracy* (Oxford University Press, Oxford, 1977), p. 25.
40 Ibid.
41 Ibid., pp. 28, 30.
42 Ibid., p. 26.
43 Ibid., p. 36.
44 Ibid., p. 35.
45 Ibid., pp. 39, 37.
46 Ibid., p. 31.
47 Macpherson, *Democratic Theory*, p. 174.

48   Macpherson, *Liberal Democracy*, pp. 51–3, 55–6.
49   Ibid., p. 61.
50   Ibid., pp. 77ff.
51   Macpherson, *Democratic Theory*, p. 123.
52   Ibid., p. 124.
53   Ibid., p. 206.
54   Ibid., p. 14.
55   Ibid., p. 35.
56   Ibid., pp. 17, 20.
57   Ibid., p. 19.

Further reading

By Macpherson

C. B. Macpherson, *The Political Theory of Possessive Individualism: Hobbes to Locke*, Oxford University Press, 1962.
C. B. Macpherson, *The Real World of Democracy*, Clarendon Press, Oxford, 1966.
C. B. Macpherson, *Democratic Theory: Essays in Retrieval*, Oxford University Press, London, 1973.
C. B. Macpherson, 'Liberal-democracy and property', in *Property: Mainstream and Critical Positions*, Basil Blackwell, Oxford, 1978.
C. B. Macpherson, *The Rise and Fall of Economic Justice and Other Papers*, Oxford University Press, Oxford, 1985.

On Macpherson

J. H. Carens (ed.), *Democracy and Possessive Individualism: The Intellectual Legacy of C. B. Macpherson*, State University of New York Press, Albany, 1993.
J. A. Dunn, 'Democracy unretrieved', *British Journal of Political Science* 4, 1974.
W. B. Leiss, *C. B. Macpherson: Dilemmas of Liberalism and Socialism*, St Martin's Press, New York, 1989.
D. Miller, 'The Macpherson version', *Political Studies* 30, 1982.
K. R. Minogue, 'Humanist democracy: the political thought of C. B. Macpherson', V. Svacek, 'The elusive Marxism of C. B. Macpherson' and Macpherson's 'Response to Minogue and Svacek', *Canadian Journal of Political Science* 9, 1976.
M. A. Weinstein, 'The roots of democracy and liberalism', in A. de Crespigny and K. Minogue (eds), *Contemporary Political Philosophers*, Methuen, London, 1976.

Part II
Embattled Liberalism

6

Michael Oakeshott: Rationalism and Civil Association

Michael Oakeshott is one of the most fascinating and distinctive thinkers to have turned his mind to the problems of political philosophy in the twentieth century (matched only, perhaps, in this respect but in a very different style, by Hannah Arendt). Unlike almost all the other writers considered in this book, he not only wrote but was born and lived all his life in England, and he is at his best a unique master of English prose. Beyond question he is the finest stylist to have written political philosophy in English this century, perhaps in any century; and besides its strictly literary qualities, his writing achieves – at its not infrequent best – a blend of subtlety, insight, lucidity, and precision which makes reading Oakeshott an unusual pleasure. But it must be added that this describes Oakeshott only at his best, for his work also displays some less pleasing qualities – namely a tendency to dogmatism, and to an unhidden contempt for his intellectual opponents so complete that, too often, he disdains to engage with their arguments but rather dismisses their views with evident scorn. Oakeshott appears as a man supremely confident of his gifts – by no means without reason.

Like several others among the major political philosophers of the twentieth century – Arendt again, Hayek, Popper (and Hobbes in the seventeenth century) – Oakeshott's intellectual interests were at first not political at all, or hardly so. His first book (and cause of his first fame), *Experience and Its Modes*, published in 1933 when Oakeshott was a little over 30, is a work of general philosophy and metaphysics in which politics is mentioned only briefly (and does not figure in the index). His two important political books appeared much later – *Rationalism in Politics* in 1962 (though the essays composing it date from 1947 to 1961) and his masterpiece, *On Human Conduct*, not until 1975 (Oakeshott was by then over 70). It is not entirely simple to characterize the political position defended by Oakeshott in these two books. *Rationalism in Politics* made him famous, or notorious, as the age's foremost spokesman for conservatism and as scourge of 'rationalism' (closely related to what Weber called rationalization): the key concept in this book is *tradition*. In *On Human Conduct*, however, Oakeshott appears more as a liberal individualist, basing his argument on the concept of *civil association*. Whether these 'two Oakeshotts' are mutually consistent, are even perhaps a single, continuous Oakeshott, is an issue which has been raised by several commentators. To call him, simply, a liberal conservative would indeed be *too* simple. My own opinion, which will be explained below, is that the 'two Oakeshotts' are not (completely) consistent with each other – or, to put it another way, that, while conservatism (of a kind) is indeed consistent with political liberalism, *political* conservatism is not.

Notwithstanding any inconsistency there may be between them, both *Rationalism in Politics* and *On Human Conduct* are outstanding books. Unfortunately, the same cannot be said, in my view, for *Experience and Its Modes*: in that book some of the central doctrines presented seem to me eccentric and implausible, and are too often scarcely argued for but rather merely stated and (at some length) elaborated. Despite this, the book cannot be ignored, both because it has been widely admired, and because it has left some traces in Oakeshott's later work. (Fortunately, I think, not too many traces. Oakeshott would not have become the great political philosopher of later years had he allowed himself to be too inhibited by the philosophical system of his first book.)

Experience and its modes

In *Experience and its Modes*, Oakeshott presented his own version of philosophical idealism, in which reality is identified with human experience, and truth defined in terms of the coherence of ideas (rather than correspondence of ideas with an external reality): thus reality is found, and truth known, when (or if) a totally coherent system of ideas (or 'world of ideas', in Oakeshott's terminology) is achieved through the ordering of experience. The endeavour to do this, Oakeshott says, is philosophy.[1] But philosophy is not the only response to experience, nor the only world of ideas that it generates. What Oakeshott calls a 'mode' of experience is, unlike philosophy, an attempt to understand reality from a specific, limited (in Oakeshott's word, abstract) point of view.[2] Oakeshott's book considers at length three such modes – called history, science and practice – while explicitly avoiding any claim that this is a complete list.[3] We must now look at what Oakeshott has to say about the three modes, and their relation to each other and to philosophy.

Oakeshott stresses that a mode of experience 'is not a separable part of reality, but the whole from a limited standpoint'. Thus history is the organization of the whole of experience *'sub specie praeteritum'*, that is, in the form of the past – or rather, in the form of the past *for its own sake*[4] (the significance of this qualification will become apparent below). This historical past, however, is known through the *present* world of experience – thus 'the past in history rests upon the present', even 'is the present'. Whatever historians may believe, their endeavour is not (cannot be) to discover '"what really happened"', but rather '"what the evidence obliges us to believe"'.[5]

Oakeshott's definition of science as a mode of experience is interesting. It is a world of ideas which springs from the desire to escape from the private world of personal experience into 'a world of common and communicable experience . . . upon which universal agreement is possible'. Its entire history 'may be seen as a pathetic [sic] attempt to find, in the face of incredible difficulties, a world of definite and demonstrable experience, one . . . independent of the idiosyncrasies of particular observers, an absolutely impersonal and stable world'.[6] The form to which this attempt has driven science is that of conceiving the world 'under the category of quantity', a world susceptible of precise measurement and described in terms of generalizations.[7] Not all 'sciences' correspond perfectly to this ideal, but it is none the less the scientific ideal; all science aspires to the condition of physics. In Oakeshott's view there is no intrinsic reason why sociology, economics, etc., cannot be sciences in this sense.[8] To become properly scientific, however, any discipline must leave behind 'the unstable categories of personal experience as such'.[9]

What now of practice? Practice is the world of everyday life, of action, and of change – more precisely, of change aimed at transforming 'what is' so as to agree with 'what ought to be' (it thus involves two kinds of knowledge, of fact and of value). As Oakeshott also says, practice is the exercise of the will, and practical experience is 'the world *sub specie voluntatis*'.[10] Politics clearly belongs to the practical world. A presupposition of practice, and thus a necessary truth of the world of practice, is human freedom; the world of practice is a world of self-determined selves. According to Oakeshott, this means that the quasi-Kantian formula, that each person is 'an "end in himself"', is likewise a constitutive presupposition of the practical world. Thus, in the practical world, truth gives freedom, and 'similarly the errors of practice are those which enslave'.[11] (This admirably liberal conclusion is unfortunately not based on a convincing argument. Is enslavement merely an *error* of practice, or do slaves not belong to the world of practice, or of agents, at all?) Not only is the practical world the world of values, in this world coherence, and therefore truth, are 'conceived in terms of value', under the sovereignty of moral and religious truth (or values).[12] Oakeshott sees a possible objection to his account of the practical world, namely, that not only human wills and desires, but also moral judgements and judgements of value, conflict with one another, so that this cannot be a coherent world. According to some, 'the most elementary lesson of life is the necessity of recognizing these irreducible differences'. But Oakeshott disagrees. These differences are an 'incidental defect' of the practical world, not an inherent characteristic of it: 'the principle of this [practical] world, as of every other, is coherence', which is also the condition of practical, as of all other, truth.[13] Notwithstanding Oakeshott's remarks about freedom, this doctrine (as Isaiah Berlin later argued) has potentially extremely *il*liberal implications. It seems very like what Berlin calls 'monistic rationalism', and is notably different from the point of view later taken by Oakeshott in his last and greatest book, *On Human Conduct*.

Let us return to *Experience and Its Modes*, and ask the question: what is the status of the knowledge, or 'truth', produced in the worlds of experience constituted by the three modes? According to Oakeshott, such knowledge and truth are at best partial. Each mode has its own (relative) validity, and the knowledge it produces is true from its own point of view, or rather is true so long as it recognizes its own limitations and relativity: that is to say, it is knowledge of a partial world, not of experience as a whole, produced by adopting a specific and limited viewpoint. The world of knowledge produced by the modes, each in its own way, is, as Oakeshott puts it, 'abstract' rather than 'concrete', that is, an abstraction from the totality of experience. But it is (apparently) inherent in the modal worlds (or those engaged in them) *not* to recognize this limitation, and to claim to produce knowledge of truth in an absolute sense, at least in principle. They thus cease to be true, and fall into error, that is, incoherence and self-contradiction.[14] In the case of history, the contradiction is between its form and its content. History, by definition, is knowledge of the past. But 'to suppose this world of history *actually* to be in the past . . . involves us in a radical contradiction'. Like all knowledge, historical knowledge is an organization if experience, and all experience is present experience. Oakeshott sums up the contradictoriness of history as follows: 'If the historical past is knowable it must belong to the present world of experience'.[15]

Science is no less self-contradictory, but in a different way. Scientific knowledge is knowledge of generalizations: more precisely, science 'seeks generalizations which will remain relevant beyond what has actually been observed'. (Indeed, science ideally seeks *universal* generalizations, which of necessity go beyond what, at any time, has been observed.) Thus, Oakeshott believes (or believed), the conclusions of science are, and can only be, claims of probability. As he also puts it, they are 'an inference from the character of the whole of observed A's to the *probable* character of any single A, whether or not it has been observed, or to the *probable* character of all As whatever' (emphases added). Scientific knowledge, then, is not really knowledge of reality at all, being merely probabilistic.[16] Further, it is merely hypothetical: a scientific 'law' does not actually assert the existence of anything: rather it asserts the (probable) dependence of a 'consequent' (effect) on some condition *if* the latter is realized. The world of science, says Oakeshott, is a world of 'supposals', which (in contradiction to its self-conception) 'has no contribution whatever to make to our knowledge of reality'.[17]

The reader will by now anticipate a similar analysis from Oakeshott of the world of practice. The argument, this time, is the following. Practice undertakes to *change* a given world of experience, thereby assuming that the latter is incoherent, and ought to be made coherent. But it never finally succeeds in bringing into existence this coherent world – if it did, practice itself would necessarily cease. From this Oakeshott concludes that a mode of experience based on the premise of change (that is, changing reality) cannot know reality in the full sense, and is therefore ultimately incoherent.[18] Nevertheless, the world of practice, alone of all the worlds, is inescapable – it is the world of our 'incurably abstract' lives.[19] History, science and philosophy, by contrast, are attempts to escape from the responsibility of living.[20] Philosophy, however, is the only world of experience capable of arriving at truth without any reservation or limitation, and in its full concreteness. As Oakeshott writes: 'Philosophy means experience without reservation or presupposition . . . in which the determination to remain unsatisfied with anything short of a completely coherent world of ideas is absolute and unqualified'.[21] Not least among its tasks is to understand and evaluate our abstract worlds of experience, such as history, science and practice. Thus *Experience and Its Modes* is indubitably a book of philosophy.

As expounded so far, Oakeshott's early philosophy may seem plausible, coherent, and even attractive. But it is now time to consider an aspect of it which seems to me definitely mistaken – indeed, hopelessly so. This issue is that of the relation between philosophy and the modes of experience, and of the modes to one another. According to Oakeshott, there can be no relation

117

whatever: each proceeds from a point of view totally exclusive of all the others. Thus, any attempt to make inferences from one world to another must by definition be a blunder and, as Oakeshott frequently repeats, it manifests *ignoratio elenchi* and commits the logical error of irrelevance. In other words, each of the worlds is totally irrelevant to all the others.[22]

Oakeshott frequently makes this point not only in a general sense, but also in relation to the specific cases. Thus: 'Philosophy is without any direct bearing upon the practical conduct of life', indeed, 'A philosophic life is a monstrosity'. Correspondingly, 'philosophy . . . depends for its existence upon maintaining its independence of all extraneous interests, and in particular from the practical interest'.[23] Oakeshott is indeed particularly eager to maintain the total separation of practice from the other worlds. No guidance for practical life can be drawn from either history or science: indeed, 'What more than anything else hinders the full development of scientific thought is the practical interest'.[24]

Needless to say, Oakeshott was aware that these are iconoclastic contentions. Can they be sustained? In my view the answer is quite definitely no. Let us consider first the relation between science and practice. Oakeshott's characterization of science itself is now somewhat dated (contrast the view of Popper) but this is not the basic point. The orthodox (and in my judgement correct) view is that every scientific law, no matter how esoteric the concepts in which it is expressed, must be in principle testable and if possible tested *by* the test of practice (observation or experiment), and if valid can be successfully applied *to* the world of practice (in so-called applied science or technology). Oakeshott is aware that this is the usual view, but he considers it an illusion. Rather, he says, 'A scientific idea must be transformed, taken out of the world of scientific experience, before it can establish itself in the world of practice'.[25] Only then can science have practical consequences, or have a bearing on the everyday world of sense perceptions from which it originally fled in the search for a stable, impersonal truth. In a sense this is true enough: however, if Oakeshott were right about the total separateness and mutual irrelevance of science and practice, such a translation from one world to the other would not be possible. Oakeshott's view, in fact, seriously misconceives the place of science in the human world, and especially its crucial role in modern, twentieth-century civilization (besides which it does no justice to science's philosophical significance). One suspects, here, a hostility to science which is of a piece with the attitude to social science in his later political writings.

Oakeshott's assertion of the total mutual irrelevance of philosophy and practice also has some dubious implications. For example, it implies that there is no such thing (or no such legitimate thing) as moral philosophy.[26] Moral philosophy is an attempt to philosophize about values, or to prescribe values philosophically – an impossibility for Oakeshott, because values belong to the world of practice. Ultimate reality (and hence philosophy) know nothing of value judgements, of moral philosophy - nor, therefore, of prescriptive political philosophy. Indeed, it is doubtful whether the Oakeshottian map of experience allows political philosophy to exist at all. Despite this, by the time Oakeshott gave his famous inaugural lecture of 1951, he was willing to apply this label to his own style of reflections on politics, but he still denied that political philosophy, being philosophy, can guide or evaluate practical politics.[27] In thus disclaiming any prescriptive intention in his own political writing, Oakeshott was, as we shall see, less than entirely frank. Some unnecessary confusion has resulted.

What of history and practice? Oakeshott admits that, in practical life, and above all in politics, people habitually draw lessons from the past, or use the past to justify their present actions, or to explain the present. He insists, however, that it is not the *historical* past that is used in such cases, but an altogether different past – the practical past. The historical past, by definition, is the past for its own sake, and its own sake only. The historical past is, must be, *different* from the present. 'The historian does not set out to discover a past where the same beliefs, the same actions, the same interactions obtain as those which occupy his own world.'[28] This notion that there exist (at least) two pasts – historical and practical – quite different from each other but each equally valid from its own point of view, seems to me extremely strange. Fortunately, Oakeshott (although he repeated his thesis as late as his essay 'The activity of being an historian' published in 1955)[29] did not allow it to influence his political writing (and, I suspect, did not fully believe it). One of Oakeshott's key political concepts – tradition – undoubtedly involves a past which does and should inform present practice. Nevertheless, Oakeshott, in the important essay 'Political education' (reprinted in *Rationalism in Politics*), which gives a lengthy exposition of the role of tradition in politics, ends by advocating that therefore 'the study of politics should be an *historical* study'[30] (emphasis added); and in the brilliant and fascinating third chapter of *On Human Conduct* ('On the character of a modern European state') he explicitly undertakes to illuminate our understanding of contemporary politics by means of a historical analysis. Even at the time when he wrote *Rationalism in Politics*, I suspect that Oakeshott did not fully believe in his doctrine of the two pasts, for in unguarded moments he uses the term 'history' in a way which contradicts it. For example, in explaining the development of science – how it came to be what it is, *now* – he remarks that, 'Historically, science, no doubt, began with crude, imperfectly apprehended attempts to find a stable world'; again, in excoriating 'the infatuation which the modern mind has conceived for "science", he remarks that 'there is little in the history of folly to which one may compare' that infatuation.[31]

In sum, it seems to me that Oakeshott's dogmatic, *a priori* insistence in *Experience and its Modes* on a total, rigid and watertight separation between different worlds of experience is a denial of precisely what we know to be most true about human life and the world in which we live. It is a philosophical dead end. It also (very fortunately) contrasts markedly with Oakeshott's later political writing, the great strength and virtue of which is its subtle and sensitive recognition of the contingency, fluidity and open-endedness of the factors that influence politics, and human life in general. The later political writing manifests a quite different spirit from *Experience and Its Modes*.

Oakeshott on Politics

One cannot be certain of the reason for Oakeshott's 'political turn', or why Oakeshott the philosopher came to focus his attention on politics more than any other topic; but the evidence of his writings suggests that it was most probably motivated by a profound dismay, even disgust, at the trend of British politics after the Second World War. Whatever the reason, Oakeshott's preoccupation with politics continued throughout the remainder of his career. As already mentioned, interpretation of Oakeshott's political philosophy must deal with the relation in his work between two themes, conservatism and liberalism, or tradition and freedom. Roughly speaking, the thematic duality correlates with two phases, or two books, *Rationalism and Politics*, published in 1962, and *On Human Conduct*, 1975. But the correlation is by no means perfect. *Rationalism in Politics*, which collects essays written from 1947 on, and is the *locus classicus* of Oakeshottian conservatism, also contains at least one 'liberal' essay ('The political economy of freedom') and another ('On being conservative') which, despite its title, is as much about liberalism as conservatism, or perhaps more accurately, seeks to deduce liberalism from conservatism. Whether it succeeds is an important question which must eventually be addressed; for the time being, however, these two essays will be ignored, and attention focused on three other major essays, all published between 1947 and 1951 (not by coincidence, during the term of the reforming post-war Labour government). These essays are called 'Rationalism in politics', 'Rational conduct', and 'Political education' (another essay from the same period, 'The Tower of Babel', must also be mentioned). For the time being we are concerned solely with Oakeshott the conservative.

'Political education' (the title given to Oakeshott's inaugural lecture at the London School of Economics) contains a famous Oakeshottian definition of politics: it is 'the activity of attending to the general arrangements of a set of people whom chance or choice have brought together', and, preeminently of 'the hereditary co-operative groups . . . which we call "states"'.[32] The striking feature of our three essays, however, is the extent to which Oakeshott treats politics, not in terms of its specific characteristics, but simply as one human practice among many, and sharing its most essential features with these others (in this respect, *On Human Conduct* affords a marked contrast). Oakeshott's political conservatism rests on an analysis of human activity in general.

More precisely, it rests on an analysis of the relation between action and knowledge. 'Every science, every art, every practical activity requiring skill of any sort, indeed every human activity whatsoever, involves knowledge.'[33] This is a commonplace. Also a commonplace, indeed proverbial, is the fact that, as we say, 'practice makes perfect', or more accurately (since perfection is rare in human life), practice vastly improves performance, and much practice is often needed before performance becomes even adequate. In other words, a great deal of knowledge of how to carry on an activity comes to us precisely in the practice of that activity, and accumulates over time as we practise more. To this banal and therefore unassailable proposition Oakeshott adds one further contention which is fundamental to his conservative philosophy: much if not all, and at any rate the most important part of this knowledge gained thorough practice, can be acquired in no other way. He therefore calls it 'practical knowledge'.[34]

There is, however, a second form of knowledge relating to activity, which Oakeshott calls (rather confusingly in my opinion, for reasons to be explained) 'technical knowledge'. Oakeshott defines this as follows: 'technical knowledge [can be] formulated into rules which are, or may be, deliberately learned, remembered, and . . . put into practice . . . whether or not it is, or has been, precisely formulated, its chief characteristic is that it is susceptible of precise formulation'.[35] This means that it can be put into a book or other written form – an instruction manual or handbook we might say. Several questions arise in relation to this 'technical knowledge'. What exactly is its value, for the carrying on of an activity? What is its relation to practical knowledge? How do we come by it in the first place?

In brief, Oakeshott's answers to these questions are as follows. On its own, technical knowledge is more or less useless from a practical point of view – it is useless until supplemented by practical knowledge, gained through practical experience. That is not to say that it is totally useless – it can serve as a starting point, to orient the learner as he sets out to master a practice. Where does it come from? Not, in the first instance – a point repeatedly stressed by Oakeshott – by any individual sitting down in advance of practice to work out *a priori* how it should be carried on: practice is logically and chronologically prior, and technical knowledge is a digest, or as Oakeshott often says, an 'abridgement', of the totality of knowledge needed for, and embodied in, the practice itself. Using again a contrast important in *Experience and its Modes*, but applying it differently, Oakeshott says that practice is concrete, while technical knowledge is abstract. The knowledge needed for practice cannot be found in a book, it cannot even be put (fully) into words.[36]

Oakeshott has a further important point to make about practical knowledge. Can it be transmitted from one generation to the next? Or must each generation start anew in learning to master the skills of practices? If the latter were the case, mankind could never make any progress, so clearly practical knowledge is passed on. But it cannot be passed on by learning the rules of technical knowledge abstracted from past practice. How then is the feat achieved? Oakeshott's answer is, by apprenticeship. By apprenticing oneself to a master of a craft, by associating oneself with (presumably older) persons experienced in a practice, 'by continuous contact with one who is continually practising it', practical knowledge can be absorbed. Thus practical knowledge, Oakeshott says, can also be called traditional knowledge.[37] But what if the practice should be faced, for one reason or another, with completely new problems? Can traditional knowledge solve new problems? Oakeshott's answer (and here his argument suddenly becomes controversial) is yes – indeed, *only* traditional, practical knowledge can solve them. No one can even recognize, much less solve, such a problem who has not absorbed the practice's traditional, practical knowledge (just as a new scientific hypothesis to explain unexpected observations can be offered only *by a scientist*, i.e. someone already steeped in the practice of scientific work and equipped with the practical knowledge needed to carry it on). But more than this: 'Both the problems [that arise in a practice] and the course of investigation leading up to their solution are *already hidden* in the activity' (emphases added).[38] Practices, traditions contain the knowledge needed to solve the problems that they encounter.

Why, now, does Oakeshott consider the distinction between practical and technical knowledge to be so important, particularly in relation to politics? The answer is simply that far too many people are unaware of, or deny, the importance of practical knowledge. They hold, quite mistakenly, that all knowledge is technical knowledge, hence can be reduced to explicit rules or formulae, and learned out of a book. Such people Oakeshott dubs 'rationalists' or, in politics, 'ideologists'.[39] The form taken by technical knowledge in politics is called by Oakeshott 'ideology' (we shall have to consider later just what that term embraces). As with technical knowledge generally, the importance of ideology is much less than the political rationalist believes: its proper role is to 'abridge' the practical knowledge of a particular political tradition, and thus to serve a largely academic, and only minimally practical, function.

Here is how Oakeshott describes the political (or other) Rationalist:

> He stands . . . for thought free from obligation to any authority save the authority of 'reason' . . . He is the enemy of authority, of prejudice, of the merely traditional, customary or habitual. His mental attitude is at once sceptical and optimistic: sceptical because there is no opinion, no habit, no belief, nothing so firmly rooted or so firmly held that he hesitates to question it and to judge it by what he calls his 'reason'; optimistic because the Rationalist never doubts the power of his 'reason' (when properly applied) to determine the worth of a thing, the truth of an opinion, or the propriety of an action. Moreover, he is fortified by a belief in a 'reason' common to all mankind.[40]

Rationalist politics, therefore, are 'the politics of perfection and they are the politics of uniformity . . . there is no place in [the Rationalist's] scheme for a "best in the circumstances", only a place for "the best". By refusing to recognize circumstance, Rationalism excludes variety. The rationalist is quick to 'reduce the tangle and variety of experiences to a set of principles, which he will then attack or defend only upon rational grounds'. Rather than recognizing the integrity and authority of a tradition, he engages in the 'corrupting enterprise' of 'rang[ing] the world in order to select the "best" of the practices . . . of others (as the eclectic Zeuxis is said to have tried to compose a figure more beautiful than Helen's by putting together features each notable for its perfection)'.[41] Like Zeuxis, the rationalist in politics is a naive and arrogant fool.

He might be less so, if he recognized the commonality between politics and other practices, and the relation therein between technical and practical knowledge. A good deal of Oakeshott's argumentation, including some of its most brilliant passages, relates to practices other than politics, but is clearly at the same time intended to illuminate politics by analogy. Among these other practices are science (already mentioned), language (it would be absurd to imagine that rules of English grammar or good English usage could be constructed in advance of the use of the language in practice) and, most memorably, cookery. All three of the essays we are engaged in examining refer to cookery, but the most extended and illuminating discussion is in 'Political education'. Cooking, Oakeshott remarks, is a concrete activity which *cannot* be generated by 'an ignorant man, some edible materials, and a cookery book'.[42] For 'the cookery book is not an independently generated beginning from which cooking can spring: it is nothing more than an abstract of someone's [prior] knowledge of how to cook'. The activity of cooking existed, and had to exist, before cookery books. What is more, 'if [the book] were [a man's] sole guide, he could never in fact begin'. The recipes in the cookery book are merely the technical knowledge of cooking: correspondingly, the recipes of rationalist or ideological politics are the politics of the cookery book.

Another, even more famous but in my view less successful, analogy used by Oakeshott to undermine rationalistic politics is that of cycling, or bloomers. Bloomers (named after their inspirer, the eponymous Mrs Bloomer) were, Oakeshott tells us, an 'extraordinary garment affected by girls on bicycles' in Victorian times,[43] plentifully illustrated in contemporary issues of *Punch*, and looking somewhat like baggy Turkish trousers. The point is that they were touted as ' "rational dress" for girl cyclists'. But are they? Their advocates had in mind the activity of propelling a bicycle, as efficiently as possible given the design of the bicycle and of the (female) human body. Traditional prejudices about female dress were to be ignored. Yet clearly they were not: otherwise the advocates of rational dress would have designed, not bloomers, but shorts. Yet, Oakeshott argues, this failure was not really, in the circumstances, a mistake. Without being aware of it, these would-be rationalists had set themselves to solve, not the problem of designing a garment maximally efficient for propelling a bicycle, but the subtler and more appropriate problem of finding the best combination of cycling efficiency with contemporary ideas of female propriety. All things considered, bloomers were indeed a more rational – more genuinely rational – solution than shorts[44] (in the twentieth century, no doubt, the reverse would be the case).

Oakeshott's tale of the bloomers gives rise to some interesting questions, but if it is intended (as appears to be the case) to illustrate the difference between technical and practical knowledge, and their respective roles in relation to practice, it must be accounted a failure. The knowledge of contemporary standards of female propriety which according to Oakeshott, un-known to themselves, constrained, and rightly constrained, pursuit of maxi-mum bicycling efficiency in this case is *not* practical knowledge as Oakeshott defines it. Practical knowledge is skill learned only in practice, and incapable of being formulated in explicit rules or instructions, or put into a book. The relevant standards of Victorian female propriety in dress are not a skill, could easily be formulated in an explicit rule (female legs must be hidden in pub-lic), must often have been so stated by contemporaries, and could have been put into a book of etiquette (if this itself were not judged a breach of propri-ety). Oakeshott has here confused the distinction between practical and tech-nical knowledge with an altogether different distinction. I shall now argue that there is a similar confusion *within* Oakeshott's concept of technical knowl-edge.

Oakeshott first introduced the concept of technical knowledge (so far as I know) in his 1947 essay 'Rationalism in politics', where it is also given the alternative name, 'knowledge of technique'. The rationalist is described as a believer in the 'sovereignty of technique', a man whose model is the engi-neer. His mind, Oakeshott says elsewhere, is an 'instrumental mind',[45] that is, he conceives of rational behaviour as behaviour aimed at a specific ex-plicit purpose or end, guided by conscious calculation of the most efficient means to the end, and nothing else. Oakeshott's remarks on cookery and bloomers exemplify this analysis. In Weberian terms, Oakeshott's rationalist thus described is a believer in *Zweckrationalität* or instrumental rationality. Oakeshott therefore can take his place among the many critics of this trend in modern Western civilization, though his reasons are very different from those of, say, Marcuse.

But interspersed with this account of technical knowledge is another, rather different one. Oddly, in *Rationalism in Politics*, Oakeshott offers as an ex-ample of 'technique' (the 'technique of driving a motor car on English roads'), the rules and maxims of the Highway Code.[46] These of course are not in-strumental rules, but (mostly) constraints that the motorist must observe as a matter of 'good road manners' or (better) good road morals. A similar puz-zlement is evoked by Oakeshott's description of the creed and catechism as part of the 'technical side' of Christianity (presumably because, like the High-way Code, they are written down).[47] However, it is not only technical rules or prescriptions that can be written down, so too can moral and other con-straining principles (like rules of propriety in female dress). In fact, Oakeshott's accounts of technical knowledge often refer explicitly to such principles: for example, he charges that the rationalist reduces morality to explicit principles and ideals, that is, to a 'technique'.[48] But that word is quite inappropriate in relation to moral principles, which are non-instrumental. It should be noted that the embodiment of Oakeshottian rationalism or technical knowledge in politics – ideology – more often than not consists of principles, not instrumentalities (cases in point, quoted by Oakeshott himself, are the American Declaration of Independence and the French Revolutionary Declaration of the Rights of Man). Again in Weberian terms, these are manifestations of *Wertrationalität*, or value-rationalism. Oakeshott is as hostile to this as to instrumental rationalism, but does not clearly distinguish the two. That mistake he emphatically did not repeat in *On Human Conduct*, the thesis of which depends precisely on drawing a sharp distinction between ends and non-instrumental rules as guides to action.

To liken ideology to technique may be a mistake, but does not in itself compromise Oakeshott's case for political conservatism: the ideological style of politics can still be seen as a wanton refusal of the 'practical knowledge' embodied in tradition. However, tradition may itself be a more problematic phenomenon in practice than in theory. We all know what the word means, but to identify or characterize a particular tradition is not so easy – indeed, it is inherent in Oakeshott's conception of tradition as an embodiment of practical knowledge that no tradition can be fully or adequately characterized in words. It is absorbed by experience and familiarity, at first by serving a political apprenticeship alongside those imbued with it (an argument, in Oakeshott's eyes, for a significant hereditary element in political life).[49] And Oakeshott continually stresses that a tradition is not fixed, finished and unchanging, but fluid and flexible, capable of responding appropriately to changed circumstances. But – the question then arises – how is one to tell whether a given political act or policy is or is not in line with the political tradition of the country? It is clear, of course, that political revolution, especially revolution in the name of an ideology, is not – but beyond that, things are not so clear. It is indeed at this point that many critics of Oakeshott accuse him of becoming hopelessly nebulous. He himself admits that 'a tradition of behaviour is a tricky thing to get to know',[50] and counsels against expecting certainty in such matters. Beyond that, he (notoriously) describes faithfulness to a tradition as 'a flow of sympathy' and 'a pursuit of intimations' inherent in the tradition and understood by those who have acquired the practical knowledge it embodies.[51] Such terms clearly give scope for a wide variety of interpretation in particular cases. Sometimes, however, Oakeshott himself offers judgements, on particular cases. For example, on the enfranchisement of women in Britain he remarks (again rather notoriously) that 'the *only* cogent reason' (emphasis added) in favour of it 'was that in all other important respects [than politics] they had already been enfranchised'.[52] The point, then, was not any alleged natural of right of women to vote but rather that, as things stood before they were admitted to the vote, 'there was an incoherence in the arrangements of society which pressed convincingly for remedy'. Incoherences, then, should be remedied, coherence pursued (a doctrine already enunciated by the youthful Oakeshott in *Experience and Its Modes*). Unfortunately, however, incoherences (even if clearly detectable) can be remedied in different, opposed ways. Incoherence is always a relation between an A and a B, which can be remedied by changing either A or B. The incoherence Oakeshott speaks of in the status of women could also have been removed by disenfranchising them in other, non-political areas. And if it be replied that the status of women was at that time *predominantly* one of enfranchisement, so that their exclusion from the right to vote was a glaring anomaly, then one has to ask how that state of affairs could have come about legitimately by Oakeshott's standards (his own argument implies that it was not always so). It is hard to see any satisfactory answer to this question.

It appears, then, that the degree and circumstances of change that Oakeshott's conservatism can accommodate are rather limited. It is not only violent or ideologically motivated revolution that is ruled out, but any substantial reform motivated by 'rationalism in politics'. To see what this means, it suffices to look at some of the examples that Oakeshott gives of that *bête noire* – the Beveridge Report, the Education Act of 1944, even the Catering Wages Act of the 1945 Labour government.[53] The first two of these are foundations of the post-1945 welfare state, which Oakeshott thus condemns as 'the progeny of Rationalism' and a violation of the British political tradition.

Or does he? Such seems to me to be the obvious interpretation of Oakeshott's position, but it must be admitted that it goes counter to some elements at least of his own self-interpretation. As I have already noted, Oakeshott's express view of political philosophy is that it is explanatory, not prescriptive or condemnatory. 'It will not help us', he writes, 'to distinguish between good and bad political projects; it has no power to guide or direct us in the enterprise of pursuing the intimations of our political tradition'. He even claims that it is not his object 'to refute Rationalism'.[54] There are times when he appears to suggest that rationalism, however mistaken and ridiculous it may be, is impotent (and therefore presumably harmless) – such seems to be the moral of the story of the bloomers, for he goes on to claim, in that essay, that because the rationalist theory is 'a misdescription of human behaviour', it is not possible 'to produce any clear and genuine example of behaviour which fits it . . . it is not merely undesirable, it is in fact impossible'.[55]

But I do not think these protestations should be taken at face value. Besides the list of misbegotten rationalist legislation that I have mentioned, Oakeshott frequently uses language of an evaluative kind which reveals his true attitude. Though rationalist politics cannot succeed in its aims, what it can do and does is to 'corrupt' politics. The rationalist in action is a man who 'turns out the light and then complains he cannot see', who can do nothing but blunder about in the darkness, making mistake after mistake. He causes 'war and chaos'.[56] In part, this is because rationalists lack, and despise, the necessary traditional knowledge; but it is also often because they seek to apply to politics an ideology abstracted from some other field (as Marx applied to politics an ideology abstracted from economic practice). Oakeshott also notes the danger that a tradition may become 'compromised' by loss of confidence – a 'malady' for which a 'remedy' is necessary (though not easy to achieve).[57] All in all, I think there is little doubt that Oakeshott wishes to warn us against 'rationalism' and to enjoin us to remain faithful to our 'traditions'.

Is this a coherent set of injunctions (to invoke Oakeshott's own favoured standard)? I fear that it is not. The reason is simple. As Popper has pointed out, there is such a thing as a *rationalist tradition*, that is, a tradition of rational criticism of tradition. Not only is this a possibility, it is actually our own tradition in the West, as Weber's analysis of rationalization indicates. Oakeshott himself frequently laments the ubiquity of rationalism in the modern world, in politics[58] and elsewhere: furthermore, this state of affairs is no sudden recent development (brought about, as Oakeshott sometimes likes to suggest, by the accession to power of new, inexperienced individuals and classes who, lacking traditional knowledge, have resort to ideologies).[59] It is no breakdown of our tradition, but is rather the logical continuation (desirable or not) of that tradition – a tradition that goes back, not only as far as the so-called Enlightenment, but (Popper argues) to the ancient Greeks, from whom our civilization has inherited so much of what it values. What is more, Oakeshott himself knows this, and from time to time admits it. The American Declaration of Independence and the French Revolutionary Declaration of the Rights of Man, after all, are hardly recent developments – they show, Oakeshott admits, that 'the rationalist habit of mind is not a fashion which sprang up only yesterday'.[60] But not only that. In the essay called 'The Tower of Babel', Oakeshott traces the rationalistic temper of Western civilization (specifically, of 'Western European morality') much further back, to 'the first four centuries of the Christian era', when 'a Christian morality in the form of a way of life . . . was swamped by a Christian moral ideology'. Our classical (Græco-Roman) moral inheritance has been similar, Oakeshott says.[61] All of this might well make Oakeshott profoundly pessimistic, but there is a more important point. In the light of this history, to laud tradition and assail rationalism is seen to be incoherent. If rationalism is genuinely an evil, so is at least one tradition (our own). Oakeshott is logically obliged to do what he refuses to do – to apply an *external* standard in judging the relative worth or worthlessness of traditions.

A somewhat similar conclusion can be reached via another argument. This requires us to do something else which Oakeshott, in the essays under consideration, fails to do (with one exception, of which more below) – to examine the specificity of politics as a practice, and its differences from other practices such as (for example) cooking. Oakeshott's analysis of cooking is perceptive, illuminating and entirely convincing: but politics is not quite like cooking. Cooking is a skill, and the skilled cook is skilled at producing the ends (dishes) he envisages: the knowledge he deploys in it can appropriately be divided into practical and technical. Politics, too, is a skill, but it is much more – above all, it is an arena in which authoritative decisions are taken and imposed, conflicting interests arbitrated, and conflicting opinions expressed as to what decisions are right and which interests legitimate. Nothing of the sort applies in cooking. The reason is simple: in cooking, all cooks are (roughly speaking) free to cook what they wish or (if they are professional cooks) what they can find a market for (subject to rules of hygiene, etc.) and all eaters are free to patronize whatever cooks they please. In such a situation, there is little reason for conflict about what dishes to make, and no need for authoritative decisions. In this sense the practice of politics is unique, and cookery (and other practices) are a poor model for it – reliance on 'practical' or traditional knowledge is not enough in politics. It should also be noted that the regime of freedom in cooking is not intrinsic to the activity, but is rather an aspect of *political* liberty in a society like our own (one can for example imagine a regime in which cooking, or cooking of a certain kind, is monopolized by a particular caste). Thus, Oakeshott's characterization of cookery (and other practices) as independent, self-contained fields for the exercise of their own intrinsic practical knowledge, and nothing else, in effect assumes that the political system is a *liberal* one. Now, Oakeshott, as we know, is a liberal, and can uphold the British political tradition in so far as it is a liberal one (not only in relation to cooking). The problem for Oakeshott the conservative, however, is that not all political traditions are liberal. Here we confront the problem of reconciling the conservative Oakeshott with the liberal Oakeshott. The moral, again, is that the liberal Oakeshott (like the anti-rationalist Oakeshott) cannot accept all traditions indiscriminately as self-validating. He must judge them by an external criterion.

As I have already noted, *Rationalism in Politics* contains an essay which seeks to reconcile the two philosophies of liberalism and conservatism ('On being conservative'). Interestingly, also, one of the three major 'conservative' essays, namely 'Political education', contains a famous passage which can be interpreted in both ways. Discussion of this passage, and of the essay 'On being conservative', can serve as an introduction to the liberal Oakeshott, whose full flowering is to be found in *On Human Conduct*.

Quotation of the passage in 'Political education' is, besides, almost obligatory in any discussion of Oakeshott's political philosophy, because it is a small masterpiece of English prose. Oakeshott writes:

> In political activity, men sail a boundless and bottomless sea; there is neither harbour for shelter nor floor for anchorage, neither starting-place nor appointed destination. The enterprise is to keep afloat on an even keel; the sea is both friend and enemy; and the seamanship consists in using the resources of a traditional manner of behaviour in order to make a friend of every hostile occasion.[62]

Let us, at the risk of pedantry, translate this imagery. Clearly a boat or ship is involved (though not actually mentioned); aboard this boat are passengers (members of society) and crew (politicians). Oakeshott's conservatism is manifest in his stipulation that the latter make use of the traditional resources of 'seamanship' (politics), but how exactly should we interpret the following metaphors: that the crew's task is solely to keep the boat afloat on an even keel, because this boat has no appointed destination? Is there anything particularly conservative about keeping the boat afloat? Or does it not rather signify, here, the maintenance of social peace and stability? The absence of an appointed destination can be interpreted in two ways: it may signify the unrealizability of any 'rationalist' blueprint for a perfect society; or, alternatively, that no single goal or set of goals (other than social peace and stability) should be authoritatively imposed, either by the crew on the passengers, or by a majority of passengers on the rest. This latter is a liberal interpretation of Oakeshott's image. It should be noted that the imposition of a rationalist social blueprint could be as illiberal as it is un-conservative; in other words, a certain *kind* of rationalism in politics is as hostile to liberalism as to conservatism. This does not, of course, mean that liberalism and conservatism are the same thing, or can necessarily be reconciled. We should not be blinded to this truth by the brilliance of Oakeshott's rhetoric.

In his 1956 essay 'On being conservative', Oakeshott presents the following argument.[63] I live, he says, in a society whose members 'engage in a great variety of activities' and 'entertain a multiplicity of opinions on every conceivable subject'. They pursue happiness, seek the satisfaction of desires, enter into relationships, and make agreements with one another. The 'multiplicity of activity and variety of opinion' are liable to produce 'collisions'. Some observers of this scene, Oakeshott says, find it deplorably wasteful and disorganized: 'it has none of the satisfaction of a well-conducted business enterprise'. Such observers may wish to replace the society described by a 'dream' of some coordinated, conflict-free human activity, in which the role of government is to impose upon its subjects the conditions necessary for realizing the dream. But that, Oakeshott continues, is not the response of the conservative, for the conservative disposition is to accept 'the current condition of human circumstances' as described above, the condition of variety and diversity. To the conservative, therefore, the proper role of government is to act like an umpire 'whose business is to administer the rules of the game' – not to impose a social dream. The function of government is the resolution of conflict and the preservation of peace. The message is similar to that of Oakeshott's maritime metaphor.

Students of Oakeshott will recognize this argument as an anticipation of the one developed at book length in *On Human Conduct*. Clearly, the dream-imposer is, in Oakeshott's terms, a 'rationalist in politics', and his antagonist is indeed, in a certain sense, a conservative, though he is also clearly a liberal. This, however, does *not* show that *political* conservatism entails political liberalism. The conservative attitude of acceptance of 'things as they are' described by Oakeshott relates to people and their ways in a complex, heterogeneous society: it does *not* relate to the political system, which Oakeshott *prescribes* must be of a certain type – it must be a liberal system of government. However, not all political regimes are liberal, nor are all illiberal regimes the consequence of rationalism – many (for example, in Russia or China before the twentieth century) have been extremely traditionalist. The political liberal, therefore, who is a political liberal for the reasons mentioned in Oakeshott's account of the 'conservative disposition', cannot be an unqualified *political* conservative, nor an unqualified upholder of political traditions. He can support only *liberal* traditions. In other regimes, he is obliged to call for *liberalization*.

If this interpretation is correct, it can be said that Oakeshott's political liberalism (which is, as we shall see a libertarian form of liberalism) may have been motivated by what he calls a 'conservative disposition' towards the heterogeneity of modern, complex society. We shall find, however, that it is not on this conservative premise that he relies in his liberal (or libertarian) masterpiece, *On Human Conduct*. Rather, he returns to the premise of *Experience and Its Modes* – namely, that, the world of practice is by definition a world populated by free agents. Hence, as he there wrote, 'Practical truth . . . is the truth that can give freedom, [while] the errors of practice are those which enslave.' And although Oakeshott restates (in somewhat different language) his view that the practical world is an 'abstract' mode of experience that takes for granted assumptions that are questionable from the standpoint of the only fully 'concrete' world of knowledge, namely philosophy, there is no suggestion, now, that the abstractness of practical understanding involves inescapable self-contradiction. In any case, as Oakeshott stressed from the beginning, the practical world is the one in which by necessity we have to live and act.

On Human Conduct, then, theorizes and postulates a world of individual agents who are in a certain sense free. In Oakeshott's words, 'The starting-place of doing is a state of reflective consciousness, the agent's own understanding of his situation, what it means to him . . . He is "free" because [his situation] is an understood situation and because doing is an intelligent engagement.'[64] An agent is one who can imagine his situation different from what it is and recognize it as alterable by his own action, can imagine alternative forms of action, choose between them, and decide what to do. In so choosing and deciding, he seeks to achieve 'a satisfaction', a 'wished-for outcome', an end or purpose, the promotion of an interest.[65] The world of agency is, of course, inhabited by a plurality of interacting agents, but – underscoring his individualism – Oakeshott declines to describe it by terms such as 'social' or 'collective', referring instead always to 'conduct *inter homines*' – for, as he remarks, 'the arts of agency are nowhere and never to be found save in the understanding of adepts'.[66]

Though thoroughly individualistic, Oakeshott's view of the human world and human conduct is far from *atomistic* (whatever exactly that term of abuse so frequently levelled at liberalism may mean): on the contrary, the focus of Oakeshott's analysis is *association*, and the different forms it can take. Given Oakeshott's conception of human beings as purposive, satisfaction-seeking agents, one basis for association is obvious – those who share the same purpose or interest, who seek to bring about the same wished-for state of affairs, may (and frequently do) associate together in order more effectively to pursue their common goal. Pursuit of such a common goal is called by Oakeshott an 'enterprise', and an association devoted to it is called by him an 'enterprise association'. Oakeshott stresses that, since such an association is devoted to realising a common want of all associates, the relation between associates is a freely chosen one, and can be freely revoked by any individual who chooses to leave the association.[67]

Enterprise associations may be small or large, short lived or long lived. Particularly if they are long lived, and the more so if they are large, pursuit of the association's common purpose (which takes the form of a sequence of decisions 'to do *this* rather than *that*', as Oakeshott puts it, in response to continuously emerging situations) entails what Oakeshott calls 'management', i.e. a procedure for taking decisions, whether by all the associates, or (more realistically) by a deputed manager or managers, but in any case acknowledged by all associates. As Oakeshott sums up, 'enterprise association is a "managerial" engagement: it is agents related to one another in the substantive activity of choosing performances contingently connected with a common purpose or interest'.[68] Furthermore, an enterprise association (if not transitory) may make use of, and its members may recognise the authority of, rules, or 'rule-like arrangements', whose desirability is to be judged (like the performances of associates) by their 'propensity to promote or to hinder' the common purpose of the association.

A (non-transitory) enterprise association, then, has rules, a set of decision-making procedures, and designated and acknowledged decision makers. Speaking loosely, perhaps, one might be tempted to say that it has a political structure, and thus to imply that the form of association known as the 'state', or political association in a stricter sense, is a kind of enterprise association. This, Oakeshott (correctly) says, is a common belief, but one which he repudiates totally. The state is a *compulsory* association; and 'compulsory enterprise association is a self-contradiction'.[69] By definition, an enterprise association is an association of agents to pursue a *common* purpose, which therefore has no place for compulsion to belong to the association or accept its decisions. It is thus intrinsically compatible with the freedom of the human agent. The state, then, is not like an enterprise association, and to understand it we need to look to other forms of association. But the state, though compulsory, *can* still be compatible with human freedom – on condition that it is not confused with an enterprise association. This is the central message of *On Human Conduct*.

It is the central message, because the state, if it is supposedly modelled on an enterprise association, but (of course) compulsory, is *not* compatible with human freedom, for in such an association (state) individuals will be forced to pursue some goal, or help to bring about some state of affairs, whether or not it is one they would freely choose. In practice it is certain that many individual citizens of an 'enterprise state' will be forced to serve a goal or goals not their own, and indeed contrary to their will. Such, as Oakeshott points out, is the inevitable implication of any conception of the state which conceives its function (and, perhaps justification) as the achievement of a substantive goal or purpose, whether military, economic, religious or whatever. Although that has been a very common conception of the state, there is an alternative. Oakeshott calls it 'civil association'.

To understand this Oakeshottian concept, we must first examine another, that of a 'practice'. In *On Human Conduct* this term does *not* (as in *Rationalism in Politics*) refer to or include such goal-oriented activities as cookery or science. Rather, practices are made up of *rules* and 'rule-like considerations' such as principles, customs, etc.[70] Practices then create obligations or duties that must be observed in human action. As Oakeshott puts it, in an important if perhaps initially obscure phrase, the obligations due to practices constitute 'an authoritative adverbial qualification' of human performances,[71] or in other words they dictate conditions which agents must observe as they pursue (alone or in an enterprise association) whatever goals they choose to pursue. These conditions, Oakeshott says, are specified by words such as 'punctually, considerately, civilly . . . legally, candidly', and so on. To be considerate, civil, or punctual is a *rule* to which one's actions should conform: very importantly, such rules do not dictate any specific 'performance' or action whatever. Thus, they leave the individual free to choose his actions in line with his own chosen purposes. Practices do not compromise human freedom, any more than enterprise associations do. Both are an inevitable part of 'conduct *inter homines*'.

Among the various practices and their concomitant rules, one kind is of particular interest to Oakeshott – namely, moral practices, conduct guided by 'morality', or moral conduct. Oakeshott does not give any very satisfactory definitions of morality or moral rules: the latter, he says, are of a particularly high degree of generality, the former he calls 'the *ars artium*; the practice of all practices; the practice of agency without further specification'.[72] But the vagueness of this is not important: the concept of morality and moral rules is not arcane – we know well enough which rules are moral ones, even if the concept is hard to define. The point for Oakeshott is that moral rules, moral practices (like all rules and practices) do not specify any particular actions, they are (as he says) not prudential, nor 'instrumental to the achievement of any substantive purpose or to the satisfaction of any substantive want'. Honesty may be the best policy, but this is not the purpose or point of the norm of honesty. Nevertheless, subscription to the terms of a moral practice is a form of human association. 'Moral relationship' says Oakeshott 'is not association for the achievement of a common purpose . . . it is relationship solely in respect of conditions to be subscribed to in seeking the satisfaction of any want'.[73] Since a moral practice prescribes only these conditions, and not any substantive performance, 'it postulates "free" agents and it is powerless to deprive them of their freedom'.[74]

'Civil association' is association in terms of a moral practice, or rather one kind of such association. Oakeshott uses a number of Latin terms (rather than their English translations which, he says, carry inappropriate implications) to designate its elements. The rules of civil association are *lex*; the individuals who subscribe to the rules are *cives*, and the condition of such associated persons is called *civitas*, or the civil condition.[75] These terms, of course, do not *define* civil association, or tell us how it differs from moral association generally. The *differentiae* of civil association are the following: *lex* specifies (among other things) its own sphere of jurisdiction; its rules are backed up by an apparatus of enforcement; and this requires procedures of adjudication to determine authoritatively when the rules have been broken (or as Oakeshott characteristically prefers to put it, not adequately subscribed to). Furthermore, an apparatus for enforcing rules (*lex*) implies also a procedure of legislation, for amending or repealing the rules, and creating new ones, in response to changing conditions and opinions; and this correspondingly implies a specialized 'office' of legislator (as well as judge or adjudicator). Ensuring 'adequate subscription' to the rules of civil association is called by Oakeshott 'ruling'.[76]

To repeat: a civil association is a kind of moral association (roughly speaking, it is a moral association whose rules are enforced) and hence it does not subserve any purpose of any of the individuals thus associated, not even a 'common purpose' of all of them. It is not enterprise association, still less compulsory enterprise association. It is compulsory *association*, but not a compulsory association for the pursuit of any goal or purpose. Thus it does not compromise individual freedom. What it does is to require of civil associates (*cives*) observance of certain rules and conditions as they go about the business, *inter homines*, of pursuing *their own* chosen goals and purposes. Such is the civil condition.

It is obvious that many of the features that define civil association are reminiscent of characteristics of the state, and it seems natural to say that it is in fact

135

Oakeshott's ideal of the state (because in it individuals are free), the obverse of his repudiation of the state conceived as compulsory enterprise association. But is it? Oakeshott tells us that he is a 'theorist' of human conduct and association, not a 'theoretician'. The latter is a 'deplorable character' who purports to be a 'tutor' to ordinary folk, able to prescribe 'correct' performances to them.[77] Once again Oakeshott as philosopher seems to eschew any prescriptive role, such as advocating a form of state corresponding to civil association rather than (compulsory quasi-) enterprise association. Once again, however, this modesty should not be taken at face value. The mask of neutrality, never very firmly in place, clearly slips from time to time. For example, Oakeshott more than once complains of the civil condition being 'corrupted' by an enterprise association conception of the state, which is also described as a 'rickety moral construction', and a tendency of which 'European peoples' ought to be 'profoundly ashamed'.[78] In his 1975 essay, 'Talking politics', Oakeshott comes clean: 'Civil association', he says, 'is particularly appropriate to the state because it is the only morally tolerable form of compulsory association'.[79] The situation is in reality just what it seems to be: civil association is indeed Oakeshott's ideal of the state, and the rival view which assimilates it to enterprise association is to be resisted, for moral as well as logical reasons.

Despite this, it would not be true to say that Oakeshott's rejection of the enterprise association model of the state is total. For one thing, it is not his style to trade in absolutes. More specifically, it may sometimes be necessary to suspend the civil condition, in order to save it from a threat of destruction, by, for example, military force.[80] In such circumstances it becomes a regrettable necessity for the state to make defence against such an attack into a common or quasi-common imposed purpose. Military conscription of persons and resources is then justified in order to save the civil order. Oakeshott thus justifies, in certain cases, defensive war – but defensive war only. To organize the state for any other military purpose is a clear case of illegitimately turning the state into a compulsory (quasi-)enterprise association.

Of course, it is not the only way of doing so. Perhaps the most fascinating section of *On Human Conduct* is its last chapter, called 'On the character of a modern European state', in which Oakeshott traces the conceptual history of that phenomenon, from about the sixteenth century on, in terms of his crucial contrast between civil and enterprise association. Not, of course, that these two coinages of Oakeshott were used by earlier theorists, but equivalent terms were available, and used, as a heritage from medieval ways of thinking. These terms are *societas* and *universitas*. *Societas* was the name given to an association, usually but not always resulting from agreement among agents, in terms of common subscription to rules: *universitas* was the name for agents associated in such a way as to constitute a single 'person' pursuing a specific purpose or end (universities in the modern sense are only one example). Both terms were used by theorists trying to define or prescribe the nature of the emerging, and developing, European state, even although the state is of course not a voluntary association. In other words, the state was in effect viewed by European thinkers as either a civil or an enterprise association.

Why as an enterprise association, or *universitas*? One reason, says Oakeshott, was the 'sacerdotal authority' once exercised by the Pope and the Universal Church, but claimed by early modern rulers or on their behalf – a development, of course, given much impetus by the Reformation.[81] Thus protection of the true faith was asserted to be a (or the main) purpose of the state. A second reason springs from the feudal institution of 'lordship'.[82] Medieval feudatories and kings were both rulers and lords – both enforcers of rules, and owner-managers of landed estates, dischargers therefore of both a political and an economic function. Although the two functions were conceptually distinguished in medieval theory, they were combined in practice, and it was thus easy enough to attribute to the state the purpose of economic development. A brilliant and influential synthesis of these two strands of thought (economic and religious) was achieved by Francis Bacon, who argued that the maximum and most beneficial development of the earth's natural resources was a divine injunction, and its organization a duty laid by God on rulers. According to Oakeshott, this vision has persisted throughout the history of European thought, though with the economic element becoming increasingly predominant and the religious diluted or transformed, in the writings of (for example) St Simon, Comte and Marx, and in the practice of the 'enlightened despots' of the eighteenth century and the Bolsheviks in the twentieth.[83] Among other reasons cited by Oakeshott for the interpretation of the state as a *universitas* or enterprise association are its penchant for waging war, and its development of a bureaucratic administration – the latter encouraging confusion between the ruler's relation to his servants, and his relation to his subjects (or the relation of the state and its citizens). As Oakeshott puts it: 'Rulers may employ clerks, but they rule subjects'.[84]

In addition to these institutional and intellectual factors, Oakeshott mentions also some features of human psychology (it is a historical or social psychology) which influenced the choice between civil and enterprise association (*societas* or *universitas*) as the ideal of the state. The emergence of the modern European state took place in a world of social change in which 'the old certainties of belief, of understanding, of occupation and of status were being dissolved'[85] as an old, communally organized way of life passed into desuetude. Individuals were faced with the need to make choices. Some relished the challenge: these were persons who not only accepted the human condition as one 'saddled with an unsought and inescapable "freedom"', but also recognized this condition as 'the emblem of human dignity and as a condition for each individual to explore, to make the most of, and to enjoy as an opportunity rather than suffer as a burden', in the exercise of self-determination, individuality, autonomy.[86] 'The state which corresponds with such persons', Oakeshott remarks, 'is some version of . . . civil association'. But a second kind of human character was also in evidence when the modern European state was born (and since): persons who 'by circumstances or temperament' could not respond to the invitation to make their own choices, for example, 'the displaced labourer', 'the dispossessed believer' or 'the helpless victim of an enclosure'. For reasons of either material or spiritual indigence, or both, such persons 'could be accommodated only in the sort of association which the analogy of *universitas* suggested for the state; namely a compulsory enterprise association in which the office of government was not to rule subjects but to make substantive choices for those unable or indisposed to make them for themselves'.[87]

Since compulsory enterprise association is, according to Oakeshott, a self-contradiction, the latter class of persons must be accounted victims of delusion at best. But actually their case is even worse – they wish to abandon the defining characteristics of human agency, almost of humanity itself. They are to be either pitied or despised. Either way, they are assuredly not the kind of person Oakeshott admires. They are called by him 'individuals *manqués*'. To the inadequacy of the individual *manqué* in the face of the modern world, there corresponds a certain kind of ruler, the 'leader'. Leaders are persons who seek and gain power by offering to take decisions on behalf of followers who are unable to unwilling to make their own, by promising them 'salvation' or arousing 'millennial expectation' among them.[88] Weber would call them 'charismatic' leaders, and it is clear that Oakeshott's view of them, in sharp contrast to Weber's, is entirely negative – there is no place for such leaders in civil association. Correspondingly, Oakeshott repudiates Weber's attitude to nationalism and the 'nation' (closely connected with his support for charismatic leadership). All states, Oakeshott remarks, are more or less arbitrary agglomerations of persons brought together by violence and historical accident – the concept of the 'nation state' in application to modern Europe, is an illusion of those who, envisioning the state as an 'integrated community . . . pursuing a common purpose, [and] under the spell of a supremely inappropriate analogy . . . have confused their dreams with the conditions of waking life'.[89] All this is quite alien to civil society, which, Oakeshott remarks, 'is not a relationship of love or affection'.[90] Nor is it the locus of emotional satisfaction or spiritual fulfilment. Civility is a cool, austere, limited (though necessary) relationship.

It is interesting to continue the comparison between Oakeshott and Weber. Unlike Weber, Oakeshott sees the alliance between charismatic leaders and their followers as a threat to liberty and individuality, and therefore – unlike Weber – he is hostile to modern democracy. The strongest statement of this hostility is to be found, not in *On Human Conduct*, but in an earlier essay, 'The masses in representative democracy'.[91] The mode of government generated by 'the aspirations of individuality', Oakeshott there argues, was parliamentary government. But modernity generated not only the modern individual, but also the individual *manqué*, who became the anti-individual. In due course, the anti-individuals (also called 'mass men'), realizing they were in the majority, pressed for and achieved universal adult suffrage, thus transforming parliamentary government into something totally different – 'popular government'. The tendency of this form of government has been to turn government into what in *On Human Conduct* is called a compulsory enterprise association.

What sort of compulsory enterprise association, exactly? Broadly speaking, an economic one, devoted to maximizing output and to distributing it appropriately. However, so far as increasing output is concerned, civil association has been the beneficiary of a huge stroke of luck, for freedom in the economic sphere – the so-called 'free market' – is also the most productive economic system, whereas the centrally planned economy is as inefficient as it is destructive of freedom. Insight into the efficiency of the free market made the classical economists into supporters of civil association, though for entirely the wrong reasons (the same is true, up to a point, of their modern-day successor, Hayek), and thus economic efficiency serves as a bulwark of civil association in the era of mass democracy. The main threat to civil association, therefore, comes from the preoccupation with economic distribution, or 'distributive justice'. As Oakeshott puts it, 'there is no place in civil association for so-called "distributive justice". . . *lex* cannot be a rule of distribution of this sort, [for] civil rulers have nothing to distribute'.[92] The 'justice' of civil association is nothing but 'adequate subscription' to its rules by purpose-pursuing individuals. The welfare state, already condemned by Oakeshott as the progeny of political rationalism, is condemned again as a manifestation of the enterprise association state,[93] answering to the needs of those who prefer security to freedom, with its attendant risk of 'frustration of one's purposes'. The beneficiary of welfare state handouts, as Oakeshott contemptuously puts it, 'enjoys the composure of the conscript assured of his dinner', and his state is one of 'compensated servility'.[94] But – even worse – the price of 'assured dinners' is servility for all, for such is the nature of the state modelled on enterprise rather than civil association.

Oakeshott is assuredly right to say that the welfare state answers to the desire (or need) for security ('social security' is its explicit purpose) – perhaps not in itself, however, such a contemptible desire. Nor is it immediately clear why the welfare state, or redistribution in favour of the poor, destroys freedom, or subjects citizens to a single, monolithic purpose such as characterizes an enterprise association. To understand and assess Oakeshott's argument here it is necessary to look more closely at the concept of a purpose and what Oakeshott understands as 'pursuing a purpose'. For example, he is emphatic that 'peace', or the tranquillity of associates, which may and no doubt should result from the civil condition, is *not* its purpose, nor the purpose of its associates, because it is not a substantive purpose at all (except perhaps in crisis situations – 'survival', Oakeshott allows, may become a 'want' but only in 'circumstances of threatened extinction').[95] In normal times, civil associates do not pursue peace or survival. Oakeshott even goes so far as to say that 'A rule obligating *cives* not to kill one another is not a conclusion to be inferred from the theorem that there is a common want (as distinct from an organic urge) to remain alive . . . and such a rule is not desirable on account of its promoting the satisfaction of this want'.[96] Surely this goes *too* far – and the mistake is failure to distinguish between wants and purposes. I may not be pursuing my survival as a purposive project, but it is certainly something I want.

Unlike peace or tranquillity, it seems, prosperity, or economic security, *is* a substantive purpose (and/or want), in Oakeshott's opinion, and so to use the state to organize pursuit of wealth, or economic security for those who need it, is to depart from civil association and take away the freedom of citizens. But is it, and does it? I think not. Rather, what it does it to increase, or to redistribute, one of the major means for achieving individual purposes (what Rawls calls a 'primary social good'). And in this respect it is in fact very like civil association. Civil association, by enforcing moral rules like the one obliging *cives* not to kill one another, creates a state of order and peace, which greatly enhances the ability of all (though not of all equally) to achieve what they want to achieve (the sheer absence of civil association corresponds to what Hobbes and other social contract theorists called the 'state of nature'). Oakeshott even admits that 'security' is an outcome of civil association (though – strangely – not its justification).[97] Why should a form of association that ensures security of person and property be considered to be a guarantor of freedom and individuality, while one that provides a broader economic security is held to destroy these goods?

A defence of the welfare state, economic redistribution, and the provision of economic security can be made in another way, still consistently with some of Oakeshott's basic premises. According to Oakeshott, civil association is enforced moral association (or enforcement of a moral practice), i.e. of moral rules, which do not specify performances but only conditions to be observed in acting. This analysis of moral rules is incomplete. Perhaps it is generally agreed that charity is a moral virtue; many would go further, and call it a moral obligation. It is easy to imagine an enterprise association devoted to charitable purposes (many in fact exist), but this does not mean that there is no moral rule obliging us to make such charitable donations as we can afford for the relief of poverty and suffering. Such a rule may be a moral rule in just as good standing as the moral rule against murder, and therefore just as eligible for enforcement by the state – the welfare state. Oakeshott's analysis of moral rules implicitly assumes that they are all *negative* (like 'Thou shalt *not* kill') but there is no reason why this should be so. If the enforcement of moral obligations is morally justified, so, too, is the welfare state. The welfare state, then, enforces moral obligations, rather than pursuit of a purpose which each individual ought to be free to choose or reject.

It is time, finally, to relate Oakeshott's theory of civil association to the theme of liberalism. In my opinion, it is indeed a form of liberalism, in fact a superb, but flawed, contribution to liberal theory. Oakeshott himself seems reluctant to accept the liberal label (though he has, quite accurately, called himself a libertarian), mainly it seems because he identifies liberalism with the theory of natural rights, which (unlike the later libertarian, Nozick) he rejects because of their absoluteness.[98] Nevertheless, the Oakeshottian theory of civil association can, with hindsight, be clearly seen to be an expression of what Rawls later called the priority of the right over the good: in these terms, rules of civil association are rules of right, and as such obligatory and enforceable, while the pursuit of purposes reflects conceptions of the good, and must be voluntary, not enforced. As Oakeshott often puts it, the former belong to the public sphere, the latter to the private. To be sure, the priority of the right over the good is necessary rather than sufficient for liberalism, in so far as enforced non-purposive rules may in principle be paternalistic in nature (a good example is the British law which forbids driving a car without wearing a seat belt) or moralistic in an illiberal sense (e.g. laws forbidding homosexual acts between consenting adults). However, Oakeshott – unsurprisingly – tends to rule these out (though – characteristically – not absolutely) by endorsing Mill's principle that (as he puts it) 'self-regarding actions should be exempt from civil conditions'.[99] This is unsurprising, given Oakeshott's vision of human life as a succession of performances *inter homines*, in which individuals are free to choose their own purposes. It is also implicit in Oakeshott's identification of 'civility' as 'a practice of just conduct' – breach of the rules of civil association could hardly be described as injustice, unless some 'harm to others' was involved. But Oakeshott's libertarian version of liberalism is flawed by his belief that state action to enforce economic redistribution amounts to enforced (quasi-)enterprise association, and severs the link between choice and action which constitutes free agency. His argument to that effect is not convincing. We shall see the argument taken up again, in a more careful and less unconvincing way, by Robert Nozick.

Notes

1   M. Oakeshott, *Experience and Its Modes* (Cambridge University Press, 1993), pp. 48, 82.
2   Ibid., pp. 71, 74.
3   Ibid., p. 75
4   Ibid., pp. 71, 106, 111.
5   Ibid., p. 107.
6   Ibid., p. 169.
7   Ibid., pp. 171, 181.
8   Ibid., p. 178.
9   Ibid., p. 176.
10   Ibid., p. 261.
11   Ibid., pp. 269–70, 308.
12   Ibid., pp. 261, 309.
13   Ibid., pp. 254–5.
14   Ibid., pp. 34, 73–4, 77–80, 330.
15   Ibid., pp. 146, 148–9, 107.
16   Ibid., pp. 174, 188, 207.
17   Ibid., pp. 215–17.
18   Ibid., pp. 304–6.
19   Ibid., p. 83.
20   Ibid., pp. 296–7.
21   Ibid., p. 82.

22 Ibid., pp. 75–6, 156–7.
23 Ibid., pp. 1, 3, 338, 354.
24 Ibid., p. 171.
25 Ibid., pp. 199, 200, 265.
26 Ibid., pp. 309, 334–5, 337–8.
27 M. Oakeshott, *Rationalism in Politics and Other Essays* (Methuen, London, 1962), p. 132.
28 Oakeshott, *Experience and Its Modes*, pp. 102–3, 105–6.
29 Oakeshott, *Rationalism in Politics*, pp. 154–5.
30 Ibid., p. 130.
31 Oakeshott, *Experience and Its Modes*, pp. 182, 312.
32 Oakeshott, *Rationalism in Politics*, p. 112.
33 Ibid., p. 7.
34 Ibid., p. 8.
35 Ibid., p. 7.
36 Ibid, pp. 10, 25, 120.
37 Ibid., pp. 8, 11.
38 Ibid., p. 99.
39 Ibid., pp. 11–12.
40 Ibid., p. 1.
41 Ibid., pp. 5–6, 131.
42 Ibid., p. 119.
43 Ibid., p. 81.
44 Ibid., p. 82–3.
45 Ibid., pp. 7, 11, 93, 96.
46 Ibid., p. 7.
47 Ibid., pp. 8–9.
48 Ibid., p. 35.
49 Ibid., pp. 23–5.
50 Ibid., p. 128.
51 Ibid., p. 126.
52 Ibid., p. 124.
53 Ibid., p. 6. Cf. also p. 36, where the post-war Labour government is referred to as 'a set of sanctimonious, rationalist politicians, preaching an ideology of un-selfishness and social service' to a population that they have done their best to deprive of 'the only living root of moral behaviour'.
54 Ibid., pp. 132, xxx.
55 Ibid., pp. 88–9.
56 Ibid., pp. 106, 32, 105, 94.
57 Ibid., p. 107.
58 For example, ibid., p. 20: 'all contemporary politics are deeply infected with rationalism'.

59   Ibid., p. 23.

60   Ibid., p. 28.

61   Ibid., pp. 75, 78.

62   Ibid., p. 127.

63   Ibid., pp. 185ff.

64   M. Oakeshott, *On Human Conduct* (Oxford University Press, London, 1975), p. 37.

65   Ibid., pp. 39, 59.

66   Ibid., p. 87.

67   Ibid., pp. 114–15.

68   Ibid., p. 115.

69   Ibid., p. 119. Oakeshott's argument here neglects the issue of collective goods and the free rider problem.

70   Ibid., p. 24.

71   Ibid., p. 55.

72   Ibid., p. 100.

73   Ibid., pp. 60, 62.

74   Ibid., p. 79.

75   Ibid., p. 108.

76   Ibid., pp. 141ff.

77   Ibid., pp. 25–6.

78   Ibid., pp. 168, 312, 317, 321.

79   M. Oakeshott, *Rationalism in Politics and Other Essays*, expanded edition (Liberty Press, Indianapolis, 1991), p. 460.

80   Oakeshott, *On Human Conduct*, p. 146.

81   Ibid., p. 220.

82   Ibid., pp. 218–19.

83   Ibid., pp. 287ff.

84   Ibid., p. 146.

85   Ibid., p. 275.

86   Ibid., p. 236.

87   Ibid., pp. 274–5.

88   Ibid., pp. 276ff.

89   Ibid., p. 188.

90   Ibid., p. 123.

91   In Oakeshott, *Rationalism in Politics*, expanded edition. Cf. pp. 364, 370–4, 376–83.

92   Oakeshott, *On Human Conduct*, p. 153.

93   Ibid., p. 311.

94   Ibid., p. 317.

95   Ibid., p. 119.

96   Ibid., p. 173.

97 Ibid., p. 117.
98 Ibid., p. 245 n. 2; Oakeshott, *Rationalism in Politics,* expanded edition, pp. 455–6.
99 Oakeshott, *On Human Conduct*, pp. 178–9.

Further reading

By Oakeshott

M. Oakeshott, *Experience and Its Modes*, Cambridge University Press, 1933.

M. Oakeshott, 'The claims of politics', *Scrutiny* 8 (1939–40).

M. Oakeshott, *Rationalism in Politics and Other Essays*, Methuen, London, 1962 (expanded edition, Liberty Press, Indianapolis, 1991).

M. Oakeshott, *On Human Conduct*, Clarendon Press, Oxford, 1975.

M. Oakeshott, *On History and Other Essays*, Basil Blackwell, Oxford, 1983.

M. Oakeshott, *The Voice of Liberal Learning: Michael Oakeshott on Education*, ed. T. Fuller, Yale University Press, New Haven, 1989.

On Oakeshott

B. Barber, 'Conserving politics: the political theory of Michael Oakeshott', *Government and Opposition* 2, 1976.

P. Franco, *The Political Philosophy of Michael Oakeshott*, Yale University Press, New Haven, 1990.

R. Grant, *Oakeshott*, Claridge Press, London, 1990.

J. Gray, 'Oakeshott on law, liberty and civil association', in *Liberalisms: Essays in Political Philosophy*, Routledge, London 1989.

W. H. Greenleaf, *Oakeshott's Philosophical Politics*, Longman, London, 1966.

K. Minogue, 'A memoir: Michael Oakeshott', *Political Studies* 39, 1991.

J. Norman (ed.), *The Achievement of Michael Oakeshott*, Duckworth, London, 1993.

Political Theory 4, August 1976: *A Symposium on Michael Oakeshott*, including 'A reply to my critics' by Oakeshott.

D. D. Raphael, 'Professor Oakeshott's rationalism in politics', *Political Studies* 12, 1964 (Oakeshott's 'Reply' is in *Political Studies* 13, 1965).

J. Waldron, 'Politics without purpose', *Times Literary Supplement*, 6-12 July, 1990, p. 718.

7
Friedrich Hayek: The Theory of Spontaneous Order

Friedrich Hayek is the twentieth-century social theorist who, probably more than any other, found himself vindicated by events – if not wholly, then at least in his central contention. He is also the one who, more than any other, himself exercised a significant political influence. Neither the fact nor the manner of this influence was predictable. Born just before the century itself, in Vienna in 1899, Hayek became between the two world wars a leading economist and standard-bearer of the celebrated Austrian school of economic theory, inheriting the mantle of such distinguished predecessors as Carl Menger and Ludwig von Mises, whose protégé he was. But in 1931, Hayek's life and career took an unexpected turn. Invited by the English economist Lionel Robbins to lecture at the London School of Economics, Hayek settled there as a professor and became, in due course, a British citizen. Such he remained until his death in 1992, despite later moves to the University of Chicago in 1950, and the University of Freiburg in 1961. It was in Britain, too, that his political influence was greatest, reaching a peak with the prime ministership of Margaret Thatcher (1979–90), who frequently invoked his name and ideas.

Yet Hayek's influence came late, after several decades during which his status was almost that of a pariah. Like so many other political theorists of his generation, Hayek's thought was shaped in response to the century's political cataclysms – the world wars, and the menacing totalitarian regimes established in Germany and Russia. Again, like many contemporaries (for example Marcuse and Arendt), Hayek saw the two totalitarian régimes as essentially similar evils. The peculiarity of his interpretation, however, was (in sharp contrast to Marcuse, in particular) to see both Stalinism and Nazism as forms of *socialism*. In other words, he accepted as accurate the self-description, National Socialism, adopted by Hitler's movement and régime. The two totalitarian systems were, to Hayek, socialism of the left and of the right respectively. From the period of the Second World War, therefore, Hayek embarked on a theoretical crusade against socialism and collectivism – a crusade which, especially in the immediate post-war atmosphere, made him an extremely unpopular figure in many quarters. Yet as the decades passed, and the instability of the apparently so successful Keynesian settlement became apparent, Hayek's teachings attracted more favourable attention. In 1974, he was awarded the Nobel Prize for economics – less, in truth, for his contribution to technical economic theory than in recognition of his philosophical defence of liberal capitalist civilization. Fifteen years later, the collapse of socialism in its Soviet-style manifestation gave him the status, before his death, almost of a prophet. The transformation from pariah to prophet was Hayek's reward for fifty years of unwavering theoretical consistency.

Three major works carry Hayek's statement of his social theory. The first, and most controversial (a description of the book's reception rather than its content), was *The Road to Serfdom*, published in 1944. Though praised by authorities as diverse as John Maynard Keynes and Joseph Schumpeter, this book also earned considerable hostility, and even abuse, for its author. Overall its reception was discouraging to Hayek, who did not seriously return to the fray until the publication in 1960 of *The Constitution of Liberty*, considered by many to be his *magnum opus*. But it must dispute that title with his last major statement, *Law, Legislation and Liberty*, which was first published between two covers in 1982, having already appeared as three separate volumes (*Rules and Order* (1973), *The Mirage of Social Justice* (1976) and *The Political Order of a Free People* (1979)). Of the many other publications that flowed from Hayek's pen during his long life, those most relevant to the present context are his critique of scientific social theory entitled *The Counter-Revolution of Science*, published in 1955, and an essay in the same field, though focusing particularly on the nature of economic science, 'The theory of complex phenomena' (included in his 1978 collection, *Studies in Philosophy, Politics and Economics*). That discussion is continued in Hayek's important Nobel Prize lecture, 'The pretence of knowledge', which was published by the Institute of Economic Affairs in 1975. Latterly Hayek's reflections on economic theory became inseparable from his forays into policy prescription, in which he sought to demonstrate the errors of so-called 'Keynesian' aggregate demand management. Several of these essays, too, were published under the imprint of the Institute of Economic Affairs. But Hayek's earlier, book-length works of technical economics, mostly written in the 1930s, and focusing largely on the problem of the trade cycle, are not without political relevance also. Finally, mention should be made of a fascinating volume of autobiographical reminiscence, entitled by its editors *Hayek on Hayek*. This includes the instructive transcript of a 1945 radio discussion of *The Road to Serfdom* in which Hayek was interrogated by two distinguished academics from the University of Chicago, both intensely hostile, and one positively abusive.

Hayek, however, kept his temper, both in the 1945 radio broadcast and throughout his scholarly career. His writing indeed, though it became a little acerbic in his later years, is on the whole a model of good manners combined with intellectual force. Hayek is in his own way a stylist, a master of clear and lucid explanation. His work totally lacks pomposity and unnecessary obscurity or complication – his aim was to convince, not to dazzle. Even those who remain unconvinced, in whole or in part, by Hayek's arguments, have no difficulty in knowing what they are. Of course, Hayek himself was influenced by the arguments of some of his contemporaries and has himself acknowledged one such influence in particular, that of Karl Popper. The relation between Hayek and Popper calls indeed for some comment. Popper, like Hayek, was a self-exiled Viennese who became a British citizen, a teacher at the London School of Economics, and a major social theorist in his own right. In fact, Hayek, who knew and admired Popper's *Logic of Scientific Discovery*, was instrumental in obtaining for Popper an academic post in London, and thus turning his compatriot into a colleague. From then on the two men were not only colleagues but close friends. The works of each contain laudatory references to the other. Nevertheless, although there are points of similarity in their views, as well as reciprocal influence, the resemblance is less than each, doubtless motivated by their strong personal friendship, seeks to suggest. To put it crudely: both are liberals, but Hayek is considerably more right wing.

A few words should also be said about the relation between Hayek and another colleague at the London School of Economics, Michael Oakeshott. Any reader of their respective works cannot help noticing important similarities in their ideas. Yet there seems to have been no close personal relationship between the two men, nor much if any mutual influence – certainly neither acknowledges such an influence. Indeed, Oakeshott's occasional references to Hayek's work are distinctly unenthusiastic, while Hayek, in sharp contrast to Oakeshott, explicitly repudiated the self-description 'conservative'.[1] This reciprocal wariness between the two men might seem a little puzzling, but there are in fact good reasons for it. Despite the significant measure of agreement apparent between them, they are also divided by very different fundamental philosophies. To put the point crudely once again:

both are liberals, but Hayek is above all an economic liberal. This makes him *less* right wing than Oakeshott, as will be shown below.

As noted above, Hayek besides being a major political philosopher has made significant contributions to the philosophy of social science. In both fields, his central preoccupation is to understand the relation between the individual and society. In the philosophy of social science, the problem is an ontological one (do the individual and the social constitute two distinct orders of being? How are they related?); while in the political sphere the problem for Hayek is how to reconcile social order with the protection of individual liberty (the preoccupation with liberty is manifest in the titles of all three of his major political books). The connection between the two problems is closer than might appear, because, in brief and summary terms, Hayek's solution to the political problem is to rely largely on the potentialities of what he calls *spontaneous* social order. In order to constitute a solution to the political problem, however, spontaneous social order (like any kind of social order, indeed) must *be* a certain kind of relation between individuals. It must, of course, also be possible – must be a phenomenon capable of existing.

Hayek's treatise on social ontology, *The Counter-Revolution of Science*, is an attack on what he calls 'scientism' (not, however, on science). Scientism is the unthinking and inappropriate application of natural scientific methods to the social sciences. The two do, of course, have something in common. However, according to Hayek, whereas the methodology of natural science is 'objectivist' (the study of objective facts, or phenomena perceptible to the senses), social science cannot be so because its data are *subjective*, that is, defined not in physical terms, but rather in terms of what people think about them. Thus, a 'tool' or a 'barometer' is to be defined, not as a thing with certain physical qualities, but as a thing 'intended for' some kind of human purpose: an aneroid barometer and a mercury barometer are both barometers, though they 'have nothing in common except the purpose for which men think they can be used'.[2] And barometers and hammers are both tools because men intend them to serve some purpose.

Clearly 'subjectivist' social science as conceived by Hayek is similar to Max Weber's *verstehende Soziologie*. Furthermore (and again similarly to Weber), the methodology of social science must be not only subjectivist, but also 'individualist' and 'compositive'. Subjectivity inheres in the minds of individuals (there are no 'group minds') and so the individual mind, its thoughts and purposes, must be the bedrock and starting point of social theory. 'The concepts and views held by individuals . . . form the elements from which we must build up, as it were, the more complex phenomena',[3]

including *social* entities and relations. This compositive or synthetic methodology of the social sciences, Hayek explains, differs from the case of natural
science, where an analytic method is appropriate. That is, in the natural
world the directly observable objects are wholes which scientists seek to
understand by analysing them into their parts (elements, atoms, fundamental
particles) which are often postulated rather than observed directly; whereas
in the social world, it is not social 'wholes' that are directly observable or
knowable, but rather 'the concepts and views held by individuals'. These
latter are the 'elements' whose structural connections we attempt to discern,
and in so doing to identify the various social 'wholes' that exist. This means
that individuals as such are *not* the elements of which social wholes consist:
certain 'concepts and views' of individuals are these elements. 'If the social
structure can remain the same although different individuals succeed each
other at different points, this is not because the individuals . . . are completely identical, but because they succeed each other in particular relations,
in particular attitudes they take towards other people and as the objects of
particular views held by other people about them'.[4]

It should be clear that Hayek's methodological individualism is not, as is
sometimes thought, a denial of the reality of social wholes. Rather, his view
is that the individual phenomena are the ones we know of directly, whereas
references to social wholes or social entities are properly to be thought of as
postulates or theories about the relations between individual phenomena.
Social wholes, then do indeed exist, 'if, and to the extent which, the theory
is correct which we have formed about the connection of the parts which
they imply'.[5] Thus, for example, the University of Glasgow is a social whole,
which no one has ever *seen* (though they have seen individuals and buildings
that belong to it, and quite likely the words 'University of Glasgow' written
for example over an entrance gate), but which (I venture to assert) exists,
because the relations between individual actions which the concept implies
do actually obtain. But Hayek insists on distinguishing between ideas of
individuals which *constitute* social phenomena such as the University of Glasgow, and explanatory or theoretical ideas *about* what social wholes exist.
Actually the distinction is less sharp than Hayek implies, since the ideas
people who belong to the University of Glasgow have *about* that organization also affect the actions and relations that constitute it. But the point
Hayek wants to stress is that the mere postulation of a social whole does not
guarantee its existence, because it is 'only' a theory (possibly mistaken) about
the relations between individuals. Thus it may be that the concept of 'social
class' or 'proletariat' postulates certain ideas and relations of individuals which,

in certain circumstances, do not obtain or hardly obtain, so that these social wholes do not then exist, or hardly exist. To suppose that social wholes are entities whose existence can be directly observed is, for Hayek, to commit the error of 'collectivism' – an error as much in the methodology of social science as it is in political philosophy, as we shall see. Hayek considers methodological collectivism to be an element or consequence of scientism, but in this I think he is mistaken. Possibly he was misled by the fact that some prominent scientistic social theorists, such as Marx and Durkheim, were methodological collectivists also.

Although all social phenomena are the result of intentional actions of individuals, it does *not* follow that all social phenomena are *intended by* any individual or individuals. Quite the contrary. In fact, Hayek believes, the task of social science is precisely to trace the undesigned results of the intentions and intentional actions of many individuals, and in particular to trace and explain undesigned social regularities and social order. 'If social phenomena showed no order except insofar as they were consciously designed, there would indeed be no room for theoretical sciences of society', no explanatory work for social scientists to do.[6] That such undesigned regularities exist is to Hayek beyond question – language is one indisputable example. Another celebrated example offered by Hayek is the formation of footpaths in 'wild broken country':

> At first everyone will seek for himself what seems to him to be the best path. But the fact that such a path has been used once is likely to make it easier to traverse and therefore more likely to be used again; and thus more and more clearly defined tracks arise and come to be used to the exclusion of other possible ways. Human movements through the region come to conform to a definite pattern which, although the result of deliberate decisions of many people, has yet not been consciously designed by anyone.[7]

Not only do undesigned social regularities, patterns and orders exist: the fact that they exist and can (like a pattern of footpaths) serve human purposes is of the greatest *political* importance to Hayek. What the footpath example is intended to demonstrate is that useful social institutions (of which a footpath or a pattern of footpaths is a simple example) can arise and function without any overall organization, without exercise of power or authority, without coercion, and thus without compromising individual liberty. The existence and use of the footpaths described by Hayek does not in the least interfere with the freedom of the individuals involved. We might, on the other hand,

151

imagine an alternative scenario in which a set of footpaths was designed and constructed by some authority, and persons travelling in the region were required by law to keep to one or other of these 'official' paths. In such a case individual travellers would be much less free: travellers would be forced to choose (coerced into using) one of a narrow range of paths, and it is possible that certain individuals would have been forced to construct the paths in the first place. Whether movement through the region would be more or less efficient than in the other case is an interesting question which will not be answered here. Hayek, however, might well expect it to be less efficient, for reasons to be explained.

When Hayek came, in his later books, to elaborate the political moral of his footpath example, he did so by placing at the centre of his theoretical system the concept of the *spontaneous social order*. The term was first used in *The Constitution of Liberty*, but it is in the later *Law, Legislation and Liberty* that the theory of the spontaneous social order receives its fullest statement. First, Hayek defines an *order* as

> a state of affairs in which a multiplicity of elements of various kinds are so related to each other that we may learn from our acquaintance with some spatial or temporal part of the whole to form correct expectations concerning the rest, or at least expectations which have a good chance of proving correct.[8]

More succinctly, an order is an ensemble of systematically (non-randomly) related elements. It may or may not be social. It may or may not be describable as a 'whole'. And, most importantly for Hayek, it may or may not be the product of deliberate design by a controlling intelligence. An apt example (not given by Hayek) of a designed, non-social order is a machine, while an example (given by Hayek) of an undesigned, non-social order is a biological organism. It is arguable, and has certainly been widely believed, that the universe as a whole is an undesigned order, though for believers in the Judaeo-Christian God it is a designed one. Indeed, as is well known, the so-called argument from design was for long a staple for natural theologians, who maintained that the orderliness of the universe must be the product of a (divine) Designer. Such arguments, according to Hayek, are fallacious. As is also well known, the sharpest controversy regarding the argument from design, which finally discredited it intellectually, focused on the Darwinian theory of natural biological evolution and the origin of species.[9] Acceptance of the Darwinian theory is, of course, acceptance of the reality of the evolution of undesigned order. In Hayek's view, the evolution of undesigned (spontaneous) social order is equally a reality: yet a secular political equivalent of the argument from design has been so influential that it required to be combated at every turn. This is the view that all social order (or all beneficial social order, and therefore the best possible social order) must result from conscious organization. The opposition between *spontaneous* social order and *organized* social order (or organization) is at the centre of Hayek's thinking.

What Hayek calls a social organization is very similar to Oakeshott's enterprise association. It is a social unit deliberately created and designed for a purpose.[10] In order to achieve its purpose it needs to have a structure of authority and to operate in accordance with definite rules – instrumental rules, consciously created to serve the organization's purpose. The rules of an organization typically assign and govern tasks to be carried out by individuals for the sake of its purpose – they are role specific rather than general, and have the same function as commands. Needless to say, Hayek is not opposed to social organizations any more than Oakeshott is opposed to enterprise associations (capitalist corporations are, after all, social organizations). What he is opposed to is any attempt to organize society as a whole, and the idea that all social order, or all valuable social order, must take the form of social organization.

The fallacious view that all (beneficial) social order must be the product of design Hayek ascribes to an erroneous philosophy, which he calls constructivist rationalism. At once, both a similarity to and a difference from Oakeshott are apparent. Oakeshott excoriated all 'rationalism in politics', without any qualifying adjective: the target of Hayek's attack is not *all* rationalism, but only that which aspires to guide, control and organize *all* social order.[11] This is a hubristic rationalism, so arrogantly over-confident of its own powers, so lacking in necessary humility, that those infected by it believe what according to Hayek is an impossibility and even an absurdity – that they possess all the knowledge needed for a total rational reconstruction of society. No individual mind, no elite, no political party can possibly have such knowledge. The illusion that this is possible, has even been achieved, is the source, Hayek believes, of revolutionary totalitarianism and collectivism, well-meaning or otherwise.

Hayek points here to a profound paradox of rationalization, in Max Weber's sense of the term. The more the rationalization of human life advances, the more knowledge mankind acquires, the more likely men are to succumb to the temptations of constructivist rationalism and to attempt a total 'rational' organization of society. Yet if they do so they destroy the foundations of further progress in knowledge and rationality. Total organization destroys individual freedom, and it is on freedom – not only freedom of thought, but also freedom to undertake what John Stuart Mill called 'experiments in living' – that such progress depends.[12] 'If we are to advance', Hayek says, 'we must leave room for a continuous revision of our present conceptions and ideals.'[13] Progress cannot be planned beforehand (the belief that it can is an extreme example of rationalistic hubris); it 'rests on the unpredictability of human action', which rational organization seeks to eliminate. Yet it is essential 'to leave room for the unforeseeable and the unpredictable'.[14] A progressive society, therefore must be a free society, based on spontaneous order. Indeed, 'the spontaneous order of a free society' is a frequently repeated phrase of Hayek's, and a statement of his ideal.

What, then, is the nature of a spontaneous order, how do they and how have they come about? As mentioned above, the clearest and best understood example of spontaneous order is the case of biological forms, the product of Darwinian evolution. Darwinian evolution, however, also has a social aspect or level. Many animal species are *social* – not only the well-known social insects, but (more relevantly) some of mankind's closest animal relations, the monkeys and apes. A likely implication of Darwinism is that human sociality at its origin was not hugely different from that of the apes, or of humanity's immediate ape-like ancestors. This is not to deny that there are also major differences, that human society has changed and developed enormously in the course of history, and is now very different indeed from the societies of other animals. Nor has this development been a process of strictly Darwinian evolution. Nevertheless, man is still an animal, and the continuities are not insignificant. As we shall later see, there is some ambiguity in Hayek's thinking, in so far as he stresses sometimes the continuities, sometimes the differences.

It is a feature of all spontaneous orders, social or otherwise, that their elements exhibit regularities of behaviour or, as Hayek puts it, follow certain rules.[15] This does not necessarily mean that the elements are conscious of the rules, or follow them consciously, since the elements may not even be capable of consciousness (an example of Hayek's is the elements of a crystal, which 'spontaneously' conform to the orderly relations that constitute the crystal).[16] In the case of animal societies, it is not certain to what extent the elements (animals) have consciousness, but it is quite certain that (lacking developed language) they cannot articulate the rules they follow, and are probably unaware that they do follow them. That they follow the rules is simply an observable behavioural fact. In primitive human societies, Hayek suggests, the situation was not greatly different. Only later in human development did social rules begin to be expressed in a verbal, communicable form – a form that could be taught, and consciously taken as a standard or norm. But Hayek makes two important points about this process. First, the earliest consciously articulated rules were not invented when first articulated – rather, they were articulations of pre-existing behavioural regularities. Secondly, in Hayek's opinion, human society still to this day rests on more rules than we are conscious of, or at any rate have put into words.[17] Ironically, perhaps, language itself is a prime example of a rule-governed order whose practitioners followed (and still follow) linguistic rules long before knowing what they were.

As we have just seen, Hayek considers the distinction between social rules which are simply behavioural regularities and those which are norms or standards to be one which is quite difficult to draw with any definiteness. However, he does recognize the normative rules that have evolved from a proto-normative stage as a separate category – a category of great importance, which he calls rules of conduct. On the other hand, another category of rules, which are behavioural regularities only, is equally important to him. These are the rules of behaviour in an exchange economy, for example: individuals 'will normally prefer a larger return from their efforts to a smaller one, and often . . . they will increase their efforts in a particular direction if the prospects of a return improve'.[18] These two kinds of rules together – let us call them rules of conduct and rules of market behaviour, a combination, one might say, of morality and individual purposiveness – together provide the structure, in Hayek's opinion, for a spontaneous social order of a kind enormously beneficial to human life. What is more, the two kinds of rules interconnect importantly at one particular point at least, namely, the institution of private property. Private property is, of course, a complex of rules of conduct, and at the same time a condition for the regularities of behaviour characteristic of an exchange or market economy.

By this stage it is clear that Hayek's social theory is no longer a neutral account of the evolution of human social structures, but is a defence of a particular kind of evolved social structure, one incorporating private property and a market economy – 'the spontaneous order of a free society'. But why is this particular sort of society so beneficial, in Hayek's view – so much more beneficial than any alternative, so much more beneficial than a totally organized society? Generally speaking, Hayek gives two kinds of answers to this question, one much more powerful than the other. One answer resorts to what can be called (despite Hayek's protestations to the contrary) a kind of Burkean conservatism. Spontaneously evolved social rules, especially rules of conduct, are subject to a kind of (semi-Darwinian and non-Darwinian) selection process. Those rules which 'work' will be preserved; those that do not will be dropped; in extreme cases of dysfunctional rules the societies in question may not survive. In this way a gradual refinement and improvement of such rules takes place over time. But whether or not this is true, it gives us no particular reason (other than a Burkean preference for experience over 'abstract reason') to prefer a society based on spontaneously evolved rules of conduct to one based on conscious design.

Hayek's other argument for the spontaneous order depends on the *benefits of freedom*, which are perhaps most vividly manifested in the economic sphere. Here, Hayek invites us to compare (or rather contrast) the free market system with the so-called 'planned' or collectivist economy, such as was called for by Marx and Engels (typical constructivist rationalists) in order to end the alleged 'anarchy' of the market. In Hayek's opinion this demand of the Marxian founding fathers shows a total lack of insight into the nature of an economy (quite characteristically, he does not accuse them of bad motives, but only of lack of understanding). The function of an economy can be stated in more or less utilitarian terms as, the satisfaction of individuals' wants by the production of goods and the provision of services. Hayek's argument for the free market, and against the socialistic 'planned' economy, rests on the role therein of knowledge.

In brief, the argument (which is by no means confined to the economic sphere, however) is that freedom can take advantage of far more knowledge than can any centralized plan[19] – especially if the planners claim a monopoly, an enforceable right to direct the entire economy (or any other social function). In the economic case, broadly speaking, two kinds of knowledge are necessary for the economy to perform its task – knowledge of what people want, and knowledge of ways of producing the goods and providing the services that are wanted. Hayek's simple but devastating point is that the amount of this necessary knowledge is enormous, as well as formidably complex and detailed. As a result, it can never be gathered together in a single human mind, or limited group of minds (such as those of the 'planners'). Not only is this economically necessary knowledge often of a highly specialized, particularized and localized nature, it continually changes as new ways of doing things are found (technological progress) and as individual tastes and desires change. The most benevolent planners, therefore, inevitably go about their task in ignorance of most of what they need to know. They are attempting the impossible, and the more impossible the more complex the economy. But their inevitable ignorance does not mean that the necessary knowledge is unavailable. For, as Hayek stresses, the quantity and detail of economically relevant knowledge means that it is inevitably dispersed among many individual minds.

No one individual possesses any very large fraction of this knowledge, but very many individuals possess a significant fraction of it. The only efficient way to use it, therefore, is to leave everyone free to make use of such knowledge as he has – to respond to those individual desires of which he knows, making use of such useful knowledge as he has of how to do so. This is precisely what the free market does – at the same time providing an incentive to those who have such useful knowledge to use it to satisfy the desires of others (as if moved by an invisible hand, as Adam Smith put it). This is the case for the market and against the centrally planned economy, which seems to have been triumphantly vindicated by the events of 1989–91.

It is worth stressing that Hayek's 'Austrian' defence of the free market is totally different from the standpoint of orthodox neoclassical economic theory, of which Hayek on the whole takes a dim view. The orthodox view focuses on the concept of 'perfect competition' and its supposed merits, a concept which Hayek holds to be not only unrealistic but absurd and even dangerous. 'It is difficult', he has written, 'to defend economists against the charge that for some 40 to 50 years they have been discussing competition on assumptions that, if they were true of the real world, would make it wholly uninteresting and useless.'[20] As every student of orthodox economics knows, 'perfect competition' is defined, *inter alia*, as a state of affairs in which all economic actors have 'perfect knowledge'. That this is an unrealistic assumption is obvious, but the significance of its unreality is not always appreciated. As Hayek points out, the case for the free market rests, above all, on the fact that *no* individual (or limited group of individuals) can ever know all economically relevant facts. If the perfect knowledge assumed by the theory of 'perfect competition' could occur in reality, it could of course also be known by the would-be planner, who could then claim, with a show of justification, the right to direct the economy. But the beginning of economic wisdom, Hayek claims, is recognition that no such claim is justified; that the would-be planner 'cannot acquire the full knowledge which would make mastery of the events possible'.[21]

The relation between the market and inevitably dispersed knowledge has, Hayek believes, further significance for economic theory. In economics, he believes, precise predictions of specific phenomena are impossible (if they were possible, planned economies would be possible). The Walrasian simultaneous equations used by economists to represent 'general relations between the prices and the quantities of all commodities bought and sold' include many unknowns which cannot all become knowns, many variables whose values are, in any particular situation, unknowable.[22] They do not permit the prediction of particular prices or quantities. All that economic theory can achieve is what Hayek calls general 'pattern predictions' (predictions that leave open a rather wide range of possibilities) of which indeed the Walrasian equations are an example (cognizant of Popper's philosophy of science, Hayek is careful to insist that such pattern predictions are falsifiable). Hayek suggests that the reason for this is that, unlike the physical sciences, economics, in so far as it describes economic markets, has to do with inherently 'complex phenomena', that is, in markets outcomes are determined by very many, rather than relatively few, interacting factors. But I doubt that this is correct – physical science also has great difficulty in making precise predictions in complex real–world situations (weather forecasting is a good example). Its successes tend to be confined to controlled situations and closed systems, such as the laboratory and the factory, of a kind which are generally unavailable to social scientists. A more interesting suggestion of Hayek's is that the competitive market should be looked on as a *discovery procedure*,[23] a system, that is to say, which enables economically relevant facts to be discovered (in fact encourages their discovery). It thus makes no sense, Hayek argues, to think of the market as working on 'given data'. It is precisely the fact that the data are not given, but have to be discovered, that makes the market such a potent and valuable instrument for the furtherance of human welfare.

To abolish the market and replace it by a central plan is, to Hayek, an act of economic madness. But is also means abolition of the spontaneous order of a free society, and its replacement by a hierarchical organization structured by commands and by rules having a similar function to commands, that is, the achievement of specific purposes. The rules of conduct of a spontaneous social order, Hayek stresses, have a totally different character. Like the rules of an Oakeshottian civil association, they do not subserve any particular purposes, but leave individuals free to pursue their own purposes and – very importantly for Hayek – make use of any knowledge they have or can acquire in order to further their purposes and at the same time (thanks especially to the market) to benefit others. Yet there is here a puzzle within Hayek's social theory – if not a contradiction, at least an ambiguity and a gap. This deserves some examination.

There are, in fact, a number of linked issues. Let us begin their investigation by considering Hayek's central concept, the spontaneous social order. When Hayek explains the meaning of this expression, it is often (and probably initially) the case that 'spontaneous' means 'grown' rather than 'made'. Clearly this is so in relation to such orders as biological organisms, animal societies and the earliest human social orders. What is more, Hayek often stresses the continuities between earlier and later human social orders, the gradual evolution from earlier to later. It is this that not infrequently gives his thought a Burkean if not a conservative cast (as mentioned above, he repudiates the label 'conservative', but often makes clear that he values tradition). Yet when Hayek discusses specifically modern society, the concept of spontaneous social order receives a somewhat different interpretation, the defining feature then being *the kind of rules* that structure such an order – specifically, regularities of market behaviour, and rules of conduct of a particular kind, namely rules independent of any concrete purpose or as Hayek often puts it, 'abstract' rules[24] (which can be made, as well as grown). Such a society Hayek has called by the name 'The Great Society', by which term he means a complex modern society whose individual members are left free by its rules to pursue their own purposes. And he adds, with obvious approval, that *only* such a society can bring and keep together, freely and peacefully – non-coercively – a multiplicity of individuals with varying goals and purposes. This clearly is the liberal Hayek speaking.

The problem is that 'rules of conduct' as such need not be liberal. And Hayek, particularly in the later volumes of *Law, Legislation and Liberty*, possibly to some degree but not wholly because of the influence of Popper, often stresses the difference between simple, primitive human societies and the complex, modern 'Great Society'.[25] Concomitantly there is a small but significant (and unremarked) modification of Hayek's terminology. Where before he spoke of rules of conduct, later he refers to rules of *just* conduct.[26] By the latter, it emerges, he means rules governing the behaviour of individuals that affects other individuals,[27] the implication being that in the Great Society, governed by these purpose-independent rules of just conduct, individuals are otherwise, broadly speaking, free. Here again, the contrast with primitive societies and their purpose-oriented rules is explicit. What is, however, less clear is how, despite continuities, this momentous change came about – on this Hayek offers only a brief speculation about the effect of commerce.[28] Is it then Hayek's opinion that all societies will 'naturally' (spontaneously) evolve into 'Great Societies' (or perhaps a single Great World Society) so long as power does not fall into the hands of collectivists or constructivist rationalists? Is market capitalism, contrary to the view of, for example, Max Weber, a natural and spontaneous growth? Hayek's answers to these questions are uncertain.

What is none the less clear is that, to Hayek, there are certain necessary conditions for the development of the Great Society, and other conditions which destroy it. Among the former is the institution of private property.

For Hayek there is an intimate link between private property and individual freedom, which he explains as follows. Freedom means 'the possibility of a person's acting according to his own decisions and plans, in contrast to [being] subject to the will of another', that is, to being coerced by another. Freedom requires an 'assured private sphere . . . some set of circumstances in [the individual's] environment with which others cannot interfere'.[29] Private property is such a private sphere – one secured by general rules rather than granted by an authority whose power over individuals' private spheres could become an instrument of coercion. But, as Hayek explains, an individual's freedom in modern society depends less on his himself owning property, than on the condition that certain vital material means 'not be all in the exclusive control of one other agent'.[30] Ownership of these material means 'should be sufficiently dispersed so that the individual is not dependent on particular persons who alone can provide him with what he needs or who alone can employ him'. Clearly this is an argument against socialism, in the sense of ownership of the means of production by the state, and in favour of capitalism, that is ownership thereof by a large number of private owners. 'The freedom of the employed', Hayek argues, 'depends on the existence of a great number and variety of employers' and would always be threatened 'if there were only one employer – namely, the state', which would then dispose of enormous powers of coercion. By contrast, 'in a competitive society, the employed [person] is not at the mercy of a particular employer', since alternative employment is normally available.[31]

This argument of Hayek's is a valuable one, but it is open to an objection. Hayek himself makes a qualification: an employee is not at the mercy of a particular employer, 'except in periods of extensive unemployment'. At the time of writing (March 1997) unemployment is extensive in almost all the developed economies of Europe, and has been so for a considerable number of years. The question thus arises: how characteristic is extensive unemployment of the capitalist market system? Economic theorists have long concerned themselves with the issue of the so-called trade cycle, which suggests that recurrent, quite extensive unemployment is a normal feature of the system. For a number of years it was believed that 'Keynesian' management of aggregate demand had solved this problem, but Hayek himself was a vocal and effective critic of such claims. As he wrote in his 1975 pamphlet, *Full Employment at Any Price?*, 'as soon as government assumes the responsibility to maintain full employment at whatever wages the trades unions succeed in obtaining, they no longer have any reason to take account of the unemployment their wage demands might have caused'.[32] Increases in total demand will then inevitably outstrip increases in productivity, and make accelerating inflation also inevitable. Either this process must continue until the market system is destroyed, or it must be ended, at the cost of producing far more severe unemployment than was prevented in the short run. This prediction of Hayek's arguably was vindicated by events. He adds that the inevitable unemployment 'is not the effect of a failure of "capitalism" or the market economy, but exclusively due to our own errors which past experience and available knowledge ought to have enabled us to avoid'.[33] But is unemployment so easy to avoid? The history of the trade cycle might suggest otherwise, and Hayek himself argued in an early book (*Monetary Theory and the Trade Cycle*) that '[cyclical] fluctuations [in economic activity] caused by monetary factors are unavoidable'; hence trade cycles are the price we have to pay for economic growth.[34] If this is true, it weakens Hayek's arguments as to the freedom of workers in capitalist systems.

Be that as it may, Hayek's preoccupation with the free society is central. It manifests itself, once again, in his discussion of law, and the rule of law. In Hayek's view, there has been much dangerous confusion surrounding these issues, mostly blameable on the ideas of legal positivists such as John Austin. In Hayek's view, the Austinian (and Hobbesian) concept of sovereignty is incompatible with the rule of law, and, contrary to Austin (and Hobbes), law should *not* be defined as the command of the sovereign. That definition equates law with the command-like rules of a social organization, rather than the abstract rules of conduct that characterize a free society. To define law as commands suggests that society as a whole should be an organization, and leads ultimately to totalitarianism. Hayek does admit (rather reluctantly) that it is normal to apply the term 'law' to the command-type rules of one specific organization – namely, the government. Such 'laws' are the rules by which the government organizes itself (and its servants) to achieve its purposes. But – except in a totalitarian system – government and society are not coextensive. Society's laws are, or can and should be, of a different type, namely, *enforceable rules of (just) conduct*. The rule of law, simply, means that the government, like everyone else, is subject to society's enforceable rules of just conduct. As Hayek stresses, these laws, unlike enforceable commands, are not coercive. They are either negative prohibitions, or enforce positive obligations only where the latter arise from voluntary acts (as in the case of contracts). They thus 'provide the framework within which the individual must move but within which the decisions are his'.[35] They do not subject us to another's will, or force us to serve another person's ends.

Enforceable rules of just conduct are not commands of the sovereign, because they are not commands at all. Also, in a free society characterized by the rule of law they do not emanate from the sovereign because in such a society there is no sovereign (defined by Hobbes and Austin as not subject to law). Where, then do they come from? There are two possibilities. They may be the result of acts of legislation, by a legislator or legislature. The mistake (one mistake) of legal positivists is to suppose that *all* laws have this source. But there is another, equally or more important, and historically prior – by spontaneous evolution from a society's rules of (just) conduct. As Hayek puts it, law is older than legislation. Legislation is a law-making function of governments, but it is a typical positivist mistake to suppose that legislation depends on governments. For many centuries, indeed, government was relatively little concerned with law or legislation, apart from to some degree organizing law enforcement. Even the representative assemblies of medieval Europe were much less legislatures than councils of consultation with the monarch and his government, and a forum of negotiation over and approval of the means for execution of the government's plans – above all, by the raising of taxes (as often as not, for the waging of war). In modern times, however, representative assemblies are thought of simply as legislatures, and the great bulk of modern law does indeed result from legislation.

Hayek is not, of course, opposed to legislation. There is no guarantee that a society's spontaneously evolved rules of conduct, enforceable or otherwise, are ideal, complete or incapable of improvement. Nevertheless, legislated law carries a danger. Legislators belong to government, and thus have a strong tendency to think of laws – societal laws included – as having the form of enforceable commands (as Austin did), rather than enforceable abstract rules of conduct. In effect, such law-making extends administration of the government's resources to administration of the whole of society, turning individuals into 'objects of administration'.[36] Individual liberty in modern society, in Hayek's view, has suffered seriously and sometimes grievously from this tendency, which at its worst culminated in Nazi and Soviet totalitarianism. It is no accident, Hayek says, that Soviet ideologues so often expressed a preference for administration over law. But Hayek believes, also, that even well-meaning and apparently inoffensive philosophies, such as 'democratic socialism', embody the same totalitarian logic. This was the message first proclaimed in *The Road to Serfdom*, and accounts for the outrage that book caused in many quarters.

What, however, is socialism? No doubt socialism is many things to many people, but to some socialism has meant state ownership of the means of production and state planning of the economy. Hayek's objections to these ideas have already been explained. To others, socialism is 'about equality', or social justice. Hayek is opposed to these ideas also. Only one form of equality is favoured by Hayek, namely equality before the law (that is, enforceable rules of conduct that apply equally and impartially to all).[37] So far as economic equality is concerned, it is of course incompatible with the market economy, championed by Hayek, which works by rewarding some more than others, and some not at all. So far as those who would be left indigent by the market are concerned, Hayek favours provision of a basic minimum by government action 'outside the market' (by means of redistributive taxation) but certainly not abolition of market inequalities. But he has further arguments against equality. It is, he asserts, incompatible with progress. Material progress depends (inter alia) on progress in knowledge: but 'new knowledge and its benefits can spread only gradually'. At first they will benefit only a few, before these benefits can spread to the many. New products like radios and refrigerators (they were of course new once) are at first expensive, affordable only by the wealthy. In other words, it is the wealthy who at first provide a market for such new goods, and make possible 'the experimentation with the new things that, as a result can later be made available' to the rest of society.[38] The point is that, in the long run, everybody benefits from this process – and it is only in this way, Hayek suggests, that material progress for all can take place. 'So long as [society] remains progressive . . . some must lead, and the rest must follow.'[39]

Hayek is unusual among champions of the market (unusually clear-sighted, or unusually honest) in his clear recognition that market inequalities also make equality of opportunity impossible. He is therefore explicitly opposed to it. Market inequality means not just unequal individuals, but unequal families. Since everyone's chances in life depend to a significant degree on family circumstances, unequal families means unequal opportunities. This, in Hayek's opinion, is no cause for concern, because 'the acquisition by any member of the community of additional capacities to do things which may be valuable must always be regarded as a gain for that community'.[40] This holds true whether the additional capacities arise from 'nature' or from 'nurture', from genetic inheritance or from economic inheritance, from intelligent parents or from a good home. '[If] it is desirable to harness the natural instincts of parents to equip the new generation as well as they can, there seems no sensible ground for limiting this to non-material benefits.' Similarly, Hayek opposes enforced equality of educational provision, on the grounds that here, too, it is socially beneficial that some should have advantages even if not all can have them, and that attempting to enforce equality will prevent some from getting the better education they might otherwise have had. Hayek freely admits that such inequality advantages people who do not in any way deserve to be advantaged. But he argues that the attempt to give everyone 'an equal start', if taken seriously, would require such a degree of collectivist organization of economy and society as to destroy freedom and the conditions of progress.[41]

Furthermore, society benefits greatly from private wealth, from 'men of independent means', however undeserved or unequal the wealth. 'The leadership of [private] individuals or groups who can back their beliefs financially is particularly essential in the field of cultural amenities, in the fine arts, in education and research', and 'above all, in the propagation of new ideas'[42] (Engels's support of Marx is a case in point). Many a good cause has benefited from the support of wealthy idealists – examples include abolition of slavery, penal reform and humane treatment of the insane. The fact that many wealthy persons waste their wealth in idleness or vulgar expenditure, while regrettable, does not in Hayek's view negate the point.[43]

Not only does Hayek oppose economic equality; more startlingly, he also opposes social justice. This does not, however, mean that he favours social *in*justice, or injustice of any kind. According to Hayek, injustice is a breach of obligation by an individual – breach of a rule of just conduct. In a free society, and a market economy, therefore, no question of *social* injustice can arise. For social injustice means an unjust distribution of wealth; while in a free society and a market economy the distribution of wealth cannot be blamed on an unjust act, because it cannot be blamed on *any* act. It is, rather, the unplanned and unintended outcome of innumerable separate acts of exchange. It is completely characteristic of the market that it produces overall outcomes not foreseeable or planned in advance, just because it is a free, spontaneous social order. But this does not mean that the distribution of wealth it produces is just, either – for justice, like injustice, is an attribute of individual actions only (of those that conform to rules of just conduct). To use the language of justice and injustice in relation to a distribution that no one has brought about or intended is, as one might put it, a category mistake. Hayek, here again, is exceptional among champions of the free market in not claiming that the inequalities it produces are just. He agrees that those who come off better thanks to the operations of the market do not *deserve* their advantages (or not necessarily so) – rather, they are luckier than their fellows. Hayek admits that the distribution of wealth in a free market is such that, *if* it had been brought about by design, it would have to be called very unjust.[44] Nevertheless it cannot be so described. Undeserved inequalities of wealth due to the free market are no more unjust than is unequal distribution of natural resources such as oil or minerals among countries. No one has brought about the in-equality; simply, some people are luckier than others. Indeed, the benefits of markets are incompatible with any proportioning of reward to merit or desert, however defined. The market does not reward men for virtue or even hard work, but for the economic value of their efforts and contributions. Market rewards are, and should be, *signals* to indicate to agents how they can use their abilities and knowledge to the greatest general advantage; they cannot at the same time be a recognition of merit, virtue or desert.

Hayek's polemic against social justice is not aimed only against applying the concept to a market order. For the term social justice is not meaningless, nor is it always inappropriate to describe a distribution of wealth as just or unjust. On the contrary, it is appropriate if and only if the distribution has been brought about and maintained deliberately. But that can be the case only if the market is abolished, and replaced by a collectivist organization of the economy – an organization so total that everyone's wealth is determined by a central authority.[45] If social justice means distribution of wealth accord-ing to merit or desert, in order to achieve it the central authority would, first of all, have to adopt and impose a definition of merit (in itself a highly contentious matter), and would then have to allocate the appropriate quan-tity of goods to all members of society (presumably allocation could not be in the form of money, which would lead to unsanctioned trades). Since market signals would no longer motivate economic activity, the economy would have to be run by commands, including direction of labour. To call for social justice is to call for such an economic system, whether the partisans of social justice know it or not. It is to call for the total extinction of all economic freedom, and all its benefits.

Despite all this, Hayek fully admits the motivating power of the concept of social justice – that, indeed, is what makes it so dangerous. It appeals to powerful, but misguided, moral sentiments – sentiments inherited, in Hayek's opinion, from mankind's early history, which was spent (like most of his history) in small face-to-face bands and troops, whose members shared com-mon ends, and corresponding feelings of solidarity.[46] Such sentiments are not appropriate to the large, and largely anonymous, Great Society, in which individuals, as they pursue their own ends, are dependent on the efforts and knowledge of millions of others who are unknown to them. Such a society has to operate on quite different principles. To apply the concept of social justice to it is to invite disaster – indeed, to invite totalitarianism. Hayek concludes: 'the phrase "social justice" is not, as most people probably feel, an innocent expression of good will towards the less fortunate . . . If political discussion is to become honest it is necessary that people should recognise that the term is intellectually disreputable, the mark of demagogy or cheap journalism which reputable thinkers ought to be ashamed to use'.[47]

It is necessary to repeat that, despite these strong words, Hayek is not an advocate of *laissez-faire* or the minimal state. Unlike Oakeshott and Nozick, he advocates state provision of a minimum income for the unfortunate.[48] But he does not see this as a matter of justice. The recipients of such a minimum income do not *deserve* it any more than the rest of us deserve the income that the market enables us to enjoy. They should receive it, simply because it is right to relieve, or better, prevent, suffering. Nor, as we shall see later in more detail, is Hayek opposed in principle to the welfare state, though he is certainly highly critical of many aspects of the way it has developed in practice. But he firmly opposes the idea that anyone has the right to a particular share of total wealth, or that the state should use its coercive power to guarantee such shares.

We have by now seen the intensity, and the grounds, of Hayek's hostility to such fundamental pillars of the socialist project as central planning of the economy, state ownership of the means of production, economic equality and social justice. It was in *The Road to Serfdom*, in 1944, that his critique was first broached, in a highly unpropitious climate of opinion. At a time when Stalin's Soviet Union was allied to the Western democracies in a life and death struggle against Hitler's Third Reich, even Hayek's suggestion that there was in fact little to choose between Bolshevism and Fascism, later commonplace enough, earned a hostile reception. Not only Marxists, who interpreted Fascism as the response of capitalism to the communist challenge, saw the Fascists and Bolsheviks as opposite poles. To Hayek, they were similar above all as hostile collectivist reactions against liberal capitalist civilization, and as such both forms of socialism.[49] Even the collectivism of moderate democratic socialism – so widely acceptable at the time that Hayek dedicated his 1944 book 'to the socialists of all parties' – threatened to become, in his view, a 'road to serfdom'. Hayek's warning, that in the process of fighting National Socialism the upholders of Western civilization were in danger of becoming like it, was to many a peculiarly offensive paradox.

In *The Road to Serfdom* Hayek explores the affinities between revolutionary socialism and Fascism at a number of levels.[50] He points out that the Marxist-influenced socialist movement was an organization of the industrial workers against the capitalist class, premised on the assumption that the 'middle class' was insignificant and would disappear. It 'completely disregarded the

rise of a new middle class, the countless army of clerks and typists, administrative workers and school teachers, tradesmen and small officials and the
lower ranks of the professions'. The economic position of members of this
class, between the two world wars, was in fact worsening relative to the
industrial workers and was even, not infrequently, worse in absolute terms.
Since the classic socialist parties had no interest in them, there were 'bound
to arise rival socialist movements' to appeal to this disadvantaged and resent-
ful class. In Hayek's view 'Fascism and National Socialism are a sort of mid-
dle-class socialism', also hostile to the capitalist system and demanding a
redistribution of wealth in accordance with their ideas of 'social justice'.[51]
Furthermore, in their organization these movements borrowed many techniques pioneered by the Marxian socialists in an attempt to integrate the
entire life of their followers into the party – party organizations for children,
party clubs for sports and games such as football and hiking, party uniforms,
party modes of greeting and forms of address and so on.[52] The bitter conflicts
between the Fascists and Nazis and the 'older socialist parties', says Hayek,
were 'very largely . . . the kind of conflict that is bound to arise between
rival socialist factions'.[53]

Despite these conflicts, the affinities between the two kinds of socialist
movement manifest themselves in some surprising ways. A strikingly large
number of Nazi and Fascist leaders in Germany and Italy, Hayek points out,
were former socialists (Mussolini is a famous example), and the same is true
of rank-and-file recruits.[54] Perhaps this is not so surprising if, as Hayek suggests, the anti-Semitism of Hitler's followers was largely founded on popular
German and Austrian hatred of a stereotypical image of the Jew as capitalist
(widespread dislike of commercial pursuits having made the latter relatively
much more accessible than, say, the professions to the alien race).[55] Was it
not, after all (though Hayek does not mention it) the orthodox German
Marxist socialist leader, August Bebel, who called anti-Semitism 'the socialism of fools'? It is also the case that some of the leading theoretical critics of
capitalist individualism, such as Johann Fichte in Germany, Thomas Carlyle
in Britain and Georges Sorel in France, have a notably ambiguous status
such that it is plausible to interpret them as precursors or allies of either
socialism or fascism or both. In his chapter entitled 'The socialist roots of
Nazism', Hayek shows in considerable detail how the arguments of leading
proto-Nazi theorists, for example Spengler and Moeller van den Bruck, explicitly endorse socialist ideas at the same time as they express hatred of
liberal individualism.[56] In these writers it is literally true that sympathy for
socialism is combined with virulent nationalism. Hayek traces their intellec-

tual pedigree back through theorists such as Paul Lensch and Johann Plenge as far as Werner Sombart. Sombart was a celebrated sociologist and, Hayek tells us, an enthusiastic Marxian socialist who, motivated by his hatred of capitalism, made the intellectual journey to an extreme militaristic nationalism. In his 'notorious' 1915 book, *Händler und Helden* (Merchants and Heroes), 'this old socialist welcomed the "German War" as the inevitable conflict between the commercial civilisation of England and the heroic culture of Germany'.[57] The message of the former socialist Sombart in this book is simple: it is to oppose the heroic warrior spirit of the Germans, which sacrifices the individual to the people and the state, to the contemptible commercial philosophy of individual happiness, individual rights and individual freedom, represented by the French and, above all, the English. In Hayek's view, Sombart's intellectual evolution was not capricious nor incomprehensible but symptomatic and representative.

If *The Road to Serfdom* was intended largely as a warning, Hayek's later books include some specific policy prescriptions and even proposals for constitutional reform (this possibly accounts for Oakeshott's dismissal of Hayek as a (rationalist?) pedlar of plans, albeit of 'a plan to prevent planning'). For example, a chapter of *The Constitution of Liberty* is devoted to social security. Here Hayek accepts the 'unquestioned necessity' of communal provision for the needy, organized by the state on a universal basis, and at a level, in a comparatively wealthy society, more generous than is 'absolutely necessary to keep alive and in health'.[58] This will involve the state using its coercive powers to compel individuals to provide financially for the needs of old age, unemployment, sickness, disability and so on, through taxation and compulsory insurance.[59] But there are two things which, Hayek says, such a state-organized system of social security should never do.[60] It should never be turned into an engine of 'social justice', aiming to ensure 'fair shares' of wealth for everyone (as distinct from relief of poverty and suffering). Secondly, the state should never enforce a monopoly of provision of such services. People should not be (here as elsewhere) subjected to 'compulsory membership in a unitary organization controlled by the state'.[61] Hayek warns that the supposed superior efficiency of such a unitary state system will in the long run be offset by the inevitable long-run inefficiency of 'all sheltered monopolies'. Hayek's opposition to state monopoly provision is asserted with particular force in relation to education, where (issues of efficiency apart) he is (like John Stuart Mill before him) above all fearful of the opportunities for control of minds that such a monopoly would create.

In another chapter of *The Constitution of Liberty* Hayek addresses the question of how to finance social security and state provision generally. Here he broaches a theme which later came to preoccupy him – the problem of democracy. Although a supporter of democracy, Hayek is not a supporter of 'majority rule'.[62] He rejects the 'sovereignty of the people', because he rejects sovereignty altogether, as incompatible with individual liberty and the rule of law. In relation to the finance of governmental services through taxation, however, what is at issue is rather individual property rights. To put it simply, Hayek fears that the taxation system in a democracy can be used by the majority to rob the minority – the wealthy minority. Progressive taxation for example (more than proportionate taxation of larger incomes) is liable to constitute injustice of this kind. Hayek makes clear that he is referring, not to income tax as such, but to the overall tax burden (progressive income tax is justified to offset the regressiveness of indirect taxation). To be just, therefore, progressive taxation must take the form, not of penalizing a minority, but of benefiting a minority – the poor minority. It is perfectly legitimate that a majority 'tax itself to assist a minority', but not that it tax a minority to benefit itself.[63] In other words, the principle of just taxation is that the highest rate of taxation in the system must be that which the majority pays.

The problems of majoritarian democracy and how to deal with them are the theme of the third volume of *Law, Legislation and Liberty*, entitled by Hayek *The Political Order of a Free People*. There is no doubting Hayek's unhappiness at the working of democracy in advanced industrial society, which he describes as 'forming organized majorities for supporting a programme of particular actions in favour of special groups'[64] – a process which paradoxically produces results contrary to the moral principles of the majority. What political scientists refer to as 'coalition formation', in a situation unconstrained or inadequately constrained by moral rules (rules of just conduct), amounts to a bargaining process among organized interests for the power to use the state's coercive force to their own advantage and at the expense of other groups. Democratic politicians trying to form a government have no option but to offer bribes to such groups – resulting in the rule of what Bentham and John Stuart Mill called 'sinister interests'.[65] Political parties are coalitions of such interests rather than unions of believers in particular principles. Thus democratic government is unlikely to result in policies that Hayek would consider either wise or just.

For this state of affairs Hayek does not blame the politicians, but rather the structure of our democracy (he calls it 'an inherent corruption which the most virtuous and decent man cannot escape').[66] The problem, as he sees it, is that democratic 'legislatures' are actually organized for (and 'legislators' attuned to) government rather than legislation in the proper sense, that is, the enactment of enforceable rules of just conduct, to which acts of government ought to be subject. Thus they enact policies that run counter to the rules of conduct which (if asked) they would endorse. The solution to the problem, then, is to restore the supremacy of rules of conduct, or the 'rule of law' – as Hayek puts it, to replace the rule of the majority by 'the rule of laws approved by the majority'.[67]

To this end Hayek proposes a radical reform of the democratic constitution – so radical a reform, indeed, that he can have had scant expectation of its ever being enacted. Probably this proposal (like Arendt's proposals for 'council democracy') should be considered less as practical politics than as the staking out of a position, or an exploration of the institutional embodiment of fundamental principles. Hayek's 'model constitution' would establish, first, a Legislative Assembly, charged with the *sole* function of determining the rules of just conduct to be enforced on society. The state's coercive powers, according to this constitution, must be exercised only in obedience to such laws. Laws made by the Legislative Assembly must be not only general in a formal sense, but *abstract*, that is, aiming not to achieve any particular purpose or to affect particular groups, but to apply to 'an indefinite number of unknown future instances'[68] (Hayek intends this to be a justiciable criterion, in order to avoid the familiar problem of pseudo-generality.) Achievement of particular purposes (policy) would be the province of a second or Governmental Assembly, whose actions would be constrained by the enforceable rules of just conduct. Both assemblies, Hayek says, would be representative democratic assemblies, but differently constituted.[69] The Governmental Assembly would be the arena of party politics of the familiar kind, chosen in the familiar way. But the higher Legislative Assembly should *not* be under the sway of party politics – it should be a forum of opinions, not of interests. Hayek suggests, therefore, that it should consist of persons elected 'at a relatively mature age, for fairly long periods' – say, fifteen years – and not eligible for re-election. This could be brought about by having an election every year in which those citizens turning 45 years of age in that year would choose representatives from their age group to serve for fifteen years. 'The result would be a legislative assembly of men and women between their 45th and 60th years, one-fifteenth of whom would be replaced every year.'[70] Men and women chosen on this basis would be in their prime and – most importantly – completely above the party battle. To complete the scheme, Hayek would create also a Constitutional Court charged with resolving conflicts between the two assemblies and ensuring that each remained within its constitutionally defined sphere of competence.

It is not necessary to go into all the details of Hayek's 'model constitution' (most of which concern the highly unfamiliar Legislative Assembly). Suffice it to say that one might think twice about entrusting the highest authority in the state to a body in relation to which one could exercise a vote only once in one's life (or never, if one was so unfortunate as to die before reaching the age of 45). As one critic has remarked, Hayek's Legislative Assembly looks rather too much like an oligarchy of the middle-aged. His scheme for the Governmental Assembly (not, however, the Legislative Assembly) also includes a most regrettable suggestion that government employees and pensioners, and other recipients of government welfare benefits, be disenfranchised: 'that civil servants, old age pensioners, the unemployed, etc., should have a vote on how they should be paid out of the pocket of the rest . . . is hardly a reasonable arrangement',[71] says Hayek. This is a sadly mean-spirited suggestion which would, of course, give governments a powerful incentive to ignore the plight of the unemployed and other needy people. It should itself be ignored.

As this regrettable coda indicates, Hayek, though in many ways remarkably clear-eyed and frank about the working of the market system, is not without his blind spots. He freely admits, for example, that the functioning of the market order has to involve, not only reward for success, but also punishment for failure and mistakes ('the principle of negative feedback'), and thus involves the disappointment of many individual hopes, 'unmerited failure' for not a few, and a considerable degree of 'risk and uncertainty' for all. It creates, but disregards, 'the pain of unfulfilled desire'.[72] Nothing or little is guaranteed in the spontaneous order of a free society – for example no guarantee can be offered that a person's gifts and talents will find fulfilling expression rather than be wasted.[73] All these aspects Hayek acknowledges, but it is arguable that he does not take them seriously enough. It is not that, like Oakeshott, he takes a totally non-utilitarian view of social institutions – on the contrary, despite some derogatory references to utilitarian philosophers of the Benthamite kind (who seem to him to be constructivist rationalists obsessed with *calculations* of utility),[74] it is clear that for Hayek a major (or the major) criterion is how best to facilitate the exploitation of useful knowledge for human benefit. His defence of the free or market society is, simply, that despite its drawbacks no other system achieves this better, or as well.

Nevertheless, others may give more weight to the drawbacks – to the negative effects on the quality of life due to what Marxists call the 'commodification of labour' (treatment of human beings as pure resources, to be employed when their employment is profitable and dismissed as soon as dismissal is more profitable), the destruction of communities when the industries on which they depend fail, the demoralizing effect of lengthy un-employment, the tendency to what Marcuse calls 'moronization' through a market-dominated system of mass culture. In effect, Hayek tells us these evils cannot be cured except by means of worse evils. Perhaps he is too defeatist. And he also seems blind, or rather half-blind, to another aspect of modern capitalism, one so much stressed by Weber – its increasing reliance on large-scale, bureaucratic organization. Here and there he does indeed notice, and indeed deplore, the effect of this fact on the modern mind-set – the fact that so many people are employed in large organizations encourages them to think of remuneration as something determined by an authority, for example.[75] Nevertheless, his continual references to the free or market order obscure the degree to which modern capitalism is hierarchical and bureau-cratic. He should be more concerned than he is (as Weber was) about the implications of this for individual freedom.

Notes

1   F. A. Hayek, *The Constitution of Liberty* (Routledge and Kegan Paul, London, 1960), pp. 397ff.
2   F. A. Hayek, *The Counter-Revolution of Science: Studies on the Abuse of Reason* (Free Press of Glencoe, 1955), pp. 26–7.
3   Ibid., p. 38.
4   Ibid., p. 34.
5   Ibid., p. 55.
6   Ibid., p. 39.
7   Ibid., p. 40.
8   F. A. Hayek, *Law, Legislation and Liberty,* vol. 1: *Rules and Order* (Routledge and Kegan Paul, London, 1973), p. 36.
9   Hayek, *The Constitution of Liberty*, p. 59.
10   Hayek, *Rules and Order*, p. 49.
11   Ibid., 5, 29.
12   Hayek, *The Constitution of Liberty*, pp. 33–5, 41, 110.
13   Ibid., p. 23.
14   Ibid., pp. 38, 29.
15   Hayek, *Rules and Order*, p. 43.
16   Ibid., p. 39.
17   Ibid., p. 19.
18   Ibid., p. 45.

19   Hayek, *The Constitution of Liberty*, pp. 22, 24–5; F. A. Hayek, *Law, Legislation and Liberty*, vol. 2: *The Mirage of Social Justice* (Routledge and Kegan Paul, London, 1976), pp. 109ff.

20   F. A. Hayek, *New Studies in Philosophy, Politics, Economics and the History of Ideas* (Routledge and Kegan Kegan Paul, London, 1978), p. 179.

21   F. A. Hayek, *Full Employment at Any Price?* (Institute of Economic Affairs, London, 1975), pp. 34–5, 41–2.

22   F. A. Hayek, 'The theory of complex phenomena', in *Readings in the Philosophy of Social Science*, ed. M. Martin and L. C. McIntyre (MIT Press, Cambridge, Mass., 1994), p. 62.

23   Hayek, *New Studies*, pp. 179ff.

24   Cf. Hayek, *Rules and Order*, pp. 45–6.

25   Hayek, *The Constitution of Liberty*, pp. 151–2.

26   Cf. Hayek, *Rules and Order*, p. 100.

27   Hayek, *The Mirage of Social Justice*, p. 33.

28   Hayek, *Rules and Order*, p. 82.

29   Hayek, *The Constitution of Liberty*, pp. 12–13, 139–40.

30   Ibid., p. 141.

31   Ibid., p. 121.

32   F. A. Hayek, *Full Employment at Any Price?* It should not be supposed that Keynes himself ever advocated such a policy. He died, in fact, many years before the full development of the demand-management strategy whose supporters invoked his name.

33   Ibid., p. 24.

34   F. A. Hayek, *Monetary Theory and the Trade Cycle*, tr. N. Kaldor and H. M. Groome (Jonathan Cape, London, 1933), p. 185.

35   Hayek, *The Constitution of Liberty*, p. 152.

36   Ibid., p. 213.

37   Ibid., p. 85.

38   Ibid., p. 44.

39   Ibid., p. 45.

40   Ibid., p. 88.

41   Ibid., p. 92.

42   Ibid., p. 125.

43   Ibid., pp. 127–30.

44   Hayek, *The Mirage of Social Justice*, p. 64.

45   Hayek, *The Constitution of Liberty*, pp. 231–2.

46   Hayek, *The Mirage of Social Justice*, pp. 42, 88.

47   Ibid., p. 97.

48   Hayek, *The Constitution of Liberty*, p. 101.

49   F. A. Hayek, *The Road to Serfdom* (Routledge and Kegan Paul, London, 1944), pp. 20, 22.

50   Ibid., p. 86.
51   Ibid., p. 87.
52   Ibid., p. 85.
53   Ibid., p. 87.
54   Ibid., pp. 21–2.
55   Ibid., p. 104.
56   Ibid., pp. 124–5.
57   Ibid., p. 126.
58   Hayek, *The Constitution of Liberty*, p. 285.
59   Ibid., pp. 286–7.
60   Ibid., p. 289.
61   Ibid., p. 287.
62   Ibid., p. 106.
63   Ibid., p. 314.
64   F. A. Hayek, *Law, Legislation and Liberty*, vol. 3: *The Political Order of a Free People* (Routledge, London, 1979), p. 3.
65   Ibid., p. 13. Cf. J. S. Mill, *Consideration on Representative Government*, ch. 6.
66   Ibid., p. 11.
67   Ibid., p. 133.
68   Ibid., p. 109.
69   Ibid., p. 112.
70   Ibid., p. 113.
71   Ibid., p. 120.
72   Hayek, *The Mirage of Social Justice*, p. 71; Hayek, *The Constitution of Liberty*, pp. 45, 82.
73   Hayek, *The Constitution of Liberty*, p. 80.
74   Hayek, *The Mirage of Social Justice*, pp. 17–19.
75   Hayek, *The Constitution of Liberty*, p. 122.

Further reading

By Hayek

F. A. Hayek, *The Road to Serfdom*, Routledge and Kegan Paul, London, 1944.

F. A. Hayek, *The Counter-Revolution of Science: Studies on the Abuse of Reason*, Free Press of Glencoe, 1955.

F. A. Hayek, *The Constitution of Liberty*, Routledge and Kegan Paul, London, 1960.

F. A. Hayek, *Studies in Philosophy, Politics and Economics*, Routledge and Kegan Paul, London, 1967.

F. A. Hayek, *Full Employment at Any Price?*, Institute of Economic Affairs, London, 1975 (includes 'The pretence of knowledge', Hayek's Nobel Prize lecture).

F. A. Hayek, *New Studies in Philosophy, Politics, Economics and the History of Ideas*, Routledge and Kegan Paul, London, 1978.

F. A. Hayek, *Law, Legislation and Liberty*, Routledge and Kegan Paul, London, 1982 (previously published in 3 volumes in 1973, 1976 and 1979).

F. A. Hayek, *The Fatal Conceit: The Errors of Socialism*, ed. W. W. Bartley III, Routledge, London, 1988.

F. A. Hayek, *Hayek on Hayek: An Autobiographical Dialogue*, ed. S. Kresge and L. Wenar, Routledge, London, 1994.

F. A. Hayek, 'The theory of complex phenomena' in M. Martin and L. C. McIntyre (eds), *Readings in the Philosophy of Social Science*, MIT Press, Cambridge, Mass., 1994.

On Hayek

N. P. Barry, *Hayek's Social and Economic Philosophy*, Macmillan, London, 1979.

J. Birner and R. van Zijp (eds), *Hayek, Coordination and Evolution*, Routledge, London, 1994.

S. Brittan, 'The wisdom of the market', *Times Literary Supplement*, 9 March 1994, p. 235.

E. Butler, *Hayek: His Contribution to the Political and Economic Thought of Our Time*, Temple Smith, Hounslow, 1983.

A. Gamble, *Hayek: The Iron Cage of Liberty*, Polity Press with Basil Blackwell, Oxford, 1996.

H. S. Gissurarson, *Hayek's Conservative Liberalism*, Garland, New York, 1987.

J. Gray, *Hayek on Liberty*, Basil Blackwell, Oxford, 1984, 1986.

C. Kukathas, *Hayek and Modern Liberalism*, Clarendon Press, Oxford, 1989.

8
Karl Popper: Critical Rationalism and the Open Society

Like his slightly older friend and colleague Friedrich Hayek, Karl Popper was born in Vienna (in 1902) but left his native Austria to settle, eventually, in Britain, where he became a citizen, and a teacher at the London School of Economics and Political Science. In Popper's case, however, departure from his homeland was not voluntary, but an exile made necessary by the rise of Fascism in central Europe in the 1930s. Having left Austria in 1937 (just a year before Hitler's invasion) Popper made his home in New Zealand, joining Hayek in London only in 1946. Unlike Hayek he continued to reside in Britain until his death in 1994. For many years Popper was a highly controversial figure, disliked in particular by the Marxist left because of his critique of revolution. Yet politically his position (as will be shown below) was far from right wing – much less so, certainly, than that of Hayek, although (as remarked in a previous chapter) the mutual friendship between the two men led them always to play down their theoretical differences. Political figures of both the moderate right and the moderate left (for example the Conservative minister Sir Edward Boyle and the Labour MP and philosopher Bryan Magee) have acknowledged his influence on them. Popper achieved fame as a champion of liberal democracy, and it is therefore perhaps not surprising that he received a knighthood from the British state in 1965.

While Hayek and Popper are both liberals, the differences between their respective brands of liberalism may have something to do with the differing intellectual starting points from which each approached politics. Whereas Hayek was first of all an economist, whose conception of a liberal society was shaped by his understanding of the free market, Popper was (and remained) a philosopher, in particular a philosopher of knowledge and of science. There is no doubt that Popper's political theory builds on his analysis of the scientific enterprise, of the conditions necessary for the growth of knowledge, and for rational thought in general. In Popper's eyes human beings are, in all areas of their activities, *problem-solving animals* – they encounter problems, try to solve them and may succeed, but in doing so always encounter (and often create) new problems. They make progress, but never achieve perfection or finality – there are always further problems to solve. They are both *rational* and *fallible* creatures who, as Popper never tired of repeating, make mistakes, but can *learn from their mistakes*. Popper's name for this philosophy of knowledge (which is at the same time a view of the human condition) is *critical rationalism*.

Clearly, the link between Popper's political theory and his epistemology is a close one, and it is a moot point whether his contribution to the philosophy of politics or of science is the more important. Certainly his *Logik der Forschung* of 1934 is a landmark in the latter field. Yet, somewhat paradoxically, because that book was not published in English translation, as *The Logic of Scientific Discovery*, until 1959, it was as a political theorist that Popper first became known to anglophone readers. His first important political work, *The Poverty of Historicism* (whose title is obviously intended as a riposte to Marx's *Poverty of Philosophy*), though not published in book form until 1957, had appeared in print in the form of three articles in the journal *Economica* as early as 1944 and 1945. (The 1957 edition added an important preface, however.) Popper's major work of political theory, *The Open Society and Its Enemies*, was published in 1945. This is a work in two volumes which develop Popper's own political philosophy through a critique of that of major figures of the past considered by Popper to be also major influences on the present – above all, Plato (in the first volume) and Marx (in the second). The later collection of essays entitled *Conjectures and Refutations* (1963) contains material on all of Popper's philosophical interests, including an important essay in political theory, 'Towards a rational theory of tradition'. It was not until 1972, with the publication of *Objective Knowledge*, that Popper's epistemology took its definitive form (more or less). Four years later came his illuminating 'intellectual autobiography', *Unended Quest*, which had previously appeared as part of a volume on Popper in *The Library of Living Philosophers*.

Before embarking on an exposition of Popper's views, it is of interest to compare and contrast some general aspects of his position with that of another great twentieth-century political theorist, Michael Oakeshott. There are some similarities, but less in their opinions than in the objects of their interests. Both are concerned with politics (in Oakeshott's terms, a part of practice), science, history and philosophy, and the relations between them, if any. But their substantive views on those questions are very different.

Oakeshott in fact (in *Experience and Its Modes*) denies all relationship between them, claiming that each is a world of its own, whereas Popper (much more convincingly) sees a high degree of mutual relevance linking philosophy, science, practice and politics. This leads to marked, but not total, disagreement on 'rationalism in politics' (to use Oakeshott's phrase). And, in contrast to Oakeshott's philosophical idealism, Popper is an uncompromising adherent of metaphysical realism (he often calls it commonsense realism) – the view that the physical world is an independent reality, and that physical science is an attempt to describe and explain that world truly – to give us 'objective knowledge' thereof.

Popper's book *Objective Knowledge* has a sub-title: 'An Evolutionary Approach'. Both title and sub-title indicate fundamental aspects of Popper's epistemology. Another fundamental element is his ontological pluralism, or theory of the *three worlds*: 'The first is the physical world or the world of physical states; the second is the mental world or the world of mental states; and the third is the world of intelligibles, or of *ideas in the objective sense*.' To the third world (or world 3) belong, for example, theories, logical relations, arguments and what Popper calls problem situations. Although the three worlds are distinct, and none is reducible to the others, they are not (unlike Oakeshottian modes) unrelated. In obvious ways the mental world (world 2) interacts with the physical world; and the world of ideas is wholly the product of the human mind. Nevertheless, once produced, it is autonomous. For example, the natural numbers, which belong to world 3, are creations of human thought, but it is nevertheless the case that certain objective truths and relations hold of them, whether or not anyone is aware of it. To a certain extent, the three worlds illustrate Popper's evolutionary perspective, for there was certainly a time when only the first or physical world existed: the mental world evolved from the physical world, and the world of ideas from the mental world.

One important interrelation between the three worlds is the following: human beings make descriptive statements (including explanatory laws and theories) about the physical world (as well as about the other worlds). These statements are *products* of the (human) mental world, they are *about* the physical world, they *belong* to the world of ideas. Despite these connections, none of the three worlds is reducible to another. Thus, descriptive statements about the physical world (for example physical science) are not (contrary to positivism) predictions about our experiences, which belong to the mental world, even though certain physical states can indeed be expected to give rise to predictable mental experiences as a result of the interaction of worlds 1 and 2. Thus the criterion of truth, so far as these statements is concerned, is not in any way subjective, does not inhere in the subjective mental world (which of course includes beliefs) but in their correspondence or otherwise with the facts of the physical world. The criterion of truth is, in other words, objective, despite the fact that every statement about the world consists of words and concepts that are human mental creations. Popper is immovably opposed to every attempt to locate the criterion of truth in the beliefs of any group or class or historical epoch – to every form of metaphysical idealism or relativism. Human beliefs cannot be in any sense the criterion of truth, because human knowledge is inherently fallible – a fact of the greatest political importance, as we shall see.

It is equally important politically that human beings are not only fallible, but rational also – more precisely, that they share, or rather can share, a common, objective rationality. This makes possible rational argument and rational agreement. Equally important, it makes possible rational criticism, in both the social and the scientific spheres. Fundamental here are the objective truths of logic, including in particular the law of contradiction, a truth of world 3 available to rational minds of world 2, which is indispensable to the objectivity of science, and to the possibility of scientific progress: for Popper's philosophy of science depends on the detection of contradictions between the universal descriptive laws characteristic of science and particular descriptions based on experience. If such an empirically generated particular description is accepted as true, then any general law which it contradicts must be accounted false – the latter is, as Popper puts it, (objectively) falsified. Empirical falsifiability is, in fact, Popper's famous criterion of a scientific statement – his demarcation criterion, as Popper typically called it. To put the matter more formally: a universal law of the form 'All As are Bs' (or 'As are always Bs', or – to adopt a formulation more appropriate to causal laws – 'Whenever A occurs, B occurs') is equivalent to a *negative* law of the form 'No A is (ever) not-B' (or, 'A never occurs without B occurring') – laws which can clearly be falsified if any particular A is found (observed) to be not-B, or if a particular occurrence of A is found (observed) without the concomitant occurrence of B. Popper stresses that the scientific *attitude* to the empirically falsifiable laws of science is to seek to falsify them, or at least to test them, by ever more stringent tests; and to acknowledge the falsification of any that fail them. The failure of Marxists (among others) to adopt this attitude is one reason why Popper brands them as unscientific, or rather pseudo-scientific.

The degree of empiricism involved in Popper's philosophy of science led critics such as Marcuse and other members of the Frankfurt School to pillory Popper as a positivist – a somewhat ironic fact, since Popper always saw himself as an enemy of positivism. In the first place, Popper explicitly distances himself from the logical positivists (the so-called 'Vienna Circle' and their followers) by stressing that his empirical demarcation criterion is a criterion of *science*, not of *meaningfulness* – metaphysics and ethics are thus by no means meaningless, even though neither is science. Furthermore, Popper's falsificationism is actually intended as a refutation of the logical positivist principle of *verificationism*, the doctrine that a meaningful statement, and *a fortiori* a scientific statement, must be empirically verifiable. Although designed to exalt the physical sciences over all other knowledge claims, the verification principle has the paradoxical consequence of making scientific laws meaningless, because empirical verification of a universal law is impossible. This is a simple matter of logic, plus the inescapable fact that observation is necessarily of particular cases: no universal statement is logically justified by knowledge of particular cases, no matter how many. Hence no matter how many empirical tests conform to a scientific law (corroborate it, as Popper says) the law is not verified. Even if all of millions of observed As have been Bs, it remains possible that the next A to be observed will turn out to be not-B. Nor does such a weight of empirical evidence show even the *probable* truth of the law, as the history of science plentifully demonstrates. In other words, inductive reasoning, relied on by the logical positivists to support their principle of verificationism, is radically unsound. All scientific laws, according to Popper's doctrine, remain unproven hypotheses or 'conjectures', whose merit (or verisimilitude) is indeed a function of the quantity and variety of their empirical corroboration, but which can never be established beyond challenge. While it is theoretically possible that we might arrive at a set of true universal physical laws that describe and explain the natural world, we can never know this to be the case. The pursuit of scientific knowledge is in principle endless.

To put the point slightly differently, scientific *progress* is unending (so long, that is, as scientists understand the nature of science, and remain fertile in the invention of new theories). Popper's philosophy of science does not involve any relativism or scepticism about truth, only fallibilism about our knowledge. It also provides clear and (Popper asserts) rational criteria for the rejection and (tentative) acceptance of scientific hypotheses, and for choosing between rival hypotheses – one should prefer whatever hypothesis has the highest degree of empirical corroboration, or verisimilitude, according to the known evidence. It is a notable fact that this conception of science has found favour with a number of very distinguished scientists – for example the physicist Hermann Bondi, and the Nobel prize-winning biologists Sir

Peter Medawar and Sir John Eccles (with the latter of whom Popper collaborated in a book about the science and philosophy of mind).[1]

It may now be a little clearer what Popper intended by giving his book *Objective Knowledge* the sub-title 'An Evolutionary Approach'. So far as physical science is concerned, his picture is not merely of evolution, but of (objective) progress. What is more, Popper believes the 'logic of scientific discovery' to be basically the same in the social as in the physical sciences – in principle, that is, or potentially, because it is clear that (partly because of misunderstandings of the nature of science, as well as a weakness for unfalsifiable verbiage, on the part of social scientists) the potential remains so far largely unrealized. We shall return to this point, and also to Popper's evolutionism. But in the meantime it is worth mentioning Popper's implacable hostility to 'dialectical logic' of the kind championed by Marcuse and other philosophers influenced by Hegel. Marcuse, it may be recalled, preferred dialectical to orthodox logic because the latter refuses to tolerate contradictions. As Popper puts it,[2] dialecticians wish to discard the orthodox law of contradiction (or 'law of the exclusion of contradictions') on the grounds that contradictions (for example between 'thesis' and 'antithesis') exist in reality, are 'the moving forces' of progress both in reality and in thought, and are thus no logical mistake but rather are extremely 'fertile'. To this Popper responds that contradictions (or rather discovery of them) may indeed be extremely fertile, and necessary to the progress of thought – but only on the condition that they are *not* tolerated, that is, are taken as a reason for criticism and a sign of the need to improve our theories and thus remove the contradictions. It should be clear how fundamental this position of Popper's is to his philosophy of science, his concept of scientific progress, and his 'critical rationalism' in general.

Let us return to Popper's evolutionism. Since the fact of evolution in the world is so important to Popper, it is not surprising that he devotes considerable attention to the Darwinian theory of evolution by natural selection – the received theory of the origin and succession of biological species. Viewed as a scientific theory, Darwinism poses some problems for Popper, since it appears not to be empirically falsifiable – such at least is Popper's view (not shared by all biologists), and it is certainly not obvious what evidence would falsify it. Popper has therefore proposed that the Darwinian theory should be considered to be, strictly speaking, not a scientific but a metaphysical theory – a highly fruitful one, which has generated many valuable *scientific* hypotheses.[3] He also suggests that, given certain premises – that there are living organisms capable of self-reproduction, and that they take a variety of forms of different degrees of 'adaptation' to their environment – it follows, 'almost tautologically', that better adapted life forms will survive better, and life forms generally evolve in a Darwinian manner. Since the premises of this argument are well-corroborated empirical hypotheses, it is not clear to me that Popper's two ways of characterizing the Darwinian theory of evolution (that it follows almost tautologically from well-confirmed premises, and that it is a metaphysical 'research programme') are consistent. But what is much more important, given the propensity of some social theorists (including Marx) to compare their theories to Darwin's, is the fact that the theory of evolution by natural selection is not, in any precise sense, predictive – it does not by itself enable us to predict what new species will evolve in the future, if only because (even if the process is totally deterministic) we cannot tell whether the environment will remain the same, or change, or how it may change.

Not only terrestrial species but also human ideas evolve, and Popper stresses the analogy between the two processes – and, more specifically, between Darwinian evolution and the evolution of scientific theories. Darwinian evolution, Popper points out, is like a series of experiments in which competing life forms are tested, and the 'unfit' are eliminated, just as scientific progress involves a 'struggle' between competing hypotheses in which those that fail empirical tests are falsified and discarded. Both processes thus illustrate what may be called 'learning by trial and error' – learning which alternative best solves the relevant problem (of life, or knowledge) by at the same time discovering which competing possible solutions are in fact errors. But there is an important difference between the two kinds of selection – as Popper puts it, in the Darwinian process, the penalty of error is death for the organism, whereas human beings who propose erroneous theories in a scientific context are not thereby condemned to death. Science is 'letting our hypotheses die in our stead', Popper says.[4] This is a great advantage that human beings enjoy compared to other organisms – and one advantage of being a rational animal.

As these last remarks suggest, Popper sees the evolution of human (including scientific) knowledge as not only analogous to, but also continuous with, Darwinian evolution. To put it another way, Darwinian evolution is also an evolution of knowledge, or of hypotheses about the nature and workings of the natural world. For organisms' ways of responding to the environment, and animals' ways of perceiving it and reacting to it, must clearly be the result of evolutionary pressure. Such ways of perceiving and reacting are solutions to life problems of the organism (not necessarily conscious solutions, of course), which incorporate 'expectations' or 'theories' about the world, implicitly premised on the assumption that certain regularities obtain therein. Popper suggests that, since the same is presumably true of human beings, all perception of the world is necessarily structured by pre-existing theories about the world – theories (or 'points of view') which are in a real sense built into animal and human sense organs by evolutionary processes. Contrary to positivism, therefore, there is no such thing as 'pure' perception, but only selective perception structured by the point of view that evolutionary pressures have built into our sense organs. This does not, of course, mean (contrary to such writers as Thomas Kuhn)[5] that our theoretical expectations cannot be falsified by our experiences, either in science or elsewhere, nor does it mean that we are incapable of rejecting the theoretical premises from which we started in favour of better ones (the contrary, Kuhnian view Popper has dubbed 'the myth of the framework').

Of course human language, capacity for the explicit formulation of ideas, and for rational criticism of ideas, make a great difference. Especially significant, Popper says, is the establishment of a *tradition of rational criticism* – a tradition essential to modern science, but one that has by no means characterized all societies in the course of human history. This view of science has enabled Popper to mount an effective critique of conservative traditionalism of an Oakeshottian stripe. The argument involves an analogy between science and politics. Modern science, including the scientific attitude, revolutionary though both were, did not spring from nowhere. The traditionalists are right, Popper believes, to stress that our beliefs at any moment are largely inherited, not created or originated by ourselves, and that this must be so – to discard all our inherited beliefs and start again, so to speak, would be an impossible act of madness which would leave us totally disoriented and unable to cope with the world. Nevertheless it does not follow that our attitude to traditional beliefs (or any kind of tradition) must be or should be *uncritical*. Popper suggests that the philosophers of ancient Greece invented a new attitude to inherited beliefs, and created a new tradition which eventually matured into the scientific tradition – namely, the disposition to discuss traditional beliefs (especially explanatory beliefs) critically. In this way they turned *myths* into *philosophy* (which Popper calls the substitution of new myths for old ones): they ceased to treat inherited beliefs as dogmas. The full flowering of this critical tradition later created the scientific tradition – which is actually, according to Popper, a duality of traditions. By this he means that each generation of scientists inherits its beliefs from its predecessors, and in this sense scientific beliefs are traditional; but scientists also inherit a second tradition, or second-order tradition – one which prescribes that first-order inherited scientific theories be subjected

183

to, and improved by, rational criticism using the empirical method, the method of attempted empirical falsification of old theories and the invention of new and hopefully better ones. As Popper emphasizes, modern science is a cultural and social phenomenon, whose objectivity and rationality depend, not on the objectivity of individuals, but on the existence of scientific communities guided by appropriate norms, such as freedom to criticize established views and acceptance of public experience as the arbiter of disputes. These norms are part and parcel of our scientific tradition.[6]

This 'rational theory of tradition',[7] as Popper calls it, should also apply to our social institutions, and thus to politics. The conservatives, like Oakeshott, are half-right, in the sense that our social institutions and mores, like our beliefs, at any moment are and must be largely inherited and traditional. To destroy them all in order to start again (in other words, the project of social revolution) would in this case also be an impossible act of madness which, once again, would leave us helpless, disoriented and insecure. Traditions give us a necessary order and predictability in our lives. But this of course does not mean that our attitude to traditions should be uncritical – on the contrary, we should try to improve them, just as (or somewhat as) scientists try to improve their theories. We should, here also, be faithful to our tradition of critical rationalism which Popper believes informs the scientific method. But Popper does not propose a complete parallel between the two spheres. Whereas in science, the tradition is in a sense revolutionary – totally new theories are proposed that are quite different from established ones, for example the quantum theory and relativity theory which superseded Newtonian physics – such an attitude is not appropriate to society and politics. Mistaken scientific theories can 'die in our stead', and so be eliminated without doing any harm; but mistaken social policies can do great damage to human lives. Hence Popper's advocacy of what he calls 'piecemeal social engineering', a programme for careful reformism that rejects revolution and conservatism alike. As the expression 'social engineering' suggests, Popper thinks of social reform as, at least in part, the application of social science. But it should be careful, even cautious – 'piecemeal' – because all our knowledge is fallible, and all human actions have unintended consequences. This political programme of Popper's gives rise to some problems, to which we shall return.

It should by now be evident, at all events, that Popper's view of science makes him – in contrast to such thinkers as Oakeshott, Arendt or Marcuse – a celebrator of modernity (not, needless to say, of all aspects of it). One well-known way in which he expresses this attitude is through a contrast between the 'open' and the 'closed' society. [8] In human history the closed type of society is primordial – Popper often refers to it as tribal society, or tribalism. Although tribal societies have varied greatly, Popper suggests that they share certain common features – certain features of their social structures and norms, and certain characteristic ways of thinking. For example, their social practices and institutions are relatively fixed and rigid, as is the place of individuals therein. The reason for this, Popper suggests, is that thinking in these societies is magical rather than rational. Behaviour is governed by taboos, often of a religious nature, and thus established ways are not subject to criticism. As Popper stresses, a consequence of this is a failure to distinguish clearly between natural and social (or conventional) regularities – both are viewed as enforced by a divine will, and thus as being equally unalterable. A person living in such a society has relatively little freedom of choice and, correspondingly, little individual responsibility for his or her actions. Members of the closed society do not experience many moral dilemmas, because the 'right' way to behave is fixed and known.

Such a society is, of course, very unlike the ones in which we live today. Popper credits the Greeks of the classical era with taking the first steps that in time created the 'open' society or, in other words, Western civilization.[9] They did so, in the first instance, by adopting a critical, rational attitude to established beliefs and institutions – by inventing, one might say, natural, moral and social philosophy, though not that alone, since the rational and critical attitude was as much practical as theoretical.[10] This, Popper tells us, was the most profound revolution in human history. Among the essential features of the open society is a great increase in freedom of various kinds – intellectual freedom (freedom to criticize established beliefs), but also freedom of the individual to choose his own way of life, his own personal relationships, his own career in a more fluid social structure ('social mobility').[11] A corollary of both rationality and social fluidity is a clear distinction between laws of nature and social norms (between nature and convention, as the Greeks put it) – the latter being variable and alterable, though the former are not. The distinction between fact and value is thus an integral part of the open society, as is the necessity for moral choice in the absence of clear guidelines. In Weberian (not Popperian) terms, the open society is disenchanted. Or is it? According to Popper, it has one possible faith, and only one – humanitarianism.[12] Popper applauds the open society for making possible a great increase in our knowledge, our capacity for 'cooperation and mutual help', and consequently, our well-being and chances of survival.[13]

Since the open society, as defined by Popper, lives by reason and by a humanitarian faith, it implies also a certain style of politics and a certain

185

system of government – namely, democracy, freedom, egalitarianism and piecemeal social engineering aimed at the elimination of human suffering. Some of these terms, notably democracy and egalitarianism, are rather vague, and will need to be clarified later. For the time being, let us concentrate on the politics of piecemeal social engineering. As remarked above, this term implies an application of social science to the solution of political problems. We must therefore consider Popper's conception of social science.

Popper often proclaims his belief in 'unity of method'[14] as between social and natural science – in other words, he believes that the logical structure of social science is fundamentally similar to that of natural science. This fundamental similarity does not, however, preclude some differences or at least peculiarities so far as social science is concerned. Like natural science, Popper believes, social science ought to consist of empirically falsifiable explanatory laws: and these laws can and should be of universal form (the view that social science laws must be limited to particular types of societies or particular periods is said by Popper to be characteristic of 'historicism', a view he rejects).[15] On the other hand, he follows Hayek in embracing 'methodological individualism', that is, the principle that social entities are theoretical 'models' of individuals' behaviour: hence 'the task of social theory' is to analyse these models *in terms of individuals*, of their attitudes, expectations, relations etc.'[16] These two postulates together seem to imply that social science needs, or even consists in, laws of individual behaviour. Yet it is not at all clear that Popper believes in such laws, or can do so, in view of some of his other theoretical commitments, especially those relating to individuality and freedom. Let us examine his views further.

One very frequently reiterated view of Popper's is his rejection of what he calls 'psychologism', that is, the view that social phenomena are explicable in terms of individual psychology, and which therefore aims at 'the reduction of social theories to psychology, in the same way as we try to reduce chemistry to physics'.[17] Why does Popper reject this? One reason is that he believes that 'psychologism' is committed to a belief in a constant human nature, or in other words, uniform laws of individual psychology.[18] Whether this is really an implication of psychologism is less important than the fact that Popper rejects it because he believes that 'the human or personal factor' makes the future essentially unpredictable.[19] Nothing, for example, can guarantee the continuation of scientific progress. No matter what institutions we create, it might be ended by 'an epidemic of mysticism' (Popper even saw some danger of this). Yet whatever the dangers of this unpredictability of the 'human factor', it is a corollary of something immensely valuable – human freedom. Human freedom makes possible 'perhaps the most powerful tool for biological evolution which has ever emerged' – critical reason.[20] Therefore 'the diversity of individuals and their opinions, aims and purposes must never be interfered with'.[21] All this may be perfectly true, but it is hard to see how to reconcile it with the idea of an individualistic social science consisting of universal laws. Or at least, with one consisting of *deterministic* laws.

Is there any other kind of sociological laws that Popper might have in mind? Another reason given by Popper for rejecting psychologism is that the social outcomes of human action depend as much on institutional conditions as on psychological propensities.[22] (This view is not in conflict with methodological individualism, so long as an individualistic account of social institutions can be given.) Popper therefore proposes, as a method of generating social generalizations, his so-called 'zero method',[23] or analysis in terms of what he calls 'the logic of the situation'.[24] Popper believes, then, that there is a logical way to behave in any given situation, whose implications can (often) be worked out (this is the 'zero method'). People do not, to be sure, act perfectly rationally, 'but they, none the less, act more or less rationally; and this makes it possible to construct comparatively simple models of their actions and inter-actions, and to use these models as approximations'.[25]

Popper gives a number of examples of this proposed methodology. One is orthodox economic theory; another, 'an explanation of the way in which a man, when crossing a street, dodges the cars which move on it'.[26] In the latter case, the relevant 'situation' is presumably the street and the cars moving on it; in the former, among many other things, the many institutions of the capitalist market economy. But it is obvious (as Popper indeed admits) that the behaviour of the street-crosser or the economic agents in a market cannot be explained in terms of their situation *alone*; it is necessary to allude also to their motives, intentions and so on (for example, the desire of the street-crosser to get to the other side; the desire of the economic agents to maximize profit or utility or whatever). This does not, of course, mean (a point much emphasized by Popper) that the agents in question necessarily achieve their purposes, or that social facts are necessarily to be explained by finding who intended to bring them about, and why (a view condemned by Popper as 'the conspiracy theory of society').[27] As Popper rightly says, economic slumps are not the result of economic agents wishing to bring about slumps: in this case as in many others, 'social life is . . . action [which] creates . . . many unforeseen reactions', and it is thus the task of social science to analyse 'the unintended social repercussions of intentional human actions'.[28] But the fact remains that, because such analyses and theories have to assume a certain sort of social 'situation' and also certain standard motivations on the part of agents, the theoretical generalizations of social science must normally be, at best, of spatially and temporarily limited application – the view rejected by Popper as characteristic of 'historicism'. Orthodox economic theory is a theory about behaviour in market economies, on the assumption that agents are driven by 'capitalistic' motives – not a universal theory of economic behaviour. Indeed, it is a concomitant of the human freedom in which Popper believes that individuals can choose different goals to pursue, even if it is also true that in a given culture certain goals can sometimes be assumed to be approximately standard. The only exceptions to this pattern – the only possible genuinely universal sociological laws – would be those derivable from universal human motivations, or 'human nature': the form of explanation rejected by Popper as 'psychologism'.

It appears, then, that Popper's philosophy of social science is a good deal less convincing than his philosophy of natural science. What is the implication of this for his political theory of 'piecemeal social engineering'? Paradoxically, it strengthens it, if anything. The fact that sociological 'laws' are applicable only to particular kinds of society (particular social 'situations') actually makes no practical difference at all, while the fact (if it is a fact) that human actions are unpredictable, and their consequences often unforeseen by the agent, reinforces the grounds for caution which underlie Popper's demand that social reform should be 'piecemeal' and tentative. If our scientific knowledge is always fallible, our social scientific knowledge is still more so. (This is not to say that the idea of basing politics on a fallibilistic conception of science is problem free – a point to which we shall return.)

Let us pursue further the implications of Popper's application of fallibilism to politics. Popper's support for piecemeal social engineering is a 'middle way', a rejection of two extremes, not only of conservatism, but also and even more, of what he calls 'holistic' or 'utopian' social engineering, that is, the project of establishing an ideal society by means of a total social reconstruction, possibly in accordance with some 'blueprint'.[29] Popper, in other words, rejects social revolution as a political method. Why? In part, we already know the answer, in so far as it has to do with the value, indeed indispensability, of traditions for human life. To abolish all existing traditions and institutions (what Popper often calls 'canvas-cleaning') would, if it were possible, leave most of us (if not the utopian social engineers) bewildered and at a loss as to how to act.[30] But there are other reasons, to do with the fallibility of all our knowledge, and especially our knowledge of social causation. This fallibility means that it is rational to prefer piecemeal to holistic engineering, for several reasons. In the first place, we have more knowledge about the effects of piecemeal changes, because we have more experience of them. Small-scale social experiments are in fact carried on all the time, by private individuals and groups as well as governments. There is a constant process of learning from the inevitable mistakes, and of adjusting expectations accordingly. But of really large-scale, or 'holistic' social reconstructions we obviously have very little experience indeed, and very little capacity indeed to predict their consequences. The history of the Marxist-inspired revolution in Russia certainly seems to bear this out. And as a matter of principle, the larger the scale of a social 'experiment', the harder it is to learn from it, since where many things are changed and many consequences thereof are produced simultaneously, it is very difficulty if not impossible to know which causes have produced which effects. The social engineer, Popper argues, should take his cue from the mechanical engineer, who never tries to put a large-scale engineering solution into practice without a long period of *applied research* – a process in the engineer tests model after model, continually adjusting both his expectations and his machinery. The social engineer cannot quite do this (he cannot isolate the system he wishes to improve), but the nearest analogue is piecemeal experimentation, undertaken in the awareness that mistakes will be made, coupled with continuous efforts to learn from and correct the mistakes. As Popper says, 'an attitude of scepticism towards one's causal theories, and of intellectual modesty, is . . . one of the most important moral duties'.[31] Holistic social engineering lacks this intellectual modesty, and is likely to lead to very big mistakes, which are very hard to correct. Again, witness the recent history of Russia.

In summary, utopian social engineering is in Popper's opinion irrational and unscientific, quite contrary to the claim made by Marx and his followers as to the 'scientific' status of their revolutionary project. It is interesting, also, to recall Marcuse's hostility to 'positivism', precisely on the grounds, among others, that a 'positivistic' or empiricist social science cannot (for reasons similar to those adduced by Popper) provide evidence in favour of revolution. For Popper, of course, this is an argument against revolution, not against (social) science. Also worth emphasizing is the contrast between Popper and Marcuse on piecemeal social engineering, which for Marcuse is of necessity a device whereby society's rulers are enabled to manipulate the other members of society to their own advantage. Popper, by contrast, has no fear of 'instrumental reason' *so long as it is applied with due caution and intellectual modesty*, in the spirit of fallibilism. To Popper, in contrast to Marcuse, it is not piecemeal but utopian social engineering that is likely to destroy human freedom.[32] Utopian blueprints for social reconstruction are bound to be too simple to give much scope to independent individual choices. Opinions are, after all, likely to differ as to what constitutes an ideal society. Utopian social engineers cannot tolerate the deviant or the unpredictable, just because human freedom threatens to frustrate the realization of their favoured blueprint. Thus, even if human liberation was the original aim of the utopian engineers, they find themselves compelled to resort to more and more coercive methods, to dictatorship, and ultimately to totalitarianism. This, of course, is seen by Popper as at least a partial explanation of the Stalinist disaster that emerged from the Bolshevik revolution of 1917, on which so many idealists pinned such high hopes. Nazi totalitarianism, of course, never had any commitment to individual freedom, but can still be interpreted as the imposition of a utopian blueprint incompatible with freedom.

Another way to describe the totalitarian systems created in Germany and Russia between the two world wars, is to say that they were attempts to recreate the 'closed' society – not a 'naturally' closed society like tribal society (which is closed because of traditional beliefs and attitudes) but an 'enforced' closed society, one which has to be enforced because it has to destroy the freedom, and therefore the rationality, that characterize the open society. Why did this happen? Like Arendt, Hayek and Marcuse, Popper tries to answer that burning question or, more accurately, to indicate some of the contributory causes. Broadly speaking, he identifies two kinds of factors – psychological and intellectual. One of the intellectual factors – the mistaken aspiration to utopian social engineering – has already been discussed; another – the intellectual error called by Popper 'historicism' will be discussed below. But these intellectual errors are of course not unrelated to the psychological factors – to the psychological effects of the growth of the open society, and the human reaction to that development. As Popper writes in the first paragraph of *The Open Society and Its Enemies*, the transition from the closed to the open society was a 'shock' from which we have still not recovered, and perhaps never will – a shock 'which is one of the factors that have made possible the rise of those reactionary movements which have tried, and still try, to overthrow civilization and to return to tribalism'. By supporting and even leading such movements 'many of the intellectual leaders of mankind' have betrayed the open society of which they are a product.

What is the nature of this 'shock', or as Popper often calls it, the 'strain of civilization'?[33] Individualism and freedom bring costs as well as benefits.[34] In the absence of unquestioned norms and social structures the individual has to shoulder the burden of responsibility – to make, for example, his own career and his own moral decisions, to be materially and morally self-reliant. A society in which individuals strive for material betterment and which encourages rational criticism makes for conflict, including conflict between social classes. Members of the open society lack the feeling of security which comes from unquestioned norms and strong communal bonds. Popper remarks that the open society is to a striking degree 'abstract', a term that here has much less favourable connotations than when Hayek uses it to refer to his Great Society: for Popper it refers to the *impersonality* of our social relations ('membership of a trade union may mean no more than the possession of a membership card and the payment of a contribution to an unknown secretary'), which can lead to a life of isolation and unhappiness.[35] This set of factors is not dissimilar to that which, according to Oakeshott, encourages the conception of the state as a compulsory enterprise association; according to Popper, it can make attractive the project to return to the closed society, in the form of totalitarianism.

The role of philosophy in this project is paradoxical. According to Popper, the invention of philosophy in classical Greece was an integral and essential part of the birth of the open society; yet the acknowledged fountainhead of the Western philosophical tradition, the most revered if not the greatest of our philosophers – Plato – was an implacable foe of the open society. Popper speaks often of the 'Great Generation',[36] the generation that lived in Athens before and during the Peloponnesian war – a period of transition from the closed to the open society. The great spokesmen of the new society, in Popper's eyes, were such men as Pericles, Herodotus, Protagoras, Democritus, Gorgias, Alcidamas, Lycophron, Antisthenes and, greatest of all, Socrates, the 'gadfly', the tireless asker of questions, the man who proclaimed that the only thing he knew was that he knew nothing. Popper, it might be said, sees Socrates as the very embodiment of critical rationalism and fallibilism, and a man who believed so intensely in this creed that he preferred to die rather than betray it. Needless to say, not all of the leading figures of the Great Generation were enthusiastic about the developing open society – some of the greatest of them were sceptical or hostile (Popper mentions the playwrights Euripides, Sophocles and Aristophanes, and the historian Thucydides). By a supreme irony, the greatest and most influential of the enemies of the open society was Socrates' devoted pupil, Plato. In an even more bitter irony, Plato's views, expressed in his political dialogues, are put into the mouth of the by now dead Socrates himself.[37]

According to Popper, Plato's political philosophy manifests two components that are characteristic of the intellectual enemies of the open society, utopianism and historicism. The utopianism (a term already explained) is in my opinion more important in Plato's case than the historicism, but it is nevertheless necessary to make clear what Popper means by the latter. Historicists, then, are those who believe that 'it is the task of science to make predictions [and therefore] the task of the social sciences to furnish us with long-term historical prophecies. They also believe they have discovered laws of history which enable them to prophesy the course of historical events'.[38] The ideal typical historicist is Karl Marx, of whom more will be said below. As for Plato, whatever his views on 'science' may have been, the point for Popper is his belief that human history (normally) conforms to definite patterns or cycles.

In Popper's description, Plato was an Athenian of aristocratic family who lived through the crumbling of the old order of aristocratic tribalism, experienced the open society of democratic Athens, and reacted with hostility to what he saw as its instability, disorder and incompetence. This experience he interpreted in terms of two theories: the theory of social change as corruption or degeneration; and the theory of forms (or ideas). The former theory is, of course, Plato's historicism: his utopianism indicates the only possible exception to the historicist theory, namely the establishment of a society so perfect as to be able to resist all change and decay. This must be the work of philosophers like Plato, of those who understand the forms or ideas, suprasensual entities which are the ultimate reality, unchanging and perfect.[39] To understand the perfect state is to understand the form (idea) of the state, and to create an ideal state on earth is to make it correspond as closely as an earthly thing can to its perfect form. Whereas Socrates confessed that he knew nothing, Platonic philosophers appear to know everything and therefore to merit omnipotent political power.

Let us look in more detail at Plato's historicism, which takes the form of a necessary succession of forms of government, each defined in terms of who rules the state.[40] The best possible state is that ruled by the wisest (philosophers) but (unless it is ideally structured) it will decay into, first, a timocracy (the rule of the noble, motivated by honour), then into oligarchy (rule of the rich), democracy (which is lawlessness) and ultimately, worst of all, tyranny.[41] This is a picture of successive degeneration. Plato, Popper says, considered himself to have lived through the last two, the two worst phases, and had some exceedingly shrewd sociological comments to make on the forces that bring about the social changes involved – above all, the weaknesses of democracy which make it vulnerable to the demagogic appeals of tyrants. (That does not mean, however, that the changes are necessary, as distinct from possible, in Popper's opinion.) Broadly speaking, the motive force of change, and hence of decline, identified by Plato is social conflict, including class conflict, but most importantly conflict within the ruling group. To create an ideal state proof against decline, therefore, is to design one that is conflict free.[42]

To this end Plato offers a blueprint of a state that is not only founded and ruled by philosophers, but so designed as to ensure the unity of the ruling class. According to Popper this ideal Platonic society has two classes, the workers (the ruled) and the governing military–philosophical class: 'the guardians are no separate caste, but merely old and wise warriors who have been promoted from the ranks of the auxiliaries'.[43] The unity of the governing class is to be maintained by appropriate education, by elimination among them of private property and economic activity, and by common ownership of women and children (in order to prevent divisive individualism and family loyalty). The class of workers (or economic class) must be totally excluded from political power (a provision that Arendt found understandable, but which arouses Popper's indignation) and rigidly separated from the governing class. In Plato's political imagery, the guardians are shepherds, the auxiliaries sheepdogs, and the workers sheep.[44] To maintain the control and ensure the unity of the ruling class, education and literature must be strictly controlled, and religious orthodoxy enforced on penalty of death.[45] More, the rulers must maintain their own power and the subjection of the economic class by uninhibited use of lies and deceit[46] – for example, the 'noble lie' (or, as Popper prefers to translate it, 'lordly lie') that members of the different classes are made of different substances (different metals, in fact), which must not be mixed. Criticism of the state's political institutions and attempts at religious innovation, Plato says in the *Laws*, should be capital offences.[47] The Nocturnal Council, charged with administering these draconian provisions, is called by Popper an Inquisition. So much did Plato come to hate individual freedom, which he equated with selfishness, and saw as the enemy of what he most cherished – the stability and good order of the whole – that he could write, again in the *Laws*:

> The greatest principle of all is that nobody, whether male or female, should ever be without a leader. Nor should the mind of anybody be habituated to letting him do anything at all on his own initiative . . . But in war and in the midst of peace – to his leader he shall direct his eye, and follow him faithfully. And even in the smallest matters he should stand under leadership. For example, he should get up, or move, or wash, or take his meals . . . only if he has been told to do so . . . In a word, he should teach his soul, by long habit, never to dream of acting independently, and to become utterly incapable of it.[48]

It is passages such as this that lead Popper to dub Plato a totalitarian, a holistic engineer who sought to strangle the open society at birth.

Since Plato has long been a revered figure, Popper's reading of his views inevitably caused controversy and even outrage; so it is worth noting that his interpretation was largely endorsed by two Plato scholars of the stature of Gilbert Ryle and Richard Robinson (despite the fact that the latter found 'serious causes of offence' in its tone and some of its details).[49] More debatable is the question of Plato's influence on later European history, which Popper believes to have been very great, describing him as 'unsuccessful in his immediate and practical undertakings, but in the long run only too successful'.[50] This I think is unproven and perhaps unprovable. Is it possible that Plato's political philosophy could be a contributory factor in the establishment of totalitarian regimes over two thousand years later? Some evidence that this could be the case is to be found in an article on Popper by Walter Kaufman, who points out that the 'official' Nazi philosopher, Alfred Rosenberg, refers to Plato in glowing terms, that special editions of a compendium of carefully chosen passages from Plato's writings were prepared and widely used in German schools in the Nazi period, and that the intellectual originator of Nazi race theory, Hans Günther, was also the author of a book on Plato.[51]

Oddly enough, the article by Kaufman in which these facts are pointed out was not intended to support Popper's thesis in *The Open Society and Its Enemies*, but emphatically the reverse – its burden is an indignant rebuttal of Popper's attack on Hegel, in the second volume of that work, as an intellectual precursor of Nazism. Indeed, Popper's account of Hegel (unlike his interpretation of Plato) has found little favour with specialists. But if Popper did misinterpret Hegel, the latter would have little right to complain, because of the notorious and monstrous obscurity of his prose – an obscurity often so impenetrable as to make one doubt if he wanted to be understood. In Popper's eyes, this obscurity is not just a literary but also a moral fault, because it is a threat to rationality, which depends for its very life on clarity of expression. Another threat to rationality is Hegel's preference for 'dialectical' over orthodox logic (discussed above). Thus, although Hegel continually proclaims himself a champion of 'reason' (*Vernunft*), he is actually according to Popper one of its deadliest enemies. And similarly with 'freedom', again championed verbally by Hegel but in reality undermined by him in so far as he redefined it in such a way as to identify it with the laws of the state (said to be the earthly incarnation of reason). If these were indeed Hegel's views, it is understandable that Popper categorized him as a dangerous enemy of the open society. Whether they really were his views is probably impossible to say. What is perhaps more important is whether his works can be, and have been, understood in this sense by his disciples.

In the two volumes of *The Open Society and its Enemies*, Hegel occupies a relatively small part of Popper's attention, by comparison with his two main subjects – Plato and Marx. Whereas Popper attacks Hegel with angry contempt, and treats Plato with a combination of intellectual respect and political hostility, his attitude to Marx is much more friendly. Marx, in Popper's eyes, was emphatically *not* an enemy of the open society – or at least, not deliberately so. Popper sees him as a man actuated by strong humanitarian feelings, and a generous indignation on behalf of the oppressed, with which he (Popper) strongly sympathizes. For example, he fully shares Marx's view of the cruelty and inhumanity of nineteenth-century *laissez-faire* capitalism (in marked contrast to Hayek). And yet Marxism is, or became, notwithstanding this, one of the deadliest threats to the open society in the history of Western civilization – because, Popper argues, Marx, despite his great intellectual gifts and many profound sociological insights, also committed some fatal intellectual errors. As with Plato, the roots of these are to be found in the mistaken doctrines of historicism and utopianism. However, the way these are combined in Marx's theory differs from the case of Plato. Unlike Plato, Marx believed in utterly inexorable and deterministic laws of history (which he also claimed to understand, and thus to be able to prophesy the future); unlike Plato, he believed in progress, and so welcomed social change (by means of revolution). Again unlike Plato, because of his deterministic historicism, he refused to construct any 'blueprints' for an ideal society – if history is predetermined this is obviously a waste of time. Despite this, his followers were forced in practice to be holistic utopian social engineers. When Lenin and the Bolsheviks seized power in the name of revolutionary Marxism in Russia in 1917, they found little or no detailed guidance in Marx's writings as to how to proceed. They had to improvise a utopian blueprint, so to speak, on the spot.

Marx's historicist prophecies are summarized by Popper as follows.[52] First, the internal logic of capitalism will bring about ever-increasing economic inequality between an increasingly wealthy bourgeoisie and an ever more impoverished proletariat; secondly, all other social classes will disappear or become insignificant; third, this social simplification and polarization will lead to a proletarian revolution; finally, the victorious proletariat will institute a classless society (socialism or communism).

Every one of these prophecies has turned out to be false. Economic inequality in capitalist systems has greatly decreased since Marx's day, and the bulk of the employed working class is far more prosperous. It is also proportionately a declining fraction of capitalist societies, because of the huge growth of the middle classes. There has been no Marxist revolution in any developed capitalist country – only in 'feudal' and/or peasant societies like Russia in 1917 and China in 1949, revolutions obviously not made by the industrial proletariat (which was tiny or non-existent) despite the rhetoric of the revolutionaries; and in no society has the revolution led to a classless society or anything remotely resembling communism as envisaged by Marx. Instead it has led to closed, authoritarian and often totalitarian societies. Yet Marx, according to Popper, was a brilliant sociologist who produced penetrating and original analyses of capitalism. Why, then were his prophecies so wrong?

One answer is that the whole conception of historicism, the basis of Marx's prophecies, rests on a fundamental mistake. Popper's argument to this effect will be discussed below. At a more specific level, also, Popper identifies weaknesses in Marx's analysis. Marx did, to be sure, correctly identify a number of important forces at work in nineteenth-century capitalism; but he made the mistake of assuming these forces must continue unchecked, leading to the results he predicted. It does not seem to have occurred to him (or if it did he chose to ignore the possibility) that new, counteracting forces could arise to check or reverse existing trends – in particular, that they might be checked or counteracted by *deliberate* action, as indeed occurred. For example, the impoverishment of the working class has been offset by (among other things) the growth in power of trade unions, and the institution of unemployment insurance and other forms of social welfare – partly as a result of working-class demands, and partly because of a realization by the capitalist class that such concessions were necessary to prevent, if not revolution, unacceptable social disorder. In brief, the two classes found a basis for compromise, and thus the Marxist prophecies (which otherwise might have come true) were frustrated. But certain of Marx's prophecies were actually, in Popper's opinion, totally baseless – for example, that if a successful revolution were carried out by or in the name of the proletariat, this must lead to Marx's communist utopia. Internal divisions among the successful revolutionaries, and tyrannical rule of the prevailing faction, are just as likely or rather much more so, given the nature of a revolution as an exercise in holistic social engineering. It is, indeed, a striking if obvious fact that Marx prophesied as inevitable that which he devoutly desired – an extraordinarily and, alas, baselessly optimistic view of history. To be blunt, much of the Marxist prophecy is nothing more than wishful thinking – or wishful thinking that seized on some of the real forces and trends at work in nineteenth-century capitalism, in order to draw from them conclusions beyond anything they could justify.

These conclusions, of course, are prophecies based on Marx's historicism. As Popper's discussion of Plato shows, historicism is a very ancient intellectual style, but Marx's historicism was of a new and modern kind, most especially in its self-conscious claim to be *scientific*. Unfortunately, it is nothing of the sort — its claim to be so testifies to a profound misunderstanding of the nature of science. Scientific laws are *not* laws of historical succession, such that, once grasped, they permit absolute, unconditional predictions. Rather, they are laws of 'constant conjunction' (as Hume put it), or constant succession, having the form, as we saw, 'All As are B', or 'Whenever A occurs, B occurs'. The latter is equivalent to a *conditional* prediction, namely, 'if A occurs, B will occur'. It does not license any absolute prediction (prophecy) whatever — neither that A will occur, nor that B will (necessarily) occur, nor that anything will occur. True, scientific knowledge does sometimes seem to license unconditional predictions — of eclipses of the sun or moon, for example, into the far distant future. But such predictions are actually dependent on the predictability, usually the stability, of the relevant initial conditions ('A will be the case' or 'A will occur'), a requirement rarely satisfied, and dependent on the *isolation* (from unpredictable or poorly understood influences) of the system in question. Strictly speaking, one can never be certain of the persistence of such isolation, but in some cases confidence can be reasonably justified. Astronomical systems are a case in point, but it is worth repeating that the environment of biological forms (which so strongly influences Darwinian evolution) emphatically is not. Neither is society.

As Popper rightly points out, the 'theory' of evolution is not a scientific law of succession, but rather a description of a unique sequence, of the succession of terrestrial life forms, and of how they are related. Logically it is similar to a human genealogy. Thus it is a *singular historical statement*; and so is any description of the succession of social forms in human history (or at least this is so if, as in the Marxist case, 'world history' is treated as a single evolving process). Popper is here stressing that these descriptions of the succession of forms (biological or social) are not general laws, capable of corroboration by experience. Somewhat strangely, Popper seems to suggest that this is a further reason against using such accounts as a basis for prediction: 'we may base scientific predictions on laws', he writes,[53] but 'we cannot hope to test a universal hypothesis nor to find a natural law acceptable to science if we are for ever confined to observation of one unique process. Nor can the observation of one unique process help us to foresee its future development. The most careful observations of *one* developing caterpillar will not help us to predict its transformation into a butterfly'.[54]

What is strange about this passage is its clear implication that (unlike a singular description, however detailed) a well corroborated universal law (or hypothesis) *does* afford grounds for prediction, just because it is a corroborable and well-corroborated generalization. Is this not a reliance on inductive reasoning, such as the 'official' Popper repudiates totally? Nor is it an isolated lapse, for part of Popper's polemic against 'utopian' as opposed to 'piecemeal' social engineering is (as we saw above) that we have far more, and more relevant, *experience* of the latter (experience which, Popper implies, makes (conditional) scientific prediction much more reliable in the latter case). Popper likens piecemeal social engineering to the work of the physical engineer, which is guided by 'principles tested by practical experiments'.[55] It seems that Popper cannot, after all, totally dispense with inductive reasoning. While Popper is right that, logically speaking, no amount of past evidence either demonstrates or makes probable the truth of a universal law, it is in fact difficult if not impossible to make sense of the concept of *rational* action (a concept central to Popperian politics and philosophy) without allowing some validity to inductive reasoning – to the use of evidence to guide behaviour.

If Popper has, after all, failed fully to solve the riddle of induction, he is in good philosophical company. His critique of historicism and utopian engineering, and the combination of the two involved in Marxism, remains cogent. These are deeply irrational and unscientific approaches to social problems. Marxism, especially (or, one should say, mainstream Marxists), is unscientific in another way – in its (their) dogmatism, which manifests a naive and reckless disregard of the inherent fallibility of all human, including scientific knowledge. Not the least of the problems of the old USSR was that, because of its Marxist foundations, an economic and sociological theory was given the status of a religion – an orthodoxy. It is hard to think of anything more absurd.

But Popper's critique of historicism goes deeper than has yet been explained. Historicism is, of course, a form of determinism – a doctrine which Popper rejects, even, controversially, at the level of physics, or world 1. More relevant and less controversial is Popper's rejection of determinism in relation to the other worlds. To put it another way, Popper believes that evolution is creative – productive of genuine, unpredictable novelty. This goes beyond the fallibilism of Popper's philosophy of science, for it implies that, even if we knew all the laws of science, not all developments could be predicted – especially, Popper believes, those of world 3, the world of ideas. Popper considers it quite absurd to suppose that, for example, the symphonies of Beethoven could have been predicted on the basis of scientific knowledge or in any other way – they are instances of human freedom and human creativity. Exactly the same is true of scientific theories, so that the idea of a 'science of science' is likewise absurd. Indeed, it is more absurd – it is a logical contradiction, if it means that the growth of scientific knowledge (or any kind of knowledge) could be predicted. To predict (in any detail) the growth of knowledge, is to claim to know now what will not be known until the future – a manifestly self-contradictory claim. Furthermore, this provides Popper with a clinching argument against historicism. If (as seems plausible) knowledge will grow in the future; and if (equally plausibly) the growth of knowledge will significantly influence the future development of human society; then the latter must be as unpredictable as the former – that is, necessarily unpredictable as a matter of logic. Among the unpredictable, and therefore inexplicable, events of human history, Popper asserts, is perhaps the most important – the birth of the open society in classical Greece. That the Greeks of the Great Generation reacted to the breakdown of their closed society 'by inventing the tradition of criticism and discussion, and with it the art of thinking rationally', Popper remarks, 'is one of the inexplicable facts which stand at the beginning of our civilization'.[56]

The open society also provides the clue, in Popper's opinion, to the popularity of historicist theories, especially in the twentieth century. (Marxism, though the most fully articulated historicist theory, was not the century's only one – there are significant elements of historicism in Nazi thinking also.) Historicism can be seen as a way of reacting to the strains of the open society, especially to its unsettling uncertainties, and to the burdens of moral responsibility that it thrusts on the individual. Historicism bears the welcome tidings that change can be fully understood and anticipated, and that, as a consequence, there is no need for moral choice, since the future is already predetermined. Comforting though such tidings may be, they are as deplorable in their effects as they are false in their comfort. For one thing they lead to a kind of amoralism, or perversion of morality, which Popper calls moral historicism – the equation of moral rightness with historical success, present or future, even if the success is, in theory or practice, the fruit of violence.[57] Both Hegel and Marx are charged by Popper with asserting this doctrine – in effect, that might is right. (Hegel, notoriously, saw war as a prime engine of historical progress, while Marx attributes a similar role to revolution.) From one point of view, historicism is an attempt to 're-enchant' the disenchanted open society by endowing history with meaning; Popper responds that history has no meaning, except the meaning we ourselves may give it (just as nature and 'life' have no meaning, other than the ends we decide to pursue).[58] By denying this, historicism encourages us to shirk our moral responsibility – to ignore or deny the truth that it is our decisions and actions that will shape history for better or worse, not 'laws' of historical development. Not uncommonly, this feature of Marxist theory in particular manifested itself in a peculiarly ironic and self-stultifying way. Popper has graphically described the paralysis of will, attributable to their historicist beliefs, which prevented the Austrian Marxists in the 1930s from offering any serious resistance to Nazism, which they interpreted as a necessary stage in the progression from capitalism to socialism (even though Marx, of course, had not predicted it). It was, indeed, only by flouting Marxist historicism that Lenin and the Bolsheviks could seize power in a country as manifestly unready for socialism as Russia was in 1917 – according to Marxist theory as well as, as it turned out, in reality.

As is well known, Marxism is not only a determinist theory, but a theory of economic determinism; not just a historicism, but an economic historicism. It therefore teaches what Popper calls the impotence of politics.[59] With this teaching Popper disagrees profoundly. When he speaks of the need to recognize our moral responsibility for the course of history, he means that we have the power, and the duty, to make a difference through political action. The power, as we saw, suffices to invalidate historicist prophecy (not least in the effect of Marxist *ideas* on Russia after 1917); the duty is to use political action to alleviate social problems, through piecemeal social engineering (they will never, of course, be definitively solved). But clearly social policy cannot be simply the application of knowledge: the knowledge must serve moral ends and values. Popper has sometimes been accused of an exaggerated analogy between politics and science which assumes, falsely, that it is obvious what are the social problems with which politics must deal. There is some merit in this charge, but not much. Popper does indeed believe that it is much easier to identify, and agree on, social problems, than it is the lineaments of a social utopia – after all, problems (unlike utopias) are phenomena we have experienced. Beyond this, the supreme ethical principle that should guide politics, Popper says, is the relief of suffering. Relying on something like a Humean concept of sympathy, he writes: 'human suffering makes a direct moral appeal, namely, the appeal for help'.[60] Contrary to utilitarianism, there is no comparable call to increase happiness. In any case we do not know what will make other people happy, and the attempt to design a society for 'maximum happiness' is liable to turn into utopianism. 'Pain, suffering, injustice and their prevention . . . are the eternal problems of public morals . . . The "higher" values should very largely . . . be left to the realm of *laissez-faire*', writes Popper.[61] Underlying this view, obviously, is a basic egalitarianism – not economic egalitarianism, but a humanitarian belief that government, whether or not it should be 'by the people' (a question to which we shall return), should be *for* the people – all of the people, impartially, and as individuals, not, as Plato and Hegel believed, for the state as a supra-individual whole.

It is this attitude that makes Popper sympathize so strongly with Marx's critique of capitalism: 'the injustice and inhumanity of the unrestrained "capitalist system" described by Marx cannot be questioned', he writes.[62] But Popper does not, of course, believe that Marx offered any cure for the situation. Rather, it needed (and needs) to be tackled by political action, by what Popper calls 'protectionism'. In the economic realm as in the realm of brute physical violence, freedom must (paradoxically) be restrained for the sake of freedom: the freedom of the strong must be restrained in order to protect the freedom of the weak. 'Nobody should be at the *mercy* of others, but all should have a *right* to be protected by the state'.[63] Unrestrained capitalism must give way to capitalism restrained by state interventionism. 'Economic power must not be permitted to dominate political power; if necessary it must be fought and brought under control by political power'.[64] And this has indeed happened, to a significant degree, despite Marx's view that politics and the state are 'essentially' impotent, economically determined, and in the long run superfluous. However, Popper's enthusiasm for 'interventionism' is tempered by fear that it might, if unchecked, lead to an over-mighty state. He therefore prescribes that it be limited to what is required by justice and equal liberty, and be effected through established laws, not left to the discretion of state officials.[65]

Notwithstanding this *caveat*, the upshot is that Popper, in refreshing contrast to so many of his contemporaries among the leading political philosophers of the century, supports strongly and without qualification what has come to be called the welfare state – the system of unemployment insurance, other forms of social insurance against disability, old age, etc., full employment policy, a guaranteed income for everyone willing to work, educational provision for all regardless of income, and so on (Popper realizes, of course, that provision of these benefits is dependent on the economic productivity of the capitalist system. But they are dependent also on political will and political action).[66] The welfare state illustrates, interestingly, not only Popper's political principle of protectionism, but also his application of fallibilism to politics.

The various measures that constitute the welfare state were instituted in order to deal with some of the urgent and manifest problems of unrestrained capitalism. As such they were a huge advance. But in course of time, partly due to changing circumstances, they have created their own problems, which the present generation must attempt to solve. This is in fact an issue high up on today's political agenda. It is widely asserted, and may be true, that the established model of the welfare state has become unsustainable, so that further 'piecemeal social engineering' is now called for.

The principle of 'protectionism' provides Popper with one part of his political programme; another part is derived more or less directly from his fallibilist epistemology. As he puts it, while there is no 'rational scientific basis' of ethics, 'there is an ethical basis of science, and of rationalism'.[67] The recognition that all knowledge is fallible naturally suggests a regime of freedom and tolerance (though not of the intolerant), of what Popper calls *reasonableness*. Recognizing our own fallibility, we will be open minded, aware that we can learn from the criticism of others. We will not be prone to resort to violence and killing as a political method. ('One does not kill a man when one adopts the attitude of first listening to his arguments'.)[68] Reasonableness 'is an attitude which does not lightly give up hope that by such means as argument and careful observation people may reach some kind of agreement on many problems of importance; and that even where their demands and interests clash, it is often possible . . . to reach . . . a compromise which, because of its equity, is acceptable to most, if not all'.[69] Popper is insistent that it is rationality and reasonableness that give us the hope of living *in peace* – not 'the irrational emphasis upon emotion and passion' which Popper believes to have been such a destructive force in the twentieth century.[70] Popper's point here relates not only to obviously 'negative' emotions such as hatred: positive emotions, such as love and loyalty, are inadequate to the political need. Since we cannot genuinely love all of humanity, political appeals to our generous emotions tend to be effective only in relation to those we know, our own social group. Appeals to emotions, even to love, thus tend to divide men rather than to unite them (nationalism is a case in point).[71] It is reason, not love, that can transcend such divisions, provide a common standard for argument and discussion, provide a basis for a universal humanitarianism, for reasonable compromise, agreement and peace. One reason why Popper so detests philosophical relativism is the political one that it denies this.

With the best will in the world, however, agreement on political issues cannot always be reached. We therefore need, as well as reasonableness, a system for taking and enforcing authoritative decisions, when necessary –

we need a state. What kind of state? How should we be governed? According to Popper, this question has continually been approached in the wrong way, not least by those two great thinkers targeted in *The Open Society and Its Enemies*, Plato and Marx. The misconception in question has been to look for an answer to the question, 'Who should rule?' Plato's answer was – philosophers should rule; Marx's was that the proletariat should rule first of all, and ultimately no one should because ruling should become unnecessary. All these answers are rejected by Popper, but so is the (supposedly) democratic answer – that the people should rule. All answers to the question of who should rule should be rejected, because the question is the wrong question. Popper gives two reasons why this is so. First of all, the question implies acceptance of the doctrine of sovereignty – in other words, the view that, so long as power is given to the right people, it can and should be unlimited. To the liberal, fallibilist Popper this is a profound mistake. All rulers are human, and therefore fallible, and should not be trusted with unlimited power. Although he is a democrat, Popper does not believe in the sovereignty of the people. He believes that *all* power must be limited.

Secondly, answering the question 'Who should rule?' fails to solve the political problem, because, Popper thinks, the doctrine of sovereignty contain a logical contradiction.[72] Is the sovereign entitled to relinquish power to someone else? If (as Plato predicted) the people in a democracy are seduced into handing over power to a tyrant, is that democratic or undemocratic? The democrat who defines democracy as rule by the people has no answer to this conundrum, and is unable to oppose tyranny in this case.

Popper's conception of democracy, therefore, is not rule by the people, but a form of government that puts limits on power – the best such system. Democracy, says Popper is 'the right of the people to judge and to dismiss their government' through the device of elections.[73] This, Popper says, is the only way in which we (the people) can protect ourselves against abuse of political power, and also bring it about that it is used to secure equal freedom for all (through, for example, what Popper calls 'protectionism' and 'interventionism'). Not the least of the merits of democracy is that it is a *peaceful* way of getting rid of rulers we dislike. One of Marx's greatest mistakes, Popper thinks, was his scornful or at best tactical attitude to 'bourgeois democracy', a system which has in fact achieved much more for the working class than his favoured method of proletarian revolution.

As the last sentence above perhaps suggests, Popper is, among all the political philosophers of the twentieth century, probably the truest son of the Enlightenment, and the doughtiest champion of modernity – of science, reason, individual liberty and representative democracy. *Conjectures and Refutations* contains an essay entitled, a little provocatively, 'The history of our time: an optimist's view' (originally delivered as a lecture in 1956) in which Popper celebrates the achievements of the democratic era. We have, in the 'developed' countries, Popper claims, 'very nearly, if not completely, succeeded in abolishing the greatest evils what have hitherto beset the social life of man'.[74] Evils such as poverty, economic insecurity, sickness and pain, slavery, lack of educational opportunity, religious and racial discrimination, and rigid class differences, have been greatly alleviated and even in some cases remedied. Human rights and human dignity are more respected in our society than they have ever been before. Of course many serious problems remain, but that is the human condition – we are fallible beings who cannot achieve utopia but only seek as best we can to solve our problems, using our resources of reason. As Popper sums up: 'In spite of our great and serious troubles, and in spite of the fact that ours is surely not the best possible society, I assert that our own free world is by far the best society which has come into existence during the course of human history'.[75] It appears that we humans have indeed been able to learn something from our many mistakes.

Notes

1 K. R. Popper and J. Eccles, *The Self and Its Brain* (Routledge, London, 1990). Medawar refers to Popper in, for example, P. M. Medawar, *Induction and Intuition in Scientific Thought* (Methuen, London, 1969).
2 K. R. Popper, *Conjectures and Refutations: The Growth of Scientific Knowledge* (Routledge and Kegan Paul, London, 1963), pp. 316–17.
3 K. R. Popper, *Unended Quest* (Fontana/Collins, Glasgow, 1976), p. 168.
4 K. R. Popper, *Objective Knowledge: An Evolutionary Approach* (Oxford University Press, London, 1972), p. 248.
5 T. S. Kuhn, *The Structure of Scientific Revolutions* (University of Chicago Press, 1962).
6 K. R. Popper, *The Open Society and Its Enemies,* vol. 2: *Hegel and Marx* (Routledge and Kegan Paul, London, 1962), 4th edn, pp. 217–18.
7 Popper, *Conjectures and Refutations*, pp. 120–35.
8 K. R. Popper, *The Open Society and Its Enemies,* vol. 1: *The Spell of Plato* (Routledge and Kegan Paul, London, 1962), 4th edn, ch. 10.
9 Ibid., pp. 171, 175.
10 Ibid., p. 176.

11 Ibid., pp. 174–5.
12 Ibid., pp. 183–4.
13 Ibid., p. 176.
14 K. R. Popper, *The Poverty of Historicism* (Routledge and Kegan Paul, London, 1957), p. 130.
15 Ibid., pp. 5, 7, 10–11, 131–3.
16 Ibid., p. 136.
17 Ibid., p. 157.
18 Ibid., pp. 152, 158.
19 Ibid., pp. 158–9.
20 Popper, *Objective Knowledge*, p. 237.
21 Popper, *The Poverty of Historicism*, pp. 158–9.
22 Ibid., p. 154.
23 Ibid., pp. 142, 158.
24 Popper, *The Open Society and Its Enemies*, vol. 2, p. 97.
25 Popper, *The Poverty of Historicism*, pp. 140–1.
26 Popper, *The Open Society and Its Enemies*, vol. 2, p. 97.
27 Ibid., p. 94.
28 Ibid., p. 95.
29 Popper, *The Open Society and Its Enemies*, vol. 1, pp. 157–8.
30 Ibid., pp. 161–4.
31 Ibid., p. 287.
32 Ibid., pp. 159–60.
33 Ibid., p. 176.
34 Ibid., pp. 73, 174, 177.
35 Ibid., pp. 174–5.
36 Ibid., p. 185.
37 Popper gives a detailed argument on Plato's departures from Socrates' views in his discussion of the 'Socratic problem': ibid., pp. 306–10.
38 Ibid., p. 3.
39 Ibid., p. 145.
40 Ibid., p. 39.
41 This is the sequence in the *Republic*. There are minor variations in the *Statesman* and the *Laws*.
42 Popper, *The Open Society and Its Enemies*, vol. 1, pp. 38, 83.
43 Ibid., p. 46.
44 Ibid., pp. 49–51.
45 Ibid., p. 143.
46 Ibid., p. 138.
47 Ibid., p. 195.
48 Ibid., p. 103.
49 Cf. ibid., pp. 332, 342; B. Magee, *Popper* (Fontana/Collins, London, 1973),

p. 93; R. Robinson, 'Dr Popper's defence of democracy', *Philosophical Review* 60 (1951), pp. 487–507.

50 Popper, *The Open Society and Its Enemies*, vol. 1, p. 169.

51 W. A. Kaufmann, *Philosophical Review* 60 (1951), pp. 465–6.

52 Popper, *The Open Society and Its Enemies*, vol. 2, pp. 136–7.

53 Popper, *The Poverty of Historicism*, p. 115.

54 Ibid., p. 109.

55 Ibid., p. 84.

56 Popper, *The Open Society and Its Enemies*, vol. 1, p. 188.

57 Ibid., vol. 2, p. 206.

58 Ibid., vol. 2, pp. 269, 278–9.

59 Ibid., vol. 2, p. 119.

60 Ibid., vol. 1, p. 284.

61 Ibid., vol. 1, p. 237.

62 Ibid., vol. 2, p. 124.

63 Ibid.

64 Ibid., vol. 2, p. 126.

65 Ibid., vol. 2, pp. 131–2.

66 Ibid., vol. 1, p. 131; vol. 2, pp. 126, 140, 181–2; Popper, *Conjectures and Refutations*, p. 370.

67 Popper, *The Open Society and Its Enemies*, vol. 2, p. 238.

68 Ibid.

69 Ibid., vol. 2, p. 225.

70 Ibid., vol. 2, p. 234.

71 Popper, *Conjectures and Refutations*, pp. 368–9.

72 Popper, *The Open Society and Its Enemies*, vol. 1, p. 123.

73 Ibid., vol. 2, p. 127. Cf. also ibid., vol. 1, p. 124.

74 Popper, *Conjectures and Refutations*, p. 370.

75 Ibid., p. 369.

Further reading

By Popper

K. R. Popper, *The Open Society and Its Enemies*, 2 vols, Routledge and Kegan Paul, London, 1945, 1952, 1957, 1962.

K. R. Popper, *The Poverty of Historicism*, Routledge and Kegan Paul, London, 1957.

K. R. Popper, *The Logic of Scientific Discovery*, Hutchinson, London, 1959.

K. R. Popper, *Conjectures and Refutations: The Growth of Scientific Knowledge*, Routledge and Kegan Paul, London, 1963.

K. R. Popper, *Objective Knowledge: An Evolutionary Approach*, Oxford University

Press, London, 1972.

K.R. Popper, *Unended Quest: An Intellectual Autobiography*, Fontana/Collins, Glasgow, 1976.

K. R. Popper, *Karl Popper: Selected Writings*, ed. D. Miller, Princeton University Press, 1985.

K. R. Popper, *In Search of a Better World*, tr. L. J. Bennett, Routledge, London, 1992.

On Popper

T. Burke, *The Philosophy of Popper*, Manchester University Press, 1983.

G. Currie and A. Musgrave (eds), *Popper and the Human Sciences*, Nijhoff, Dordrecht, 1985.

M. Freeman, 'Sociology and utopia: some reflections on Karl Popper', *British Journal of Sociology* 26, 1975.

M. H. Lessnoff, 'The political philosophy of Karl Popper', *British Journal of Political Science* 10, 1980

H. Lubasz, 'Popper in utopia', *Times Higher Education Supplement*, 25 December 1981, p. 10.

B. Magee, *Popper*, Fontana/Collins, London, 1973.

A. O'Hear, *Karl Popper*, Routledge and Kegan Paul, London, 1980.

P. A. Schilpp (ed.), *The Philosophy of Karl Popper*, 2 vols, Library of Living Philosophers, Open Court, La Salle, Illinois, 1974 (includes Popper's 'Intellectual autobiography' published separately as *Unended Quest*, and replies to critics).

C. Simkin, *Popper's Views on Natural and Social Science*, E. J. Brill, Leiden, 1993.

J. Shearmur, *The Political Thought of Karl Popper*, Routledge, London, 1996.

9
Isaiah Berlin: Monism and Pluralism

Isaiah Berlin, like so many of the significant political philosophers of the twentieth century, was an immigrant – in Berlin's case, from Russia to Britain. By comparison with Arendt, Marcuse, Hayek and Popper, however, Berlin arrived in his adopted country at a much younger age. Born in the Latvian capital Riga (then a Russian city) in 1909, he was in England by 1921, having fled St Petersburg with his family after the revolutions of 1917. Berlin, therefore, was a refugee from Bolshevism rather than Nazism; members of his family, however, died at the hands of the Nazis in Latvia in the Second World War. Thus Berlin's experience of the political traumas and the totalitarian regimes of the twentieth century was direct and personal, and they shaped his political thought as much as did his largely English education. Most of Berlin's adult life was spent in Oxford, as (*inter alia*) Fellow of All Souls, Professor of Social and Political Theory (1957–67) and first President of Wolfson College. At the end of his life Berlin was, despite his foreign roots, a leading member of the English intellectual establishment, admired for his wit, learning and brilliance as a lecturer, knighted in 1957, and famous as a champion of liberalism. I shall suggest, however, that the last-mentioned part of his reputation is open to question.

In the early part of his academic career, Berlin was a colleague and admirer of the leader of Oxford linguistic philosophy, J. L. Austin, to whose 'circle' he belonged. Berlin's work in the 1930s did not at first betray any particular interest in politics, being largely concerned with technical philosophical problems. But the publication, in 1939, of his first book – on Karl Marx – signalled a change of direction towards the field in which he was to win distinction, namely the history of ideas, with particular emphasis on their social and political bearing. According to Berlin himself, the motive for this change was a desire to work in a field in which he could expect to know more at the end of his career than at the beginning. It is not, of course, only Berlin who knows more as a result of his life's efforts. However, Berlin's quest was never merely for knowledge, but above all aimed at a historically informed understanding of the role of ideas in our time. Conceptually, that role is understood by Berlin in terms of an opposition between the 'monism' which he opposes, and the 'pluralism' which he champions. Historically, Berlin's opposition is, especially, between the 'Enlightenment' and the 'Counter-Enlightenment' (though it is not confined to these two moments). Thus he has written (at book length) on Vico and Herder, and on J. G. Hamann; and (at lesser length) on Machiavelli, Montesquieu, de Maistre, Sorel, J. S. Mill, Herzen, Tolstoi and others, besides more general essays on intellectual movements of the eighteenth and nineteenth centuries. Many of these essays have been collected in three anthologies, entitled *Russian Thinkers* (1978), *Against the Current* (1979) and *The Crooked Timber of Humanity* (1990). Another anthology, *Concepts and Categories* (1978) collects early philosophical articles as well as two significant contributions to political philosophy, 'Does political theory still exist?' and 'Equality'. But Berlin's most famous contribution to political philosophy, which is at the same time an historical exploration of politically relevant ideas, is not a book or an article or an essay, but a lecture – Berlin's celebrated 1958 inaugural lecture as Professor of Political and Social Theory, 'Two concepts of liberty'. This was later reprinted (along with 'Historical inevitability' and two other pieces) in *Four Essays on Liberty* (1969).

Why should Berlin write, in 1961, an article entitled 'Does political theory still exist?'[1] Not because he himself doubted its existence, but rather because, as he says, of a widespread belief in the 'death of political philosophy' among contemporaries: a belief which he attributes to the absence of any 'commanding work of political philosophy' written in the twentieth century. In view of the contributions already made, before 1961, by Oakeshott, Arendt, Hayek and Popper, to say nothing of the Frankfurt School, this seems a distinctly odd analysis. A better explanation of the belief in political philosophy's demise is to be found in the introduction to the second series of papers collected under the title *Philosophy, Politics and Society* by Peter Laslett and W. G. Runciman, in which Berlin's 1961 article is reprinted. The editors cite their own statement, in the introduction to an earlier collection published in 1956, that, 'For the moment, anyway, political philosophy is dead',[2] and attribute that belief to the hegemony of what they call 'Weldonism', that is, the opinions of the Oxford linguistic philosopher T. D. Weldon. For Weldon (as, ironically, for the young Berlin), philosophy is linguistic analysis, and prescriptive political theory, therefore, is not philosophy but un-philosophical moralizing. Presumably, Berlin, by 1961, repudiated this implication or interpretation of linguistic philosophy. More interesting, however, is Berlin's reason for proclaiming, not only the continuing existence of political philosophy but the necessity of its existence. The problems of political philosophy are of a kind that cannot be solved by logical analysis or empirical evidence alone, or by both together. This does not, however, mean that the problems are meaningless or trivial; rather, it reflects the fact of fundamental disagreements about values. As Berlin puts it, political philosophy presupposes 'a world where ends collide'.[3] Political philosophy exists because of the plurality of values. It exists if and only if value-pluralism is true, and value-monism false. In a society dominated by a single goal, where 'no serious questions about political ends or values could arise', there would be technical problems but no political problems – no politics.[4] The existence or at least the legitimacy of politics itself – not just of political philosophy – is a consequence of value-pluralism, that is, of the legitimacy of a plurality of values. This latter is the *leitmotiv* of Berlin's thinking on political theory; the relation between value-pluralism and liberalism must be a central issue in any discussion of his political thought.

Berlin's assault on monistic thinking in politics begins, perhaps, in his 1953 lecture on 'Historical inevitability'. In Berlin's view, the belief in historical inevitability, or historical determinism, which he rejects in the name of human freedom, manifests monistic thinking in at least two distinguishable ways. Most fundamental is what Berlin calls the teleological outlook, which takes many forms, but always involves belief in a 'single "cosmic" over-all scheme which is the goal of the universe', or at least of humankind[5] – a single purpose or plan which makes the universe or human history intelligible. The word 'plan' is here significantly ambiguous: it signifies both a goal (though not, in this case, of any human agent, but rather of history or the universe as a whole) and also a pattern of interrelations among elements which subserves the goal. Historical or any other explanation, from this point of view, means showing the place that each individual item has in the overall plan. As Berlin puts it, 'to understand is to perceive patterns',[6] and to explain an historical event or action is to show it to be 'a necessary consequence of its place in the pattern'. This is a view, Berlin suggests, which owes very little to respect for empirical reality, and everything to a metaphysical attitude – almost, one might say, to a metaphysical yearning. To use Weberian terms, it is an attitude which rejects the disenchantment of the world.

Yet, paradoxically, that attitude not infrequently pays homage to science, and seeks to invoke its authority in support of its favoured teleology – the most obvious examples are Comte and Marx. It is this union which spawns the doctrine of historical inevitability in its most recent form, the belief in natural laws of history. And this 'scientism' (to use Hayek's term) is also a manifestation of monism – in this case, the insistence on a single valid method of understanding and explanation. Berlin calls it an 'infatuation',[7] the product of a 'naive craving for unity and symmetry at the expense of experience',[8] and he rejects it, as he rejects all forms of monistic teleology, because all are 'forms of determinism', which claim or imply that the individual's freedom of choice is 'ultimately an illusion'.[9]

Berlin distinguishes two forms of the doctrine of historical inevitability, one 'benevolent', the other 'less amiable.[10] The former (exemplified by the utopias of Bacon, Condorcet, St Simon, Owen and Comte) rests, Berlin says, on a 'belief in the possiblity (or probability) of happiness as the product of rational organization', a belief that 'unites all the benevolent sages of modern times'. It is, however, quite unclear (and Berlin does nothing to clarify the problem) how such a belief is even compatible, logically speaking, with historical determinism, never mind a form of it. More germane is Berlin's 'less amiable' form, exemplified by Hegel and Marx – less amiable because, Berlin says, each uses his version of historical teleology to justify the destruction of any human beings so foolish as to oppose or obstruct history's necessary movement towards its *telos*. This, Berlin says, is the attitude of the '*enragé* prophet'[11] who looks to history to wreak vengeance on those he hates.

In summary, Berlin identifies the belief in historical inevitability with a monistic style of thinking which is anti-individualist in two senses – it justifies individual suffering for the sake of a supposed greater good, and it denies the reality of individual freedom and individual choice. As he himself points out, he has not shown – has not even argued – that the belief in historical inevitability is false; rather, he seeks to show that it has implications which are unacceptable. In particular, he argues that these implications are at variance with the ordinary assumptions of human beings, including historians and 'natural scientists outside the laboratory'.[12] This is shown by the language that we all use (here Berlin seems to draw on the precepts of linguistic philosophy to which he adhered as a young man), language which presupposes that choices between alternative courses of action are open to individual agents, that it makes sense to think or argue about the best course of action, and that therefore human beings are, at least up to a point, responsible for their actions, and thus appropriate objects of moral judgement, praise and blame. Whether or not all this rests on an illusion, 'to make a serious attempt to adapt our thoughts and words to the hypothesis of determinism [would be] a fearful task',[13] verging on the impossible. Nor is there any good reason to try, since no one has shown any version of historical determinism to be true.[14] Plainly Berlin wishes to go on conceptualizing human beings as free agents, not only because to do so comes naturally, but because he values them as such. So far, then, Berlin appears as a defender of individual freedom against philosophical monism.

The same theme appears, in greater elaboration, in what is probably Berlin's most celebrated contribution to political philosophy, the lecture on 'Two concepts of liberty'. In this piece, the contrast between monism and pluralism is made explicit, and the latter championed against the former. The political context of the lecture is also significant – namely, the so-called Cold War between the liberal West and the Marxist or Stalinist East.[15] From this point of view, Berlin's lecture appears as a defence of the Western liberal tradition against its enemies, including Bolshevism – even although that particular enemy is not given any explicit predominance in Berlin's argument, but is rather set in a large context of the history of ideas. Specifically, Berlin aims to show how the contrast between monism and pluralism has manifested itself in two very different concepts of liberty, which he calls 'negative' and 'positive'.

These two concepts need to be defined with some care. At times, Berlin uses a kind of shorthand contrast between 'freedom from' (negative) and 'freedom to' (positive) which has also sometimes been used by commentators and critics, but which is at best uninformative and at worst misleading. It is uninformative in relation to 'negative liberty', which Berlin believes to be the normal (unphilosophical) conception of freedom, according to which a person is free if, or to the extent that, his or her actions are not subject to deliberate interference or coercion by other human beings. It is misleading in relation to 'positive liberty', which is defined by Berlin as self-mastery, or self-direction or self-government. A man is free, in this sense, if or to the extent that he is his own master.

Are these really two different concepts, or simply two different ways of saying the same thing? Berlin is somewhat ambivalent about this. He remarks at one point that they 'may seem' to be at no great logical distance from each other – yet, historically, they 'developed in divergent directions not always by logically reputable steps until, in the end, they came into direct conflict with each other'.[16] This comment suggests a frequent criticism of Berlin's argument (made, for example, by C. B. Macpherson), namely, that his 'positive liberty' is not one but several concepts – a family of concepts related historically, but not necessarily logically. This criticism has considerable justice. Nevertheless, Berlin's two definitions *are* of different concepts – there are many factors other than deliberate interference or coercion by other persons that can prevent one from being one's own master. One – as critics of Berlin have again pointed out – is poverty. According to Berlin's negative or normal concept of liberty, poverty may make one unable to do what one wishes, but does not in itself diminish one's freedom. It is an evil, no doubt, but not *that* evil. But poverty, or at least extreme poverty, can certainly prevent one from being one's own master. Freedom is a great good, and 'negative' freedom is a great good, in Berlin's view; but it is not the whole of good, it does not alone ensure (though some minimum amount of it is necessary for) a good life. It does not ensure self-mastery.

So much Berlin is happy to admit. But what else, besides poverty or the coercive interference of others, can prevent a person from achieving self-mastery? It is in giving answers to this question that the philosophers – or certain philosophers – have been so fertile and ingenious that the 'positive' concept of liberty came to be interpreted in ways which are in direct conflict with the normal or negative concept. In this way they have in the end created an *illiberal* concept of liberty – a sham, or, as Berlin puts it, 'a specious disguise for brutal tyranny'.[17] How did this happen?

Self-mastery is mastery of the self by the self. But what is the self? It has long been a tradition of Western philosophy, from Plato onwards, to conceive the individual 'soul' as divided into a number of distinct faculties – in Plato's conception, a trinity, consisting of reason, spirit and passion or desire. More typically, the trinity came to be reduced to a duality, or opposition, between reason and passion (or passions, or desires). But if these two faculties of the soul are *opposed*, which must dominate if the individual is to be genuinely his own master? The question answers itself. Self-mastery, or 'real' freedom according to the positive conception, requires that the individual is guided by reason, or that his reason rules his passions or desires. Thus self-mastery can, paradoxically, be prevented by one's own desires. This conception is buttressed by the common human experience of seeking (sometimes successfully, sometimes not) to control or subdue one's passions for the sake of some nobler or more rational purpose. The 'true' or at least the 'higher' self must be the rational self, or the rational faculty within the self. What are the consequences for the concept of freedom of this hierarchical and dualistic conception of the self?

There are several. One is what may be called the Stoic conception of freedom, or (in Berlin's words) 'the retreat to the inner citadel', or the concept of 'the rational sage who has escaped into the inner fortress of his true self'.[18] To have desires is always to risk frustration, whether or not this results from the deliberate opposition of other men. But that thwarting of one's desires does not impinge on one's liberty, if those desires are really alien to one's true or rational self. One should, therefore, make every effort to rid oneself of all frustrated desires, perhaps even of all desires, since all desires may be frustrated. A person thereby becomes not less but more free – free of the passions that might enslave his reason, or that might be used by others to manipulate him contrary to his reason. The desire to lose all desire is most characteristic of Stoics such as Epictetus, but Berlin detects elements of this view of freedom also in Rousseau and even Kant. His main *political* objection to it is that it implies that a ruler who is able, by conditioning or otherwise, to induce his subjects to abandon desires which he dislikes, can claim to have liberated them.[19]

Another version of the positive concept of freedom harks back to Berlin's critique of historical inevitability. To resist the inevitable is by definition irrational; correspondingly, if the true self is the rational self, to be free is to understand what is inevitable and to accept it. For thinkers such as Hegel and Marx, therefore, to grasp and submit to the necessary course of history is to be liberated. But knowledge is not the only possible liberator – indeed, sometimes it is not a possible liberator, for in some people, or perhaps most people, reason may be too weak, or perhaps there may be insufficient time to 'educate' them. If only truth can liberate, those who have not grasped the truth can and must be liberated by those who have. The rational must liberate the irrational by forcing them to behave rationally. 'Once I take this view, I am in a position to ignore the actual wishes of men or societies, to bully, oppress, torture them in the name, and on behalf of, their "real" selves'.[20] According to Berlin, the authoritarianism of such thinkers as Fichte and Comte derives from these conceptions, as do 'many of the nationalist, communist, and authoritarian creeds of our day'. And not only of our day – the Jacobins of the French Revolution relied on them as much as the Bolsheviks of the Russian Revolution.

But what kind of truth is it that is known to the rational, and justifies their coercing the irrational in order to liberate them? Not all such 'liberators' have been, like Hegel and Marx, historicists in Popper's sense of the term. It should be noted (though Berlin does not) that that brand of historicism fuses fact and value in a very specific and characteristic way – that is, it proclaims, or assumes, that the necessary direction of history, its *telos*, is *good*, so that to resist it is not only futile but evil. Something similar applies also to Comte.

For such thinkers, therefore, the issue of *moral* knowledge hardly arises as a separate issue. But this is not true of all the 'rationalist' philosophers discussed by Berlin. Particularly crucial here is the role of Kant. Kant certainly did not confuse or identify fact and value, but he did identify morality and reason. According to Kant's categorical imperative, morality is that which I can will without contradiction to be a universal law. Immorality therefore is irrationality, and to be rational is to be moral. Hence to be free (from the heteronomy of domination by the passions) is likewise to be moral.[21] According to Kant, no law of which, as a rational being, I should approve, deprives me of any portion of my freedom. True freedom is subjection to such laws, 'for this dependence is the work of my own will acting as law-giver'.[22] As Rousseau (whose influence both Kant and Robespierre acknowledged) had put it, to subject oneself to the General Will (which is one's own moral will) is to receive civil and moral freedom; and whoever disobeys the law made by this moral General Will can and must be forced to be free.

Berlin's survey of the career of the positive concept of liberty depicts the transformation of self-mastery into enslavement by dint of what he calls 'rationalism', that is, the view that human reason can determine what is true or right. But the doctrine in question is not merely rationalism – it is 'monistic rationalism'. This Berlin explains as follows. Not only is reason capable of solving correctly every intellectual and moral problem, there is only one, unique, correct answer to any such problem. Not only that, but the true answers to all such problems must be mutually consistent and compatible – there can be no conflicts 'within' reason. To put it another way, truth is the unique set of rationally discoverable and mutually consistent correct answers to all questions. There is 'one unique pattern which alone fulfils the claims of reason'.[23] The rational person acts and lives in accordance with this pattern; the rational society is organized in accordance with it; the rational state enforces it through its laws. There is only one way to be rational, and only one legitimate way to live. Monistic rationalism is also value-monism.

Berlin rejects value-monism totally, and proclaims his belief in a *pluralism of values*. 'The world that we encounter . . . is one in which we are faced with choices between ends equally ultimate, and claims equally absolute, the realization of some of which must inevitably involve the sacrifice of others . . . The necessity of choosing between absolute claims is [thus] an inescapable characteristic of the human condition'.[24] Because of the multiplicity and incompatibility of human ends, 'the possibility of conflict – and of tragedy – can never wholly be eliminated from human life, personal or social'. There are many goods that are potentially realizable in human life, but not all can be fully realized by one person or one society – that, to Berlin, is an objective fact. Human beings must choose which goods they will seek to realize and to what extent, but no single choice is the uniquely correct or objectively rational one. It is this state of affairs that gives value to freedom to choose – freedom in the negative or normal sense; makes it, indeed, an indispensable value for human life. But it is not the only value, for here, too, pluralism reigns; while (negative) liberty is indispensable, it cannot be unlimited, but must be curbed in order to accommodate other values such as security, equality, and happiness. 'That we cannot have everything is a necessary, not a contingent truth'.[25]

Some critics of Berlin's famous inaugural lecture have complained that the evils analysed therein are blamed on the wrong culprit – there is nothing intrinsically illiberal about the 'positive' concept of liberty as self-mastery or self-direction, which has been deformed into illiberality only because philosophers and others have combined it with a rationalistic conception of the self and a monistic conception of reason. This riposte is perfectly justified, yet it is of secondary importance. Whatever the title of Berlin's lecture, it is precisely monistic rationalism, or value-monism, which is his target, here as throughout his political philosophy. Elsewhere Berlin cites Alexander Herzen's remark that the modern era has invented a new kind of human sacrifice – the sacrifice of human beings to an ideal.[26] The monistic theories which underpin such sanguinary ideals are, to a certain kind of mind, a source of considerable emotional and intellectual satisfaction, but they also manifest, Berlin suggests, a kind of immaturity. He champions instead 'the ideal of freedom to choose ends, without claiming eternal validity for them'.[27] This may be less exciting, but it is by far more humane, and corresponds better to the truth.

It is undoubtedly the argument of the inaugural lecture that is the principal source of Berlin's reputation as a champion of liberalism, a position which, as we have seen, he once again founds on his principles of pluralism and anti-monism. Yet Berlin's later writings cast doubt both on this reputation, and on the logical link between pluralism and liberalism. The problem, in fact, is already present in the argument of the inaugural lecture, though it may not be readily apparent. Plurality of values, or of goods, or of legitimate ends, is not *alone* a sufficient premise for liberalism – that requires another premise, or value judgement, that coercion is *per se* an evil, and the exercise of autonomous choice a good. For if that is not so, the plurality of legitimate ends affords no argument against coercion, so long as the coerced action tends to realize one at least of the plurality of legitimate ends. The monistic coercer may be mistaken in thinking he is promoting the only good, but can still be promoting good. (It will not, furthermore, help to postulate *variety* as an intrinsic good, since that too could be achieved by coercion.) To put the problem another way: does or can the plurality of values include illiberal values? Pluralism in itself does not rule this out, hence the need for the further premises indicated. An interesting question therefore arises: does Berlin wish to exclude illiberal values from the legitimate plurality of values? The inaugural lecture suggests that he does; but some of his later writings cast doubt on this.

Having identified as the key issue of political philosophy the opposition between monism and pluralism, Berlin, in most of his later writings, set about tracing the manifestations and development of these opposed ideas in the history of Western political thought – and, in particular, to assemble a gallery of 'pluralist' intellectual heroes. It is this enterprise which casts doubt on or at least qualifies his liberalism. But before examining this matter, we shall first glance briefly at Berlin's application of pluralism to another central concept of political philosophy, namely equality. Berlin's paper on 'Equality',[28] which predates the inaugural lecture by a couple of years, expresses the following views. Equality in the treatment of human beings is a principle that requires no justification, because it is simply an application of the formula that similar cases should be treated similarly. Since all human beings by definition belong to the class of human beings, they should be treated identically, unless there is a sufficient reason not to do so. In other words, unequal treatment of humans requires justification. In Berlin's view, such justification frequently exists. The person who takes the contrary view is called by Berlin the 'fanatical egalitarian'.[29] In the language later adopted by Berlin he could be called an egalitarian monist – one who believes equality to be the only value, or at least believes that equality should never be compromised for the sake of any other value. Berlin takes the contrary, pluralist view. 'Equality is one value among many'.[30] Thus it must sometimes be compromised for the sake of other values, such as efficiency and liberty. Good music is a value that justifies the unequal authority wielded by the conductor of an orchestra; the value of freedom justifies departures from economic equality. What is worth mentioning about this argument is that, while pluralist, it gives no privileged place to liberty among the plurality of values – if any value is accorded special status, it is not liberty but equality.

Let us now turn to Berlin's assessments of individual thinkers in relation to the monism–pluralism polarity, and in particular his search for the roots of pluralism – what might be called an effort to establish a pluralist roll of honour. In this context it is not surprising to find a celebration of John Stuart Mill

('John Stuart Mill and the ends of life', included in the *Four Essays on Liberty*). Other heroes are more unexpected, and more problematic. Machiavelli is praised for discovering 'the uncomfortable [pluralist] truth . . . that not all ultimate values are compatible with each other',[31] that the individualistic and other-worldly morality of Christianity is not compatible with the civically oriented, militaristic ethic of classical paganism, and that one must choose between them – even although Machiavelli chose, and invited rulers to choose, a ruthless version of the latter that had no qualms about trampling on the rights and liberties of individuals. Not only is there nothing liberal about Machiavelli's pluralism, Berlin's attitude to it begins to make his own pluralism look like relativism. This is an issue to which we shall return.

Machiavelli, however, although admired, is not the brightest star in Berlin's pluralist galaxy. Two later thinkers vie for that title – the Italian Giambattista Vico, and the German Johann Gottfried Herder. The greatness of the early eighteenth-century Neapolitan, Vico, Berlin tells us, is that he was the 'father both of the modern concept of culture and of . . . cultural pluralism',[32] the doctrine that 'each authentic culture has its own unique vision, its own scale of values',[33] and must be understood on its own terms. Vico applied his version of pluralism to history, seen as a succession of distinct human cultures, rather than a single story of progress or regress. The moderns are not superior to the ancients, or vice versa: rather, each have their characteristic values and virtues. The values of Homeric Greece are not those of classical Athens, nor of Renaissance Italy, nor of eighteenth-century France; each culture gives space for the flourishing of certain virtues, but at the expense of others. In history, all gain involves loss. Berlin comments:

> it follows that the very notion of a perfect society, in which all the excellences of all cultures will harmoniously coalesce, does not make sense . . . [It] entails that the perennial idea of the perfect society, in which truth, justice, freedom, happiness, virtue coalesce in their most perfect forms, is not merely Utopian . . . but intrinsically incoherent; for if some of these values prove to be incompatible, they cannot – conceptually cannot – coalesce . . .[34]

If Vico was the originator of cultural pluralism, that conception found its classical formulation in the work of Herder (1744–1803). Whereas Vico 'thought of a succession of civilizations', Herder 'went further and compared national cultures in many lands and periods'.[35] The word 'national' is important – Herder is the prophet of the nation (*Volk*) as the human cultural unit *par excellence*. Berlin explains his views as follows.

Values are not universal: every human society, every people . . . possesses its own unique ideals, standards, ways of living and thought and action. There are no immutable, universal, eternal rules or criteria of judgment in terms of which different cultures and nations can be graded in some single order of excellence . . . Every nation has its own traditions, its own character . . . its own centre of moral gravity, which differs from those of every other: there and only there its happiness lies — in the development of its own national needs, its own unique character.[36]

Human beings are naturally divided into these exclusive cultural groups, defined by 'bonds of common descent, language, soil, collective experience'.[37] Greeks are Greek, Indians Indian, Persians Persian, Frenchmen French. 'Cultures are incommensurable; each is of . . . infinite value . . . [None] is superior to any of the others.'[38] All men are shaped by their national culture and tradition, and can develop fully as human beings only by remaining faithful to it, indeed can never escape it.

It is obvious that the cultural pluralism of Vico and Herder as Berlin understands it has nothing to do with liberalism, is indeed incompatible with it, since liberalism is just the sort of universal principle which these thinkers (Berlin says) repudiate. Equally obviously not all civilizations or national cultures are liberal, or respect the liberty of the individual — yet all, according to Herder, are (Berlin says) equal. It may seem surprising (at least at first sight) that, despite his great admiration for Herder, Berlin writes scathingly of nationalism in several articles. However, he is careful to distinguish 'nationalism' from 'national consciousness', and from pride in national character.[39] Nationalism, as Berlin defines it, is the belief in the intrinsic superiority of one's own nation, such as to justify fighting for it in any conflict 'no matter at what cost to other men'.[40] Nationalism, Berlin says, is 'an inflamed condition of national consciousness', usually caused by some form of collective historical humiliation.[41] Berlin clearly sees Herder as the champion, in those terms, of national consciousness, not nationalism, and agrees with him. The problem is, however, that belief in the superiority of one's own nation is not (contrary to what Berlin implies) an 'inflamed' or merely pathological exaggeration of national consciousness — it is a normal part of it. Aggressive attitudes to other nations are not unusual, historically (even if genocide and 'ethnic cleansing' are relatively rare and extreme manifestations thereof). Herder's sophisticated belief in the equality of all national cultures is not part of any of them — it is in fact a universal principle underivable from any of them, and foreign to them.

Implicitly, then, if not explicitly, Herder and Berlin do apply *some* universal standards to national cultures, and find them (partially) wanting. But the number of universal principles each is prepared to apply in this way is strictly limited (and does not include, be it noticed, any strong principle of individual liberty). While the exact degree of Berlin's agreement with Herder is not clear, there is no doubt that he sees Herder as a master-exponent of pluralism, to which he (Berlin) also subscribes. This raises again the issue of relativism. Herder, as depicted by Berlin, is clearly a relativist, though he fell foul of the familiar paradox of relativism, in the form described above. Berlin, however, explicitly repudiates relativism, and seeks to distinguish it from pluralism. We must examine whether he succeeds.

He deploys two lines of argument. First, Berlin argues that his position (and also that of Herder and Vico) is not relativism, but an appeal to us as members of one culture, 'by the force of imaginative insight',[42] to enter into, and understand the values and ideals of other cultures, no matter how remote in time and space; and to accept these alien values and ideals, though we do not share them, as valid, rational, and fully human. This is possible, Berlin contends, 'because what makes men human is common to them, and acts as a bridge between them'.[43] There are, however, limits to this. 'Ends, moral principles, are many. But not infinitely many: they must be within the human horizon.' Berlin imagines a culture in which men worship trees, for no other reason than 'because they are made of wood', and asserts that such a bizarre culture, if it really existed, would be incomprehensible – beyond the bounds of imaginative sympathy. What is not clear, however, is whether all cultural values which *are* familiar and comprehensible, are to be accepted as valid. The results of that would be catastrophic. It would not allow Berlin to condemn slavery, for example, as he explicitly wishes to do,[44] nor religious intolerance, the Inquisition, or (probably) genocide. The same considerations refute Berlin's second argument, which is that the possibility of understanding other cultures implies *some* common human values. It does not. We can perfectly well understand what we condemn – precisely because we are human, and know how morally fallible human beings are. Likewise, and for the same reason, common values need not be approved. To condemn that which ought to be condemned, and to approve that which ought to be approved, we need the universal principles which, Berlin tells us, Herder denies. Berlin's limited pluralism needs such universal principles. Yet, curiously, liberal principles are not among them. Berlin's pluralism, though it began as a defence of liberalism, ends up endorsing one of liberalism's bitterest foes – communitarianism. A doctrine so broad that it finds little to choose between these two bitterly opposed philosophies is perhaps too broad.

Berlin's paradoxical hostility to universal principles has another surprising but logical consequence – a markedly sceptical attitude, verging on hostility, to the Enlightenment, and sympathy with the Romantic Counter-Enlightenment. The Enlightenment, according to Berlin, was shot through with monistic thinking: the view, as Berlin rather imprecisely puts it, 'that the light of truth is everywhere and always the same'.[45] To one aspect of this attitude Berlin is right to object – the infatuation with science, which 'alone can save us' and solve our problems, and whose method should allegedly be adopted in all spheres.[46] But Berlin objects to more: to the Enlightenment's beliefs in a fundamentally uniform human nature, and in universal moral principles (laws of nature).[47] For this universalist vision, Berlin tells us, the Romantic movement substituted a totally different one: that each man be true to his own ideals, whatever they are.[48] The question of the 'truth' of these ideals, or of which of two clashing ideals is 'true', scarcely arises, or is of secondary importance. Berlin sees this as the substitution of pluralism for monism and (despite the admitted excesses of Romanticism) a liberation from monistic tyranny. Berlin's analysis of the difference between Enlightenment and Romantic thought is acute, but the logic of his value judgements is questionable. Quintessential Enlightenment thinkers such as David Hume and Adam Smith, who certainly believed in an essentially uniform human nature, were also quintessential liberals; such convinced believers in universal moral principles as Kant and Voltaire were outspoken defenders of individual liberty. And why, logically, should they not be? On the other hand, Romantic hostility to universal reason, as Berlin admits, not infrequently culminated in an extreme irrationalism. Though he does not endorse it, Berlin seems to feel the fascination of this irrationalism, and to be more sympathetic towards it than one might expect from a liberal. His book-length study of Hamann (*The Magus of the North*) is a case in point. Others are his relatively sympathetic accounts of two extreme anti-rationalist and anti-Enlightenment thinkers, both of whom may be called precursors of fascism – Joseph de Maistre and Georges Sorel.[49] De Maistre, after all, was in Berlin's terms a pluralist, who scoffed at the Enlightenment's universalism in these often-quoted words: 'There is no such thing as *man* in the world. In the course of my life I have seen Frenchmen, Italians, Russians etc: I know, too, thanks to Montesquieu, that one can be a Persian. But as for *man*, I declare that I have never met him in my life.' This presumably is one reason why Berlin salutes de Maistre for the depth and accuracy of his political insight – despite or because of the fact that the words quoted are intended to pour scorn on the idea of human rights. Sorel, too, according to Berlin, saw through the monistic fallacy according to which the world is a 'rational harmony', championing instead heroic, uncompromising conflict in which men risk death for the sake of their values. Berlin recognizes Sorel as a ferocious enemy of liberal democracy, but credits him as 'the first to formulate . . . in clear language [the] revolt against the rational ideal of frictionless contentment in a harmonious social system in which all ultimate questions are reduced to technical problems' – a vision of a closed world which repels 'the young to-day' (1971).[50] If nothing else, the cases of de Maistre and Sorel show once again that pluralism and rejection of monistic rationalism have no necessary connection with liberalism. They also make one wonder whether Berlin's remarkable capacity for empathy with all manner of ideas and casts of mind, which is his great strength as an intellectual historian, does not also have its drawbacks. Sometimes one might wish that (in the words of a recent British prime minister) he would understand a little less, and condemn a little more.

In his famous inaugural lecture, Berlin sought to base liberal politics on a pluralist metaphysic; in later work, the emphasis is on pluralism alone. Whether or not the original project was deliberately abandoned, it has to be accounted a failure. From a liberal point of view, the fundamental problem is a failure to make certain necessary distinctions. Berlin endorses, indiscriminately, a plurality of conflicting 'values', 'ideals', 'ends' and 'goals', without any sense that the differences between these concepts might be important. Equality, for example, is referred to sometimes as a 'value', sometimes as an 'end'.[51] But is equality an end? It might indeed be an end of social policy, but it can hardly be an end pursued by the individual in private life. It is, in fact, surprising (from a liberal point of view) that, when Berlin gives specific examples of the plurality of legitimate values or ends, it is rare, even in the inaugural lecture, that anything that could serve as an end or goal of private life is mentioned[52] – rather, he refers to such social *desiderata* as harmony, peace, security and justice (as well as equality and liberty). The point is that, while liberalism can and should be largely agnostic in relation to private ends, it cannot and should not be so in relation to the structure of society. Liberalism requires a liberal society, governed by quite definite liberal principles. To put it crudely, private ends should be free, while social *desiderata* have to compromise with one another. The need to *choose* (to which ends one will devote one's life) is quite different from the need to *compromise* (between a variety of social principles). The latter has nothing to do with cultural relativism.

Berlin (to remain liberal) badly needs a distinction between (privately pursued) *ends* and (publicly enforced) *rules*, of the kind that plays such an important role in the liberal theories of Oakeshott and Hayek. To put it in different terms, he needs something like the distinction made (or used) by Rawls, between the *right* and the *good*. Liberalism means leaving people free, within limits, to pursue their own conceptions of the good: the limits are provided by certain rules of right, publicly enforced. Rawls's elaboration of this idea will be examined in the next chapter.

Notes

1 In P. Laslett and W. G. Runciman (eds), *Philosophy and Society*, second series (Basil Blackwell, Oxford, 1964), p. 1.
2 Ibid., p. vii.
3 Ibid., p. 8.
4 Ibid.
5 I. Berlin, *Four Essays on Liberty* (Oxford University Press, London, 1969), pp. 51–2.
6 Ibid., p. 52.
7 Ibid., p. 51.
8 Ibid., p. 43.
9 Ibid., p. 58.
10 Ibid., p. 60.
11 Ibid., p. 62.
12 Ibid., p. 69.
13 Ibid., p. 72.
14 Ibid., p. 113.
15 Cf. ibid., pp. 121, 131.
16 Ibid., p. 131.
17 Ibid.
18 Ibid., pp. 135, 139.
19 Ibid., pp. 139–40.
20 Ibid., p. 133.
21 Ibid., p. 147.
22 Ibid., p. 152.
23 Ibid., p. 147.
24 Ibid., pp. 168–9.
25 Ibid., p. 170.
26 I. Berlin, *The Crooked Timber of Humanity: Chapters in the History of Ideas* (John Murray, London, 1970), p. 16.
27 Ibid., p. 172.

28 I. Berlin, *Concepts and Categories: Philosophical Essays* (The Hogarth Press, London, 1978), p. 82.
29 Ibid., p. 92.
30 Ibid., p. 96.
31 I. Berlin, *Against the Current: Essays in the History of Ideas* (The Hogarth Press, London, 1979), p. 71.
32 Berlin, *The Crooked Timber of Humanity*, p. 59.
33 Ibid., p. 9.
34 Ibid., pp. 67, 65.
35 Ibid., p. 10.
36 Ibid., p. 37
37 Ibid., p. 38.
38 Ibid., p. 39.
39 Ibid., pp. 176, 245.
40 Ibid., p. 177.
41 Ibid., p. 245.
42 Ibid., p. 10.
43 Ibid., p. 11.
44 Ibid., p. 18.
45 Ibid., p. 52.
46 Ibid., p. 34.
47 Ibid., pp. 55–6.
48 Ibid., pp. 70, 192.
49 Cf. 'Joseph de Maistre and the origins of fascism', in Berlin, *The Crooked Timber of Humanity*; 'Georges Sorel', in Berlin, *Against the Current*.
50 Berlin, *Against the Current*.
51 Cf. Berlin, *Concepts and Categories*, pp. 95–6.
52 'Knowledge' and 'happiness' (mentioned by Berlin) could be either individual or social goods – but Berlin shows no interest in the distinction.

Further reading

By Berlin

I. Berlin, *Karl Marx: His Life and Environment*, Thornton Butterworth, London, 1939 (4th ed, Fontana, London, 1995).
I. Berlin, *Four Essays on Liberty*, Oxford University Press, London, 1969.
I. Berlin, *Vico and Herder: Two Studies in the History of Ideas*, Hogarth Press, London, 1976.
I. Berlin, *Russian Thinkers*, Hogarth Press, London, 1978.
I. Berlin, *Concepts and Categories: Philosophical Essays*, Hogarth Press, London, 1978.

I. Berlin, *Against the Current: Essays in the History of Ideas*, Hogarth Press, London, 1979.

I. Berlin, *The Crooked Timber of Humanity: Chapters in the History of Ideas*, John Murray, London, 1990.

I. Berlin, *The Magus of the North: J. G. Hamann and the Origins of Modern Irrationalism*, John Murray, London, 1993.

I. Berlin, *The Sense of Reality: Studies in Ideas and Their History*, Chatto and Windus, London, 1996.

On Berlin

C. J. Galipeau, *Isaiah Berlin's Liberalism*, Clarendon Press, Oxford, 1994.

J. Gray, 'On negative and positive liberty', in *Liberalisms: Essays in Political Philosophy*, Routledge, London, 1989.

J. Gray, *Berlin*, Fontana, London, 1995.

I. Harris, 'Isaiah Berlin: *Two Concepts of Liberty*', in *The Political Classics: Green to Dworkin,* ed. M. Forsyth and M. Keens-Soper, Oxford University Press, 1996.

R. Kocis, *A Critical Appraisal of Sir Isaiah Berlin's Political Philosophy*, Edwin Mellen Press, Lewiston, NY, 1989.

Part III
Contemporaries

10
John Rawls: Liberal Justice

The work of John Rawls in political philosophy has been a most remarkable and even extraordinary phenomenon. His major work, *A Theory of Justice*, despite its rather anodyne title, has had by far the greatest impact on the field of any in recent times. For a decade or so after its publication in 1971 it totally dominated the subject in the English-speaking world, and provoked a huge body of reviews, commentaries and criticisms. Just why this should be so, and whether Rawls's work really merits so much attention, are questions to which answers can only emerge, if at all, in the course of this chapter. Suffice it to say, for the present, that Rawls's political philosophy is certainly a unique and, perhaps, uniquely ambitious enterprise. Its uniqueness is in a way paradoxical: ideologically, Rawls's views are far from unfamiliar. He is a supporter of the contemporary socio–political synthesis, which combines liberal democracy, the market economy and the redistributive welfare state. What is unique, and ambitious, is his attempt to provide a systematic, uni-fied, justifying theory for this synthesis. The words 'systematic' and 'unified' deserve emphasis. It is only a slight exaggeration to say that the core of Rawls's political philosophy resembles a geometrical theorem, in which the elements of the synthesis are deduced as conclusions from appropriate, if not self-evident, premises. Some of Rawls's critics believe that this makes his theory excessively abstract and lacking in sociological realism. Whether or not this is so, what is true is that in the exposition (and assessment) of Rawls's theory it is necessary to pay an unusual degree of attention to sustained, close, logical argument.

This, no doubt, is not unconnected with the fact that Rawls, born in 1921 in Baltimore, has spent his whole adult life as an academic philosopher, sucessively at the elite American universities of Princeton, Cornell, MIT and

Harvard. He is the author to date of two books only, *A Theory of Justice* in 1971, and *Political Liberalism* in 1993. To what extent the latter book constitutes a significant revision of Rawls's theory is a matter of controversy. Each book was preceded by a series of articles, beginning with the celebrated 'Justice as fairness' in 1958, in which the position ultimately expounded in book form was adumbrated, elaborated and refined – often in response to the objections of critics. In a sense, therefore, the articles are subsumed in and superseded by the books, and we need not pay attention to the former, except for 'Justice as fairness', in which Rawls announced and commenced his project.

That project is extremely specific – it is to define and defend a conception of *social justice*. This is a strictly limited problem of political philosophy (more limited, perhaps, than the lack of any adjective in the title of Rawls's *magnum opus* might suggest), even though Rawls has chosen to focus on it because, as he tells us, he considers justice to be the primary, indeed the indispensable, virtue of social systems.[1] Even though Rawls's conception of social justice turns out to be more comprehensive than that of many theorists, it is not (he insists) 'an all-inclusive vision of a good society'.[2] Rawls, we may note, concerns himself with a concept (social justice) which another theorist, Friedrich Hayek, has dismissed as a 'mirage', as we saw in an earlier chapter – or, worse, one which Hayek sees as unrealizable except at the cost of the total destruction of freedom and all its benefits. Whether these strictures are really applicable to Rawls's theory is an issue to which we shall return.

What is (social) justice, in Rawls's view? It is the virtue that social systems display when, or if, they are able to solve in the correct way a certain problem, which Rawls calls the 'problem of justice'. Society, according to Rawls, should be conceived as 'a cooperative venture for mutual advantage',[3] more or less self-sufficient, and necessarily governed by rules. The individual members of society, therefore, share common interests, but – crucially – there is also conflict of interests among them. 'Persons are not indifferent as to how the greater benefits produced by their collaboration are distributed, for in order to pursue their ends they each prefer a larger to a lesser share.' They press on one another incompatible claims to a larger rather than a smaller share of the benefits, and seek to shape the rules of society accordingly. This is the problem of justice. Justice is achieved when, or if, 'the proper distribution of the benefits and burdens of social cooperation' is achieved,[4] when (as Rawls also puts it) the basic rights and duties assigned to individuals by the rules of society correspond to this proper distribution. More precisely, the rules of society's major institutions, what Rawls calls its 'basic structure', must so assign the fundamental rights and duties of individual members of society. Rawls assumes that the assignment of these rights and duties, of social advantage, cannot be completely equal. 'Inequalities [are] presumably inevitable in the basic structure of any society.'[5] The issue is to define how and whether such inequalities can be just.

A striking feature of Rawls's theory of justice is that it is a social contract theory.[6] Thus, Rawls deliberately and explicitly set out to revive a very ancient and for centuries very popular style of political argument, but one which, before he wrote, had fallen into desuetude and was generally thought to belong in the philosophical museum. Properly to understand Rawls's theory, therefore, it is necessary to say something about social contract theory in its earlier incarnations. We shall find the differences thereof from Rawls's theory to be as significant as the similarities. One reason why it is important to be clear about this is that it is Rawls's revamped version of the social contract that provides the premises for his quasi-deductive argument.

So-called social contract theory (it should really be called political contract theory) was traditionally a method of trying to solve what is known to specialists as the problem of *political obligation*. This 'problem' (it is really a family of problems) has to do with such questions as the justification of political authority, how far it properly extends, why and whether individuals have an obligation to obey rulers, on what conditions, etc. The method used to answer these questions by social contract theorists such as Hobbes, Locke and Rousseau, was to offer a description of the state of human society in the absence of political authority (the so-called 'state of nature'), stressing the shortcomings of this 'state of nature', and to postulate the necessity for individuals therein to solve their problems by agreeing together to establish, and submit to, political authority, on some stated terms. This is the 'social contract'. Commentators differ as to whether the 'state of nature' and the 'social contract' were considered by the theorists to be actual historical phenomena preceding political authority, or whether these ideas were rather the fruit of a thought experiment in which political authority was 'thought away' from existing reality, and the resulting state of affairs deduced or imagined. But either way, the putative contract establishing political authority was held to be binding on citizens and the source of political obligation.

There are many serious problems with this style of argument, which explain its virtual disappearance from political philosophy after the eighteenth century. Rawls, however, revived it in a modified form, because it seemed to him particularly suited to solving the problem of justice, at a theoretical level. The reason is as follows. The problem of justice arises from incompatible claims to the benefits of social cooperation – from *disagreement*. The problem might be solved, therefore, if the disagreement could be transformed, in some suitable way, into *agreement* – an agreement, or social contract, among those concerned (all members of society) as to the proper distribution of the benefits, or rather, the proper principles that should regulate the distribution – a social contract on *principles of justice*, as Rawls calls them. The basic intuition is that what is agreeable to all concerned, under appropriate conditions, can be taken as definitive of justice.

It is, of course, useless to look to people, just as they are, to make this agreement, or to try to imagine what agreement they would make. In the first place, there is no likelihood that they could reach any agreement at all. Secondly, if they could reach an agreement, it would undoubtedly be greatly influenced by their relative bargaining skills and unequal bargaining power. This has two consequences. Any possible agreement would be unpredictable, and (since it would reflect unequal bargaining power) there is no reason to think it would be just. It is, for example, believed by many that the wage contract in a capitalist society is unjust, for precisely the latter reason. To deal with this problem, Rawls, in the article 'Justice as fairness', simply postulated, as a feature of his social contract model, that the 'contractors' 'are sufficiently equal in power and ability to guarantee that . . . none is able to dominate the others'.[7] This would make the contract a *fair* one. Two comments are in order. First, all this makes clear that, in Rawls's case, the social contract is a *thought experiment* and nothing else (a point he himself makes explicit). Second, Rawls has not yet wholly solved his problem: though the relation between the 'contractors' is now a fair one, there is still no satisfactory way of working out what principles of distribution they would agree on (though Rawls at first thought otherwise). In *A Theory of Justice*, therefore, Rawls adopted a somewhat different approach.

Before this is explained, there is a point which needs to be reiterated and emphasized. Unlike the older version of social contract theory, the Rawlsian version makes no use of a 'state of nature'. The older theories thought of men in a highly unsatisfactory, ungoverned state, having a *common interest* in being governed, and therefore agreeing to establish a government. In Rawls's theory, which is a theory of justice, the imagined contractors have to find a way of resolving a *conflict of interest*. This is not, of course, because Rawls thinks men in society have no common interests (as some of his critics seem to suggest), but because it is conflicting interests that give rise to the problem of justice. The Rawlsian contract, quite deliberately, models only one side of human nature and the human condition. The situation in which it occurs is not (unlike the 'state of nature') realistic, nor is it intended to be so. It is not an unsatisfactory state of life, from which the social contract enables men to escape. We shall shortly see that it is not even realizable, in any possible world. There is no reason why it should be. In *A Theory of Justice*, Rawls calls it 'the original position', but makes clear that it is a pure analytic construction.

How should it be constructed? It must reflect the problem of justice (conflicting interests), it must enable the solution of the problem by agreement, and it must ensure the agreement is a *fair* one. Thus, Rawls postulates that the imagined contractors are self-interested, in a specific sense: each is concerned only to protect, indeed to maximize, his capacity to pursue *his own* ends or purposes (however noble or unselfish in some sense these might be). (Rawls calls this feature 'mutual disinterest'.)[8] Also, in order to make this motivation effective, and equally effective, for all parties, Rawls postulates that they are rational, in the specific sense of being able to work out the relation between means and ends, and hence to know what circumstances do and do not promote their own ends. It is the opposed interests of rational, self-interested persons that justice must reconcile – reconcile justly.

To make this possible, Rawls introduces into his original position a celebrated and hugely important innovation – the so-called 'veil of ignorance'. This means that

> no-one knows his place in society, his class position or social status . . . his fortune in the distribution of natural assets and abilities, his intelligence, strength, and the like . . . The parties do not [even] know their conception of the good or their special psychological propensities.[9]

Why not? Because, in summary, Rawls wishes his contractors to be ignorant of any features which distinguish them from their fellow contractors. By this move, Rawls solves two problems at once. He removes all grounds for disagreement between his rational, self-interested contractors, and thus (it is hoped) the uncertainty as to what they would agree on. Secondly (and more controversially), Rawls believes that the veil of ignorance also makes the relation of the contractors to each other a *fair* one. In the first place, none of them will know of anything which gives him a bargaining advantage over his fellows – there can thus be no bargaining, and no exploitation of bargaining advantage. Secondly, contractors are deprived of any rationale for proposing or supporting regulatory principles biased in their own favour. Since they are required to agree on *general principles* of distribution, no one can simply propose (say) that he and his friends should get all the benefits. But it would not be hard for a contractor to think of formally general principles that would have the same effect – were it not for the veil of ignorance. The veil of ignorance makes all the contracting parties equal, indeed the same. It imposes, alongside their self-interest, a kind of impartiality. Rational self-interested persons, thus circumstanced, can agree on principles that deal impartially with their conflicting interests, and are thus fair to all. Such is Rawls's idea. The premise of his 'theorem' is therefore this: principles which would be agreed by rational self-interested persons, subjected to the veil of ignorance, to regulate the distribution among them of the benefits of social cooperation, are principles of justice.

Before we go on to see what Rawls deduces from this premise, some points need to be clarified. Thanks to the veil of ignorance, the Rawlsian contractors are unaware, not only of any attributes of themselves which might give them special bargaining power, but also (more controversially, as we shall see later) of what Rawls calls their 'conception of the good' – in other words, of the purposes which they wish to pursue throughout their lives. Is this not, one might object, a piece of ignorance too far? How can they intelligibly be perceived as rationally self-interested, if they have no specific purposes to pursue? But there is no real problem. Rawls stipulates that the motive of all contractors is to enjoy, to the maximum degree possible, so-called 'social primary goods', that is 'things that every rational man is presumed to want' because 'they normally have a use whatever a person's rational plan of life'.[10] They are all-purpose means, which are distributed by the structure of society. Among them are 'rights and liberties, powers and opportunities, income and wealth', matters which have long been a focus of social conflict both actual and theoretical. The Rawlsian contractors know that their society is subject to the 'circumstances of justice' (conflict of interest), that they are individuals with purposes to pursue, and that therefore they should seek, since they are rational, maximally to enjoy the social primary goods. That is all they need to know, for Rawls's purposes.

Rawls also stipulates, perhaps controversially, a particular interpretation of rational self-interest, such that it excludes *envy*.[11] This, I believe, is perfectly justified, given Rawls's definition of envy, and because it follows from the definition of his contractors as mutually disinterested. By envy Rawls means a disposition to be made unhappy, not by one's own misfortune, but solely by the good fortune of others. An 'envious' person, thus defined, is made happier if the good fortune of a more fortunate person is made to disappear – say, his greater wealth is confiscated – even though no more of the wealth (or other goods) accrues to the envious person as a result. This envious person is not one who wants another's goods, but is a pure 'dog in the manger'. Besides the absurdity of such an attitude, it is ruled out by the sense in which Rawlsian contractors are self-interested. They are interested purely in their own fortune, not that of others. They are not made happy or unhappy by either the good or the bad fortune of other persons.

It will be seen that Rawls has constructed his contracting situation, the 'original position', with considerable care – naturally enough, since this is the premise from which everything else will follow. For each feature of the original position Rawls has offered a justification. But is the overall design really justified? Must we really accept it as the right premise from which to derive principles of justice? Rawls cannot prove that we must; he simply hopes that we do, if not at once, then on reflection. He hopes that the design of his original position reflects widely held convictions about justice. If so, the premises of his argument are (relatively) uncontroversial, or as he puts it 'weak'. His hope is to derive from his 'weak' premises, 'strong' (that is, relatively controversial) conclusions.[12] The object of the exercise is to convince us of the validity of those relatively controversial conclusions by deriving them from premises which we find acceptable. That, at least, is how Rawls describes his enterprise in *A Theory of Justice*. In *Political Liberalism*, he puts it somewhat differently: his premises, he now claims, represent a *democratic* conception of justice,[13] and his argument therefore is addressed only to those who have such a conception. This may mean, those who live in, and participate in, a democratic political culture, but not those who do not (say, the inhabitants of China or Saudi Arabia). To the latter, apparently, he has nothing to say.[14] To some of Rawls's critics, and indeed his admirers, this change seems to introduce an unfortunate element of relativism into his position.

Rawls has another way of characterizing and justifying his enterprise. His theory of justice, he says, embodies and spells out a conception of society as a relation between *free and equal* persons. This idea can be applied to the social contract on which the theory is based: justice is that to which free and equal persons would agree (or, that to which persons, placed in circumstances of equality, would freely agree). The Rawlsian social contract models this conception of society and of persons. It remains to be seen what Rawls thinks it implies. It is worth stressing, however, that Rawls's theory, unusually, seeks to do justice to *both* the freedom and the equality of persons.

Yet individuals in society are not equal and, in Rawls's opinion, cannot be equal. How can this be justified? How can it be acceptable to the Rawlsian contractors in the original position? Let us pose the question as follows. Asked to choose between an equal and an unequal distribution of social primary goods, on what conditions would Rawlsian contractors prefer an unequal distribution? Would they accept inequality on the grounds that, or on condition that, it maximizes total utility (the criterion proposed by 'utilitarians')? In Rawls's opinion, the answer is definitely no. Maximization of an aggregate pays no attention whatever to the distribution of the aggregate among persons – and, by definition, each Rawlsian contractor is concerned only with his own fate. As Rawls remarks, utilitarianism could theoretically justify slavery, but no rational self-interested person could accept that form of inequality, if he himself might be among the slaves.

The answer to our question is in fact simple. A rational, self-interested Rawlsian contractor will prefer inequality to equality if and only if inequality is more advantageous to him than equality, in terms of enjoyment of social primary goods. Rawls now argues that, because of the veil of ignorance, such a contractor can be confident that he will benefit from inequality if and only if *all* members of society so benefit. The veil of ignorance means that, knowing nothing that differentiates him from his fellows, the contractor cannot predict what position – high or low – he will occupy in an unequal society. Therefore he can opt for an unequal society only if it makes everyone better off than would equality. This yields what Rawls calls the general conception of justice: social primary goods 'are to be distributed equally, unless an unequal distribution of any, or all of these [goods] is to everyone's advantage'.[15] Or: inequality is just, if and only if, it benefits everyone.

Actually this is only a first approximation, because the condition it places on just inequality is, taken literally, much too easy to satisfy. Rawls believes that strict equality in the distribution of primary social goods is in fact impossible. Whether it is or not, it would surely be intolerably inefficient. Equal income and wealth, for example, would mean doing without the incentives of a market economy, and would, in all probability, result in an extremely low level of wealth for all. Almost any degree of inequality of wealth could be better for everyone, economically speaking, than that. But that does not mean that such extreme inequality is just, in Rawls's view. To simplify the argument, let us imagine an economically unequal society divided into two classes, rich and poor (*within* each class, by hypothesis, everyone is equal). How great a difference between rich and poor does justice allow? Rawls's answer is: to be just, the difference, *in its entirety*, must benefit both classes. In other words, it must be impossible, *in the long run*, to benefit the poor by transferring wealth to them from the rich. Of course, in the short run it is always possible to do this, up to the point where the difference between rich and poor is wiped out. But in the long run, too much equality harms the poor as well as the rich, by destroying economic incentives. There is some degree of inequality which optimizes, or maximizes, the economic prospects of the poor class. At this point, the inequality between the two classes, *in its entirety*, benefits both classes, more than would any lesser degree of inequality. This defines the just degree of inequality: inequality is just if and only if it maximizes the benefits of the poorer class. To return to the original position, this is the rule (or principle) that would be acceptable to the Rawlsian contractors behind the veil of ignorance, given that each wishes to be confident that he will benefit by *all* social inequality. This result can be generalized in two senses. If society consists of n economic classes instead of two, economic inequality is just (other things equal) if and only if it maximizes the wealth enjoyed by the poorest class. Secondly, the principle can be extended to cover all social primary goods: all social primary goods are to be distributed equally, unless an unequal distribution of any or all of them benefits everyone; in which case the distribution must maximize the benefits of the least favoured class.[16] Or, more simply: distribution of social primary goods must maximize the social primary goods enjoyed by the least favoured class. This is the famous *maximin principle*, which sums up Rawls's general conception of justice.[17] (Actually this is a slight oversimplification, but can be treated as accurate for the time being.)

The general conception of justice is Rawls's first deduction from his social contract premise, but it is not the last. The general conception in turn serves as a premise for what Rawls calls the special conception of justice, which applies the general conception to special circumstances, that is, to a particular kind of society. In truth, it applies it to the kind of society Rawls is most interested in – a society like his own. To be more precise: Rawls is particularly interested in applying his conception of justice to a society which has achieved a reasonable level of wealth. We now have to see what difference such reasonable prosperity makes, in Rawls's opinion, to social justice.

It makes it, for one thing, more complicated. In the formula that expresses Rawls' general conception of justice, a number of social primary goods are listed, without any distinction as to their relative importance. In a sufficiently prosperous society, Rawls thinks, that ceases to be appropriate. In such a society (he argues in *A Theory of Justice*) certain individual rights and liberties – called by Rawls 'basic liberties' (though some might better be called basic rights) – assume an importance greater than other social primary goods, so much so, that they merit 'lexical priority' over the other goods. The special conception of justice expresses this by taking the form of *two* principles, one governing the basic liberties, the other 'social and economic' primary goods, with the former having priority over the latter. These are Rawls's famous 'two principles of justice',[18] as follows:

First principle
Each person is to have an equal right to the most extensive total system of equal basic liberties compatible with a similar system of liberty for all.

Second principle
Social and economic inequalities are to be arranged so that they are both
(a) to the greatest benefit of the least advantaged . . . and
(b) attached to offices and positions open to all under conditions of fair equality of opportunity.

The 'two principles' stated above need a good deal of explanation.

What, first of all, are the basic liberties? Rawls offers the following list: 'political liberty (the right to vote and to be eligible for public office) together with freedom of speech and assembly; liberty of conscience and freedom of thought; freedom of the person along with the right to hold (personal) property; and freedom from arbitrary arrest and seizure as defined by the concept of the rule of law'.[19]

But he adds that this list is illustrative, not definitive – there are indications that he would wish to add to it, for example, freedom of association, freedom of movement and freedom to choose one's occupation.[20] One oddity of the Rawlsian two principles is that they say nothing about 'non-basic' liberties. These are clearly not thought to merit the priority conferred by the first principle, but none the less they presumably are still social primary goods, and by no means insignificant. Their absence is puzzling.

Be that as it may, the 'basic' liberties are a rather familiar list of political and civil rights. So-called political liberty is in fact the rights that make up what Rawls calls 'constitutional democracy', or the just constitution (in a reasonably wealthy society) while the other basic liberties are the individual rights long prized by traditional liberalism. Social justice as understood by Rawls not only embraces these political and civil liberties, but asserts their priority; which is to say that, for Rawls, in a society that has achieved a level of material progress sufficient to make universally possible the 'meaningful' enjoyment of these rights (not in Rawls's view an extremely high level of material progress), no loss or diminution of these liberties can be adequately compensated by gains in terms of other social primary goods such as (more) wealth. From the standpoint of the original position, no rational self-interested person would accept such an exchange; from the standpoint of the

238

general conception of justice, no less-than-equal enjoyment of basic liberties can be advantageous even if it permits increased enjoyment of other social primary goods – even if it allows one to be very much richer. Theoretically, inequality of basic liberties could be justified if it enhanced the *basic liberties* of all, including those with a less than equal liberty.[21] However, it is clear that Rawls does not consider this to be a real possibility. In effect, enjoyment of the basic liberties (in a reasonably prosperous society) must be equal. They are rights of citizenship, and as such 'are required to be equal by the first principle, since citizens of a just society . . . have the same basic rights'.[22]

The second principle, Rawls explains, applies to a different aspect of the social structure, 'to the distribution of income and wealth, and to the design of organizations that make use of differences in authority and responsibility, or chains of command'.[23] The former is to be regulated by part (a) of the second principle, the latter by part (b). But here Rawls adds a second priority rule: part (b), the principle of fair equality of opportunity, has (in a reasonably prosperous society) priority over part (a). In other words, under the special conception of justice, the requirement to maximize the wealth of the poorest class holds only given the securing of maximum equal basic liberties and fair equality of opportunity. If the wealth of the poorest could be increased by some diminution of basic liberties, for example, justice does *not* require that this be done. The poorest are not benefited by increasing their wealth at the expense of their own basic liberties, and they have no just claim to increase their wealth at the expense of anyone else's.

I will postpone for the time being discussion of the very important issue of the justification of these priority rules – obviously we must return to it. Before that, however, it is necessary to note certain modifications to his two principles introduced by Rawls, in response to criticism, in *Political Liberalism*. First of all, Rawls concedes that his formulation of the first principle, as above, falsely implies that the various basic liberties enjoyed by a person can be summed, and maximized. On the contrary, as Herbert Hart pointed out,[24] they can conflict (for example, the right of free assembly can conflict with the right to own personal property). Such conflicts must be resolved in terms of the *point* of the liberties (viewed from the original position) – thus, it is not unjust to limit freedom of assembly by a suitable law of trespass. So Rawls now reformulates his first principle as follows:

Each person has an equal right to a fully adequate scheme of basic liberties which is compatible with a similar scheme of liberties for all.[25]

Furthermore, Rawls concedes also that it is not sufficient to confine the priority of basic liberties to societies prosperous enough to make their enjoyment 'meaningful'. From the standpoint of the original position, no contractor would be satisfied with that. He would insist that *he* must be prosperous enough to allow meaningful enjoyment of the liberties (which are useless if one is starving). Because of the veil of ignorance, this imposes the condition that, for the priority of basic liberties to be applicable, *every* citizen must be well enough off materially to enjoy them in a meaningful way. Really this was always implicit in Rawls's argument, though not spelt out. He admits, in *Political Liberalism*, the need to precede the (previously) first principle with 'a lexically prior principle requiring that citizens' basic [material] needs be met'.[26] Though Rawls does not say so explicitly, this in effect means that the 'special conception' of justice consists of *three* principles, in which rules for the distribution of wealth are divided between two principles: one for basic needs (which have an even higher priority than basic liberties) and one for wealth in excess of basic needs (which has a lower priority than basic liberties). (I shall argue below that this latter principle is really two principles, so that *four* principles in all are required to express Rawls' special conception of justice.)

The relative priority assigned by Rawls to the two social primary goods, wealth and liberty, having been clarified, it remains to make explicit the thinking behind his position. To a very poor person, nothing is more important than provision for his material needs. But once this is achieved, further increase in wealth, though desirable, becomes much less pressing. From the standpoint of being able effectively to pursue one's purposes, and live one's life as one wishes to live it, the guarantee of certain liberties – the basic liberties – becomes more important. This is *not* a value judgement in an ethical sense. It is, in Rawls's opinion, the judgement of a rational self-interested person behind the veil of ignorance.

Rawls's position has been much criticized. Would it really be contrary to one's interest to win a fortune by surrendering any one of the basic liberties, even in part? Many find that hard to accept. To assess this issue, it is necessary to consider the 'basic liberties' separately. As Rawls admits, not all are equally basic.[27] For example, political liberty is less basic than liberty of the person, that is, the status of a 'free' person as distinguished from a slave or a serf. The latter is indeed so basic that insisting on its priority does seem rational. Likewise 'freedom from arbitrary arrest and seizure, as defined by the concept of the rule of law'. But what about other 'basic' liberties, such as freedom of speech and assembly, liberty of conscience and freedom of thought, freedom of association and the right to vote? In *Political Liberalism*, Rawls offers an argument which lays particular stress on 'liberty of conscience', which he defines as 'liberty as applied to religious, philosophical and moral views of our relation to the world'[28]. Rawls assumes that it is normal for individuals to affirm such views, which form the ground-plan, so to speak, of what he often refers to as their plan of life, and of their conception of the good. They are, he believes, so integral to an individual's personality that they are 'non-negotiable . . . They are . . . forms of belief and conduct the protection of which we cannot properly abandon or . . . jeopardize for the kinds of considerations covered by the second principle of justice'. One cannot give up one's right to live according to one's philosophy of life. Other basic liberties are basic either because they are in one way or another necessary to the implementation or preservation of liberty of conscience,[29] or because they are essential 'for the adequate development and full exercise . . . of moral personality'.[30] Without going into the details of this argument, it might be remarked that Rawls seems to stipulate a highly moralized conception of the 'human essence' (as Macpherson might put it), in place of the neutral notion of individual self-interest which was his original premise.

A similar impression is given by Rawls's justification of the (lesser) priority of fair equality of opportunity. The ground of this is what he calls the 'Aristotelian principle', namely: 'human beings enjoy the exercise of their realized capacities (their innate or trained ability) and this enjoyment increases the more the capacity is realized, or the greater its complexity'.[31] Self-realization in this sense, Rawls claims, is one of the most important goods that an individual can enjoy.[32] It is this good that equal opportunity protects, and that is why it is more important than material wealth above the level of basic needs. We seem here to be in the realm of J. S. Mill's distinction between higher and lower pleasures, or C. B. Macpherson's contrast between consumption of utilities and exercise of human powers. Once again one feels that Rawls's personal value judgements are being smuggled into the argument, in the guise of rational self-interest.

Despite the high value Rawls attributes to self-realization, he recognizes that 'fair equality of opportunity' is an ideal that 'can be only imperfectly carried out, at least as long as the institution of the family exists'.[33] Equal opportunity means that, 'assuming that there is a distribution of natural assets, those who are at the same level of talent and ability, and have the same willingness to use them, should have the same prospects of success regardless . . . of the income class into which they are born'.[34] We saw in a previous chapter how Hayek showed that this is impossible, without abolishing the freedom of parents to do their best for their children, or else by imposing total economic equality (which would both destroy freedom and impoverish society). Rawls shows that he is aware of these facts. However, it is still possible to 'maximinimize' opportunities, that is, to arrange matters so as to maximize the opportunities of the least-advantaged class, as much as is compatible with the priority of basic liberties.

It is now possible to state Rawls's 'special conception of justice' in terms of four principles. The principles, which apply to any society wealthy enough to provide for the basic material needs of all its members, are as follows, in order of priority:[35]

1 The basic material needs of everyone must be provided for.
2 Each person has an equal right to a fully adequate scheme of basic liberties which is compatible with a similar scheme of liberties for all.
3 Opportunities to achieve desired social positions must be so distributed by the social system as to maximize the opportunities of the least advantaged class.
4 Economic inequality must be so arranged as to maximize the wealth of the poorest class.

In Rawlsian terminology, the fourth principle goes by the name of the 'difference principle', presumably because it is in the economic realm particularly that Rawls considers inequality to be inevitable and just inequality to be possible, on certain conditions. The difference principle has given rise to much controversy, and we shall return to it. First, however, we should note how Rawls's special conception of justice prescribes a particular set of social institutions. In a very obvious sense, the principle of equal basic liberties prescribes a particular political system – a liberal democracy. The other principles, which regulate the socio-economic structure, prescribe a combination of market economy and welfare state. The former is needed for economic efficiency, as great as is compatible with the priority of basic liberty (indeed, many such as Hayek would argue that it is simply the most efficient economic system available), which is necessary for the satisfaction of the difference principle. The market does not, of course, itself satisfy that principle – the distribution of wealth it produces has no connection with social justice. To provide for everyone's basic needs, and to satisfy the difference principle, governmental intervention and redistribution of wealth are required. As Rawls puts it, the government must guarantee a 'social minimum' by such devices as 'family allowances and special payments for sickness and unemployment', or by a negative income tax.[36] The principle of fair equality of opportunity (or maximinimization of opportunity) requires that the government ensure free schooling for all through either a public school system or subsidy of private schools.

Thus Rawls, so to speak, completes his 'theorem'. Starting from his social contract premises, he has deduced, first, a general (maximin) conception of justice, second a more complex special conception of justice applicable to economically developed countries (such as those of Western Europe and the USA), and finally a set of social institutions consisting of liberal democracy, the market economy and the welfare state. The whole enterprise could be described as an attempt to demonstrate the coherence, and exhibit the philosophical foundations, of political liberalism – or of Rawls's preferred version thereof.

Of course the various steps in Rawls's argument are far from unchallengeable, as we have already seen. Let us now turn our attention to the difference principle (which of course is simply an application of Rawls's general, maximin conception of justice to economic distribution), and to the controversies to which it has given rise. As Rawls makes clear, the difference principle expresses a very specific attitude to the productive skills and capacities of individuals, and of the material productive assets they are able to create: that they should be considered a common asset,[37] rather than, in any absolute sense, the private property of individuals. This is precisely the 'common ownership of society's accumulated productive resources' demanded by C. B. Macpherson. But Rawls goes further than Macpherson. He gives *reasons* why this should be the case. 'No one *deserves* his greater natural capacity' (emphasis added) – to be abler than another person is simply good fortune. Thus it is just that the abler benefit from their greater ability only if they also thereby benefit the less fortunate. In this way Rawls feels justified in excluding any principle of desert from distributive justice. It is worth stressing that this enables him to sidestep the attack launched on the concept of social justice by Hayek. Hayek, as we saw in an earlier chapter, asserted the incompatibility of social justice and freedom because he assumed that the former implies distribution to individuals in accordance with their merits. Rawls's difference principle, however, is not like that.

Another aspect of the difference principle, however, gives Rawls considerable trouble. Innate advantages do not automatically yield useful skills and talents – they need to be developed, by effort, resolution and other virtues. Different individuals, of course, manifest these virtues to unequal degrees. Does this not mean that some are more deserving than others – deserve more benefits? Rawls thinks not: 'the superior character that enables [someone] to make the effort to cultivate his abilities . . . depends in large part upon fortunate family and social circumstances for which he can claim no credit'.[38] But how far can this view be taken? Does it imply – as it seems to – that persons unwilling to do any work cannot be blamed for idleness, and are entitled to benefit by the abilities and efforts of others, under the terms of the difference principle? Would the poorest class, whose advantages must be maximized according to the difference principle, be, in a Rawlsian society, the class of idlers, those who do no work at all throughout their lives, and are provided for (if necessary) by society?

Rawls is, not unnaturally, reluctant to accept this conclusion. In *Political Liberalism*, he seems to swing to the other extreme. His theory of justice, he remarks, 'takes as its fundamental idea that of society as a fair system of cooperation over time',[39] and therefore applies to those individuals who are 'normal and fully cooperating members of society'.[40] It does not, therefore, apply to the permanently disabled (but should it not, from the standpoint of the original position, and the veil of ignorance, and given Rawls's view that we do not observe our abilities or disabilities? I will do Rawls the favour of interpreting him to mean only that the difference principle does not apply to the disabled – presumably they are still entitled to satisfaction of basic needs).[41] But what qualifies one for the status of a 'normal and fully cooperating member of society'? How many years of one's life must one work? How many days per week, and hours per day? Rawls remarks, in a footnote, that 'those who surf all day off Malibu must find a way to support themselves, and would not be entitled to public funds'.[42] But what about those who surf half the day off Malibu or anywhere else, and work the other half? Two things seem clear: Rawls has not succeeded in solving this problem, and he has not, as he hoped, succeeded altogether in excluding the concept of desert from his conception of justice. Perhaps there is no solution here, except the libertarian one, of leaving everyone free to work or idle as they will, and take the consequences.[43] After all, the right to decide how much of one's time to give to 'cooperation', and how much to devote to one's own concerns, is surely one of the most basic liberties.

Another range of issues arises in relation to the difference principle as the embodient of Rawls's maximin conception of justice, or maximin conception of rational choice in the original position. In brief, Rawls argues that it is rational for his contractors to focus on the fate of the poorest or least advantaged class, because the veil of ignorance makes it impossible for anyone to know they will not belong to that class. On the other hand, it is argued by Rawls's critics, they may not belong to it, for all they know; so it would surely be rational for them to pay attention to the fate of other classes, indeed it would be irrational not to. According to one widely accepted model of rational choice, known as expected utility maximization (expected, that is, on the basis of the probability of the various possible, differently valued outcomes) the rational chooser behind the veil of ignorance seeks to maximize the *average*, not the minimum, advantage. On grounds such as these, John Harsanyi, for example, has criticized Rawls, and championed the justice of utilitarianism – or, to be more precise, the principle of maximizing average utility (to use Rawls's own terminology). Such a society could, of course, be extremely unequal – much more unequal and therefore much more risky than Rawlsian justice allows. It holds out the prospect of far worse fates – but also of far better ones. Does not the latter by definition outweigh the former, if average benefit is greater?

Rawls is aware of this argument, and seeks to counter it.[44] Several counter-arguments are suggested, but only two will be considered here. One is called by Rawls 'the strains of commitment'. The point is that his imagined contractors are making not merely a choice, but a commitment, to which they will have to remain faithful. That is the nature of a contract. They cannot, Rawls says, commit themselves to a principle which may, if they are unlucky, have consequences so disastrous that they find they cannot accept them. Utilitarianism is such a principle, and therefore cannot be rationally chosen in the original position; the difference principle, on the contrary, can be so chosen. Furthermore, to choose a principle that may lead one into total disaster is irrationally reckless, even if it might also lead to enormous wealth. One can see this if one thinks of the contractors as heads of families, choosing not just for themselves but for – that is, in the interest of – their children. No responsible parent seriously concerned to protect his children's interests could risk disaster on their behalf, even if this also opened a chance of great riches – and this shows that risking disaster is contrary to a person's rational self-interest. A further argument may be added. The principle of insurance is widespread in our society, and is generally held to be rational. Yet insurance, by definition, involves a sacrifice of expected utility in order to avoid disaster (much lesser disaster, often, than might result to an individual from a utilitarian principle of justice, which could bring him enslavement or starvation). The modern welfare state – what Rawls calls a guaranteed social minimum, or, in more abstract language, the difference principle – is, of course, a form of social insurance, or, as it is significantly often called, social security. Its function is to answer to the natural human desire for insurance against the inherent insecurity of the market economy. If less extreme than the insecurity of the state of nature described by Hobbes and other social contract theorists, market insecurity (the obverse of its freedom) is still pervasive enough (as Macpherson noted), and so can justify a parallel argument. Just as government provides physical security, the welfare state promises economic security. And this argument suggests that (contrary to the well-known views of Robert Nozick, to be discussed in the next chapter), a contractarian justification for a government-provided social minimum could be sustained, even without the Rawlsian veil of ignorance.

None of these arguments, however, appears able to justify the Rawlsian social minimum – the *maximum* minimum (given equal basic liberties) prescribed by the difference principle. The Rawlsian maximin appears to be, in a sense, at the opposite extreme from the maximization of average utility; the rational choice of Rawlsian contractors would likely fall somewhere in between. Yet in spite of this, it needs to be pointed out that Rawls's difference principle *already* contains within it significant concessions to utilitarianism, or, perhaps better, to the principle of efficiency in the economic sense. It is, in fact, a blend of justice and efficiency. The difference principle stipulates that social and economic equalities be arranged so as to maximally benefit the poorest class. Greater inequality than this is unjust. But what about *lesser* inequality? Suppose transfers from rich to poor are in this sense excessive, and actually impoverish the poor – is *that* unjust? Rawls's answer is no. Such an inequality, he says, is just, because the advantages of the better off also advantage the poor; but it is not the *best just* situation.[45] In the language of welfare economics, it is not Pareto optimal: the fortunes of both rich and poor could be improved by moving to the distribution prescribed by the difference principle, which *is* Pareto optimal, *as well as just*, and is therefore the 'best just arrangement'. All this implies, of course, that equal distribution of wealth would be just. It would, however, be extremely inefficient economically, even if possible. It would, perhaps, be the 'worst just arrangement'. What Rawls's difference principle enables us to do is to take maximum advantage of economic efficiency, consistent with distributive justice, as Rawls understands it. That is actually the meaning of Rawls's contractarianism. To put it another way: the Rawlsian contract stipulates that everyone starts equal, then seeks to show how far away from equality we may move without injustice.

Of course this egalitarian bias, implicit in the veil of ignorance, is not acceptable to everyone. It prevents the 'well endowed' (to use Nozick's phrase) from taking full advantage of their abilities. Rawls, as we saw, justifies this on the ground that they do not deserve to. However, there is another aspect of the veil of ignorance which is more troublesome. The Rawlsian contractors are also deprived of knowledge of their 'conception of the good'[46] – deliberately so, in order to prevent anyone from trying to impose his own conception of the good on others. But is this reasonable? Many doubt it, even if they accept that it is reasonable to prevent an individual from profiting by unearned advantages. A conception of the good is not an unfair advantage, but something which, Rawls admits, a person must take with utmost seriousness. Why should he be bound by an agreement so designed as to exclude his conception of the good from any influence? This problem is the focus of Rawls's second book, *Political Liberalism*. Indeed, it explains its title, for Rawls's argument is to stress that his liberalism is 'political, not metaphysical'; or political, not comprehensive. It is a limited liberalism, confined to and suited to the political sphere. Comprehensive or metaphysical liberalism, exemplified by Kant and J. S. Mill, has a characteristic conception of the good (the good life for men), expressed in the values of individuality and autonomy.[47] Rawls's political liberalism eschews such values: it is concerned with the right, not the good. The point is, that it should be able to win the allegiance of many different, and competing, comprehensive philosophies, with their characteristic conceptions of the good.

For Rawls, a fundamental fact of our world is a pluralism of conceptions of the good – of philosophies of life.[48] The issue is: how can this plurality of doctrines (religious and secular) coexist justly? But there is a prior question: should they coexist? Is it not possible that one philosophy is true, and the rest should yield? Perhaps. But there is no way of showing this, because of what Rawls calls the 'burdens of judgment'.[49] Given this, a plurality of conflicting doctrines is (to use a word that bulks large in *Political Liberalism*) *reasonable*.[50] To put it slightly differently, our society is marked by a reasonable plurality of beliefs. Many conflicting doctrines cannot all be true, but all may be reasonable, in the sense that they cannot be shown to be false. According to Rawls, liberalism is, in turn, a reasonable response to the reasonable plurality of beliefs (or better, liberalism is *the only* reasonable response to a reasonable plurality of beliefs). It is a reasonable response, to recognize the reasonableness of beliefs one does not believe to be true, and to tolerate them. This is political liberalism. It can, Rawls says, operate as an 'overlapping consensus'[51] shared by men wedded to comprehensive philosophies otherwise conflicting – and, for Rawls, it is what justice requires. Political liberalism is tolerant of *reasonable* beliefs only; thus a politically liberal person is tolerant of beliefs he considers false only if they (or those who espouse them) are like-

247

wise tolerant – for to be intolerant in the face of a reasonable plurality of beliefs is unreasonable. Such intolerance is unjust. This, ultimately, is why it is justified to deprive Rawls's contractors in the original position of knowledge of their conception of the good, and to use this ignorance to derive liberal conclusions, in the form of a right to liberty of conscience and other basic liberties. Of course, the argument is circular, in the sense that no illiberal person will accept the propriety of Rawls's premises, but not viciously so. It displays the basis and nature of the case for liberalism.

The argument just rehearsed is of particular significance, because it illustrates a fundamental feature of Rawlsian liberalism, namely, what he calls the priority of the right over the good.[52] In asserting this priority (as well as more generally) Rawls claims to follow Kant;[53] but in fact an explicit distinction between the right and the good seems to have originated with the English moral philosopher W. D. Ross. Ross's well-known book, *The Right and the Good*, is a polemic against G. E. Moore's utilitarian account of moral obligation ('the right act').[54] In Moore's 'ideal' version of utilitarianism, the good is defined as the enjoyment of beauty and personal affection, and the right or obligatory act as that which is 'productive of the greatest good producible in the circumstances'.[55] Ross denies this. Our duties are to *other people*, which depend *inter alia* on their past actions and our relations with them, not simply on their status as potential enjoyers of the good. Our duty, then, is to bring about the right distribution of the good, not simply to maximize it. The right – the morally obligatory – is independent of the good. Maximization of the good is not morally obligatory.

Although Ross does not speak of the priority of the right over the good, that follows tautologically from his argument – the right is (by definition) the obligatory, maximizing the good is not. Ross's argument has, however, nothing to do with liberalism, nor, explicitly, with politics. Nevertheless, the obligatory is liable to become the subject matter of politics – that which is to be enforced using the coercive power of the state. Rawls follows Ross in understanding the right as the obligatory, and therefore as that which society should impose through state action. His principles of justice define 'the right' in this sense. But for Rawls, the right is prior to the good in a specifically liberal sense, which departs radically from Ross. Ross considered 'the good' to be knowable and objective. Rawls, by contrast, stressing the 'burdens of judgment', asserts the reasonable pluralism of conceptions of the good. State compulsion, therefore should not endorse any single conception of the good, but leave individuals free and able to pursue their conception of the good, within the limits and conditions set by the principles of justice – equal basic liberties, and a just distribution of wealth. (This of course does not imply the state's *neutrality* as to conceptions of the good, as is sometimes falsely asserted to be definitive of political liberalism – on the contrary, it forbids pursuit of all conceptions of the good that conflict with the principles of right.)

We shall see in the next chapter that the 'libertarian' liberal Robert Nozick fully shares Rawls's view as to the priority of the right over the good. However, although he like Rawls claims to follow Kant, he has a very different conception of the right.

Notes

1 J. Rawls, *A Theory of Justice* (The Belknap Press of Harvard University Press, Cambridge, Mass., 1971), p. 3.
2 J. Rawls, 'Justice as fairness', in *Philosophy, Politics and Society* (second series), ed. P. Laslett and W. G. Runciman (Basil Blackwell, Oxford, 1964), p. 133.
3 Rawls, *A Theory of Justice*, p. 4.
4 Ibid., p. 5.
5 Ibid., p. 7.
6 Rawls, 'Justice as fairness', p. 132.
7 Ibid., p. 138.
8 Rawls, *A Theory of Justice*, p. 13.
9 Ibid., p. 12.
10 Ibid., p. 62.
11 Ibid., p. 143.
12 Ibid., p. 18.
13 J. Rawls, *Political Liberalism* (Columbia University Press, New York, 1993), p. 3.
14 Ibid., pp. xx–xi, 14.
15 Ibid., p. 62.
16 Cf. ibid., p. 303.
17 Ibid., pp. 152–3.
18 Ibid., p. 302.
19 Ibid., p. 61.
20 Ibid., p. 310; Rawls, *Political Liberalism*, p. 181.
21 Rawls, *A Theory of Justice*, p. 302.
22 Ibid., p. 61.
23 Ibid.
24 H. L. A. Hart, 'Rawls on liberty and its priority', in *University of Chicago Law Review* 40 (1973), pp. 542–7; reprinted in N. Daniels (ed.), *Reading Rawls: Critical Studies on Rawls' 'A Theory of Justice'* (Blackwell, Oxford, 1975).
25 Rawls, *Political Liberalism*, p. 5.

26 Ibid., p. 7.
27 Rawls, *A Theory of Justice*, p. 247.
28 Rawls, *Political Liberalism*, p. 311.
29 Ibid., pp. 309, 313, 335.
30 Ibid., pp. 293, 298–9.
31 Rawls, *A Theory of Justice*, p. 426.
32 Ibid., p. 84.
33 Ibid., p. 74.
34 Ibid., p. 73.
35 Cf. R. G. Peffer, *Marxism, Morality and Social Justice* (Princeton University Press, 1990), p. 14.
36 Rawls, *A Theory of Justice*, p. 275.
37 Ibid., p. 101.
38 Ibid., p. 104.
39 Rawls, *Political Liberalism*, p. 14.
40 Ibid., p. 20.
41 Cf. ibid., pp. 157, 166.
42 Ibid., p. 182 n. 9.
43 Rawls seems in effect to accept this, when he toys with the idea of treating leisure as a social primary good alongside income (ibid., pp. 181–2 n. 9).
44 Rawls, *A Theory of Justice*, pp. 164–83.
45 Ibid., pp. 78–9.
46 Rawls, *A Theory of* Justice, p. 12.
47 Rawls, *Political Liberalism*, p. 199.
48 Ibid., p. 153.
49 Ibid., pp. 54–5.
50 Ibid., p. 144.
51 Ibid., lecture IV.
52 Rawls, *A Theory of Justice*, p. 31.
53 Ibid., p. 31 n. 16.
54 W. D. Ross, *The Right and the Good* (Hacket, Indianapolis/Cambridge, 1988), p. 3.
55 Ibid., pp. 8–9.

Further reading

By Rawls

J. Rawls, *A Theory of Justice*, The Belknap Press of Harvard University Press, Cambridge, Mass., 1971.

J. Rawls, 'Justice as fairness', *Philosophical Review* 67, 1958, and in *Philosophy, Politics and Society* (second series), ed. P. Laslett and W.G. Runciman, Basil Blackwell, Oxford, 1964.

J. Rawls, 'Social unity and primary goods', in A. Sen and B. Williams (eds), *Utilitarianism and Beyond*, Cambridge University Press, 1982.

J. Rawls, 'The priority of right and ideas of the good', *Philosophy and Public Affairs* 17, 1988.

J. Rawls, *Political Liberalism*, Columbia University Press, New York, 1993.

On Rawls

B. Barry, *The Liberal Theory of Justice: A Critical Examination of the Principal Doctrines in 'A Theory of Justice' by John Rawls*, Clarendon Press, Oxford, 1973.

N. Daniels (ed.), *Reading Rawls*, Blackwell, Oxford, 1975.

A. Esheté, 'Contractarianism and the scope of justice', *Ethics* 85, 1974.

C. Fried, 'Justice and liberty', in *Nomos* 6, ed. C. J. Friedrich and J. W. Chapman, Atherton Press, New York, 1963.

C. Kukathas and P. Pettit, *Rawls: A Theory of Justice and its Critics*, Polity Press, Cambridge, 1990.

S. Macedo, 'The politics of justification', *Political Theory* 18, 1990.

C. B. Macpherson, 'Rawls's distributive justice', in *Democratic Theory: Essays in Retrieval*, ch. IV, Oxford University Press, London, 1973.

R. Nozick, 'Distributive justice', *Philosophy and Public Affairs* 3, 1973–4 (reprinted as ch. 7 of *Anarchy, State and Utopia*, Basil Blackwell, Oxford, 1974).

R. Replogle, 'Sex, God and Liberalism', *Journal of Politics* 50, 1988.

M. J. Sandel, *Liberalism and the Limits of Justice*, Cambridge University Press, 1982.

S. Strasnick, 'Social choice and the derivation of Rawls' difference principle', *Journal of Philosophy* 73, 1976.

11
Robert Nozick: The Minimal State

The contribution of Robert Nozick to the political philosophy of the twentieth century is an important, but somewhat puzzling one. Born in New York City in 1938, Nozick became a colleague of John Rawls at Harvard University in 1963, and published his major book, *Anarchy, State and Utopia*, in 1974, three years after the appearance of Rawls's *A Theory of Justice*. The two books, and authors, manifest some similarities, as well as some striking differences. Nozick's book, like Rawls's, gives a tight, logical argument from explicit premises to conclusions in support of his thesis, namely (in Nozick's case) a defence of what he calls the 'minimal state'. Like Rawls, Nozick claims Kant as his inspiration. Nevertheless, his premises, conclusion and thesis are very different from those of Rawls, of whom Nozick is, indeed, highly critical. *Anarchy, State and Utopia* argues for an extreme and extremely controversial libertarianism: the Nozickian 'minimal state' is 'limited to the narrow functions of protection against force, theft, fraud, enforcement of contracts and so on'.[1] Above all, it is a state forbidden to engage in any economic redistribution whatever, under any circumstances whatever. Nozick's book, like Rawls's, touched off an avalanche of critical discussion, much of it hostile. Many commentators found its conclusions quite unacceptable, much though they were impressed, often, by the quality of Nozick's arguments. While defending his highly controversial thesis, Nozick at the same time admitted that his argument for it was incomplete. Early in the book, Nozick frankly admits that it does not present 'a finished, complete and elegant whole', with all arguments fully worked out. Gaps remain. Nozick adds that, in his opinion, 'there is also a place for a less complete work containing unfinished presentations, conjectures, open questions and problems'.

In view of all this, one might expect that, in the quarter century since the publication of *Anarchy, State and Utopia*, Nozick would have taken the opportunity to answer his critics, and made an effort to fill in the admitted gaps in his argument. But he has not. Indeed, he has written very little at all on political philosophy since 1974, preferring to publish works on other philosophical topics. But he has not neglected political philosophy entirely. A book published in 1989 (entitled *The Examined Life: Philosophical Meditations*) contains a somewhat surprising essay with a somewhat curious title, 'The zigzag of politics', in which the thesis of *Anarchy, State and Utopia* is, more or less, renounced. Nozick writes: 'The libertarian position I once propounded now seems to be seriously inadequate'.[2] Whereas that position was marked by the absolutism with which Nozick defended a narrow range of principles, he now (with a nod to Isaiah Berlin) acknowledges 'multiple competing values'. The theory of justice expounded in *Anarchy, State and Utopia*, Nozick now says, is at best a defence of just one of these competing values, not an absolute, but 'one that sometimes could be overidden or diminished in trade-offs'. And it may not even be an adequate theory of justice. In brief, Nozick seems to have changed his mind. However, a careful perusal of *Anarchy, State and Utopia*, undertaken with the benefit of hindsight, suggests that the matter may be a little more complex. There are a number of indications – hints – that the theory elaborated in his famous book was not one Nozick wished to see applied in practice. It was, perhaps, more by way of being an academic exercise, in the sense of a working out, to their logical conclusions, of certain seemingly very reasonable premises, to the exclusion of other considerations. As such, however, *Anarchy, State and Utopia* remains an important book, and one which cannot be omitted from any survey of political philosophy in the twentieth century. I shall at first discuss it without paying any attention to the complicating issue of whether Nozick believed or believes its arguments to be true.

Anarchy, State and Utopia is divided into three parts. The first is a justification, against anarchism, of the minimal state; the second argues against any more-than-minimal state, and in particular any state which uses its coercive powers to bring about economic redistribution; while the theme of the third is that the minimal state is 'inspiring as well as right',[3] and constitutes a 'framework for utopia'. The whole edifice, however, rests on a moral principle, or a moral philosophy, which supplies its premises. With these we must begin.

As noted in the previous chapter, the premises of Nozick's argument may be described as a version of what Rawls calls the priority of the right over the good, but with a very different conception of the right. Nozick himself calls it a 'side constraints' morality,[4] which means that the pursuit of all goals, however desirable or strongly desired, must be subordinated to certain moral side constraints. These side constraints are absolute, because they forbid any infringement of the rights of individuals. Their content is thus, Nozick says, Kantian. The most fundamental principle on which his argument rests, he says, is the 'Kantian imperative' (for Kant, a categorical imperative), which lays down that 'individuals are ends and not merely means'.[5] Therefore, they 'may not be sacrificed or used for the achieving of other ends [than their own] without their consent'. Their right not to be so used or sacrificed must be respected, always and absolutely. Sometimes, it is argued by some theorists, the rights of individuals can rightfully be sacrificed for the good of society; but Nozick disagrees. There is no 'social good' which can be advanced in this way, only separate individuals who enjoy goods or suffer evils. Contrary to utilitarianism, harm to one individual cannot be outweighed or justified by a greater gain to another or others. 'There is no justified sacrifice of some of us for others'.[6] As Nozick puts it, his side-constraints morality reflects the separateness and inviolability of individual persons. And he adds that he is also opposed to what he calls a 'utilitarianism of rights'[7] – namely, the principle of minimizing the total amount of rights violation. This can be illustrated by a familiar argument about the justification of punishment. An objection often made to the utilitarian theory of punishment runs as follows: if, in certain circumstances, framing and punishing an innocent person would be the easiest or even the only way to deter crime, then that, according to utilitarianism, is what should be done. This would be to violate the rights of one person in order to minimize the total amount of rights violation. Yet (it is said by the critics of utilitarianism) it is an obvious abuse. Nozick's side constraints morality bans all such actions. No one is ever entitled to violate the rights of an individual, for any reason whatever.

Naturally enough, Nozick argues that states and governments are bound by Kantian moral side constraints, just like any other agent. Their coercive powers, therefore, must never be used to force some people to serve the ends of others. This is the foundation of the libertarianism defended in *Anarchy, State and Utopia*. Or perhaps it is not quite the foundation, for Nozick does offer a further justification of it. The justification has to do with Nozick's conception of 'an elusive and difficult notion: the meaning of life'.[8] The issue is what, in a disenchanted world (to use Weberian terminology not used by Nozick), can make human life meaningful, or worth living. Nozick's idea is that human beings can lead meaningful lives because they have the capacity to regulate, indeed live, their lives in accordance with some overall conception they choose to accept – some conception of the good, as Rawls might say. When a person does this, but only then, he or she lives in a meaningful or worthwhile way. This is indeed a very widely accepted premise of liberalism; but not all who accept it agree with the conclusions derived from it by Nozick.

Nozick's Kantian imperative creates a prima facie case against coercion, regardless of who the coercer is, or the purpose thereof. It therefore creates a prima facie case against the state, which is an intrinsically coercive institution. To anarchists, it creates not just a prima facie but a conclusive case against the state. The first part of *Anarchy, State and Utopia* is devoted to showing that the anarchists are wrong. The state, Nozick argues, is justified – so long as it remains the minimal state.

The structure of Nozick's argument in the first part of his book depends on the fact that it is intended as a refutation of anarchism. What has to be refuted is the anarchists' quite plausible view that the state, by its very nature, 'must violate individuals' rights and hence is intrinsically immoral'.[9] Nozick adopts a very traditional starting point for his argument – the state of nature, (or, in the technical sense of the word, anarchy), used to justify the state by many a social contract theorist. Nozick, however, though a state of nature theorist, is not a social contract theorist. Nevertheless, like the social contract theorists, Nozick is interested in what the state of nature would be (rather than was) like, and what people living in a state of nature would do about it. But what *would* the putative state of nature be like? The old social contract theorists, such as Hobbes, Locke and Rousseau, gave very different accounts of it. Probably none of them really knew, and Nozick does not claim to know either. Fortunately, however, he argues that he does not need to know, but only to postulate a theoretically appropriate description. Given that the aim of the argument is to convince the anarchist, it should start from a description of anarchy, i.e. the state of nature, which is 'the best anarchic situation one could reasonably hope for'.[10] This is not the extremely pessimistic Hobbesian scenario (which an anarchist might object to as biased and unrealistic), but a more optimistic one, somewhat like Locke's version – a state of nature in which people generally, though by no means always, act as they should (that is, for Nozick, obey the 'Kantian imperative'). For Nozick's purpose it is essential that moral rules are operative in his state of nature (as indeed they are, in Locke's state of nature). Nozick's proposed strategy to refute anarchism is to 'show that the state would be superior even to this most favoured situation of anarchy . . . or would arise [from it] by a process involving no morally impermissible steps'.[11] It is not entirely clear whether Nozick thinks of these as two alternative strategies, or as parts of a single one.

The latter is more probable, for Nozick certainly uses the second argument (the state would arise, in a morally permissible way, from the state of nature) in a way that depicts the individuals involved as acting in a rational, self-interested way. I shall argue later that this argument, interesting though it is, does not succeed, and that Nozick would have done better to rely on the first argument alone.

Nozick has a further reason for using a quasi-Lockean state of nature as the starting point of his argument. Although he claims that he takes seriously the anarchist argument against the state, it would be more accurate to say that he takes seriously one particular brand of anarchism — what he calls individualist anarchism, or (as it is often called) anarcho-capitalism. The anarcho-capitalists (such writers as Murray Rothbard, John Hospers, James Martin and David Friedman),[12] like all anarchists, object to the state, but this is not because they object to coercion, or the enforcement of rules. What they object to is that a single institution (the state) should claim a monopoly of coercive rule-enforcement. They object to the state, not on behalf of the coerced, but on behalf of unfairly excluded (private) coercers. They object to a monopoly of 'coercive services' financed by compulsory taxation, instead of being provided through competitive market mechanisms. The anarcho-capitalists resemble Locke in their belief, not only in natural rights, but in the specific rights of self-defence, and of *punishing* those who violate rights. Unlike Locke, they believe that anyone, but in practice and in particular specialist firms, should be free to sell to individual purchasers the service of protection against invasions of their persons and property, just like any other goods and services that are traded on the free market. A free market in coercive enforcement, they believe, is the most efficient and the only just way to achieve protection of rights. They believe, in other words, in a quasi-Lockean state of nature developing into a capitalist market in protection of rights, instead of being superseded by the state. We shall see that Nozick's argument for the (minimal) state is, to a considerable extent, a response to such ideas.

Let us remind ourselves of Locke's views. According to Locke, the state of nature 'has a law of nature to govern it' which, in Nozickian terms, imposes moral side constraints that protect individual rights (because human beings were not 'made for one another's uses').[13] But the law is not always obeyed; therefore, every person has a right of self-defence against transgressors, a right to punish them to a degree appropriate to their transgression, and a right to exact compensation for injuries. Such a situation, Locke says, is subject to serious inconveniences. Many people will lack the power to enforce their rights effectively. The right to be judge in one's own case leads to biased judgement, and to unjust or excessive punishment (or punishment so considered by its victims). This in turn leads to violent feuding ('war', as Locke calls it). According to Locke, the remedy is obvious: to establish, by compact, a civil government.

According to Nozick, however, Locke's conclusion is too quick. After all, as many critics of social contract theory have pointed out, the scenario of a large number of individuals, inhabiting a substantial and continuous territory, coming together to invent and submit to the state by unanimous agreement, is not very plausible. It is more likely that they would first try out smaller-scale solutions, or as Nozick says, explore the possibilities of solving their problems through various 'voluntary arrangements and agreements persons might reach', *within* the state of nature.[14] The first such arrangement, Nozick suggests, would probably be to combine the power of a number of individuals by banding together in mutual protection associations, in which 'all will answer the call of any member' for defence against and punishment of rights violators. But this would be a burdensome and inefficient arrangement. To avoid having to act on frivolous and unjustified complaints, the associations would need to weed them out by means of quasi-judicial procedures. But even this would probably not reduce the burdens on members of the associations to tolerable levels. They would therefore resort, Nozick says, to 'division of labour and exchange',[15] or, in other words to the anarcho-capitalist solution. 'Some people will be *hired* to perform protective functions, and some entrepreneurs will go into the business of selling protective services'. They will establish commercial 'protective agencies'. Nozick now goes on to argue that this anarcho-capitalist scenario would still not be satisfactory, and would therefore evolve further.

Why, and how? Nozick asks, 'What will occur when there is a conflict between clients of different agencies [and] they reach different decisions as to the merits of the case?'[16] One agency will try to protect its client while the other tries to punish him. These, it must be remembered, are by definition agencies equipped with coercive force. So they can and will 'do battle'. Instead of war between individuals in the state of nature there is likely to be war between protective agencies – not a satisfactory state of affairs.

In Nozick's view, however, the problem will solve itself through the establishment, in each geographical area, of a single 'dominant protective agency'. In each area, either one agency will defeat its rivals in battle and thus put them out of business, or, if not, the rival agencies, in order to avoid the wasteful costs of war, will

agree to resolve peacefully those cases about which they reach differing judgments. They agree to set up, and abide by the decisions of, some third judge
or court [in these cases] (or they might establish rules determining which
agency has jurisdiction under which circumstances). Thus emerges a system of
appeals courts and agreed upon rules about jurisdiction and the conflict of
laws. Though different agencies operate, there is one federal judicial system of
which they are all components.[17]

Nozick now asks, 'Is the dominant protective association a state?'[18] If the answer were yes, Nozick would have invented a new version of social contract
theory. But the answer is, very nearly, but not quite. The dominant protective
agency does not have a *monopoly* of protective services in its area. Even if, by
hypothesis, it faces no commercial rivals therein, there may still be individuals
(called by Nozick 'independents'), who are not protected by it, because they
have chosen not to buy its protective services, but instead to enforce their own
rights. To turn the dominant protective agency into a state, the independents
must be incorporated into it. Nozick argues that this will happen, that it will be
accomplished *by force*, and that this exercise of force is morally justified.

It is an apparent oddity of Nozick's argument in *Anarchy, State and Utopia*
that, although he sees no moral problem in the use of force against rival
agencies by the protective agency that becomes the dominant one, he feels
called upon to offer an extremely lengthy and complex justification for its
coercive incorporation of independents. The reason seems to be this. The
'warfare' depicted between protective agencies arises as each seeks, against
the other, to enforce its interpretation of the rights of its clients. The dominant protection agency achieves its dominance (in one of Nozick's scenarios)
because its success in protecting its clients induces its rivals to cease trading, not because it forcibly prevents them from offering protective services. The incorporation of independents, on the other hand, involves forcibly depriving
them of their 'natural right' to punish rights violators.

How is this to be justified? Nozick's lengthy and complex argument
amounts to this.[19] The independents who enforce their own rights, unlike
the dominant protective agency, do not have a relatively reliable and impar-
tial judicial procedure for determining guilt and appropriate punishment.
Given people's tendency to favour themselves when they are judges in their
own case, right-enforcement by independents creates a serious risk of unjust
punishment of the agency's clients. Therefore, the agency, on behalf of its
clients, is entitled to prohibit right-enforcement by independents against them.
Furthermore, it has the power to do so, and will do so.

But it cannot stop there. The dominant protective agency that monopolizes right-enforcement is now a state, but not a just state. Nozick calls it the 'ultraminimal state'. It is unjust because it does not protect the rights of all – only of those who buy its protective services. Those who do not are forbidden to enforce their own rights. The ultraminimal state therefore must (morally) become the minimal state – must not only monopolize forcible protection of rights, but also forcibly protect the rights of all.

This completes Nozick's argument against anarchism. The independents, who had to be forced into subjection to the state, are, precisely, anarchists, so if their forcible subjection is justified, anarchism is wrong, and the (minimal) state is justified. To put it another way, the state is justified, even without universal consent, or a social contract.

But Nozick still has another problem to solve. *On what terms* is the minimal state to protect the rights of those who did not choose to buy the services of the dominant protective agency? Are they to be forced to pay the 'economic' price of these services? No doubt – if they can afford it. But what if they are too poor to afford it? Nozick must say, and does say, that they too must have their rights protected – in other words, 'those of scanter resources' must be subsidized by their wealthier fellows.[20] But in saying that wealthier citizens of the minimal state have an obligation to subsidize those too poor to pay the full economic cost of its protective services, is Nozick not in effect saying that the minimal state – even the minimal state – not merely may but must use its coercive power to enforce economic redistribution from rich to poor? Nozick needs to deny this, and does so. What is involved is, he says, not redistribution, but *just compensation* for forcible deprivation of 'natural rights'.[21] But this is unconvincing. Poor ex-independents are not necessarily anarchists at all. They may well be persons who could not afford to buy the dominant protective agency's services, but would have bought them if they could. They would, therefore, have freely accepted the incorporation–plus-subsidization deal that Nozick insists be offered them by the minimal state. No *forcible* incorporation, therefore, is necessary in their case, and hence no issue of compensation arises. What *is* necessary for their incorporation is subsidization. These 'reluctant independents' therefore, are genuinely the beneficiaries of redistribution. This is important, because it increases Nozick's difficulties in distinguishing morally between the minimal and the more-than-minimal state.

Other difficulties beset Nozick's argument. If we grant that the dominant protective agency may, can and will incorporate independents either by force or by offering subsidies, another question arises: what *level* of rights protection is it to offer them? The question arises because, as Nozick himself points out, private protective agencies, as commercial enterprises operating in the normal way, would offer clients a *variety* of protective packages, at different prices, to cater for more or less extensive or elaborate protection.[22] States, however, are supposed to provide the same protection of rights to all citizens, regardless of what taxes they pay. Nozick does not explain how this would or could come about, as the dominant protective agency transmutes itself into the minimal state. Would it involve more cross-subsidization – in effect more forced redistribution? Would it happen at all? What these conundrums suggest is that there is a much greater difference between a commercial protective agency – even a dominant one – and a state – even a minimal state – than Nozick allows, or than his argument can cope with. This conclusion is reinforced by some further considerations. For example, Nozick admits that he has given no good reason why the dominant protective agency would be entitled to force independents to accept its jurisdiction *in relation to disputes between independents (anarchists)*[23] – so it is not actually entitled to have the monopoly over right-enforcement characteristic of a state. Again, Nozick notes that independents not wishing to pay the 'price' (tax) charged by the dominant protective agency should by rights be entitled to refuse to do so, at the cost of forgoing protective services.[24] Real states, however, would prosecute such people for tax evasion, but would nevertheless otherwise protect their rights on the same basis as those of any other citizen. The upshot is that Nozick has not really succeeded in his aim of showing that a system of private, commercial protective agencies, such as the anarcho-capitalists favour, would evolve, by morally justified steps prompted by rational self-interest, into a minimal state.

Nozick could and should refute the anarcho-capitalists by a different argument – that is, by showing how unsatisfactory would be a regime of private, commercial, protective agencies or even of a single dominant agency. For one thing, their services would probably be expensive, since they would have to carry out functions of detection, apprehension of rights violators, judicial determination of guilt, and punishment. The rich would be much better able than the poor to buy their protective services. It is quite possible that a large proportion of the population would not be protected by them at all. Nor, as purely commercial agencies, would they normally provide the 'public goods' aspect of policing, which cannot be sold to individuals and is therefore difficult if not impossible to provide via the market – for example, routine patrolling of neighbourhoods in order to discourage and detect crime. In sum, what could evolve, short of the state, from the Lockean state of nature, would be so unsatisfactory as to justify establishing the state, if necessary imposing it by force on anarchists, so long as it provides equal protection of rights for all.

Refuting the anarchist case against the state is not a very controversial exercise. Much more controversial is the argument pursued in part II of *Anarchy, State and Utopia*, which seeks to demonstrate that any more-than-minimal state is unjust – more particularly, that state economic redistribution violates individual rights, and therefore must be excluded. The argument rests on Nozick's most celebrated contribution to political philosophy, his theory of economic justice (or, as he often calls it, of justice in holdings). This he calls the 'entitlement theory'.

In order to explain his entitlement theory, Nozick contrasts it with two other types of theory, which he rejects. One such type consists of 'end-state' principles, which 'hold that the justice of a distribution [of wealth] is determined . . . by some *structural* principle(s)'.[25] This means that two distributions are to be judged equally just if they have the same structure (or 'profile'), but different persons occupy different positions in the structure; for example, 'my having ten and your having five, and my having five and your having ten are structurally identical distributions'. Any principle that limits or regulates inequality, such as Rawls's difference principle, belongs to this category. Nozick objects to *all* end-state principles because they are *non-historical*, that is, treat as irrelevant to the justice of a distribution *how it came about*, how individuals acquired their holdings. Nozick's entitlement theory consists of historical principles of justice.

Some historical principles, however, must be ruled out; namely, those which belong to the category of 'patterned' principles of justice. Such a principle 'specifies that a distribution is to vary along with some natural dimension(s)'. It has the form 'to each according to his –' where the blank is filled in by 'moral merit, or needs, or marginal product', or anything else.[26] Nozick's argument against patterned principles generalizes Hayek's argument against social justice: they are incompatible with any freedom whatever for individuals to use their wealth as they choose. If a patterned distribution were established at any moment, it would of necessity be destroyed if persons could freely (and hence unpredictably) transfer some of their 'holdings' to others by means of purchases, gifts, loans, etc. Nozick asks us to choose a patterned distribution, according to taste, and to imagine it established. Then individuals use their money to buy what they want, and the pattern is destroyed: some have proportionately more than the pattern prescribes, others proportionately less. But are not all better off (having realized what economists call the 'gains of trade')? Why is the new, pattern-disrupting distribution not as just as the original patterned one, since it came about, starting from the original distribution, by the free choices of all involved? As Nozick sums up: 'Liberty upsets patterns'.[27] This argument of Nozick's is surely unanswerable. Quite rightly, his entitlement theory prescribes no pattern.

Nozick's entitlement theory of economic justice consists of three principles. First is a principle of justice in *acquisition*, which prescribes how a person may become the owner of a previously unowned thing. Second is a principle of justice in *transfer*, which specifies how one can legitimately come to own something already owned by someone else. The third principle prescribes *rectification* of injustice. According to Nozick's entitlement theory, a distribution is just (or, everyone is entitled to his or her holdings) if and only if everyone has acquired what they own through a sequence of transactions in accordance with the principles of just acquisition and just transfer.

The previous paragraph gives only the general shape of the entitlement theory – we need also to know the specifics of the three principles. The principle of rectification is in an obvious sense subsidiary, and discussion of it can be postponed. None the less, it will be seen to be important. Nozick's view of justice in transfer is straightforward: a person becomes the (new) legitimate owner of something already legitimately owned if and only if the previous owner freely alienates it to him or her – whether by a gift (charitable or otherwise), a bequest, a market exchange, or whatever. According to Nozick, this is implicit in the very concept of legitimate ownership. It follows that taxation by the state to provide welfare services – a forced transfer – is unjust. To Nozick, such forced redistribution violates the Kantian imperative: it uses some persons for the benefit of others. It is morally on a par with theft.

What about just acquisition (without which, of course, the question of just or unjust transfer cannot arise, in Nozick's historical theory)? Here, famously, is one of the gaps in the theory, for Nozick does not give a clear answer. Notoriously, and to the perplexity of many commentators, Nozick discusses Locke's labour theory of acquisition at length, finds it wanting, but does not put anything definite in its place. I believe, however, that in practice Nozick's theory of just acquisition is little different from Locke's. Certainly he believes that, as a general principle, labour creates entitlement. When *new* goods are *produced*, entitlement to them depends on how they were made. 'Whoever makes something, having bought or contracted for all other held resources used in the process . . . is entitled to it', Nozick writes.[28] It seems to follow that a person is entitled to appropriate unheld resources in order to make things, and if he uses only unheld resources to make something, he must become the rightful owner of what he makes. And if it is permissible to appropriate unheld resources in order to make something, it would seem illogical not to permit appropriation of unheld resources, just in order to use them directly (Locke, though not Nozick, calls all these transactions 'mixing one's labour' with the appropriated resources).

A similar conclusion can be gathered from Nozick's celebrated argument that 'taxation of earnings from labour is on a par with forced labour'.[29] It is, Nozick says 'seizing the results of someone's labour, [which] is equivalent to seizing hours from him'; it forces him to devote some of his hours of labour to ends not his own. Those who tax the earnings of a person's labour, therefore, treat him as if, during these hours, they *owned* his person and abilities. They flout 'the classical liberal notion of self-ownership' in favour of 'a notion of (partial) property rights in *other* people'.[30] Taxation of earnings from labour is not only theft; it is equivalent to (partial) enslavement.

Whatever the merits of this argument, the point is that it asserts the injustice of 'seizing the results of someone's labour', which by rights ought to belong to him. Thus, something a person makes out of unheld resources must, by this reasoning, become his property. If it did not, others would be entitled to seize it and, by Nozick's argument, thereby establish partial ownership, or partial enslavement, of its maker. Labour, in other words, is a just title to original acquisition.

Needless to say, this principle has nothing to do with socialism or opposition to capitalism (any more than has Locke's labour justification of property). By the just 'earnings' of labour, Nozick means what people are prepared to pay for it, or its product, in the market. Furthermore, he would include in the category 'labour' all forms of economic activity, including management; and he remarks that it would be desirable, and should be possible, to extend the argument against taxation of earnings from labour to 'interest, entrepreneurial profits, and so on'.[31] He does not give this extended argument – that is one of the acknowledged gaps in Nozick's argument. Nevertheless, he asserts that any policy designed to 'give each citizen an enforceable claim to some portion of the total social product' is objectionable in the same way as taxation of earnings of labour.[32] State redistribution is morally on a par with (partial) enslavement. There is thus no right to life, in the sense of a right to have what is necessary to sustain life.

Nevertheless Nozick does place a limit on the right to appropriate – he calls it the 'Lockean proviso'.[33] This may be a misnomer. Locke imposed, as a condition on appropriation, that 'enough and as good' be left for others. Nozick's 'Lockean' proviso, however, is that appropriation must not *worsen* the situation of others. But compared with what? Nozick admits that he cannot give a fully satisfactory answer to the 'question of fixing the [right] baseline [for comparison]'.[34] Despite this gap in the argument, Nozick emphasises that 'a system allowing appropriation and permanent property' so greatly 'increases the social product' and provides so many 'sources of employment', that the 'Lockean' proviso '(almost?) never will come into effect'.[35] It will come into effect only in cases of 'catastrophe', because 'the baseline for comparison is so low'. Why is the baseline so low? Though Nozick does not say so explicitly, he appears to take as the baseline for comparison a situation of *no property*, where everyone is free to use everything. As Hume convincingly argued long ago, such a state of affairs would indeed be catastrophic – a quasi-Hobbesian war of all against all. The 'Lockean proviso', thus interpreted, is indeed easy to satisfy. Even catastrophe might satisfy it. So it is not surprising that Nozick is able to conclude that 'the free operations of a market system will not actually run afoul of the Lockean proviso'. Even if the free market provides the disabled (for example) with nothing at all, it does not *worsen* their situation. They cannot justly claim more than they have, even if they have nothing.[36]

It is not surprising that such a stark theory has not been found acceptable by many. Only two points will be made about it here. The first is that Nozick's conclusion does not follow from his premises. His basic premise, we may recall, is the value of a 'meaningful' life, defined as a life shaped in accordance with an 'overall plan' of a person's own choosing. It would, however, be absurd to argue that a wealthy person, taxed as part of a redistributive scheme to help the poor, is thereby prevented from living a meaningful life. On the contrary, it is arguable that many more meaningful lives would be made possible in this way. The value of meaningful life does not justify Nozick's side-constraints morality, which in fact seems to embody the principle that no individual's life should ever be made *less* meaningful, even in the slightest degree, by coercing him, for whatever purpose – almost, that no *moment* of an individual's life should ever be made 'meaningless' for him in this way, whatever the cost.

But – secondly – there is some reason to think Nozick never intended that his entitlement theory of justice should be put into practice. To do so is, in fact, probably impossible. According to the entitlement theory, a distribution of holdings *now* is just if and only if it is the result of a sequence of just acquisitions and transfers, from the very beginning of human history to the present. What this tells us is that the present distribution, in every country, is hopelessly unjust. It has been massively influenced by the violent acts of which history is full. What then should we do? Theoretically, we should apply Nozick's principle of rectification of injustice, i.e. bring about the distribution that *would* exist if acts of unjust appropriation had not occurred. But this is unknowable and impossible. Nozick writes:

> One *cannot* use the analysis and theory presented [in this book] to condemn any particular scheme of transfer payments, unless it is clear that no consideration of rectification of injustice could apply to justify it.[37]

These words may come as a surprise. In any case, it appears (presumably to Nozick, also) that the stated condition for application of the theory cannot be satisfied, at least where transfers to the poor are concerned, and perhaps not at all.

There are some surprises, also, in the third and final part of Nozick's book, which argues that the minimal state provides the best 'framework for utopia'. Utopia, or 'the best of all possible worlds',[38] is one that allows as many people as possible to live as nearly as possible as they wish to live (to live meaningfully, one might say). It was argued, above, that the minimal state is far from doing this. Nozick, however, claims that the minimal state provides the best framework for utopia because it facilitates a society which contains

> a wide and diverse range of communities which people can enter if they are admitted, leave if they wish to, shape according to their wishes; a society in which utopian experimentation can be tried, different styles of life can be lived, and alternative visions of the good can be individually or jointly pursued.[39]

And he goes on to argue that this pluralistic, libertarian, utopian vision can even make room for the desired lifestyle of anti–libertarians: it can contain many and various *communities*, including anti–libertarian ones. Because it allows 'great liberty to choose among communities . . . particular communities internally may have many restrictions . . . which libertarians would condemn if they were enforced by a central state apparatus'. Communities may ban capitalism, or enforce economic redistribution among their members, and they may refuse to allow individual members to opt out of their arrangements.[40]

Why? What is the relevant difference between states and communities? Nozick addresses this question, but does not satisfactorily answer it. He cannot argue that communities are joined voluntarily, for it is possible and normal to be born into a community; nor that one is free to leave a community, since many states also allow this freedom. He even allows the possibility of a society without 'functioning capitalist institutions', such being the will of all its communities; there might for the same reason not be 'any viable non-communist communities', and recalcitrant individuals would then have no alternative but to conform. 'Still, the others do not force [them] to conform, and [their] rights are not violated.'[41] This seems to be a distinction without a difference. Nozick almost seems to admit as much when he writes, in the last sentence of this section, 'I do not see my way clearly through these issues'.[42]

It is possible, with hindsight, to see these difficulties as preparing the way for Nozick's recantation in the article 'The zigzag of politics'. In this article, he now argues for the right of a democratic majority to use the apparatus of the state to pursue their 'joint goals', because of 'the symbolic importance [to us] of an official political concern with issues or problems, as a way of marking their importance or urgency'.[43] Nozick now considers this form of collective self-expression to be an important aspect of meaningful life. Thus, helping those in need through state action can, appropriately and legitimately, express our concern for our fellows. To some this new, more permissive approach to state welfare provision may still seem unsatisfactory. Nozick still does not argue that the indigent have any right to help, nor that the wealthy, or anyone else, have any obligation to help them – only that this *may* be done, via the state, if a majority so wish.

It is a strange stance for an erstwhile individualist. However, Nozick endeavours to make provision for 'conscientious objectors' to such state-financed policies;[44] they could demand that their taxes not be used to further them, but he diverted to some other government programme, or to charity. Of course this is hopelessly impractical – and it is not clear, on Nozickian premises, why an individual should be compelled to contribute to any goal whatever. The upshot of Nozick's second thoughts is simply confusion. It is the original libertarianism of *Anarchy, State and Utopia*, however unpalatable, that is his significant contribution to political philosophy.

Notes

1   R. Nozick, *Anarchy, State and Utopia* (Basil Blackwell, Oxford, 1974), p. ix.
2   R. Nozick, *The Examined Life: Philosophical Meditations* (Simon and Schuster, New York, 1989), p. 292.
3   Nozick, *Anarchy, State and Utopia*, p. ix.

4   Ibid., p. 29.
5   Ibid., pp. 30–1.
6   Ibid., p. 33.
7   Ibid., p. 30.
8   Ibid., p. 50.
9   Ibid., p. xi.
10   Ibid., p. 5.
11   Ibid.
12   Cf. ibid., ch. 2 n. 4.
13   J. Locke, *The Second Treatise of Government and a Letter Concerning Toleration*, ed. J. W. Gough (Basil Blackwell, Oxford, 1957), p. 5.
14   Nozick, *Anarchy, State and Utopia*, p. 11.
15   Ibid., p. 13.
16   Ibid., p. 15.
17   Ibid., p. 16.
18   Ibid., p. 22.
19   Ibid., chs 4–5.
20   Ibid., p. 112.
21   Ibid., pp. 110ff.
22   Ibid., p. 13.
23   Ibid., p. 109.
24   Ibid., p. 113.
25   Ibid., p. 153.
26   Ibid., p. 156.
27   Ibid., p. 160.
28   Ibid.
29   Ibid., p. 169.
30   Ibid., p. 172.
31   Ibid., p. 170.
32   Ibid., p. 171.
33   Ibid., pp. 175–82.
34   Ibid., p. 177.
35   Ibid., p. 179.
36   Ibid., p. 182.
37   Ibid., p. 231.
38   Ibid., p. 298.
39   Ibid., p. 307.
40   Ibid., p. 320.
41   Ibid., pp. 321–2.
42   Ibid., p. 323.
43   Nozick, *The Examined Life*, pp. 287–8.
44   Ibid., p. 290.

Further reading

By Nozick

R. Nozick, *Anarchy, State and Utopia*, Basil Blackwell, Oxford, 1974.
R. Nozick, 'The zigzag of politics', in *The Examined Life: Philosophical Meditations*, Simon and Schuster, 1989.

On Nozick

G. A. Cohen, 'Robert Nozick and Wilt Chamberlain: how patterns preserve liberty', in J. Arthur and W. A. Shaw (eds), *Justice and Economic Distribution*, Prentice-Hall, Englewood Cliffs, N.J., 1978.
J. A. Corlett (ed.), *Equality and Liberty: Analyzing Rawls and Nozick*, Macmillan, Basingstoke, 1991.
J. Exdell, 'Distributive justice: Nozick on property rights', *Ethics* 88, 1977.
J. Paul (ed.), *Reading Nozick: Essays on Anarchy, State and Utopia*, Rowan and Littlefield, Totowa, N.J., 1981.
J. Waldron, 'Historical entitlement: some difficulties', ch. 7 of *The Right to Private Property*, Clarendon Press, Oxford, 1988.
J. Wolff, *Robert Nozick: Property, Justice and the Minimal State*, Polity with Basil Blackwell, Oxford, 1991.

12
Jürgen Habermas: Discourse Ethics and Democracy

Jürgen Habermas, born in 1929 in Düsseldorf, is the only political philosopher discussed at length in this book whose main works were not written in English. Students of Habermas who do not read German must rely on translations. Nevertheless, Habermas is, at the time of writing, a dominating presence in English-speaking social and political theory, as elsewhere. His thought has gone through a number of phases; politically, however, he has always placed himself on the radical left. He first came to prominence as the leading representative of the new generation of the Frankfurt School and of its 'critical theory', the origin of which between the two world wars was discussed earlier in relation to Herbert Marcuse. In 1956 Habermas became an assistant to one of its chief luminaries, Theodor Adorno, who had returned to the Frankfurt Institute for Social Research in its post-war reincarnation. From 1964 to 1971, and again from 1982 to 1994, Habermas was Professor of Philosophy and Sociology at Frankfurt. But Habermas, though the heir of Frankfurt thought, is not straightforwardly its continuator. The definition of his position has been, in stages, his definition and redefinition of his relation to the Frankfurt tradition; in the end, it is fair to say, he left it behind.

Habermas is an extremely prolific writer, the author of many books and articles, not all of which can be mentioned here. In what follows Habermas's books will be referred to by their English titles, but it is necessary, also, to distinguish between 'continuous' books (translated as such from German) and collections of essays (likewise, of course, translated, but not always collected into book form in the same combinations in both languages). In the former cases German publication dates will be given.

The key book in the earlier phase of Habermas's intellectual career is *Knowledge and Human Interests*, published in 1968. (The year, which marked the culmination of the student protest movement of the 1960s, is significant.) This is the book in which Habermas appears most recognizably as the heir of the Frankfurt school. To the same phase belong two essay collections, *Toward a Rational Society* and *Theory and Practice*. Thereafter Habermas's thought began to develop in new directions. One of these is represented by his book *Legitimation Crisis* (1973) which, however, turned out to be something of an intellectual dead end, and will therefore not be mentioned again. Much more significant is a trend in Habermas's thinking which had, somewhat paradoxically, already been signalled much earlier, in fact in his first important book, *The Structural Transformation of the Public Sphere* (published 1962), but was thereafter somewhat lost to view. This trend was resumed, and spelled out at much greater length and in much more abstract form in a two-volume work of 1981, considered by many to be Habermas's *magnum opus*, *The Theory of Communicative Action*. This work contains, among other things, an explicit settling of accounts with the earlier writers of the Frankfurt school, especially Horkheimer and Adorno. A number of essay collections contain discussions of related themes – notably, *Communication and the Evolution of Society, Moral Consciousness and Communicative Action* and *Justification and Application*. Finally, Habermas applies his 'theory of communicative action' explicitly to law and government in *Between Facts and Norms*, published in 1992.

As remarked above, Habermas is an extremely prolific writer. He is also an extremely difficult one (this is just as true of his original German as of the English translations of his work). The style of his writing is (with the sole exception of the early *Structural Transformation of the Public Sphere*) long winded, repetitive and extraordinarily abstract. It shows few signs of literary skill and can rarely be read with much pleasure. Habermas is himself a voracious reader and an encyclopaedic scholar who delights in incorporating the ideas of other writers into his own synthesis, typically after subjecting their work to lengthy survey and assessment – a trait which contributes greatly to lengthening his books, but does not make them more readable or easier to follow. In all probability the difficulties and defects of Habermas's style have actually served to increase his appeal in certain quarters, and in a way this is even a good thing, for, despite all stylistic criticism, Habermas has undoubtedly produced a significant and interesting body of theory – in contrast to a number of contemporaries of high reputation, in whom an obscure and hyperabstract prose masks poverty of ideas.

Knowledge and Human Interests is the first major book published by Habermas after becoming professor at Frankfurt in 1964. It reflects and responds to the mood of radical rebelliousness that dominated the 1960s, and is thus able to

270

connect itself with the 'critical theory' of the earlier Frankfurt School, which was then rediscovered and much admired by the 'revolutionary' left (considerably to the embarrassment, it must be said, of its original progenitors, Max Horkheimer and Theodor Adorno, who by then had changed their views considerably and, unlike Herbert Marcuse, had abandoned revolutionary and even political aspirations). This does not mean, however, that Habermas was ever an advocate of revolutionary violence. In line with earlier Frankfurt 'critical theory', *Knowledge and Human Interests* is written against 'positivism' and, more particularly, 'positivist' social science, considered by Habermas to be both philosophically naïve and politically harmful. Positivism naïvely supposes that *science* is straightforwardly knowledge of the world as it actually is, that the 'scientific' approach is the best or only way to knowledge, and should therefore be applied to the social world just as it has already been applied so successfully to nature – in order to produce a social science fundamentally similar to natural science. Another tenet of 'positivism' is that all knowledge is of *facts*, not of values (such as morality, etc.), since judgements of value cannot be established by scientific methods. Science, including social science, is thus of necessity 'value free' (as Max Weber proclaimed long ago).

The naïvety of this view is that it neglects the relation between knowledge and human interests – indeed, the dependence of human knowledge on human interests, and hence on human purposes and values. Natural science is shaped by the character of the human interest in the natural world, just as much as by the natural world itself. According to Habermas (drawing on C. S. Peirce and Wilhelm Dilthey), 'the empirical sciences contain information about reality from the viewpoint of possible technical control'.[1] That is – our interest in the natural world is fundamentally that we wish to use it for our human purposes, and natural science answers to that interest. It is not just a lucky accident that natural science affords us 'technically exploitable knowledge',[2] nor is it inherent in nature as such that knowledge of the world must be usable in this way. Rather, it is inherent in us, and in the 'technical' character of our interest in nature, by which natural science is structured. The goal of this 'empirical-analytic' science is the discovery of universal empirical laws, which enable human beings to manipulate nature for their purposes (as Habermas puts it, 'nomological knowledge is technically exploitable').[3] This goal is determined 'anthropologically'.

Unlike Marcuse, Habermas has no objection to such an 'instrumental' attitude to nature which (like Popper) he sees as continuous with (though much more systematic and effective than) the common-sense knowledge of the world that serves purposive human action. It arises from 'structures of human life', of a species which must labour in order to live. Here Habermas makes contact with Marx, to the extent of agreeing that it is through work and the exigencies of work that man comes to know the natural environment. But he parts company with Marx (and rejoins Marcuse and the old Frankfurt School) by repudiating the extension of this 'natural science' to society. That is the mistake of positivism, into which Marx unwittingly and regrettably fell.

For the way we relate (must relate) to fellow human beings in social interaction is, Habermas insists, quite different from the way men relate to the natural environment, imposes a different sort of exigencies, and therefore requires a different sort of knowledge. Or rather, as we shall see, two different sorts of knowledge. Human beings *qua* social beings *interact* with one another, and to do so they need to *understand* one another. This they do through a shared *language* (in a phrase which would come to bulk much larger in his thought, Habermas refers to this language-based human interaction as *communicative action*).[4] It necessarily follows, in Habermas's opinion, that the character of our interest in the social world, and therefore of our knowledge of it, must differ from our technical interest in and knowledge of the natural world. This interest and knowledge appropriate to society Habermas calls 'practical' or 'practically effective' knowledge.[5] Unfortunately the terms are not particularly apt, at least in English. A more informative if also more cumbersome expression used by Habermas to designate the interest and knowledge in question is 'action-orienting mutual understanding'.[6]

Knowledge constituted by this interest exists at two levels. In the first place, all normal human beings acquire it through socialization processes, which provide them with a linguistically structured picture of their social world and enable them to participate in it. But secondly, there is also a 'scientific' level of this kind of knowledge. The sciences which seek such knowledge are called by Habermas, variously, hermeneutic sciences, hermeneutic–historical sciences, and cultural sciences.[7] It seems that for Habermas these three terms are synonymous – a synonymy that may beg some questions. Here Habermas's viewpoint appears to be influenced (perhaps over-influenced) by that of Dilthey. 'Hermeneutic' means interpretive, and was originally applied to those disciplines concerned with the interpretation of texts. Dilthey expanded the term to apply to the 'human sciences' in general. It is true that these sciences involve, as Habermas says, an effort to 'grasp' or understand the shared mental world that structures the interactions of social human beings. Still, understanding a society is not quite like understanding a text, and involves much more than understanding its language.

272

However, it is clear that Habermas does not wish to confine social knowledge to the so-called 'practical' kind, or to the 'hermeneutic' sciences. The reason is that these sciences are not *critical*. They confine themselves to, and in a certain sense accept, established world-views and traditions. They do not address the issues of social *power* and social *constraints* and the questions of legitimation to which these give rise.[8] To put it another way, hermeneutic sciences fail to answer to the third of the 'knowledge-constitutive human interests', the *emancipatory* interest,[9] or interest in knowledge that 'free[s] consciousness from its dependence on hypostatized powers'.[10] How this weakness is to be remedied is a subject to which we shall return. First, however, we should examine Habermas's views as to the implications of positivistic social science.

In a summarizing statement, Habermas puts the charge against positivism in the following words:

> The positivist self-understanding of the nomological sciences lends countenance to the substitution of technology for enlightened action. It directs utilization of scientific information from an illusory viewpoint, namely that the practical mastery of history can be reduced to technical control of objectified processes . . . squeeze[s] the conduct of life into the behavioural system of instrumental action. The dimension in which acting subjects could arrive rationally at agreement about goals and purposes is surrendered to . . . mere decisionism among reified value systems and irrational beliefs.[11]

These, Habermas says, are once again consequences of slighting the 'emancipatory knowledge-constitutive interest'.

This key passage requires translation. It must be stressed that Habermas's critique of positivism is both philosophical and political. The positivist doctrine of value-free science (implying that value judgements are not knowledge, are not even rational) reduces political choices to arbitrary decisions by 'leaders' instead of rational democratic discussion and agreement (on 'enlightened action') – even in political systems supposedly 'democratic'.[12] Positivism's equation of knowledge with nomological science implies that 'rational' politics must take the 'instrumental' form of applying laws structured for 'technical control' – presumably, over human beings. In this connection Habermas refers, with obvious and understandable distaste, to a number of 'behavioural' techniques predicted by the futurologist Herman Kahn, including propaganda techniques, techniques of genetic control, and even techniques to influence the brain by means of electronic stimulation.[13] Positivistic, technical social science, in other words, becomes in Habermas's eyes a vehicle enabling some persons to exercise power over others. Sometimes this exercise of power takes on a 'technocratic' cast. Technical experts can claim power on the positivistic grounds that they are the possessors of the only rationally validated and relevant social knowledge. They then, Habermas says, use science and technology as an 'ideology'.

It is fairly clear that Habermas's critique is based in part on a *moral* position of a more or less Kantian kind. Technical knowledge is knowledge that allows the object of knowledge to be treated as a means to the ends of the knowledge-user. Such knowledge, perfectly appropriate in relation to the natural world, is morally unacceptable in relation to human beings. And yet, somewhat puzzlingly, Habermas does not seem to reject totally, or not totally consistently, 'nomological' social sciences (or, as he also calls them, 'systematic sciences of social action') such as economics, sociology and political science. However, the law-statements of these sciences are suspect for Habermas. It is necessary to distinguish, he says, between those which capture 'invariant regularities of social action as such', and those which serve an ideological function, namely, the 'freezing' of 'relations of dependence that can in principle be transformed'.[14] In other words, Habermas apparently sees many (though not all) social 'laws', not only as weapons for the exercise of power (by the powerful over the powerless) in given social structures, but also (through a false claim that these laws are universal and unalterable) as helping to perpetuate the unequal societies in which technical control of the powerless can be effected. What Habermas has in mind may be something like this. A sociological law, of the form 'if X is done, people will do Y', can be used to control or manipulate people, and thus expresses 'relations of dependence'. But the claim that such a statement is an invariable and universal social law may be true only if it is believed to be true – if people believe that no alternative social structure could alter the case, or that there is no way they could resist the outcome Y. If this *is* believed, the universal law in question may become a sort of self-fulfilling prophecy, thus 'freezing . . . relations of dependence that can in principle be transformed'. But Habermas concedes that not all universal social laws are like this – some are genuine social universals. Whether the latter are necessarily 'technical' laws oriented to control (of people) is not clear.

Habermas's remedy for the limitations and defects of both nomological and hermeneutic social science is critical theory, or 'critique', including in particular the critique of ideology. Integral to this approach is what Habermas calls 'self-reflection',[15] by which he means, in the first place, the achievement of a reflective awareness of the limitations of positivism. In self-reflection, 'information about lawlike connections sets off a process of reflection in the consciousness of those whom the laws are about', and thus *frees*, or at least can free the latter from subjection to the 'laws' in question. 'The . . . unreflected [unreflective?] consciousness, which is one of the initial conditions of such laws, can be transformed', so that the law becomes inapplicable in such a case. This kind of critical self-reflection is emancipatory – it serves the emancipatory cognitive interest because it produces a knowledge capable of liberating men from 'dependence on hypostatized powers'. It is worth pointing out that this method of liberation operates entirely at the level of consciousness. Habermas, unlike Marx or Marcuse, does not go on to advocate violent – or any other – political action as a means of liberation. It is not entirely clear whether he considers the change of consciousness sufficient in itself.

Habermas is, of course, right to suggest that people can be stimulated to liberate themselves through reflection on their condition, and also (in all probability) that they can 'falsify' a supposed law if reflection leads them to a desire to do so. However his political critique of 'nomological' social science seems misplaced. Though some laws of this kind certainly *can* (if they are true) be used as a means of objectionable social and psychological manipulation, this is not inherent in the idea of social laws or even social technology. What Popper would call piecemeal social engineering can clearly be used for good ends as well as bad, nor is there necessarily anything oppressive or manipulative (in a pejorative sense) about the means employed. Keynesian demand-management techniques (for example curing unemployment through budget deficits) are a case in point – the only thing wrong with them is that, apparently, they no longer work. Even self-reflection (as Habermas calls it) could be described as a technique of emancipation – certainly it is suggested by him as a *means* to that *end*. Like Marcuse, Habermas wrongly identifies the means–end relation with the use of resources (natural or human) as means – obviously the former is a broader category. Habermas seems to recognize the force of this criticism in his later work, in which his critique of instrumentalism in society becomes much more complex and qualified.

The fact that it is possible to speak of a technique of emancipation suggests that the latter is not really a 'knowledge-constitutive cognitive interest' comparable to our technical interest in nature and our so-called practical interest in the workings of our society. Freedom, or as Habermas also puts it, responsible autonomy (*Mündigkeit*),[16] is a value and a goal for some, but not for all. It is one value and one goal among others, however highly prized by Habermas. In *Knowledge and Human Interests*, he proclaims the contrary: 'The human interest in autonomy and responsibility is not mere fancy, for it can be apprehended a priori.'[17] This claim is part of Habermas's quarrel with positivism: contrary to the latter, he believes in objective, rational values. The case for autonomy as an objective, a priori interest or value is, however, no more than hinted at in *Knowledge and Human Interests* – it is said to be inherent in 'what raises us out of nature', namely, *language* (in brief, because true knowledge depends on free discussion). Habermas seems to have realized that he had not done enough to establish his position on this point. In his later work, the enterprise of demonstrating the possibility of rational, objective values becomes dominant. It remains linked to the analysis of language, and to the relation between (equal) freedom and truth. The notion of an emancipatory knowledge-constitutive interest seems, however, to have been given up. Its role is taken over by a minute analysis of the concept of 'communicative action' – a concept that Habermas, in *Knowledge and Human Interests*, introduced in relation to 'practical' rather than emancipatory knowledge.[18]

The *Theory of Communicative Action* is Habermas's *magnum opus*. In it he distinguishes a number of 'models' or types of action, of which only two need concern us, namely 'teleological' action and 'communicative' action.[19] Teleological action is defined as action aimed at attaining an end of the agent by the choice of appropriate (or apparently appropriate) means[20] – thus it is more or less identical with the kind of action Max Weber called *zweckrational*, a term which literally means 'purposively rational' but is often translated as 'instrumentally rational'. As we shall see, the fact that a concept of rationality here enters almost into the definition of action is highly significant. We can also note the continuity between this kind of action and the 'technical interest' which bulks large in Habermas's earlier work. In this kind of action, only a single agent need be involved, oriented to the physical world as a possible source of means to his or her ends. But as Habermas notes, an agent may adopt a similar attitude to other human beings – other agents – 'when there can enter into the agent's calculation of success the anticipation of decisions' by another agent or agents. This sort of teleological action is called by Habermas *strategic* action. It should be noted (though Habermas does not do so explicitly) that strategic action is not necessarily (indeed, not normally) unconstrained by moral and other norms – in fact, morally unconstrained strategic action would be a monstrosity.

Habermas's second, contrasting kind of action is communicative action, which he defines as follows. It 'refers to the interaction of at least two subjects capable of speech . . . who establish interpersonal relations . . . The actors seek to reach an understanding about the action situation and their plans of action in order to coordinate their actions by way of agreement'.[21] Language, as Habermas says, is central to this model. As we shall see, the definition quoted hints at, and even assumes, a whole moral and political philosophy. Much more detailed consideration of this will be necessary, but for the time being it should be noted that the philosophical implications of the concept of communicative action depend on the fact that, in Habermas's view, there corresponds to communicative action its own appropriate form of rationality – communicative rationality; just as, to the technological or strategic form of action, there corresponds the strategic or teleological or instrumental form of rationality, meaning the rational adaptation of means to ends.[22] Indeed, it is true to say that for Habermas communicative rationality is the more fundamental and comprehensive form. It is a key concept of Habermas's thought, which must be fully explained and examined. Before doing so, however, we may note how Habermas makes use of it in order to mount a critique of Weber's socio-historical conception of the 'rationalization' characteristic of modern Western civilization, and also of the interpretation of the Enlightenment offered by his Frankfurt predecessors, Max Horkheimer and Theodor Adorno.

As was explained at some length in an earlier chapter, Weber analysed the recent history of Western civilization in terms of two kinds of rationalization – rationalization of action, and rationalization of thought. The former largely pertains to *Zweckrationalität*, instrumental rationality, the purposive adaptation of means to ends. It is manifest in bureaucratization, modern technology and profit-maximizing capitalism. Rationalization of thought means above all modern science, which feeds into the rationalization of action via technology. Although these forms of rationalization have brought great benefits in the form of enhanced knowledge and efficiency, Weber's analysis of their effects also has a major pessimistic component. Rationalization of thought implies the 'disenchantment' of the world (in the scientific world-view nature is a-moral, and there are no objective values); while the main casualty of rationalized action, or efficiency, has been individual freedom and autonomy. The Frankfurt theorists, Horkheimer and Adorno, adopted and accentuated the pessimistic side of Weber's analysis of Western rationalization, which they identified with the idea of Enlightenment (or 'the Enlightenment' – the ambiguity is deliberate). They also, as Habermas points out, like their colleague Marcuse, merged this Weberian vision with their version of Marxism: they 'interpret Marx in this Weberian perspective. Under the sign of an instrumental rationality that has become autonomous, the rationality of mastering nature merges with the irrationality of class domination'.[23] As Habermas points out, this merger actually represents a reversal of Marx's own view.

Habermas challenges Weber's version of Western rationalization, and therefore also Adorno and Horkheimer's fusion of Weber and Marx. Not that he denies the historical phenomena alluded to by Weber, nor their importance; however, he argues that they represent only one side of the rationalization process, and in a significant sense not its most important one. In Habermas's opinion, Weber did not deal adequately with what he calls 'the rationalization of world views'.[24] This bears directly on the issue of disenchantment and the loss of objective values. As Habermas points out, these are relatively late outcomes of Western rationalization. In the high tide of Enlightenment thought, as represented most paradigmatically, perhaps, by Condorcet, science itself was seen – naïvely – as a model for the 'rationalization of social life', for political emancipation, and for 'the moral perfection of human beings'.[25] Condorcet confidently compared the 'moral and political' with the 'mathematical and physical' sciences. The confidence and the comparison are intellectually untenable, and inevitably collapsed. Habermas's project is to reinstate the Enlightenment belief in rational evaluation, but on a sound philosophical basis. To do so he has resort to the concept of communicative rationality.

Communicative rationality, Habermas suggests, is more fundamental and also 'wider' than the instrumental rationality emphasized by Weber.[26] Instrumental or purposive rationality – the efficient adaptation of means to ends – is not a peculiarly human achievement, even if it is human beings who have carried it to the greatest heights. It can be observed in the behaviour of animals generally, and is indeed a condition of their survival. What is peculiar to human beings is language, and the possibilities of rationality and rationalization at quite a different level that language creates – precisely because it is a vehicle of communication and argument ('argumentation'). Instrumental rationality itself is, of course, greatly enhanced by the human power to talk, argue and rationally convince: but in Habermas's view this is not the most important aspect of communicative rationality.

Because human beings are linguistic beings, Habermas contends, human actions are linked in a peculiar and specific way with linguistic expression, and therefore with what he calls 'criticizable validity claims'.[27] Thus, any goal-oriented action rests on a certain factual belief or beliefs about the world which, if true, make the action rational. If asked to explain or justify his action (always a possibility among linguistic human animals) the agent would be expected to state in words the relevant factual belief(s). He is thus committed to the truth of these beliefs, or, in Habermas's language, to a validity claim of a certain type, namely, that what he says is true. But such a claim is inherently criticizable – it is open to others to point out contrary evidence, etc. A rational person, therefore, must be committed to defending or modifying his factual beliefs in the light of relevant evidence. Whether he defends or modifies his beliefs, the agent, in so far as he is rational, is committed to adopting (and acting on) beliefs that would be adopted by all rational participants in such a 'discourse' – in principle, if not necessarily in practice (due to lack of time, insufficient evidence, etc.). Rationality is in this sense linked to agreement or consensus.

For Habermas claims as to truth are not the only kind of validity claims inherent in human action and speech. Only one other kind of validity claim need concern us – the most important one, namely, what Habermas calls 'rightness'[28] or, as we might say, normative justification.

> In contexts of communicative action, we call someone rational not only if he is able to put forward [a factual] assertion and, when criticized, to provide grounds for it by pointing to appropriate evidence, but also if he is following an established norm and is able, when criticized, to justify his action by explicating the situation in the light of legitimate expectations.[29]

In other words, human actions take place in a normative as well as a factual context, implying 'normative' validity claims as well as truth claims, claims which are inherently criticizable and (if the actions and agents are to be accounted rational) call for rational justification. 'The agent makes the claim that his behaviour is right in relation to a normative context recognized as legitimate.' But there is a significant difference between facts and norms – the former cannot be criticized in their turn, but the latter can. The rational agent, or speaker, therefore claims rightness also for the norms according to which he acts.[30] How such a claim can be made good (or, in Habermas's favoured terminology, 'redeemed') is, needless to say, a highly vexed question. Suffice it to say, for the time being, that Habermas believes that, here again, rationality implies an orientation or 'intention' towards discursive consensus just as in the factual sphere.

So far, we have seen how Habermas links rational action with communicative rationality and both with (intended or potential) agreement. But Habermas makes a stronger claim: namely, that 'reaching agreement' is the 'inherent telos' of human speech itself.[31] (To be absolutely accurate, what he says is that 'reaching *understanding* is the inherent telos of human speech'. However,

Habermas normally treats 'understanding' and 'agreement' as synonyms, and does so explicitly in this context.) In other words, communicative rationality is in some sense inherent in human language-use. 'A communicatively achieved agreement, or one that is mutually presupposed in communicative action . . . has to be accepted as valid by the participants . . . Processes of understanding aim at an agreement that meets the conditions of rationally motivated assent to the content of an utterance'. But what does Habermas mean by his claim that agreement/understanding is the telos of human speech? Certainly not that every 'speech act' aims at such agreement/understanding. 'Not every linguistically mediated interaction is an example of action oriented to reaching understanding'. Some uses of language are, in Habermas's terminology, strategic, for example. What Habermas wishes to claim, he says, is 'that the use of language with an orientation to reaching understanding is the *original* mode of language use',[32] on which instrumental or strategic uses of language are parasitic. In support of this claim, he appeals to the English philosopher J. L. Austin's well-known distinction between illocutionary and perlocutionary speech acts. 'In my view', Habermas writes, 'Austin's distinction between illocutions and perlocutions accomplishes' precisely what he (Habermas) needs. Unfortunately, his argument here appears weak.

Austin, in his book *How To Do Things With Words*, analyses speech acts by distinguishing locutionary, illocutionary and perlocutionary acts. The locutionary act uses words to convey a proposition (it 'says something'); the illocutionary act is the action a speaker performs *in* saying something (for example promising, commanding or making a statement); a perlocutionary act is an *effect* brought about in the world through saying something, through an effect on a hearer or hearers (for example, frightening someone). The point stressed by Habermas is that the essential components of the speech act are the locutionary and illocutionary ones; perlocutionary effects (and intentions) are external to the speech act as such, and such intentions may indeed be deliberately concealed by the speaker from his interlocutors. According to Habermas, this implies that the instrumental or strategic use of language is extrinsic to the nature of language as such. 'The communicative intent of the speaker and the illocutionary aim he is pursuing follow from the manifest meaning of what is said', but not so in the case of perlocutionary, and therefore strategic intentions. Thus, Habermas concludes, instrumental or strategic exploitation of language is not 'an original use of language'.[33] Communicative action, on the other hand, does not *consist* of speech acts or instances of language use, but rather of those interactions that are *mediated* linguistically, 'in which all participants pursue illocutionary aims and *only* illocutionary aims, with their mediating acts of communication'.

Habermas seems to suppose that the pursuit of illocutionary aims necessarily involves the pursuit of agreement/understanding. Of course, it is true (and banal) that communication cannot function unless the *meaning* of what is communicated is understood, and understood similarly, by all those involved. Habermas, however, claims that 'speech acts function as a coordinating mechanism for *other* actions', and that to pursue illocutionary aims *'without reservation'* means to seek to 'harmonize [participants'] individual plans of action with one another'.[34] This, Habermas says, defines communicative action. Now, it is clear that this coordination or harmonization is not the same thing as normative agreement; if Habermas thinks it is, his argument rests on an equivocation. But more probably his point is that the coordination of action that is facilitated by a successful illocutionary act (a promise, a command, or a baptism, etc.) depends on mutual uptake, and acceptance, of certain social conventions which the use of language, so to speak, hooks into. In this sense illocutionary acts imply a certain normative consensus. But if this is the argument, it is still unconvincing. This type of normative consensus is quite different from the discursive or argumentative consensus earlier said to be implicit in communicative rationality.

Even if Habermas's attempt to strengthen his argument by incorporating Austin's theory of speech acts is a failure, it does not follow that his key concept of communicative rationality is meaningless or insignificant. Far from it. It is this concept that Habermas uses to correct Weber's overly pessimistic account of occidental rationalization. To do so, he borrows from the phenomenologist philosopher Husserl the idea of the lifeworld. The lifeworld has undergone its own historical process of rationalization, in the sense of communicative rationality. The meaning and significance of this must now be explained.

What is the lifeworld? According to Habermas, it is one of two aspects or components of society, the other being the (social) 'system'.[35] The second volume of *The Theory of Communicative Action* indeed bears the title, *Lifeworld and System*. The lifeworld, Habermas tells us, is the substrate in which communicative action is 'embedded', the 'horizon within which' communicative action moves.[36] It consists of a set of 'common background convictions' about the world, society, etc., which are taken for granted by society's members, a stock of accepted interpretations that facilitate and shape the processes of reaching understanding and agreement of which communicative action consists.[37] As Habermas remarks, 'language and culture are constitutive for the lifeworld'. New situations are interpreted through the inherited cultural contents of the lifeworld, they are interpretable because they are not completely new; problematic situations are negotiated and negotiable in a similar way and for a similar reason. 'Communicative actors are always moving *within* the horizon of their lifeworld; they cannot step outside it . . . The structures of the lifeworld lay down the forms of the intersubjectivity of possible understanding'.[38]

Habermas has two main concerns in relation to the lifeworld. One, as already noted, is to analyse historically the rationalization of the lifeworld, a process which he rates positively. The other is to analyse the relation between lifeworld and system, again charting a historical development – here his evaluation is largely negative. Habermas's view of modernity is as a struggle between these two powerful historical forces. Depending on the outcome, our salvation hangs in the balance.

Habermas's history of the lifeworld (a schematic one, of course) is as follows. In terms reminiscent of Horkheimer and Adorno's *Dialectic of Enlightenment*, Habermas describes the lifeworld of 'archaic societies' as based on a 'mythical understanding of the world' – that is, a mythical *world-view*.[39] Myths fulfil 'the unifying function of worldviews', but do so in a (relatively) non-rational way. By this Habermas means (drawing on various sociologists and anthropologists, above all Emile Durkheim) that they fail to make (or to make clearly) certain distinctions that seem obvious and necessary to us, notably those between things and persons, between nature and culture, and between language and the world. As a result, the presuppositions of communicative rationality – namely, that communicative action implies *criticizable* validity claims – are seriously underdeveloped. 'The concept of the world is dogmatically invested with a specific content that is withdrawn from rational discussion and thus from criticism.'[40] This characterization is very much like Popper's description of the closed society.

Turning again to Durkheim, Habermas further characterizes the lifeworld of early human society as based on 'the authority of the sacred', which in such societies is the source of moral or proto-moral rules. In these societies it is perhaps not easy to distinguish such rules from rules of what Habermas calls 'ritual'. 'Ritual actions' he writes, 'take place at a pregrammatical level'.[41] Habermas's thesis of the rationalization of the lifeworld, and of world-views, is expressed as follows:

> the socially integrative and expressive functions that were at first fulfilled by
> ritual practice pass over to communicative action; the authority of the holy is

gradually replaced by the authority of an achieved consensus. This means a freeing of communicative action from sacrally protected normative contexts.[42]

There was, however, an intermediate phase, referred to by Habermas as 'the linguistification of the sacred'. By this term, Habermas refers to the development of the scriptural religions, a process which, from his point of view, is significant as a means 'for religious worldviews to connect up with communicative action'.[43] As a result, 'the validity basis of tradition shifts from ritual action over to communicative action. Convictions owe their authority less and less to the spellbinding power and the aura of the holy, and more and more to a consensus that is not merely reproduced but *achieved* ... communicatively ... The validity basis of norms of action changes [and] depends on reasons', if not yet exactly on reason, since 'authorization' is still dependent on 'the justificatory accomplishments of religious worldviews'. The promise of the Enlightenment was to bring this historical trend to completion, to base consensus on reason alone, or, in Habermas's terms, on 'the authority of the better argument',[44] or communicative rationality. In this historical sequence, Habermas detects a 'developmental logic', 'learning processes' leading to increased rationality. Its end point is a state of affairs 'in which traditions ... have become reflective and ... undergo continuous revision'. It seems to be a world in which, finally, nothing is sacred, except reason. Whether reason alone can generate an integrating consensus is just the issue on which Habermas differs from Weber, Durkheim and many others.

This brings us to a central Habermasian concept – discourse ethics. Discourse ethics depend on communicative rationality. As noted above, communicative rationality, for Habermas, depends on the readiness of agents and speakers to enter into argumentation, if challenged, in order to 'redeem' (rationally defend) implied validity claims of truth and rightness. It is rightness, in the moral or ethical sense, that is at issue here. 'By entering into a process of moral argumentation, the participants continue their communicative action in a reflexive attitude with the aim of restoring a consensus that has been disrupted. Moral argumentation thus serves to settle conflicts of action by consensual means.'[45] According to Habermas, this argumentative extension of communicative action holds the key to objective, rational morality; that is, it indicates a *procedure* for the generation of valid moral norms. The procedure is an idealised form of argumentation, which Habermas calls 'discourse'. Discourse is argumentation that takes place in an 'ideal speech situation'.[46] (These terms will be explained shortly.) The distinctive idea of discourse ethics, Habermas says, is expressed by the following principle:

283

> Only those norms can claim to be valid that meet (or could meet) with the approval of all affected in their capacity *as participants in a practical discourse.*[47]

Habermas's 'ideal speech situation' (the locus of 'discourse') is, like Rawls's original position, an idealization designed to ensure impartiality among all affected. It involves conditions of 'symmetry' (or equality) of rights and power between all participants in the discourse (that is, all those whose interests are affected by the issue in question – that these two categories of persons are identical is axiomatic for discourse ethics) such that 'the structure of their communication rules out all external or internal coercion other than the force of the better argument and thereby also neutralizes all motives other than that of the cooperative search for truth'.[48] All points of view can be freely expressed. Of course, real life is rarely quite like this, but Habermas maintains that these conditions for the validation of norms are presupposed by the very nature of argumentation. (Habermas even claims that to deny this involves a so-called 'performative contradiction' – for example, to claim to have convinced a person of something by means of lies is allegedly 'non-sensical'.[49] I doubt that this is so. But it perhaps suffices that to claim any moral authority for assent engineered in this 'strategic' manner is obviously untenable.)

Habermas makes clear – and it needs to be stressed – that he is not claiming merely that ideal discourses are fair to all involved; rather he claims that, ultimately – if continued long enough – they constitute a procedure that generates moral truth, or true moral norms, or (more precisely) true norms of justice.[50] Valid norms are those which all can accept, in a 'practical discourse' in an ideal speech situation. Such norms express a kind of 'general will', and embody what Habermas calls 'generalizable interests'.[51]

The main problem with Habermas's discourse ethics is, of course, that it is not clear why participants even in an ideal discourse, committed at the start to differing normative views, should ever reach agreement. Compared to Rawls's construction of contractors in the original position (discussed in a previous chapter), Habermas has set himself an infinitely harder task, by refusing to employ a 'veil of ignorance', or to limit the issues to be settled to what affects enjoyment of primary goods. It is true that Habermas does seek to limit the scope of discourse ethics in one way. 'It covers' he says 'only practical questions that can be debated rationally, that is those that hold out the prospect of consensus. It deals not with value preferences but with the normative validity of norms of action (sic)'.[52] This distinction between 'norms of action' and 'value preferences' is Habermas's version of that made by

Rawls between the right and the good, or the just and the good – 'value preferences' are conceptions of the good life. These, Habermas implies, are for individuals to decide for themselves. Unfortunately, however, Habermas destroys the force of the distinction by admitting (as he surely must) that 'values' can be '*candidates* for embodiment in norms that are designed to express a general interest'.[53] They therefore cannot be excluded from the ideal discourses of discourse ethics.

Habermas devotes a good deal of space to comparing his own approach to moral theory with that of Rawls, and also of Kant (Rawls, it will be recalled, considers himself to be a Kantian). He sees both similarities and differences.[54] Both Kant's categorical imperative, and Rawls's contractarian theory of justice, define morality in universalist terms, that is, as what is rationally acceptable to all affected – as does discourse ethics. But there is a large difference also. Both Kant and Rawls 'operationalize the standpoint of impartiality in such a way that every individual can undertake to justify basic norms on his own'[55] – including the moral philosopher himself. Thus, Rawls defends his well-known 'principles of justice'. That is, Habermas says, Rawls and Kant handle moral questions 'monologically', not 'dialogically' or 'discursively'. Habermas considers this to be a mistake. 'It is not enough for each individual [separately] to reflect on whether he can assent to a norm . . . What is needed is a "real" process of argumentation . . . [for] only it can give the participants the knowledge that they have collectively become convinced of something.'[56] For this reason, Habermas does not see it as his task to defend specific substantive moral principles. That is the task of a discourse among those who encounter moral problems and conflicts, who will feed into the discourse the relevant circumstances, interests, etc. The philosopher cannot rightly prejudge the outcome of ethical discourses. Rawls's principles of justice, for example, cannot be confirmed until they have been tested by such a discourse.

In spite of this, I believe that Habermas's ethical theory is, in reality, also monological. The reason is this. The validating discourse relied on in discourse ethics is an ideal discourse, not a real one (it is noteworthy that in the passage cited above the word 'real' is in quotation marks). In real life the conditions of Habermas's ideal speech situation are never perfectly realized, and probably cannot be, if only because of time constraints. Furthermore, the set of persons affected by any norm that might be agreed is likely to include persons not yet born. Therefore, it is always possible for Habermas or anyone else who believes in discourse ethics to reject the terms of any agreement reached in an actual dialogue. In doing so, he applies his estimate of the distorting effect of departures from the conditions of the ideal discourse. If discourse ethics is to be applied in practice, the moral agent can only reach a conclusion as to what agreement, if any, *would* be reached in an ideal discourse. The latter is ultimately a heuristic device usable in one thinker's mind – that is, monologically.[57]

Despite all reservations, Habermas's conception of communicative rationality as a basis for moral objectivity is not to be dismissed. In particular there is something persuasive about his analysis of the historical development of moral argumentation and its role in the lifeworld, and his characterization of it as a 'learning process'. This helps to validate Habermas's view of his moral philosophy as being, at the same time, a kind of 'reconstructive social science'.[58] Nor is it only the historical learning process that lends support to this idea – Habermas suggests that the point is reinforced by *individual* learning processes of the kind described by such psychologists as Jean Piaget and Laurence Kohlberg. Kohlberg, in particular, is known as the author of a theory of development of moral consciousness, in which the individual advances from stage to stage as he or she matures. According to Kohlberg,[59] the succession of stages is invariant – there is only *one* such succession, available to all – though not all individuals advance to the final or 'highest' stage, and the likelihood of an individual doing so is a cultural variable. To cut a long story short, this sequence culminates in a moral attitude consonant with discourse ethics (roughly, the claim is that the morally mature person views morally right decisions as stemming from principles rationally acceptable to all affected – these principles are seen as universal and binding on all human beings).[60] Needless to say, Habermas's appropriation of Kohlberg gives rise to many controversial issues, such as: is Kohlberg's theory empirically accurate? If so, does it really 'fit' discourse ethics as Habermas claims? And if it does, why exactly does that support discourse ethics? Unfortunately it is not possible to discuss these issues in any detail here.

Let us return to issues of social evolution. We have dealt above with the lifeworld and its rationalization; but the lifeworld is only one component of society. Society, Habermas suggests, is to be conceived as 'simultaneously . . . a lifeworld [and] a system'.[61] Habermas uses the term 'system' in a very particular way, to refer to certain particular kinds of social interaction – roughly, that kind in which attitudes of social actors to other social actors are primarily strategic rather than communicative. It includes, for example, the capitalist market and bureaucratic administrations[62] – those areas so much stressed in Max Weber's rationalization thesis, in the *zweckrational* (instrumentally rational) sense. Social evolution has not been only a process of rationalization of the lifeworld: it has been, also, one of *differentiation and uncoupling* of lifeworld and system,[63] and of growth in the scale and complexity of the latter. Habermas describes the process thus:

> the lifeworld . . . is at first coextensive with a scarcely differentiated social system . . . [Later,] system mechanisms get further and further detached from the social structures through which social integration takes place . . . Modern societies attain a level of system differentiation at which increasingly autonomous organizations are connected with one another via delinguistified media of communication: these systemic mechanisms – for example, money – steer a social intercourse that has been largely disconnected from norms and values.[64]

As can be seen from the above quotation, Habermas views the growth of the 'system' with considerable suspicion. In fact, his attitude to it has something of Weber's ambivalence: while recognizing its inevitability and the benefits it brings, he also sees it as, potentially, a threat to the integrity of the lifeworld, communicative action, and communicative rationality. The danger is of what Habermas calls the 'colonization' and therefore distortion of the lifeworld by the system.[65] In modern societies, this is what has actually happened, to a degree far beyond what is tolerable. 'Systems' have too much power or rather facilitate the exercise of power free from adequate normative restraint in too many areas. Habermas calls this the 'technicization of the lifeworld'.[66] One of its effects is to restrict and distort the lifeworld's communicative processes.[67] Among the examples of this 'sociopathology' that Habermas mentions are such familiar phenomena as 'the destruction of urban environments as a result of uncontrolled capitalist growth, [and] the over-bureaucratization of the education system'.[68] The key to a morally adequate society is to keep the 'system' in its proper place.

How is this to be achieved? For many years, Habermas would have argued that a necessary condition was the achievement of socialism (not, of course, on the Soviet model) and the consigning of capitalism to the dustbin of history. The revolution in Eastern Europe that began in 1989 has modified his views. Writing in 1990, Habermas explicitly accepts the market economy, and admits the irrelevance of 'forms of ownership' to the central issue[69] – that of controlling the 'system' and eliminating its pathological side effects. This, as Habermas says, is a matter of political action.

The political application of Habermas's moral and social theory is set out systematically in *Between Facts and Norms*, first published in German in 1992. Before considering this, however, we should look at a much earlier book by

Habermas on a political subject, *The Structural Transformation of the Public Sphere*. Not only is this among the first books Habermas wrote, it is also, among his major works, much the most accessible – it stands out among them for concreteness and attention to historical detail. In the second volume of *The Theory of Communicative Action,* Habermas picks out, as areas that ought to be protected from 'systemic' domination, the 'private' and 'public' spheres of life.[70] The private sphere includes, he says, family life, neighbourhood and voluntary association. What Habermas means by the public sphere needs lengthier explanation.

In his early book, Habermas notes that the idea of the public sphere (*Öffentlichkeit*) was not current (in Western Europe – Britain, France and Germany) until the eighteenth century.[71] It was a bourgeois institution, or at least arose out of certain needs and aspirations of the bourgeois class. The need of this class for economically relevant information – on wars, harvests, taxes, etc. – created the first so-called 'political journals'. 'News itself became a commodity.' The upper bourgeoisie (merchants, bankers, entrepreneurs and manufacturers) 'was the real carrier of the public', and was a reading public.[72] As the state authorities too, in the pursuit *inter alia* of mercantilist economic policies, began to use the press to promulgate to the 'public' information, ordinances and propaganda, this public was provoked 'into an awareness of itself as [the state's] opponent, that is, as the public of the now emerging public sphere of *civil society*. For the latter developed to the extent that the public concern regarding the ... sphere of civil society was no longer confined to the authorities but was considered by the subjects as one that was properly theirs'. The 'social structures' of this emerging public sphere included the famous coffee houses of eighteenth century London and provincial English cities (where Addison and Steele's *Spectator* and *Tatler* were eagerly devoured), the equally famous Parisian *salons*, and the German *Tischgesellschaften* (dining societies). These arenas served equally for discussion of social, political, literary and intellectual issues, and brought the bourgeoisie into socially promiscuous contact with aristocrats and leading intellectuals.

Habermas evaluates these developments extremely positively. The word 'discussion' is key here, and foreshadows the theory of communicative action. Very importantly, the participants in the discussion, despite disparities in social background, treated one another as equals.[73] What developed was 'the critical judgment of a public making use of its reason', 'rational–critical public debate', by *private* persons on political issues, aiming to challenge and even control the domination of state authorities.[74] At about the same time in Britain, the press was freed from censorship and other restrictions. 'Public opinion' was born, and became a factor to be reckoned with. In Britain it gained power as Parliament increasingly asserted its authority *vis-à-vis* the king. Of course, this 'public' was itself an élite, a small minority of the total society, and not without its social and political biases as a result. Nevertheless, Habermas considers that it represented also a genuine and highly salutary rationalization: 'Bourgeois culture was not mere ideology.'[75]

> The clichés of 'equality' and 'liberty', not yet ossified into revolutionary bourgeois propaganda formulae, were still involved with life. The bourgeois public's critical public debate took place in principle without regard to all preexisting social and political rank and in accord with universal rules ... The results that under these conditions issued from the public process of critical debate lay claim to that morally pretentious rationality that strove to discover what was at once just and right.[76]

As this quotation hints, the eighteenth-century golden age was not to last – was not to preserve its autonomy from the onslaughts of the 'system'. The rules of rational discussion of the bourgeois public sphere proved unable to accommodate the democratic demands of the working class, and (in the nineteenth century) politics radically changed its character. Conflicts were settled less by discussion than by the threat of force, 'under the "pressure of the street" '.[77] Nineteenth-century franchise reform in Britain created a mass electorate at the same time as socio-economic developments were creating a mass society, and 'public opinion' became (in the usage of liberal thinkers like Tocqueville and J. S. Mill) a pejorative expression. The 'public sphere' was breaking down.[78]

A corollary of this, according to Habermas, was a gradual destruction of the separation of state and society, and a great enhancement of the role and reach of the former.[79] The older public sphere was replaced by a 'private sphere' of economic activity only; more and more, this economic sphere and the state together (the 'system', in Habermas's later terminology) predominated in society. The public sphere was subsumed into 'the realm of consumption', a market-driven enterprise which partly panders to and partly manipulates an uncritical and un-political mass culture.[80] An index of the degeneration of the public sphere, Habermas suggests, is the phenomenon of 'public relations',[81] a strategically motivated endeavour by 'systemic' powerholders (again I am employing the terminology that Habermas developed later), which contradicts the very concept of publicness. Habermas's estimate of modern parliamentary democracy (writing in 1962) is much the same as that of Joseph Schumpeter[82] – in reality it consists largely of manipulation of voters by the political élites. But whereas for Schumpeter this *is* democracy (so long as the élites compete freely and are freely recruited) for Habermas it is a sham.[83]

Although this analysis has clear resemblances to the views developed by the older Frankfurt school (Horkheimer, Adorno and Marcuse), it also overlaps to a considerable and surprising extent with those of right-wing thinkers such as Hayek – not, of course, in relation to the capitalist market, but rather the expanded modern state. The expansion of state activity in the late nineteenth and twentieth centuries, with the concomitant increase in state bureaucracy and its impact on society, represents to Habermas (again using his later terminology) an unwelcome increase in the influence of the 'system'. This applies, furthermore, also to the welfare state. Provision of welfare services is not part of, and does not depend on, the public realm. Habermas writes:

> Citizens entitled to services relate to the state not primarily through political participation but by adopting a general attitude of demand – expecting to be provided for without actually wanting to fight for the necessary decisions. Their contact with the state occurs in the rooms and anterooms of bureaucracies; it is unpolitical and indifferent, yet demanding. In a social-welfare state that above all administers, distributes and provides, the 'political' interests of citizens [are] constantly subsumed under administrative acts.[84]

Because of this, welfare policy can be and is used to engineer electoral support which 'amounts to no more than an act of acclamation within a public sphere temporarily manufactured for show or manipulation'.[85] In the second volume of *The Structure of Communicative Action* (1981), the welfare state is called 'the model case for the colonization of the lifeworld' by the system.[86] In a manner surprisingly reminiscent of Oakeshott, the 'welfare paradigm' is seen as involving a regrettable surrender of 'autonomy' for the sake of 'well-being' (though the prospect is held out of pursuing the social-welfare project in a better way).[87] It turns 'citizens' into 'clients' and makes acceptable to them the absence of genuine political participation.[88]

Between Facts and Norms is Habermas's most extended application of his theory to government (the rather opaque title is his characterization of law). It is easy enough to see how Habermas's concepts of communicative rationality and discourse ethics suggest a certain style of *politics*, but their relation to *government* is more problematic. It may not be surprising that Habermas sees his theory as underpinning a particular conception of democracy which is highly participative, resting on an extensive 'public sphere' – a conception often referred to in recent literature as 'deliberative' or 'discursive' democracy, and which Habermas has helped to make popular and even fashionable. Democracy, Habermas says, is the institutionalization of the theory of argumentation, 'through a system of rights that secures for each person an equal participation in the process of legislation'.[89] He also claims that 'the democratic principle states that only those statutes may claim legitimacy that can meet with the assent of all citizens in a discursive process of legislation'.[90]

These two propositions are not the same, and may even be contradictory. The point is a simple one. The equal rights of political participation inherent in democracy include voting rights, which are combined with principles for taking decisions on the basis of some kind of majority or plurality system. Democracy is a system, *inter alia*, for the making of *laws*, which are then imposed on all citizens, regardless of their opinions. At first sight, Habermasian discourse ethics seems to imply that no laws, or authoritative decisions of any kind, can be imposed unless they are accepted *unanimously* by all affected. No democracy has worked or could work in this way.

What, then, is Habermas's view of law, which is, by its nature, coercive? According to Habermas, it 'steps in to fill the functional gaps in social orders whose integrative capacity is overtaxed'.[91] This appears to be an admission that the conditions of ideal discourse are never achieved in actual societies.[92] The function of law is to enforce valid norms none the less. 'The state becomes necessary as a sanctioning, organizing and executive power because rights must be enforced.'[93] The problem remains, however, of ensuring that the right laws are enforced by the governmental system, and of what the bearing of 'democracy' is on this problem. Habermas devotes a good deal of space, in *Between Facts and Norms*, to arguing for the improbable proposition that 'popular sovereignty and human rights presuppose each other',[94] but the argument is quite unconvincing (or else I have not understood it). For example, Habermas claims that individual liberties and the political rights of democratic citizens 'make each other possible' – but this, even if true, does not mean that either guarantees the other, or even makes the other probable. It is necessary to admit that democracy does not entail societal justice. This remains true, even if decision making is preceded by lengthy, democratic discussion. And the problem becomes even more serious, in the light of Habermas's remark that democratic legislation, since unlike morality as such it relates to a particular political community, may justifiably give effect, not only to universal norms, but also to collective goals and values.[95] In reality, this may mean the imposition of majority goals and values on the minority.

Habermas makes two other remarks that seem to address this issue. Admitting that majority decisions following political argumentation may always be 'fallible', he suggests that the decision's legitimacy depends on its being treated as an 'interruption' of a discourse which is 'in principle resumable'.[96] 'The outnumbered minority give their consent to the empowerment of the majority only with the proviso that they themselves retain the opportunity in the future of winning over the majority with better arguments.' No doubt – but there is no guarantee that their 'better arguments' will be heeded any more in the future than in the past. The problem remains.

Habermas's other remark is obscure, to say the least:

> Legitimate law is compatible only with a mode of legal coercion that does not destroy the rational motives for obeying the law: it must remain possible for everyone to obey legal norms on the basis of insight . . . therefore, law must not *compel* its addressees but must offer them the option, in each case, of foregoing the exercise of their communicative freedom and not taking a position on the legitimacy claim of law, that is, the option of giving up the performative attitude to law in a particular case in favour of the objectivating attitude of an actor who freely decides on the basis of utility calculations.[97]

This may (or may not) mean that the 'actor' can agree to accept the principle of (democratic) legislation on pragmatic grounds ('on the basis of utility calculations') even though he does not expect, in particular cases, always to accept the legitimacy of the law made. (The reader is invited to work out for herself whether this is a defensible interpretation.) Whether or not this is Habermas's argument, it would seem reasonable enough. What it amounts to is the idea that deliberative democracy is the best available compromise between the theory of discourse ethics and political reality.

Notes

1   J. Habermas, *Knowledge and Human Interests*, tr. J. J. Shapiro (Heinemann, London, 1972), p. 162.
2   Ibid., p. 191.
3   Ibid., pp. 302, 308.
4   Ibid., pp. 191–2.
5   Ibid., pp. 310, 191
6   Ibid., pp. 195.

7   Ibid., pp. 191, 193, 309.
8   Ibid., p. 313.
9   Ibid., p. 314.
10 Ibid., p. 313.
11 Ibid., p. 316.
12 Cf. J. Habermas, *Toward a Rational Society*, tr. J. J. Shapiro (Heinemann, London, 1971), pp. 67–8.
13 Ibid., p. 117.
14 Habermas, *Knowledge and Human Interests*, p. 310.
15 Ibid.
16 Ibid., p. 311.
17 Ibid., p. 314.
18 Ibid., p. 192.
19 J. Habermas, *The Theory of Communicative Action,* vol. 1: *Reason and the Rationalization of Society*, tr. T. McCarthy (Heinemann, London, 1984), p. 95.
20 Ibid., p. 85.
21 Ibid., p. 86.
22 Ibid., pp. 10, 14.
23 Ibid., p. 144.
24 Ibid., p. 180.
25 Ibid., pp. 146–7.
26 Ibid., p. 10.
27 Ibid., p. 15.
28 Ibid., p. 307.
29 Ibid., p. 15.
30 Ibid., p. 307.
31 Ibid., pp. 286–7.
32 Ibid., p. 288.
33 Ibid., p. 293.
34 Ibid., pp. 294–5.
35 J. Habermas, *The Theory of Communicative Action,* vol. 2: *Lifeworld and System*, tr. T. McCarthy (Polity Press, Cambridge, 1987), p. 120.
36 Ibid., p. 119.
37 Ibid., p. 125.
38 Ibid., p. 126.
39 Habermas, *Reason and the Rationalization of Society*, p. 44.
40 Ibid., p. 51.
41 Habermas, *Lifeworld and System*, p. 56.
42 Ibid., p. 77.
43 Ibid., p. 88.
44 Ibid., p. 145.
45 J. Habermas, *Moral Consciousness and Communicative Action*, tr. C. Lenhardt and

S. W. Nicholsen (Polity Press, Cambridge, 1990), p. 67.

46 Ibid., p. 88.

47 Ibid., p. 66. Emphasis in the original.

48 Ibid., pp. 88–9.

49 Ibid.

50 Ibid., pp. 68ff., 65–6,105.

51 Ibid., p. 78.

52 Ibid., p. 104.

53 Ibid.

54 Ibid., pp. 63, 65–6.

55 Ibid., p. 66.

56 Ibid., p. 67.

57 In *Between Facts and Norms* (MIT Press, Cambridge, Mass., 1996), Habermas himself calls it a 'thought experiment' (p. 323). He also admits the fallibility of participants in actual discourses (p. 324).

58 Habermas, *Moral Consciousness and Communicative Action*, pp. 15–16.

59 Ibid., p. 117.

60 Ibid., pp. 123–5.

61 Habermas, *Lifeworld and System*, p. 120.

62 Ibid., pp. 150, 154.

63 Ibid., p. 153.

64 Ibid., p. 154. 'Power' is also mentioned as a systemic steering mechanism (ibid., p. 183). The debt to Talcott Parsons is explicit.

65 Ibid., p. 196.

66 Ibid., p. 183.

67 Ibid., p. 187.

68 Ibid., pp. 293–4.

69 J. Habermas, 'What does socialism mean to-day?', *New Left Review* 183, Sept–Oct 1990, pp. 16–17.

70 Habermas, *Lifeworld and System*, p. 310.

71 J. Habermas, *The Structural Transformation of the Public Sphere* (Polity Press, Oxford, 1989), p. 2.

72 Ibid., pp. 21, 23.

73 Ibid., p. 36.

74 Ibid., pp. 24, 28.

75 Ibid., p. 160.

76 Ibid., p. 54.

77 Ibid., p. 132.

78 Ibid., p. 140.

79 Ibid., p. 142.

80 Ibid., p. 160.

81 Ibid., p. 193.

82 J. A. Schumpeter, *Capitalism, Socialism and Democracy* (George Allen and Unwin, London, 1943), chs 21–2.
83 For a somewhat more optimistic revision of this view, see the new 'introduction' added to the 1990 edition (in German) of *The Structural Transformation of the Public Sphere*. An English translation is in C. Colhoun (ed.), *Habermas and the Public Sphere* (MIT Press, Cambridge, Mass., 1992), cf. p. 438.
84 Habermas, *The Structural Transformation of the Public Sphere*, p. 211.
85 Ibid., p. 222.
86 Habermas, *Lifeworld and System*, p. 322.
87 Habermas, *Between Facts and Norms*, pp. 418, 410.
88 Habermas, *Lifeworld and System*, p. 350. The same formula is repeated in *Between Facts and Norms*, p. 404.
89 Habermas, *Between Facts and Norms*, p. 110.
90 Habermas admits that this assent may involve compromise rather than moral agreement, in the political case (ibid., pp. 166–7).
91 Ibid., p. 42.
92 Cf. ibid., pp. 115–16.
93 Ibid., p. 134.
94 Ibid., p. 450.
95 Ibid., pp. 152–4.
96 Ibid., p. 179.
97 Ibid., p. 121.

Further reading

By Habermas

J. Habermas, *Toward a Rational Society*, tr. J. J. Shapiro, Heinemann, London, 1971.
J. Habermas, *Knowledge and Human Interests*, tr. J. J. Shapiro, Heinemann, London, 1972.
J. Habermas, *Theory and Practice*, tr. J. Viertel, Heinemann, London, 1974.
J. Habermas, *Legitimation Crisis*, tr. T. McCarthy, Heinemann, London, 1976.
J. Habermas, *The Theory of Communicative Action,* vol. 1: *Reason and the Rationalization of Society*, tr. T. McCarthy, Heinemann, London, 1984.
J. Habermas, *The Theory of Communicative Action,* vol. 2: *Lifeworld and System*, tr. T. McCarthy, Heinemann, London, 1987.
J. Habermas, *The Philosophical Discourse of Modernity*, tr. F. G. Lawrence, Polity Press, Cambridge, 1987.
J. Habermas, 'Law and morality', *Tanner Lectures on Human Values*, VIII, 1988.
J. Habermas, *Moral Consciousness and Communicative Action*, tr. C. Lenhadt and S. W. Nicholsen, Polity Press, Cambridge, 1989.

Contemporaries

J. Habermas, *The Structural Transformation of the Public Sphere*, tr. T. Burger, Polity Press, Cambridge, 1989.

J. Habermas, 'What does socialism mean to-day?', *New Left Review* 183, September/October 1990.

J. Habermas, *Justification and Application: Remarks on Discourse Ethics*, tr. C. Cronin, Polity Press, Cambridge, 1993.

J. Habermas, *Between Facts and Norms*, tr. W. Rehg, Polity Press, Cambridge, 1996.

J. Habermas, *The Habermas Reader*, ed. W. Outhwaite, Polity Press, Cambridge, 1996.

On Habermas

R. J. Bernstein (ed.), *Habermas and Modernity*, Polity Press, Cambridge, 1985.

C. Colhoun (ed.), *Habermas and the Public Sphere*, MIT Press, Cambridge, Mass., 1992 (includes Habermas's new 'introduction' to the 1990 German edition of *The Structural Transformation of the Public Sphere*).

P. Graham, 'Habermas's rectifying revolution', *International Politics* 33, March 1996.

T. McCarthy, *The Critical Theory of Jürgen Habermas*, MIT Press, Cambridge, Mass., 1978.

W. Outhwaite, *Habermas: A Critical Introduction*, Polity Press, Oxford, 1994.

D. M. Rasmussen, *Reading Habermas*, Basil Blackwell, Oxford, 1991.

R. Roderick, *Habermas and the Foundations of Critical Theory*, Macmillan, Basingstoke, 1985.

J. B. Thompson and D. Held (eds), *Habermas: Critical Debates*, Macmillan, London, 1982.

S. K. White, *The Recent Work of Jürgen Habermas: Reason, Justice and Modernity*, Cambridge University Press, 1988.

13
Conclusion: The End of History?

In 1989, Francis Fukuyama published an article suggesting that the collapse of Soviet-style communism marked the end, not just of that socio–political system, not just of the 'short twentieth century', but of 'history' itself. Admittedly, the title of his article was 'The end of History?', with a question mark; and he explained in a later book (*The End of History and the Last Man*, 1992) that he was referring not to history but to History, with a capital H.[1] Nevertheless his thesis was provocative enough, no doubt intentionally. Fukuyama wrote that

> liberal democracy may constitute the 'end point of mankind's ideological evolution', and the 'final form of human government' and as such [be] the 'end of history'. That is, while earlier forms of government were characterized by grave defects and irrationalities that led to their eventual collapse, liberal democracy [is] arguably free from such fundamental internal contradictions . . . To-day's stable democracies [are] not without injustice or serious social problems. But these problems [are] ones of incomplete implementation of the twin principles of liberty and equality on which modern democracy is founded, rather than flaws in the principles themselves . . . The *ideal* of liberal democracy [cannot] be improved on.

Putting aside the oddity of identifying History with political history (or the history of systems of government), Fukuyama's provocative thesis is of considerable interest. It rests, as he explains, on what he takes to be a democratized interpretation of Hegelianism put forward by Alexandre Kojève.[2] According to Kojève's Hegel, world history, or world historical progress, should not be seen as driven by economic forces, nor as taking the form of ever-increasing material wealth; rather, it has been powered by men's 'struggle for recognition' by their fellows, and characterized by an increasingly widespread achievement of that recognition – of mutual respect among men. According to Fukuyama's Kojève, liberal democracy is the culmination of history's centuries-long struggle by the enslaved masses for recognition as equals by their (former) masters. It is the achievement of universal mutual respect – in idea, if not fully in actuality. It is therefore the end of History.

Much in this thesis can be accepted, but it does not follow that History is at an end. The end-of-History thesis rests on the following claims: (1) the principles of liberty and equality are now universally accepted, or soon will be; (2) liberal democracy embodies the principles of liberty and equality; (3) the principles of liberty and equality, and hence their liberal democratic embodiment, can never be superseded in the future. The third claim is rash, to say the least. Like Hegel's own, Fukuyama's thesis rests on a highly eurocentric view of History. Chinese civilization, for example (which can hardly be dismissed as insignificant) never rested on, and never generated, principles of liberty, equality or liberal democracy. While it is true that China is now governed by a regime that endorses and appeals to various Western ideologies, it is not certain that the Westernization of China is more than skin deep. Also, there is at least one non-Western ideology that still appears to have a lot of life in it, namely Islam, whether mainstream, radical or fundamentalist. I am not clear whether Islam, or any of its branches, would claim to embody principles of liberty and equality, but it seems to me quite imaginable that they could do so. If so, this demonstrates, what should in any case be obvious, that radically opposed interpretations of the principles of liberty and equality are perfectly possible. Almost certainly, defenders of Islamic values would deny, in all sincerity, that the treatment of women in Islamic culture betokens any inequality of respect for women, or any belief in women's inferiority.

The general point can be reinforced by considering some of the writers discussed in earlier chapters of this book. The work of Isaiah Berlin, for example, demonstrates how mutually contradictory have been the various concepts of liberty, even within the Western tradition. Berlin reminds us, also, that ideals of liberty and equality are at least partly in conflict with each other: to embody both therefore requires a compromise, and numerous alternative compromises are possible. Of all the theorists discussed, it is John Rawls who most explicitly characterizes his own theory as an interpretation of the democratic principles of liberty and equality. It is, of course, only *an* interpretation, even if Rawls considers it to be the most favoured one. Few if any of the philosophers I have discussed would dissent from the principles of liberty and equality, but they differ quite radically as to what that implies. To some, liberty and equality require free market capitalism, while to others they are destroyed by it. To some (such as Rawls), they imply an extensive welfare state, while others (such as Nozick) have described the welfare state as a kind of enslavement. In my opinion, there is actually a profound tension, even contradiction, between democracy (based on the postulate of equal power) and capitalism (which inevitably generates unequal wealth, and therefore also unequal power). However, capitalism may well be inescapable, from the standpoint of economic efficiency (as Weber suggested). In that case, the modern Western polity, contrary to Fukuyama, actually contains a profound internal contradiction. For many reasons, therefore, it seems that History still has many questions to answer. It is unlikely that a history of political philosophy in the twentieth century, still less the 'short' twentieth century, will be the last.

Notes

1   F. Fukuyama, *The End of History and the Last Man* (Free Press, New York, 1992), pp. xi–xii.
2   Ibid., part III, 'The struggle for recognition'.

Index

Index